*psychoanalysis*

*and literature*

HENDRIK M. RUITENBEEK was born in Leyden, Holland, in 1928. He took his doctorate at the University of Leyden and came to the United States in 1955. He is now a naturalized citizen. Dr. Ruitenbeek is a practicing psychoanalyst in New York City, and he also teaches psychology at New York University.

Dr. Ruitenbeek is the author of *The Rise and Origin of the Dutch Labour Party* (published in Holland in 1955) and of *The Individual and the Crowd: A Study of Identity in America* (1964). He has edited the following anthologies for the Dutton Paperbacks series: *Psychoanalysis and Social Science* (1962), *Psychoanalysis and Existential Philosophy* (1962), *Varieties of Classic Social Theory* (1963), *Varieties of Modern Social Theory* (1963), *The Dilemma of Organizational Society* (1963), and *The Problem of Homosexuality in Modern Society* (1963). Another anthology called *Psychoanalysis and Contemporary American Culture* has just been published. He is currently preparing a study of the influence of Sigmund Freud on American life and thought.

# *psychoanalysis*
## *and literature*

Edited, and with an introduction, by
HENDRIK M. RUITENBEEK

A *Dutton*  *Paperback*

New York
E. P. DUTTON & CO., INC.
1964

## FIRST EDITION

## ACKNOWLEDGMENTS

Grateful acknowledgment is made to the following for permission
to quote from copyright material:

Alfred Kazin: *Psychoanalysis and Literary Culture Today*. Reprinted from *Partisan Review*, Winter 1959, Vol. XXVI, No. 1, by
permission of the author and editor.

Ernest Jones: *The Death of Hamlet's Father*. Reprinted from the
*International Journal of Psychoanalysis*, Vol. XXIX, No. 3, 1948,
pp. 174–176, by permission of the editor.

Marie Bonaparte: *Psychoanalytic Interpretations of Stories of
Edgar Allan Poe*. Reprinted by permission of the publishers, Imago
Publishing Company, Ltd., London.

Clarence P. Oberndorf: *Psychoanalysis in Literature and Its
Therapeutic Value*. Reprinted from *Psychoanalysis and the Social
Sciences*, New York, International Universities Press, Inc., 1947,
by permission of the publishers. Copyright, 1947, by International
Universities Press, Inc.

Kenneth Burke: *Freud—and the Analysis of Poetry*. Reprinted
from the *American Journal of Sociology*, Vol. 44, 1939, by permission of the author and the editor. Copyright, 1939, by the
University of Chicago Press.

Ludwig Jekels: *The Riddle of Shakespeare's* Macbeth. Reprinted
from *Selected Papers* by Ludwig Jekels, London, Imago Publishing Company, Ltd., 1952, by permission of the publishers.

### Acknowledgments

George Devereux: *Why Oedipus Killed Laius*. Reprinted from the *International Journal of Psychoanalysis*, Vol. XXXIV, No. 2, 1953, pp. 1–10, by permission of the editor.

Simon O. Lesser: *The Source of Guilt and the Sense of Guilt—Kafka's* The Trial. Reprinted from *Modern Fiction Studies*, Spring 1962, Vol. 8, No. 1, by permission of the author and editor.

Norman N. Holland: *Shakespearean Tragedy and the Three Ways of Psychoanalytic Criticism*. Reprinted from *The Hudson Review*, Summer 1962, Vol. XV, No. 2, by permission of the author and editor.

John Skinner: *Lewis Carroll's Adventures in Wonderland*. Reprinted from *American Imago*, Vol. IV, 1947, pp. 3–21, by permission of the editor.

Mark Kanzer: *The "Passing of the Oedipus Complex" in Greek Drama*. Reprinted from the *International Journal of Psychoanalysis*, Vol. XXIX, No. 2, 1948, pp. 1–4, by permission of the editor.

Lionel Trilling: *Freud and Literature*. Reprinted from *The Liberal Imagination* by Lionel Trilling, New York, The Viking Press, Inc., 1950, by permission of the author and publishers. Copyright, 1940, 1947, 1950, by Lionel Trilling.

A. Bronson Feldman: *Zola and the Riddle of Sadism*. Reprinted from *American Imago*, Vol. XIII, 1956, pp. 415–425, by permission of the editor.

Heinz Kohut: Death in Venice *by Thomas Mann: A Story about Disintegration of Artistic Sublimation*. Reprinted by permission of the author.

Harry Slochower: *Incest in* The Brothers Karamazov. Reprinted from *American Imago*, Vol. XVI, 1959, pp. 127–145, by permission of the editor.

Frederic Wertham: *An Unconscious Determinant in* Native Son. Reprinted from the *Journal of Clinical Pathology*, Vol. VI, 1944–45, pp. 111–115, by permission of the author and editor.

# ONTENTS

# INTRODUCTION

Psychoanalysis has had a twofold influence on contemporary literature: it has given the reader and the literary critic new insights, and it has opened for the writer new areas of understanding—both of himself and of the material with which he works. Consequently, criticism has grown perceptive in new directions; drama, poetry, and the novel—all have new materials and new tools with which to use those materials.

Freud was himself much interested in poetry, plays, and novels and drew many insights from his own concern with literary works. In such papers as "The Relation of the Poet to Day-Dreaming," Freud deals with the sources of creativity and particularly with the mystery of the interaction between writer and reader. "The Theme of the Three Caskets," and "The 'Uncanny' " show other sides of Freud's interest in literature. In "Character-Types in Psychoanalytic Work," Freud brings the clinical and the critical together as he explores the character of Ibsen's Rebecca West and shows how subtly the playwright embedded the incest theme in what is apparently another study of the interplay between individual and individual and between the individual and the dictates of his society.

It is especially appropriate that Freud was himself a master of German prose. He received the Goethe prize, we should remember, not because of his contribution to the scientific understanding of human behavior but because of his contribution to German literature.

Nevertheless, Freud is sometimes charged with having "reduced" literature to the expression of a neurosis. He is thus said to be responsible for literature's apparent contemporary loss of faith in itself and its mission or, if that term be rejected, of its peculiarly significant function in the world. Freud did believe that the artist was essentially neurotic and that the writer found in his work "substitutive gratification" for his "thwarted desires." In Freud's words:

The artist is originally a man who turns from reality because he cannot come to terms with the demand for the renunciation of the instinctual satisfaction as it is first made, and who then in phantasy-life allows full play to his erotic and ambitious wishes. But he finds a way of return from this work of phantasy back to reality: with his special gifts he moulds his phantasies into a new kind of reality, and men concede them a justification as valuable reflections of actual life. Thus, by a certain path he actually becomes the hero, king, creator, favourite he desired to be, without pursuing the circuitous path of creating real alterations in the outer world. But this he can only attain because other men feel the same dissatisfaction as he with the renunciation demanded by reality and because this dissatisfaction, resulting from the displacement of the pleasure-principle by the reality-principle, is itself a part of reality.*

Most contemporary psychoanalysts reject Freud's opinion. Poetry is not necessarily the expression of the poet's neurosis, they contend. Yet if one scrutinizes what Freud has actually said in the passage just quoted, one sees how far his position is from any mere "reductionism." Instead, Freud recognizes that the writer, because of his special gifts, is able to reconcile us, as well as himself, with reality and so to achieve a more constructive relationship with the bases of existence.

As Freud's own use of literary material shows, psychoanalysis has drawn upon literature. Knowledge of psychoanalysis (and knowledge derived from personal experience in analytic treatment) has helped novelists and playwrights understand and present a fuller version of the human person. (But let no one read that statement to mean writers who lived before Freud created less deeply than those who have

* Sigmund Freud, "Formulations Regarding the Two Principles in Mental Functioning," *Collected Papers,* IV:19.

*Alfred Kazin**

# PSYCHOANALYSIS AND
# LITERARY CULTURE TODAY

## I

There is a young Englishman on Broadway who shouts every night that he is angry, very angry. Yet when we open John Osborne's play *Look Back in Anger*, and try to find out just what he is angry about, we make a curious discovery: he is not angry on specific grounds, as people often are; he is angry at his inability to feel anger, angry that he lacks a cause to be angry about. At one moment, after complaining that "nobody can be bothered. No one can raise themselves out of their delicious sloth," he says, very wistfully indeed for an angry man—"Was I really wrong to believe that there's a—kind of—burning virility of mind and spirit that looks for something as powerful as itself? The heaviest, strongest creatures in this world seem to be the loneliest. Like the old bear, following his own breath in the dark forest. There's no warm pack, no herd to comfort him. That voice that cries out doesn't *have* to be a weakling's, does it?"

This is the truest note in a play which emotionally and artistically seems rather contrived. It is not intensity of feeling but the longing for this intensity that is behind Mr. Osborne's confused and rather forced emotions. And equally, this same pseudoviolence, expressing the dearth rather than the excess of feeling, has struck me in several contemporary literary works that parade an air of militancy and rebelliousness— Norman Mailer's *The Deer Park*, Jack Kerouac's *On the Road*, Tennessee Williams' *Camino Réal* and other plays, the books of essays that Henry Miller has published from California, Allen Ginsberg's *Howl*. What puts all these works

* ALFRED KAZIN is one of Ameria's foremost literary critics and the author of many books and articles. This article was delivered before the Conference on Psychoanalysis and The Image of Man (sponsored by the National Psychological Association for Psychoanalysis, Inc., to honor the seventieth birthday of Theodor Reik), May 18, 1958, at the Waldorf-Astoria Hotel, New York City.

together in my mind is the fact that this essential lack of
feeling, of direction and point, is accompanied by the same
extreme yet abstract violence of sexual activity and description. I am reminded of the Marquis de Sade, that famous
sexual rebel, that supposed martyr to the cause of sexual
freedom—when one actually opens his books, he turns out to
be not a rebel at all but a fantasist whose idea of sexual
pleasure is always something so extreme, perverse, and
complicated that only the mind can imagine it—as only the
mind can stage it. This is the situation in Norman Mailer's
*The Deer Park*, a book that was acclaimed by some left-wing
critics as an indictment of Hollywood, and is based in part
on the enforced exile from the industry of Communist direc-
tors and writers who would not give the names of Party members to the investigating committees. One discovers very
soon in reading his book that Mailer is not interested in the
political significance of his material, though he feels that he
*should* be; he is concerned with sex as an ultimate expression
of man's aloneness. *The Deer Park* takes place mostly in a
famous desert resort, and despite the urbanities of luxurious
American living, I had the sensation that these people really
were in the desert, and with nothing to talk about, nothing
to think about, nothing to feel, they were like Eskimos
whiling away the eternal boredom of the igloo with unending
sexual intercourse.

The sensation of claustrophia, of something profoundly
cheerless and inhuman, that I got from Mailer's book was
intensified by his article in *Dissent*—"The White Negro:
Superficial Reflections on the Hipster." Mailer's theme is that
the Negro has been forced by discrimination into an outlaw
state in which he has developed the primitive and uninhibited
sexuality that white men are not allowed to indulge. As
modern capitalist society becomes inwardly more demoralized,
certain advanced sectors of white society—the more naturally
rebellious, intelligent, and unafraid—become white versions
of the Negro, seek to become hipsters (spiritual outlaws)
rather than "squares" (conventionally conformist men and
women). On the model of the Negro, they can find in the
sensations of unprecedented orgasm that direct, blazing,
ultimate contact with reality of which so many people are
deprived by conventional, inhibited middle-class life.

Anyone with experience in Marxist literature will recognize

come after.) From a reading of *The Interpretation of Dreams*, for example, the novelist can derive a notion of the unconscious life clearer than that with which he may be merely intuitively familiar. Freud linked the dream to motivation and gave the writer a new tool with which to explore, and to present the inner life of his characters. In *Freudianism and the Literary Mind*, Frederick Hoffman even suggests that the *avant-garde* took from Freud the notion of employing absurdities in their work. By *absurdities* Hoffman means the repudiation of logic and syntax for the illogical in thought and the nongrammatical in phrase. In this way, contemporary writers take us inside their own version of experience rather than merely describe that experience for us to observe from outside. Hoffman may be going too far. Ever since the beginning of Romanticism, if not long before, writers have been trying to awaken their audiences and frequently they have used some version of shock treatment in order to do so. One may well wonder how intimately the early Dadaists were acquainted with psychoanalysis, although some of the new ideas may have trickled down into European literary circles before World War I.

Ever increasing familiarity with psychoanalysis has undoubtedly made many poets aware of what recourse to the unconscious can do for their vocabularies and their imagery. Condensation, displacement, multiple determination, and secondary elaboration—such as those to be found in Freud's description of dream work—are being consciously employed in poetic works.

Language is obviously as essential to literature as are the media used by the plastic artist; and the truly creative writer —although the quality of his achievement may fall short of distinction—is the one who finds new ways to use words and brings fresh kinds of words into his writing. Because the writer uses words, and the same words as common speech, moreover, he must have subjects, too, and here also Freud's influence has been great. Whether as a causative factor or as a kind of symptom of social change, knowledge of psychoanalysis has made it possible for writers, and especially American writers, to deal more fully and frankly with a greater variety of human behavior than they were able to handle before.

*Three Contributions to the Theory of Sex*, for example,

has given playwrights and novelists material for a radically revised concept of the parent-child relationship. Conflict between the generations, and especially between father and son, had long been a staple theme of the novel, but the concept of the Oedipus complex gave a new dimension to that theme. Furthermore, the theme now was developed in new ways, especially in the United States where social change affecting the structure of the family was paralleled by the intellectual change represented by the introduction and popularization of psychoanalysis. Freud showed that Oedipus' fate was one determined not only by the rivalry between father and son but also by the son's unsatisfied longing for, and his retaliation against, the mother who betrayed him as an infant. This theme is universal, for it is a universal fate. But it has had its most acidulous expression in the work of American writers, perhaps because the mother concept has long held a position of such unique importance in American culture.

Throughout the history of literature the artist has portrayed men's struggle against incestuous impulses, dependency, guilt, and aggression. Psychoanalytic interpretation of human experience has made it possible to treat these themes more completely and with more thorough understanding. (Again, this does not mean that we have better novelists or greater playwrights in the post-Freudian world than we had in earlier times; it does mean that the contemporary novelist must show some genuine understanding of psychological reality if he means to be taken as a serious and significant writer.) Through the insights of psychoanalysis, writers are able to see their work in a new dimension and to handle their subject—the human condition as it is embodied in the predicament of particular individuals—with greater freedom and depth.

The reader and the critic have also profited. The increase in psychological sophistication and awareness has undoubtedly made it possible for much contemporary writing to find a wide audience. Conversely, that same increased knowledge and awareness have made it possible for readers to draw fresh meaning from the great works of our literary heritage. We have become ever more sensitive to the hidden significance of plot, character development, and language, and far more willing to search a book for its multiple layers of meaning.

(We may also be far too willing to import layers of meaning into what has only a rather superficial existence, but all good things have their abuses.)

Freud observed that in spite of the connection between neurosis and literary creation the analyst must hold his peace before genius. Not so the literary critic who feeds on—and feeds—genius. To the critic, psychoanalysis has given invaluable help, even though the professional analyst may at times think that the critic is misusing the vocabulary and the ideas of psychoanalysis. The poet, too, may object: he may well argue that he did not intend to hide the meaning of his work; still less did he intend the meaning which his critic has inserted. We have learned from the psychoanalyst that all speech, like all dreaming, may have a latent meaning. The critic, using methods akin to and derived from, although not at all identical with those of the analyst, can apply analytic insights to a writer's plots and characters and so learn more both about the writer and his methods. In this fashion, the critic takes the reader behind the façade and into the real structure of a literary work.

In this brief introduction to an anthology which is itself selective rather than comprehensive, it is not possible even to survey the whole range of the critic's application of psychoanalysis to literary works. I should, however, like to cite a few examples: Eduard Hitschmann's contribution is noteworthy, especially in the excellent studies of Goethe and Schopenhauer in his *Great Men*. Ernest Jones' *Hamlet and Oedipus* shows how these plays take on new meaning once subjected to the scrutiny of the psychoanalyst. And if we may consider Martin Luther as a writer—and certainly we should give that title to the man who helped create modern German prose—then we cannot overlook Erik Erikson's work. In *Young Man Luther*, really a biographical study of a historical personage, we have a model example of the way in which psychoanalytic concepts can be applied to history and to literature. Erikson combines the caution and the boldness which constitute the dual imperative of the scholar or the critic who applies psychoanalytic methods to the life and work of even a living writer.

Determining the forces which influence a man is a perilous undertaking. The practicing psychotherapist, with his patient before him, knows how difficult a task their joint effort can be. Working with a dead man's writings or with the stories, poems, and plays of living men whom one may never meet is even more hazardous. Information is apt to be limited or distorted. The person working with that limited information is himself bound by his own problems and attitudes—many of which he may not have thoroughly explored and which may be activated by elements in the very book he is studying.

With due recognition of these limitations, I have chosen the articles in this anthology to show how psychoanalysis has increased our understanding of particular creative persons and how it has deepened our appreciation of certain literary works.

In the opening essay, Alfred Kazin, a distinguished American literary critic, sets forth some of the relationships which he sees as existing between psychoanalysis and literature. Later in the volume, taking a somewhat different point of departure, Lionel Trilling states a literary critic's present position on the place of Freud and Freudian concepts in the making and the study of contemporary literature. These essays, I hope, sound the key for this anthology which is intended to enhance the enjoyment of the reader and the student of literature as well as to open a few doors for those whose major concern is increasing their appreciation of psychoanalysis.

Ernest Jones, who has been mentioned earlier, interprets the meaning of the death of Hamlet's father. His essay, however, deals with the death of all fathers and what that death means to all sons. For the psychoanalyst has this in common with the poet: each is always concerned with the particular instance and each, by his concern with the particular moves to the universal, the poet by his art, the analyst by his awareness that the problem of any patient bears some existential likeness to the problems of all men. Later, Norman N. Holland examines and appraises the general range of psychoanalytic criticism of Shakespeare.

Edgar Allan Poe has been a favorite subject of biographical speculation ever since his death. Marie Bonaparte works backward from his stories to interesting interpretations of the role of the mother and father in Poe's life.

Clarence Oberndorf was one of the outstanding personalities in American psychoanalysis. His work on the history of the movement in the United States is well known. Just as well known is his interest in the relationship between literature and psychoanalysis, as evidenced by his study, *The Psychiatric Novels of Oliver Wendell Holmes*. In "Psychoanalysis in Literature and Its Therapeutic Value," Oberndorff explores another facet of the subject which has occupied so much of his attention.

Like Poe, Lewis Carroll has been something of a puzzle to biographers. His readers have long felt that there was more in *Alice* than met the eye of even so astute a plumber of the ambiguous as William Empson. As in Poe's case, the psychoanalytic approach has proved valuable. Phyllis Greenacre's excellent inquiry called *Swift and Carroll: A Psychoanalytic Study* offers many penetrating insights into the dynamics of Carroll's personality. It also casts light on that other classic, *Gulliver's Travels*. Rather than attempting to make a mosaic of significant short passages, however, I have chosen to present John Skinner's elaboration of Carroll's pathology in "Lewis Carroll's Adventures in Wonderland."

Turning to the drama, we have Ludwig Jekel's psychoanalytic study of Macbeth. George Devereux, who is renowned for his use of psychoanalytic concepts in the study and treatment of contemporary American Indians, here deals with Laius, father of Oedipus. Mark Kanzer's essay on the Oedipus complex in Greek drama takes us away from Sophocles and into the work of other classic poets as they present the theme of antagonism between father and son and their rivalry for possession of the desired woman.

Simon O. Lesser, whose *Fiction and the Unconscious* is an interesting instance of the critic's use of analytic insights, applies these to the part played by guilt in Kafka's *The Trial*. Kafka, like Poe and Carroll, has been a constant source of interest to biographers and has been much discussed from the psychoanalytic point of view. It is worthwhile recalling, perhaps, how strongly Kafka himself rejected the suggestion that his relation to his own father could be profitably explored by the use of psychoanalysis.

We close the anthology with four essays on particular works: A. Bronson Feldman, author of *The Unconscious in History*, surveys Zola's novels with sadism as his psychoanalytic key to their significance. Heinz Kohut examines *Death in Venice* in terms of Thomas Mann's sublimation of his own impulses. Harry Slochower studies the theme of incest as Dostoevsky deals with it in *The Brothers Karamazov*. Finally, Dr. Frederic Wertham, whose *Seduction of the Innocent* has made his name familiar to many lay readers, deals with some of the unconscious processes in Richard Wright's *Native Son*.

HENDRIK M. RUITENBEEK

*psychoanalysis*

*and literature*

immediately in this essay the adaptation to the hipster of the myth of the proletariat. Mailer's essay is a completely Marxist-revolutionary essay. Although the characters are the same, their names are different; and although the plot is really the same, too, the real difference is that the play is not on the boards; nothing is really taking place except theoretically. There *was* a proletariat once, and a bourgeoisie; people did suffer from starvation, inhuman hours, physical violence. But Mailer's picture of the Negro and of his revolutionary, unprecedented orgasms gives even the interested and sympathetic reader the sense that all this is being relayed to him from far away, for it is all a mental construction. Nothing here is taken from the real life of struggle, from life as actual conflict; it is an attempt to impose a dramatic and even noble significance on events that have not genuinely brought it forth. So desperate is Mailer for something to be revolutionary about, as Osborne is, that after telling us contemptuously that modern psychoanalysis merely softens the patient up by adapting him to modern middle-class society, he says that by contrast, two strong eighteen-year-old hoodlums beating in the brains of a candy-store keeper do have courage of a sort, "for one murders not only a weak fifty-year-old man but an institution as well, one violates private property, one enters into a new relation with the police and introduces a dangerous element into one's life. The hoodlum is therefore daring the unknown, and so no matter how brutal the act, it is not altogether cowardly."

Jack Kerouac is a far less gifted and intelligent writer than Mailer, but in his recent best seller, *On the Road,* one finds this same loneliness of emotions without objects to feel them about, this same uprush of verbal violence which, when one looks at it a little closely, seems to be unnaturally removed from the object or occasion. Kerouac, indeed, writes not so much *about* things as about the search for things to write about. When he celebrates the "kick" of ecstasy brought about by drink, drugs, and jazz, it is the relief of having so strong a sensation that impresses him, not his communion with some object in ecstatic relatedness. And it is significant that his highest praise is for "the mad ones, the ones who are mad to live, mad to talk, mad to be saved, desirous of everything at the same time, the ones who never yawn or say a commonplace thing, but burn, burn, burn like fabulous yellow roman candles exploding like spiders across the stars and in the middle you can see the blue centerlight pop and everybody goes 'Aww!' "

Though it may seem a far step from the raucous and self-advertising propaganda of Kerouac's bohemian group to the professional theater world of Tennessee Williams, the very subject of Williams' plays is always this same loneliness. When Williams, minus the stage lights and hocus-pocus of his director, is read for himself, as in his execrable fiction, *The Roman Spring of Mrs. Stone* and the stories collected in *One Arm,* one discovers that his subject is not merely the fantasy world of the utterly lonely, but that in fantasy even the sexual fulfillment of his characters has a brutal and mechanical quality, as if one mental category dully followed another without any stimulus or color from direct experience. In the title story of *One Arm,* a Negro masseur not merely violates his white patient, but literally butchers him; this same hellish oppression of sexual fantasy, like a nightmare from which the dreamer may never escape into the unpatterned relief of the real world, dogs us in some of the more violent stories of Carson McCullers, in the most recent novel by Nelson Algren, *A Walk on the Wild Side,* and in the last section of Paul Bowles's *The Sheltering Sky,* where a young American wife, maddened after her husband dies in the desert, is captured by an Arab and added to his harem.

I wish I could describe some of these new novels and plays in greater detail, for what is most striking about so many of them is the fact that despite the surface sexual violence, they seem little concerned with sex itself, with the *physicality* of sex; in many of these books there are simply not enough people about, in actual human relation of any sort, for sexual activity to take place. On the contrary, many of the newer writers use sex exactly as a drunken and confused man uses profanity—as a way of expressing anger, irritation, exasperation, and thus of breaking through the numbing despair of isolation. And indeed, isolation of the most crippling and stupefying sort, the kind of isolation that makes it impossible to break the lockstep of one's thoughts, the isolation that imagines anything because it has contact with nothing, but which, in the imagination of loneliness, cannot give us the color, the tactile feel of anything, only the abstract category to which the experience belongs, is the really significant experience behind this literature.

Yet this loneliness does not call itself that; it calls itself revolutionary. In a long and now celebrated American poem simply called *Howl,* the young poet Allen Ginsberg has taken Whitman's long line and has described a hallucinated tour of America that reverses Whitman's celebration and becomes an exultant nightmare of denunciation:

*I saw the best minds of my generation destroyed by madness,*
*starving hysterical*
*naked,*
*dragging themselves through the negro streets at dawn looking for*
*an angry fix,*
*angelheaded hipsters burning for the ancient heavenly connection*
*to the starry dynamo in the machinery of night,*
*who poverty and tatters and hollow-eyed and high sat up smoking*
*in the supernatural darkness of cold-water flats floating*
*across the tops of cities contemplating jazz,*
*who bared their brains to Heaven under the El and saw Moham-*
*medan angels staggering on tenement roofs illuminated,*
. . . . . .

*who cowered in unshaven rooms in their underwear, burning their*
*money in wastebaskets and listening to the Terror*
*through the wall,*
*who got busted in their public beards returning through Laredo*
*with a belt of marijuana for New York. . . .*

Now this abstractness contrasts very sharply with the lyric and sensuous imagery with which sexual desire or activity used to be described by writers who were famous for their prophetic, unconventional concern with the subject. I have not the space to spell out in its required and fascinating detail the kind of imagery which one finds in Whitman's "Out of the Cradle Endlessly Rocking," in the love scenes of D. H. Lawrence's *Sons and Lovers,* in the glorious pages of Colette, who could portary sex as the union not only of man and woman but of man and the whole physical world of earth sounds and earth smells, of colors and nuances; in those pages of Proust where, despite the pain of Swann's jealousy of Odette, one feels the gasping sharpness of real desire and the excitement of the great city that is its background and stimulus. Perhaps I have made it too easy for myself by contrasting so many classically sensuous writers with American writers who have never had the same tradition of art as the celebration of the natural world. But as Albert Camus

confessed in his recent Nobel Prize speech, even someone
brought up in the pagan and sunlit world of North Africa
finds himself unable to describe the sensuous joy of life as
he once did. As man increasingly loses his connection with
the world, the great world, the only world, he finds himself
playing the moralist and the revolutionary as part of the same
imposture—the purpose of which is to perform *some* action,
to see oneself performing any role.

## II

Much of the fiction and poetry I have been describing has
been influenced by the theories of Wilhelm Reich, and in the
terms in which I have been describing them, illustrates the
use of psychoanalytical terminology for the sake of an utterly
hypothetical rebelliousness, in which a gangster beating out
the brains of an old storekeeper is seen in the ritual of a
revolutionary terrorist destroying the old order. Turn to the
enormously fashionable and influential literary criticism
written under the inspiration of Dr. Jung, and you find in
academic and philosophical circles the use of psychoanalysis
not as socialism but as religion. In a recent effort to summarize the Jungian conception of literature—the book takes its
very title from the loneliest character in American literature,
Melville's Ishmael—James Baird explains that what orthodox
Christians regard as sacrament is really a symbol, and that
since art itself deals with symbols, art itself may be viewed
as a religious ritual. To anyone who has followed the development of literary criticism since the vogue of neo-
orthodoxy began with Eliot, this is old stuff; phrases like
symbol, symbolic action, ritual, myth, are the mainstay of
fashionable academic criticism. But the themes I have been
stressing in this paper—isolation and forced rebelliousness—
are paralleled in the pseudometaphysics of the following.
For just as art is really a religious ritual, so religion is really
art; sacrament, says Mr. Baird, is symbol "representing corporateness in which the individual is subsumed, and ultimately these new compensatory symbols transcend the
artist in the collective of the archetype."

The abstraction of his created form as sacrament singularly en-
visions the corporateness of man in a religious act. . . . Each man
worships alone on his island. The sacrament which he creates invokes for his comfort and his "salvation" a world of the ideal
where what he remembers of lost symbols in mixed with what his

heretical allegiance to non-Christian (Oriental) custom supplies. Whether this custom, displayed to him through the aperture of his Oriental journey as experience, was mastered or merely "sampled" cannot very much matter. His symbol suggests the possibility of a new sacramental corporateness. As a maker of sacramentalism he belongs to an unconscious artistic community of his age because, as artist, he is like other workers who find art a better means of affirmation than existential courage. He has cast off convention and traditional theology, and in his act of creating, he descends to the true primitivity of religiousness; he returns to the authority of primitive feeling and the emotive life.

There is not a phrase here which refers to anything real; neither art nor religion, neither the so-called primitive feeling nor the emotive life, means anything in this context. But Mr. Baird is not bogus: he is not pretending that he believes in God; he is pretending that out of something which is not religion, religion may come again, so that human beings who have lost the traditional objects of their belief, but not the habit of belief, may have something to believe in again. Just as the Reichians want to believe in Socialism again, because they don't, so the Jungians write as if religion could be had back for the asking. It is all so easy, so fatally easy—this Socialism that carefully avoids society; this religion that dares not say that God exists. It is easy because everything is based on what the self wants, what the self needs or thinks it needs, and nothing on what the world is really like. The world—the surrounding and not always friendly reality of nature, history, society—has disappeared for these writers, and has taken with it everything which has given measure and definition to man's struggles in the world, everything which has given man a sense of his possibilities and his limits, of his guilt as well as his desire, of his tragedy as well as his happiness. These writers are not concerned with winning over nature, with forcing it to yield up its secrets; they are searching for a world they can believe in again, and get angry at again. They are tormented not by the pains of heroism, but by the inability to feel heroic—and often by the inability to feel anything. The human catastrophes visited upon our generation by totalitarianism seem too great to understand, to describe, to cope with. History has become meaningless to them, and private life a search for sensations—either of unprecedented orgasm or of God—that may make them feel real to themselves.

This pervasive sense of unreality is authentic, and as usual the writers—those whom Ezra Pound saluted as the "antennae of the race"—see ahead of everyone else. For the middle-class world which all of us have depended on so long has itself, as a value system, ceased to exert any real authority, to arouse real respect. The sense of unreality that I have been describing arises naturally out of the bewilderment of people who recognize that history has taken still another turn, and that the solid middle-class virtues on which so many of us depended, so that we could meaningfully oppose them, are no longer believed in seriously enough for opposition to mean anything. The real tragedy of our time, as Nietzsche correctly foresaw, is a nihilism so total, so pervasive, so defeatist even in the midst of the greatest luxury the world has ever known, that it is no wonder that unimaginative people try to turn back the clock of modern science, to blame Marx and Darwin and Freud for robbing us of the illusion of our omnipotence in the universe. These people are hopeless, yet there is one element of tragic truth in their indictment of the modern spirit: more and more people lack the sense of tradition with which to assimilate the endless shocks and changes of the twentieth century. Just as Marx could not anticipate heirs who would completely lack his culture and tradition, who in the name of his great insights into capitalist society would create a society far more tyrannical and unjust, so Freud, himself so rooted in the Hebraic tradition, the English tradition, the nineteenth century tradition, the scientific tradition, could not have predicted the destruction of Western civilization at Auschwitz, Maidenek, Belsen. He could not have imagined a psychoanalytically oriented psychiatry divorced from the humanistic and moral tradition, a psychiatry that would be used for market research in consumer motivation and even for the manipulation back to "normal" of political deviants. Psychoanalysis has depended so much on the intellectual and literary tradition out of which it arose, and of which it is an essential part, that now that this tradition of cultivation and intellectual freedom no longer commands allegiance as it used to, one sees an increasing divergence between writers, who are concerned with the tradition itself, and therefore with Freud's classic insights, and those psychoanalysts who, lacking the needed cultural reference, foolishly and self-indulgently suppose that they are living in the same world of bourgeois morality which made Freud grasp the necessary reactions of repression, guilt, and shame. In the last few years, the kind of psychoanalytical comment on literary works which used to be so arresting and valuable has come to seem a wholly mechanical jargon. Significantly, it has become the staple of the most pedantic and academic research, unrelated to living literature; for as with all things academic, this perspective is based on admiration of the static, the enclosed, on the literary tradition that neatly folds itself up and files itself away.

Equally, the use of psychoanalysis as a kind of pampering to merely bourgeois tastes and self-delusions, to the lap-dog psychology of Americans whose only problem is to reduce and to save on income tax, is in itself a literary scandal. In this connection I would point to several things. One: the myth of universal "creativity," the assumption that every idle housewife was meant to be a painter and that every sexual deviant is really a poet. From this follows the myth that these unproductive people are "blocked"; whereupon how easy for the hack and the quack to get together! Second: the use of psychoanalytical jargon as a static description of the personality of the artist. There is no doubt that although neurosis can cripple creative artistry or hinder it entirely, talent is always quite separate in function—if not in theme— from the emotional chaos of neurosis, which provides no clue whatever to the reality of creative life. But perhaps the theme I have been stressing in this paper—the contemporary use of psychoanalysis in order to find identity rather than freedom —is seen here, too, since the more unreal people become to us, the more we try to pin them down with a descriptive formula, usually gained these days from psychoanalysis. If we approach literature exclusively by way of the writer's personality, psychoanalytically considered, we not only get even further away from the real experience of literature than we were before, but we obliterate even the fundamental cultural respect for the health of the creative self in our eagerness to label the writer ill.

A recent example of this is the introduction by Mrs. Diana Trilling to a new selection of the letters of D. H. Lawrence. Mrs. Trilling confesses that Lawrence no longer means as much to her as he did in rebellious youth, and one believes her, since her analysis of Lawrence's work is based not on his real and marvelous creativity, but on an Oedipal conflict which she insists is the root of his ultimate failure as a

novelist. More than one great poet, or poetic talent, has
known the same kind of failure, which is probably rooted in
the gap between the poetic realization of reality, which is
always fundamentally "personal," and the kind of novelistic
instinct which specializes in *story*—an instinct that Lawrence
never really had. But instead of paying the homage to him
that his genius deserves—and calls for—homage that would
at least see Lawrence as possessing the defects of his genius,
Mrs. Trilling regales us with the kind of clinical hindsight
which, divorced from literary humility and appreciation, has
made this kind of writing a terror to anyone who simply
cares for literature.

I think it was this institutionalized conjunction of sex and love
that threw Lawrence into the despair of the war years. The conflict raging in the world was an externalized expression of the
private sexual struggle which was to absorb so large a part of his
emotional energies for the rest of his life.
This is no irrelevant private point I'm making, no psychoanalytical advantage I'm trying to take of Lawrence, need I make
that clear? The conflict which was crystallized in Lawrence when
he and Frieda finally married seems to me to be the essential
conflict, and contradiction, that runs through all his work.

This may not be an irrelevant private point, but it shows
an attitude toward literature which has nothing to claim for
literature itself. It is odd that the very people who are so
quick to see suppressed and wasted creativity in people who
are merely emotionally ill should always wish to deny the
fundamental creativity of the greatest writers, like Kafka and
Lawrence and Dostoevski—a mistake that in the case of the
latter, Freud pointedly refrained from making. Yet the reason
for this relentless psychologizing of art, so often equally
irrelevant to both art and psychology, is that it gives the
analyst, whoever he may be, the chance to share in the
creativity of his subject. There is a sad perversion here of
what, in genuine literary criticism, *is* an act of appropriation.
Henry James said that the true critic is so much in love with
art that he tries to "possess" it—to include it in his personal
experience, which means to increase his power of enjoyment
and understanding, and thereby of instruction to others. But
as Ernst Kris has pointed out, the rise of a wholly "esthetic"
attitude toward life—I should call it pseudoesthetic in effect—
is an attempt to appropriate not the work of art itself, which

does exist so that we may possess it, but the artist himself. It exists so as to give us "status" and "prestige" in a world where the old bourgeois claims of money and social position, though they support the life of art, are felt not to be as real in advancing one's prestige as creativity itself. And the myth of creativity, the endless search for it in modern times, is simply a search for identity on the part of people who believe that they can find it in an experience, that of the real creator, utterly foreign to themselves.

I could go on here to speak of many related aspects; of "taste," of corruption, of the demonstrable fact that while psychoanalysis has added nothing to the creation of art, it has added a great deal, perhaps too much, to our modern concern with art. But in conclusion it is more important to note that the most signal fact about our experience today is that it is utterly unprecedented. The protagonist of middle-class literature, from Goethe to Thomas Mann, from Blake to D. H. Lawrence, from Rousseau to Proust, naturally saw life as a struggle against convention. Under the slogan of nature as freedom and truth, man saw himself as a hero reuniting man to the natural destiny of which he had been robbed by the gods. If there had been no profound tradition of repression, no moral code to bind us, Don Juan could never have been a hero or Anna Karénina a heroine; there would have been no guilt to suffer and no rebellion to honor. But the great human symbol of contemporary literature, I suggest, is no longer the rebel, since there is no authoritative moral tradition that he can honestly feel limits and hinders his humanity. It is the stranger—who seeks not to destroy the moral order, but to create one that will give back to him the idea of humanity.

*Ernest Jones**

# THE DEATH OF
# HAMLET'S FATHER

When a poet takes an old theme from which to create a
work of art, it is always interesting, and often instructive, to
note the respects in which he changes elements in the story.
Much of what we glean of Shakespeare's personality is
derived from such studies, the direct biographical details
being so sparse. The difference in the accounts given in
*Hamlet* of the way the King had died from that given in
the original story is so striking that it would seem worth
while to look closer at the matter.

The most obvious difference is that in the Saxo-Belleforest
saga the murder is a public one, with Shakespeare a secret
one. We do not know, however, who made this change, since
an English play called *Hamlet*, thought to be written by Kyd,
was extant some twelve years before Shakespeare wrote his;
and he doubtless used it as well as the Belleforest version.
That play no longer exists except in a much later and much
distorted German version, but a Ghost probably appeared
in it, and one can hardly imagine any other function for him
than to disclose a secret murder. There is reason to suppose
that Shakespeare may himself have had a hand in the Kyd
play, but at all events he made the best possible use of the
alteration.

In the old saga Claudius (there called Feng) draws his
sword on his brother the King (Horvendil)[1] at a banquet
and slays him "with many wounds." He explains to the assembled nobles that he has done this to protect his sister-in-
law (Geruth) from ill-treatment and imminent peril of her
life at the hands of her husband—a pretext evidently a reflection of the infant's sadistic conception of coitus. Incidentally,
in the Saxo saga (though not with Belleforest), there had

* ERNEST JONES is generally credited with introducing Freudian
psychoanalysis to the English-speaking world. He is the author of
the definitive biography of Sigmund Freud and was founder and
for twenty-five years President of the British Psychoanalytic Society. Numbers in parentheses indicate references at end of article.

here been no previous adultery with the Queen, so that Feng is the sole villain, and Amleth, unlike Hamlet, unhesitatingly kills him and reigns in his stead as soon as he can overcome the external obstacles. In *Hamlet*, as is well known, the plot is intensified by the previous incestuous adultery of the Queen, which convulses Hamlet at least as much as his father's murder and results in an animus against women that complicates his previously simple task.

In the *Hamlet* play, on the other hand, Claudius disclaims all responsibility for his brother's death and spreads a somewhat improbable story of his having been stung to death by a serpent while sleeping in an orchard. How he knew this we are not told, nor why the adder possessed this quite unwonted deadliness. There is much to be said about that "orchard," but we may assume that it symbolizes the woman in whose arms the king was murdered. The Ghost's version was quite different. According to him, Claudius had found him asleep and poured a juice of hebona into his ears, a still more improbable story from a medical point of view; he further tells us that the poison rapidly spread through his system, resulting in all his smooth body being barked about, "most lazar-like, with vile and loathsome crust." Presumably its swift action prevented him from informing anyone of what had befallen him.

The source of this mysterious poison has been traced as follows (1). Shakespeare seems to have taken the name, incidentally misspelling it, from the juice of "hebon," mentioned in a play of Marlowe's, who himself has added an initial letter to the "ebon" (ebony) of which the walls of the God of Sleep were composed (Ovid.) Shakespeare apparently went on to confound this narcotic with henbane (hyoscyamus), which at that time was believed to cause mortification and turn the body black (7). Two interesting beliefs connecting henbane with the ear are mentioned by Pliny: (1) that is is a remedy for earache, and (2) when poured into the ear it causes mental disorder.

The coarse northern butchery is thus replaced by a surreptitious Italianate form of murder, a fact that has led to many inquiries, which do not concern us here, concerning Italian influence on Shakespeare. The identical method is employed in the Play Scene, where a nephew murders his uncle, who was resting after coitus, by dropping poison into

Richard III. Hamlet says he got the Gonzago story from an
Italian play, but no such play has yet been traced. But there
had been two instances of murder in an unhappy Gonzaga
family. In 1538 a famous Duke of Urbino, who was married
to a Gonzaga, died under somewhat suspicious circumstances.
Poison was suspected, and his barber was believed to have
poured a lotion into his ears on a number of occasions. So the
story goes: whether poison thus administered is lethal to
anyone with intact tympanums is a matter we must leave to
the toxicologists. At all events the duke's son got the unfortunate barber torn in pieces by pincers and then quartered. In
the course of this proceeding the barber asserted he had been
put on to commit the foul deed by a Luigi[2] Gonzaga, a
relative of the duke's by marriage. For political and legal
reasons, however, Luigi was never brought to trial (2).
Furthermore, in 1592 the Marchese Rudolf von Castiglione
got eight bravos to murder his uncle the Marchese Alfonso
Gonzaga, a relative of the Duke of Mantua. Rudolf had
wished to marry his uncle's daughter and had been refused;
he himself was murdered eight months later.

The names used make it evident that Shakespeare was
familiar with the story of the earlier Gonzaga murder, as he
possibly was with the later one too. The "poison in the ear"
story must have appealed to him, since he not only used it
in the Gonzago Play Scene—where it would be appropriate—
but also in the account of Hamlet's father's death.

If we translate them into the language of symbolism, the
Ghost's story is not so dissimilar from that of Claudius. To the
unconscious "poison" signifies any bodily fluid charged with
evil intent, while the serpent has played a well-known role
ever since the Garden of Eden. The murderous assault had
therefore both aggressive and erotic components, and we
note that it was Shakespeare who introduced the latter
(serpent). Furthermore, that the ear is an unconscious
equivalent for anus is a matter for which I have adduced
ample evidence elsewhere (5). So we must call Claudius's
attack on his brother both a murderous aggression and a
homosexual assault.

Why did Shakespeare give this curious turn to a plain story
of envious ambition? The theme of homosexuality itself does
not surprise us in Shakespeare. In a more or less veiled form
a pronounced femininity and a readiness to interchange the
sexes are prominent characteristics of his plays, and doubtless

of his personality also. I have argued (6) that Shakespeare wrote *Hamlet* as a more or less successful abreaction of the intolerable emotions aroused by the painful situation he depicts in his Sonnets, his betrayal by both his beloved young noble and his mistress. In life he apparently smothered his resentment and became reconciled to both betrayers. Artistically his response was privately to write the Sonnets (in the later publication of which he had no hand) and publicly to compose *Hamlet* not long afterward, a play gory enough to satisfy all varieties of revenge.

The episode raises again the vexed question of the relation between active and passive homosexuality. Nonanalysts who write on this topic are apt to maintain that they represent two different inborn types, but this assertion gives one an unsatisfied feeling of improbability, and analytic investigation confirms these doubts by demonstrating numerous points of contact between the two attitudes. Certainly Claudius's assault was active enough; sexually it signified turning the victim into a female, that is, castrating him. Hamlet himself, as Freud (3) pointed out long ago, was unconsciously identified with Claudius, which was the reason why he was unable to denounce and kill him. So the younger brother attacking the older is simply a replica of the son-father conflict, and the complicated poisoning story really represents the idea of the son castrating his father. But we must not forget that it is done in an erotic fashion. Now Hamlet's conscious attitude toward his father was a feminine one, as shown by his exaggerated adoration and his adjuring Gertrude to love such a perfect hero instead of his brother. In Freud's opinion homosexuality takes its origin in narcissism (4), so that it is always a mirror-love; Hamlet's father would therefore be his own ideal of himself. That is why, in such cases, as with Hamlet, suicide is so close to murder.

My analytic experience, simplified for the present purpose, impels me to the following reconstruction of homosexual development. Together with the narcissism a feminine attitude toward the father presents itself as an attempted solution of the intolerable murderous and castrating impulses aroused by jealousy. These may persist, but when the fear of the self-castration implied gains the upper hand, that is, when the masculine impulse is strong, the original aggression reasserts itself—but this time under the erotic guise of active homosexuality.

According to Freud, Hamlet was inhibited ultimately by his repressed hatred of his father. We have to add to this the homosexual aspect of his attitude, so that love and hate, as so often, both play their part.

## NOTES

[1] It was Shakespeare who changed this name to Hamlet, thus emphasizing the identification of son and father.

[2] From whom Shakespeare perhaps got the name Lucianus for the murderer in the Play Scene.

## REFERENCES

1. H. Bradley, "Cursed Hebenon (or 'Hebona')," *Modern Language Review*, XV, 1920.

2. G. Bullough, "The Murder of Gonzago," *Modern Language Review*, XXX, 1935.

3. S. Freud, *The Interpretation of Dreams*, Allen & Unwin, London, 1945.

4. ———, "Certain Neurotic Mechanisms in Jealousy, Paranoia and Homosexuality," *Collected Papers*, II.

5. Ernst Jones, *Essays in Applied Psycho-Analysis*, Internat Psa. Press, London, 1923.

6. ———, *Hamlet and Oedipus*, Norton, New York, 1950.

7. W. Thiselton-Dyer, *Shakespeare's England*, Vol. I.

*Marie Bonaparte*[*]

# PSYCHOANALYTIC INTERPRETATIONS OF STORIES OF EDGAR ALLAN POE

## TALES OF THE MOTHER

### 1. "BERENICE"[†]

After his stormy departure from West Point in March, 1831, Poe found himself readopted, this time by his aunt, Mrs. Clemm. He thus once more found himself in contact with his little cousin Virginia, not yet nine at the time. We know how important a place Virginia was destined to fill in his affections, his life and work, and how successfully she came to reincarnate, in the poet's unconscious, both his baby sister and the fragile, poetic, dying mother who was to remain the one great love of his life. We shall not, therefore, be surprised to find that Virginia served as the unwitting Muse, who first called Poe's genius as a writer of imaginative prose to life, in what we know as *The Tales of the Folio Club,* to which the gruesome story "Bernice" belongs.

Egæus, heir to the ancient castle of his fathers, scion of a feudal race—a race of visionaries—unites in his person the conflicting symptoms of various mental disorders. First, he describes his schizoid tendencies:

The realities of the world affected me as visions, and as visions only, while the wild ideas of the land of dreams became, in turn,— not the material of my every-day existence—but in very deed that existence utterly and solely in itself.

He then speaks of his tendency to obsessional rumination, which he thus distinguishes from the ponderings of the average daydreamer:

In my case the primary object [of his musings] was *invariably frivolous,* although assuming, through the medium of my dis-

[*] MARIE BONAPARTE was one of Sigmund Freud's most illustrious pupils. For many years she was President of the French Psychoanalytic Institute and is the author of *Female Sexuality.*

[†] "Berenice," *Southern Literary Messenger,* March, 1835, 1840; *Broadway Journal,* I, 14.

tempered vision, a refracted and unreal importance. Few deductions, if any, were made; and those few pertinaciously returning in
upon the original object as a centre. The meditations were *never*
pleasurable; and, at the termination of the reverie, the first cause,
so far from being out of sight, had attained that supernaturally
exaggerated interest which was the prevailing feature of the
disease.

As to the third mental disorder with which Egæus is afflicted
—and which enables him to accomplish the fearful deed that
brings the tale to a close—this will become evident later.

Egæus, who doubtless reproduces in compact and exaggerated form several psychoneurotic traits of his creator, even
to his opium-taking,[1] also resembles Poe in having a girl
cousin. When the tale begins, this girl is well, as Virginia
herself must then have been.

Ah! vividly is her image before me now, as in the eary days of
her light-heartedness and joy!

Yet another and most ancient image, that of the mother,
beloved ever more as her strength failed, made it impossible
for any of his heroines to remain well long! A few lines
further and we find:

. . . all is mystery and terror, and a tale which should not be
told. Disease—a fatal disease—fell like the simoom upon her frame,
and, even while I gazed upon her, the spirit of change swept over
her, pervading her mind, her habits, and her character, and, in a
manner the most subtle and terrible, disturbing even the identity
of her person!

Thus the little cousin, Berenice or Virginia, gradually loses
her identity and is amalgamated with the beloved mother of
the past who, likewise, succumbed to what must have seemed
to the child Edgar a vague and equally incomprehensible
disease. For Poe, it was inevitable that this change must take
place, Love being equated for him with Beauty touched by
Death. And Egæus himself confesses as much when he says:

During the brightest days of her unparalleled beauty, most
surely I had never loved her. . . . And *now*—now I shuddered in
her presence, and grew pale at her approach; yet bitterly lamenting her fallen and desolate condition, I called to mind that she had
loved me long, and, in an evil moment, I spoke to her of marriage.

As the period of their nuptials approaches, we find Egæus, one mild winter afternoon, in his castle library. "The recollections of my earliest years are connected with that chamber," he has already told us, and, "Here died my mother. Herein was I born." In that chamber also, as in Egæus-Edgar's mind, there hovers "a remembrance which will not be excluded; a memory like a shadow. . . ."

Thus, with a poet's prescience, Poe informs us that unconscious memory exists. But what in essence are these unconscious memories that haunted him? "There is," writes Edgar-Egæus, "a remembrance of aërial forms—of spiritual and meaning eyes—of sounds, musical yet sad. . . ." How subtly this evokes the sylphlike Elizabeth Arnold, the ailing singer and actress. And this "remembrance which will not be excluded" is "like a shadow, too, in the impossibility of my getting rid of it while the sunlight of my reason shall exist."

Small wonder then that, one day, as Egæus, now the betrothed of Berenice, sits meditative and absorbed in this haunted library where his mother died, the shadow should take form in the same way as it was to re-embody itself in Edgar's cousin Virginia, by entering her as that family disease to which they were all prone; the same disease which, under the same roof, was carrying off his brother Henry. The miracle—dreaded yet desired—takes place. Suddenly, as Egæus fancies himself alone with his books, Berenice is there before him. "Perhaps she had grown taller since her malady."[2] Elizabeth Arnold, Poe's frail and sylphlike mother, need not have been taller than the little Virginia, her niece, to appear tall in her son's memory. Who has not had the experience of finding that objects and places, remembered from infancy, appear strangely shrunk when seen as an adult? Our measure of our surroundings is proportionate to our size. Besides, those who dominate us, as adults dominate the child, are magnified in the mind's eye. Thus, most people have attributed superhuman or gigantic stature to their gods and goddesses, who are but the human parents infinitely enlarged.

Egæus gazes long at the emaciated figure of the apparition, and then his "burning glances" fall on her face:

The forehead was high, and very pale, and singularly placid; and the once jetty hair fell partially over it, and overshadowed the hollow temples with innumerable ringlets now of a vivid yellow,

and jarring discordantly, in their fantastic character, with the
reigning melancholy of the countenance. The eyes were lifeless,
and lustreless, and seemingly pupil-less, and I shrank involuntarily
from their glassy stare to the contemplation of the thin and
shrunken lips. They parted; and in a smile of peculiar meaning,
*the teeth* of the changed Berenice disclosed themselves slowly to
my view.

This portrait combines features from two different models.
The lofty, pale, and singularly placid forehead would seem
to have been Virginia's . . . although Elizabeth Arnold's
brow, under the jet-black hair which "overshadowed the
hollow temples with innumerable ringlets," might answer
to the same description. . . . The change in the color of the
hair from black to yellow, as a result of her disease—a
phenomenon unknown to clinical observation—is, however,
more difficult to explain. This puzzled me for some time but,
one day, reading Coleridge's *Rime of the Ancient Mariner,* I
was struck by the singular appearance of Life-in-Death—
the fantastic passenger who is seen with Death, on the
phantom ship, by the Ancient Mariner—for the hair of Life-
in-Death is the same startling yellow.[3] Poe's admiration of
Coleridge, which dated from his early youth, is well known.
We cannot escape the conclusion that, influenced by Coleridge, this yellow hair had become a symbol of Life-in-Death
to him: "the Nightmare . . . who thicks man's blood with
cold."

In two other works, the poems "Eulalie" and "Lenore,"
Poe's heroines have yellow hair, like Berenice. In "Eulalie"
there is no tragic note and misfortune is mentioned only as
being adjured *not* to appear. But in "Lenore" we see the
color of her hair as she lies on her bier:

The life upon her yellow hair but not within her eyes—
The life still there, upon her hair—the death upon her eyes.[4]

This would seem to confiirm our theory that "yellow" hair
had, indeed, come to symbolize for Poe the Life-in-Death
with which each of his heroines was endowed and, deep in
his unconscious, first and foremost his own mother.

In the first version of "Berenice," the heroine had "golden"
hair, turned by her illness into "ringlets now black as the
raven's wing,"[5] which at first sight, might seem to weaken
our argument. But we shall see later that fair (not specifically

"yellow") hair is a symbol, with Poe, for infidelity to the *dark-haired* mother who, in the first version of "Berenice," reappears as the fair cousin; much in the way that the dark-haired Ligeia is re-embodied in the fair Rowena. The fact that Poe inverts the sequence of events in the last version of this tale, by changing Berenice's "golden" hair in her prime to "yellow" hair as she lies dying, shows how powerfully Coleridge's symbol of Life-in-Death dominated Poe's unconscious.

If now, in Poe's description of the "new" Berenice, we turn to the eyes, they are clearly those of a corpse, modeled doubtless on the fixed and glassy eyes which Poe, as a child, would have seen as those of his dead mother. This would also seem to be true of the teeth, and Poe's obsession with *teeth*, which now develops in Egæus, was doubtless born at his mother's bedside. The consumptive's drawn and emaciated lips would have revealed her teeth (the teeth we encounter in so many of Poe's tales), and the description that follows, of Berenice in her coffin, would seem to corroborate this opinion.

For, after Egæus has spent a night, a day, and another night in his library, haunted by visions of Berenice's teeth, a great cry is heard and a messenger appears to announce her death. He then sees her again in her coffin. One of her fingers seems to move; the bandages about her jaws breaks asunder, and her teeth, exposed, seem to grin hideously at him.

Poe himself judged it better to suppress this episode in the last version of the story. Possibly it reproduced a memory all too real.

But now another form of mental disease takes possession of the hero; an epileptoid attack, followed, as is generally the case, by amnesia. Doubtless, this improbable transformation of an obsessional schizoid into an epileptic, with subsequent amnesia, to some extent symbolizes the infantile amnesia that masked the unconscious sources from which Poe drew this frightful tale. In any case, the hero, yielding to a sudden impulse, visits the grave, disinters Berenice's body and, utilizing instruments that belong to the family physician, extracts all her thirty-two teeth. Berenice, however, proves not to be dead, but "live-in-death," that is, in a state of catalepsy and, during this brutal act, comes to herself, screaming wildly. Help comes, but too late. Egæus, back once more in the fatal library, is found by a servant with his garments muddy and clotted with gore. His fearful crime is

revealed as Berenice's teeth fall from their box and are
scattered on the floor. On this, the tale ends.

It will appear to some of our readers that, whatever psychoanalysis may say, the sexual factor plays no part in this tale.
What more obvious than that Poe, when a child of three,
saw his dearly loved mother die; that this fearful image was
thus graven on his unconscious; and that thus, throughout
life, it tended to reappear in his writings? True, the reader
will continue, these narratives are sometimes extremely
terrifying, but therein lies the narrator's peculiar gift.

Such an oversimplified explanation, however, cannot explain Poe's *predilection* for tales of solely this type and, in
effect, such a predilection can be explained only by adducing
a sexual factor. If Poe so frequently and with such satisfaction reproduces the illness, death, and burial (usually the
premature burial) of his mother, it was because nascent
erotic factors had irredeemably crystallized round her at
a moment when, so to speak, she was adorned with these
appanages of sickness and death, even though it was a death
which—as in childhood and the unconscious—seems non-
existent and only a parting to be followed by a return.

From an analytic point of view, "Berenice" shows us yet
more. As we have already seen, Poe's sexual impotence was
conditioned by a fixation on the mother and on a mother
who was dying and later, a corpse; thus implying a moral
upheaval in Poe against all sexuality, since sexuality to him
could mean only both sadistic destruction and necrophilia.
And the danger of sexuality, the punishment that threatens
all who yield, is shown, as in "Berenice," by the manner in
which Egæus is obsessed by her teeth. And indeed, in
psychoanalysis, many cases of male impotence reveal, though
more or less buried in the unconscious—strange as it may
seem to many a reader—the notion of the female vagina being
furnished with teeth, and thus a source of danger in being
able to bite and castrate. That Poe's unconscious, too, held
this fantasy, is testified by many of his tales. Mouth and
vagina are equated in the unconscious, and, when Egæus
yields to the morbid impulse to draw Berenice's teeth, he
yields both to the yearning for the mother's organ and to be
revenged upon it, since the dangers that hedge it about make
him sexually avoid all women as too menacing. His act is
therefore a sort of retributive castration inflicted on the

mother whom he loves, and yet hates, because obdurate to his sex-love for her in infancy. We shall meet the same theme again in "The Black Cat."

This concept of the *vagina dentata* and its consequent menace is, however, also a displacement (in this case downward) of a factor with roots deep in infantile experience. We know that babes which, while toothless, are content to suck the breast, no sooner cut their first teeth than they use them to bite the same breast. This, in each of us, is the first manifestation of the aggressive instinct, as many a mother can testify. Abraham, in his fine study of the evolution of human libido,[6] splits the first of the most important stages through which the libido passes, namely, the oral phase, into two parts: before and after the cutting of the child's teeth. The second of these he terms the *cannibal* phase. If, in fact, the child were not restrained, it might really try to eat, as well as suck, the breast on which it feeds. But, by gentle taps when it bites too hard, or by being deprived of the breast and, later, when the sense of what "one should not do" has been instilled by ever severer and more numerous moral injunctions (education in cleanliness being the first great step), the memory, or rather the fantasy of biting the mother's breast must become charged, in the unconscious, with past feelings of wickedness. And the child, having learned by experience what is meant by the law of retaliation when he infringes the code—codes so deeply ingrained in our unconscious race memories—begins, in his turn, to fear that the bites he wished to give his mother will be visited on him: namely, retaliation for his "cannibalism."[7]

The child knows, therefore, from experience, that the wish to bite and devour flesh, even that of his fellows, is a profound biological instinct. He attributes it to others, and with reason. Are there not tribes today, in Australia, which devour their children at a kind of family banquet?[8] The father would seem to have preserved this ghastly appetite even later into human history than the mother. It was Kronos from whom the mother of Zeus hid her son, to save him from his father's gluttony. But in ancient times, too, the mother must sometimes have been guilty of devouring her offspring as, nowadays, does in our domestic hutches. Traces of this barbarous age still survive in our myths, legends, and fairy tales, in the

persons of ogres and ogresses. The teeth of Berenice are thus
the fellows—though "vaginalized" or "genitalized" in the
unconscious—or the ogress who eats the children in Perrault's
version of "The Sleeping Beauty."

## 2. "LOSS OF BREATH"*

That Poe, throughout life, retained his "innocence," an
innocence determined by his impotence, is testified not only
by what we know of his life, but by his works: works which,
according to Baudelaire "contain not a single passage in any
way licentious or even sensual"—or, we would add, of the
fulfillment of love. There is no clearer evidence of this, to
the analyst, than the story "Loss of Breath."

"Loss of Breath," which forms part of the first series of
*The Tales of the Folio Club*, is also a tale of the "grotesque,"
to which Poe added the subtitle "A Tale à la Blackwood,"
though, later, he changed this into "A Tale neither in nor out
of Blackwood." Today, "Loss of Breath" seems to the reader
somewhat like those "surrealist" films which present a series
of unlinked images emanating from the unconscious.

Poe begins by declaring that "The most notorious fortune
must in the end, yield to the untiring courage of philosophy
—as the most stubborn city to the ceaseless vigilance of an
enemy." As examples he cites Samaria, Nineveh, Troy, and
Azoth, which latter "opened at last her gates to Psammitticus,
after having barred them for the fifth part of a century."

Following this preamble, which would appear totally unrelated to the subject, did we not recall that captured cities
often represent captured women, Poe, without transistion,
embarks on his tale:

"Thou wretch!—thou vixen!—thou shrew!" said I to my wife
on the morning after our wedding, "thou witch! thou hag!—thou
whipper-snapper!—thou sink of iniquity!—thou fiery-faced quintes-
sence of all that is abominable!—thou—thou—" here standing upon
tiptoe, seizing her by the throat, and placing my mouth close to

* "Loss of Breath, A Tale neither in nor out of 'Blackwood' ":
*Southern Literary Messenger*, September, 1835; 1840; *Broadway
Journal*, II, 26.
My quotations are taken from *The Broadway Journal* text, re-
vised in accordance with MS notes by Poe in a copy of the tale
given by him to Mrs. Whitman, and follow the *Virginia Edition*,
Vol. 2.

her ear, I was preparing to launch forth a new and more decided epithet of opprobrium, which should not fail, if ejaculated, to convince her of her insignificance, when, to my extreme horror and astonishment, I discovered that *I had lost my breath.*

Such are the terms in which Poe pictures the morning after a wedding. In place of the genital act performed in darkness, we have a verbal and sadistic attack in the day, which these insults represent while, at the very moment the husband seizes his wife to attack her, we find his powers suddenly fail and that, for want of breath, he cannot "ejaculate" the penetrating words.

The phrases "I am out of breath," "I have lost my breath," and so on, are often enough repeated in common conversation; but it had never occurred to me that the terrible accident of which I speak could *bona fide* and actually happen! Imagine—that is if you have a fanciful turn—imagine, I say, my wonder—my consternation—my despair!

Our hero, however, does not lose his self-possession.

Although I could not at first precisely ascertain to what degree the occurrence had affected me, I determined at all events to conceal the matter from my wife, until further experience should discover to me the extent of this my unheard-of calamity. Altering my countenance, therefore, in a moment, from its bepuffed and distorted appearance, to an expression of arch and coquettish benignity, I gave my lady a pat on one cheek and a kiss on the other, and without saying one syllable, (Furies! I could not), left her astonished at my drollery, as I pirouetted out of the room in a *Pas de Zéphyr.*

Thus the hero of the tale can once more boast, in the words of Rousseau. *"Et le chemin des passions me conduit à la philosophie véritable"* (And I was led to true philosophy by the path of passion).

Poe's real impotence, too, must have seemed to him the "truest philosophy." In spite of his "consternation" and "despair" at losing his "breath" for good, he, also, must have put a good face on his ill fortune. His consolation was to make a virtue of necessity, as the impotent so often do. He alone was capable of pure love! No one before had felt such ardent or ethereal passion! Nor would anyone after him! Thus, as of right, he could despise those who—like John

Allan with his harem—wallowed in the mire of fleshy delights. And since irony is a way to overcome misfortune, he could turn his impotence into a "humorous tale." Poe's humor, however, is always sinister and but thinly covers his ill-hap.

Yet, we ask, why should Poe rob his hero of breath for wishing to shout into his new bride's ear? Doubtless, the fact that the hero is *shouting*, when he should be thinking of doing something else, has its relation to his recent encounter— when the story was written—with the young cousin who would soon become his child-wife. We see here a defense reaction against the later temptations of carnal desire, plus memory traces, from deep in the past, of the manner in which this impotence was established. This must have happened before he was three, while still in the anal-sadistic stage, for his libido, then fixated on the beloved mother never, thereafter, renounced its object, and rendered him impotent for life.

Behold me then [continues the hero], safely ensconced in my private *boudoir*, a fearful instance of the ill consequences attending upon irascibility—alive, with the qualifications of the dead—dead, with the propensities of the living—an anomaly on the face of the earth—being very calm, yet breathless. . . .

We could ask no better description of the impotent man's plight.

Yes! breathless. I am serious in asserting that my breath was entirely gone. I could not have stirred with it a feather if my life had been at issue, or sullied even the delicacy of a mirror.

But now our hero discovers that he is not wholly speechless, as he at first feared. By lowering his voice to "a singularly deep guttural," he can emit sounds dependent "not upon the current of the breath, but upon a certain spasmodic action of the muscles of the throat."

These, the analyst would be inclined to interpret as an intestinal, pregenital language, replacing the strictly genital type of speech symbolized by respiration, the guttural sounds marking a regression to an earlier infantile, and hence impotent, stage of libidinal development.

Nevertheless, the unfortunate hero throws himself into a chair and is assailed by the most sombre reflections. He even thinks of suicide but rejects this with a shudder. Meanwhile "the tabby cat purred strenuously upon the rug, and the very water-dog wheezed assiduously under the table; each taking to itself much merit for the strength of its lungs, and all obviously done in derision of my own pulmonary incapacity."

Eventually he hears his wife go out and, assured he is alone, with palpitating heart returns to the scene of the disaster.

There, after locking the door, he begins a vigorous search. He thinks it possible, he tells us, "that concealed in some . . . closet or drawer, might be found the lost object of my inquiry. It might have a vapory—it might even have a tangible form." Male potency, which we here find symbolized by breath, has, of course, its "tangible form." We shall see later why Poe's unconscious here prefers to symbolize it as "vapory" breath.

Long and earnestly did I continue the investigation: but the contemptible reward of my industry and perseverance proved to be only a set of false teeth, two pair of hips, an eye, and a bundle of *billets-doux* from Mr. Windenough to my wife. I might as well here observe that this confirmation of my lady's partiality for Mr. W. occasioned me little uneasiness. That Mrs. Lacko'breath should admire anything so dissimilar to myself was a natural and necessary evil. I am, it is well-known, of a robust and corpulent appearance, and at the same time somewhat diminutive in stature. What wonder then that the lath-like tenuity of my acquaintance, and his altitude, which has grown into a proverb, should have met with all due estimation in the eyes of Mrs. Lacko'breath.

The undersized husband, we now learn, has a successful rival in the person of the lank, skinny Mr. Windenough, who has no difficulty in using *his* "breath." Small wonder, thinks Mr. Lacko'breath, since women are made that way! He resigns himself to the inevitable, and thus again demonstrates how truly philosophical he is. The identity of his lucky rival we shall seek to discover later.

"My exertions," continues our hero,

proved fruitless. Closet after closet—drawer after drawer—corner after corner—were scrutinized to no purpose. At one time, however, I thought myself sure of my prize, having in rummaging a dressing-case, accidentally demolished a bottle of Grandjean's Oil of Archangels—which, as an agreeable perfume, I here take the liberty of recommending.

Soon convinced of his error, however, he returns with a heavy heart to his boudoir—

there to ponder upon some method of eluding my wife's penetration, until I could make arrangements prior to my leaving the country, [for] . . . In a foreign climate . . . I might, with some probability of success, endeavour to conceal my unhappy calamity —a calamity calculated, even more than beggary, to estrange the affections of the multitude. . . .

Mr. Lacko'breath, thereupon, begins to memorize an entire tragedy, that of *Metamora*, where the tones of voice beyond his range are unnecessary whereas, for the leading role, "the deep guttural was expected to reign monotonously throughout."

For some time he practices his part "by the borders of a well frequented marsh," as Demosthenes by the seashore and, when he feels sufficiently sure of his progress, determines to make his wife believe him "suddenly smitten with a passion for the stage":

In this, I succeeded to a miracle; and to every question or suggestion found myself at liberty to reply in my most frog-like and sepulchral tones with some passage from the tragedy—any portion of which, as I soon took great pleasure in observing, would apply equally well to any particular subject. It is not to be supposed, however, that in the delivery of such passages I was found at all deficient in the looking asquint—the showing my teeth—the working my knees—the shuffling my feet—or in any of those unmentionable graces which are now justly considered the characteristics of a popular performer. To be sure they spoke of confining me in a straight-jacket—but, good God! they never suspected me of having lost my breath.

Let us pause here to recall the mediocre tragedian—as contemporary testimony unanimously affirms—who was Poe's father and who must often, in Edgar's hearing, have memorized aloud and ranted his "matamorish"[1] parts, in the guttural tones affected by indifferent tragedians. Edgar, it is true, was only eighteen months, when his father abandoned the family in New York, but unconscious memories reach far into the past. Since indifferent tragedians are legion, those who subsequently entered Mr. Placide's company—with which Edgar's mother stayed till he was three—might well, by fusing with his memories of his father, have helped to keep that memory alive. We have no means of knowing whether, or how often, Edgar was taken to the theatre to gaze with wondering eyes at his mother rehearsing, but it seems unlikely that so precocious a child, the son and grandson of players, would be kept away from the stage on which his mother spent her life and where, it is said, he even himself appeared.[2]

To us, therefore, it would seem that although Mr. Lacko'-breath primarily represents Poe in his impotent aspect, certain details reveal his father, the ranting tragedian. Like Poe's father, Mr. Lacko'breath is suddenly "smitten with a passion for the stage"—a passion which, in fact, made David Poe abandon his home and his father, the general. In other words, Poe, in this grotesque character, ironically identifies himself with his father or, rather, his father with himself. We have here a sort of posthumous revenge which the unconscious takes on the father; it is as though the child deep in Poe sought to insinuate, in this burlesque of the wish, that his father, the envied rival as regards the mother was, possibly, no more potent than himself!

There is, however, another character, so far but briefly mentioned by the narrator, who, nevertheless, is of prime importance as regards the hero, and who will emerge in all his glory only toward the end of the tale. This is Mr. Lacko'-breath's successful rival, the fortunate Mr. Windenough, whom we here see in all the panoply of potency, with far more breath than he needs; indeed, with more than anybody, as we shall see. In him we see the father in all his potency, the begetter to whom the mother belongs and whom she prefers above all others, as witness the love letters guarded so preciously in the drawer where they are found. This imaginary packet of letters, and what they reveal, reminds us, however, of other and real letters; letters which played so important and, possibly, a similar part in Poe's life; namely, the packet left by Elizabeth Arnold, which contained her miniature, her sketch of the port of Boston, a pocketbook, some locks of hair, and a jewel case, and which was all she could bequeath her two children when she died, before Edgar went to the Allans, and Rosalie to the Mackenzies. The jewel case, apparently, accompanied Rosalie when she

visited Fordham in 1846. Later, Mrs. Clemm is thought to
have burned the letters. During his life, Poe is said to have
treasured them, as he did everything connected with his
mother. Had he read them, however? It seems doubtful,
given his repressions and his fears of discovering what,
doubtless, he suspected and what, possibly, they contained:
proof of his mother's infidelity and the illegitimacy of his
sister.

Be that as it may, there was certainly doubt, at the time,
about Rosalie's legitimacy. The date of her birth is uncertain,
and our only record, as we have said, is the much later entry,
in the Mackenzie family Bible, that Rosalie was born at
Norfolk in December, 1810: that is, six months after David
Poe's disappearance in New York. Whether he did, in fact,
die in October, 1810, as reported at this time in the single
newspaper cutting we possess, or after Rosalie's birth, we
know that, when she was born, he had vanished from his
wife's life, a fact which, given Elizabeth Arnold's profession,
would well have sufficed to breed gossip. John Allan would
certainly have made the most of these doubts, since he but
little approved his wife's fostering of a child of strolling players. In the bitter and recriminatory letter John Allan wrote
to Henry Poe in November, 1824, he manages to insert:

Between you, your poor sister Rosalie may not suffer. At least she
is half your sister and God forbid my dear Henry that we should
visit upon the living the errors of the dead.[3]

It was doubtless the wish to refute such insinuations—
which must cruelly have hurt the pride of a charity child—
that made Poe, with his usual indifference to dates, advance
that of his father's death and even, for instance, write in a
letter to his cousin, William Poe:

My father David died when I was in the second year of my age,
and when my sister Rosalie was an infant in arms. Our mother
died a few weeks before him,[4]

a statement which, apart from the first assertion, was clearly
untrue, as Poe, indeed, must have very well known. The key
to the mystery which so preyed upon him, and thus made him
alter these dates, doubtless lay in this packet of old letters.
Did anyone ever read them? Possibly Mrs. Clemm, before

burning them. In any case, if the loving, simple Muddy ever discovered the secret, she took it with her to the grave.

Of one thing, however, we may be sure: fact or fantasy, the idea that his mother had betrayed his father assumed enormous importance in Poe's unconscious life. As a result, it finally remained as fact in his psyche, whatever the basis for it in the past, much in the way that the young Napoleon reacted to Lætitia Bonaparte's supposed intrigue with Governor de Marbeuf.[5]

In the case of Elizabeth Arnold, the supposition seems more likely to be true. The infidelity of the ailing English actress seems more credible than that of the "Corsican Cornelia." I have not been able to discover on what grounds Hervey Allen asserts that "all the authentic dates and the known facts show that the suspicion which was thus afterward thrown upon the memory of Mrs. Poe was not only cruel but untrue." [6] We have no real record of Rosalie's birth, and those concerned at the time thought that Elizabeth Arnold's letters were best burned: one may therefore wonder whether Hervey Allen's defense of his heroine is not dictated by the Puritan American attitude to such matters, in spite of the present prevalence of adultery, in America as elsewhere, and the general tolerance with which it is regarded.

I myself incline to the view of adultery, given the lapse of over a century, but nothing can now be affirmed. Yet, it seems to me that in Mr. Windenough, Poe combines characteristics of both his mother's lover and her husband and this by a wholly unconscious process of which he could not be aware. So, too, our dreams are constructed and remain, for the most part, un-understood. It is, in fact, the analyst's task to unravel the latent meaning thus hid in our dreams and waking fantasies.

The principal and characteristic feature of this imaginary character, a feature common to both husband and real or imagined lover, is power of breath; that breath which engendered Henry, Edgar, and subsequently Rosalie. We shall now examine the symbolism of this breath and seek to determine how Poe, impotent, came to choose breathing and breath as symbol of male potency.

In that outstanding work, *The Madonna's Conception through the Ear*,[7] Ernest Jones demonstrates that, as origin-

ally conceived, the legend of the Annunciation implied that
the Virgin was impregnated by the angel's words and the
breath of God or the Holy Ghost, which are one, entering
her ear.[8] In St. Augustine's words: *"Deus per angelum
loquebatur et Virgo per aurem imprægnebatur."* In their
breviary the Maronites are equally explicit: *"Verbum patris
per aurem benedictæ intravit"*[9] and, in a hymn to Thomas
à Becket as to St. Bonaventura, we find:

> Gaude, Virgo, mater Christi,
> Quae per aurem concepisti,
> Gabriele nuntio.
> Gaude, quia Deo plena
> Peperisti sine pena
> Cum pudoris lilio.

Jones also quotes a French version of this hymn of the
seventeenth century:

> Rejouyssez-vous, Vièrge, et Mère bienheureuse,
> Qui dans vos chastes flancs conçeutes par l'ouyr,
> L'Esprit-Sainct opérant d'un très-ardent désir,
> Est l'Ange l'annonçant d'une voix amoureuse.[10]

Again, St. Eleutherius thus addresses the Virgin: "O Vierge
bénie, rendue mère sans la coopération de l'homme! Car ici
l'oreille fut l'épouse, le verbe angélique l'époux."[11]

Following Jones, we might add many a similar quotation
from the Fathers of the Church and other ecclesiastical
writers, but content ourselves with observing (to quote this
author) that myths relating to the conception of gods or
heroes by the ear are not special to Christianity, though there
it possibly reaches its highest perfection. Shigemuni, the
Mongol savior, for instance, having chosen the most perfect
of earthly virgins, Mahænna or Maya, for mother, impregnated her while she slept by entering her right ear while, in
the Mahabharata, Kunti, the very pure virgin and later mother
of the hero Karna (whose name signifies breath), is similarly
impregnated by the sun god.

Now, it is just this channel that Poe's burlesque hero
chooses through which to approach his wife. The difference
in attitude between a religious legend and an extravaganza
in no way affects the significance of the symbols on which

they are based, and it is here worth recalling that Rabelais's Gargantua was also born from his mother's ear.

We shall now turn from the female ear as a receptive organ, to the engendering male breath and ignore the symbolism of the Dove, to which Jones consecrates a chapter, for this will not concern us here since Poe, in his story, omits the bird, offspring of the wind, in favor of wind itself, or breath. Nevertheless, this extensively documented work demonstrates that breath and, by extension, all aspects of wind, are endowed with fecundative powers. Thus the mouth, as orifice, serves at times as a female symbol; it may also readily become, thanks to its phallic tongue and its ability to spit or blow, a male potency symbol.

The concept of breath as a creative and fecundating force is thus expressed in Genesis: "And the LORD God formed man of the dust of the ground, and breathed into his nostrils the breath of life; and man became a living soul."[12]

Or in the words of the Psalmist: "By the word of the LORD were the heavens made; and all the host of them by the breath of his mouth."[13]

If from the theogony of the Old Testament we turn to mythology and folklore, we find winds universally conceived as fecundating. And not only of the earth and the fruits thereof, but of animals and women, whether mortals or goddesses. Was not Hera, in Greek mythology, made pregnant by the wind, to whom she bore Hephæstus; and do not the women of the Aruntas of Central Australia fly shrieking to their huts when the west wind blows, believing it bears the seed of children?[14] At one time, it was believed by the ancients that the women of Cyprus could conceive only in this manner, and an infinite number of such beliefs might be cited. Similar beliefs have also been attached to animals. Freud, in his study *Leonardo da Vinci*, has noted the ancient belief that all vultures were female and conceived by presenting the cloaca to the wind,[15] a belief so widely held that Origen cites it to substantiate the Virgin Birth of Jesus. In Samoa, a similar capacity is attributed to snipe[16] and, in antiquity, by St. Augustine to the mares of Cappadocia,[17] by Virgil to those of Bœotia,[18] and by Pliny to those of Lusitania.[19] Aristotle[20] and Pliny[21] both tell us that partridges might also be similarly fertilized should the wind blow from the cock, a legend which recalls the pollenation of certain plants, and leads us back to the common origin of all these

tales of wind fertilization. Clearly, all such tales and beliefs
are in origin anthropomorphic, and were projected upon the
winds of heaven only when the father himself had been
relegated there.

How was it, however, that in the unconscious, men came
to substitute breath, or wind (that is, the breath of our
Father in Heaven), for the generative fluid, and what "flows"
from the mouth for what issues from the penis? We have
already shown that the mouth, as an orifice furnished with
tongue, saliva, and breath, may symbolize both male and
female genitals. Nevertheless, there is a connecting link,
and one so far unmentioned, which provides us with the
first and infantile prototype of an organ strikingly able to
blow. This is the anus, whose functions—with due apologies
to civilized adults, in whom anal erotism is strongly repressed
—are charged, for the child, with intense libidinal interest.
Object as one may that breathing is far more important and
vital than breaking wind, it is the latter which most interests
the child. Here a distinction must be made between vital and
libidinal. Though our lives depend on respiration as on the
circulatory system, analysis shows that we do not find these
represented in the unconscious to anything like the same
extent as the functions which carry a libidinal charge, be they
anal, oral, phallic or, later, truly genital. One must be asth-
matic to worry about breathing. Displaced from below, however, it is intestinal flatus which invests the vital act of
respiration with the libidinal interest we find attached to it
in story, myth, and legend.

That this importance actually attaches to flatus we have
abundant proof, not only from contemporary psychoanalyses
but also from writings handed down to us from earliest
antiquity.

"The *pneuma*" (of the Greeks), writes Jones.

coursed through the entire body, regulated nutrition, generated
thought and semen, and, according to Aristotle, conveyed to the
head movements of sensation that had been transmitted to it from
without through the medium of the sense organs; on the state of it
depended the health of the individual.

With the Greeks, the

conception of respiration was a singularly broad one, many processes being included under the term besides that of breathing.

Aristotle, for example, positively states that the pneuma of the body, the importance of which we have just noted, is not derived from the breath, but is a secretion resulting from processes going on within the body itself (primarily in the intestine), and Galen says, even more explicitly, that the psychic pneuma is derived in part from the vapours of digested food.

Again,

the Greeks thought of the respiratory and alimentary systems as being throughout closely connected. . . . They not only identified the absorption of air, its subsequent changes within the body, and its final excretion, with those of food, but ascribed to the influence of the former the process whereby the latter becomes sufficiently rarefied to be carried over the body; the underlying idea, with of course many modifications, seems to have been that the inspired air reached the stomach, either through the blood-stream or through the œsophagus (which they believed led to the heart), and there digested the food, the internal pneuma being the product of this, and thus representing a combination of air and food. From this point of view (concludes Jones), it is clear that pneuma was not merely a symbolic equivalent of intestinal gas, but was actually and grossly identical with it. . . .[22]

The Vedic conception was similar to that of the Greeks. To the Indian philosophers, five Prânas, or breaths, were to be distinguished in man. The first, or true Prâna, the "up-breathing," means essentially the breath proper. The second, Apâna, the "down-breathing," is the wind of digestion, residing in the bowels. It originates in the navel of the primeval man . . . and presides over the organs of evacuation and generation. The third, the

Vyâna, or "back-going" wind, unites the breath proper to the wind of digestion and courses through the blood vessels. The Samâna, or "all-breathing," unites the Prâna to the Apâna, and carries the food over the body. These two last-mentioned breaths evidently make up together the Greek "internal pneuma." Finally, the Udâna, the "up- or out-breathing," sometimes called the wind of exit, dwells in the throat, and either brings up again or swallows down that which is eaten or drunk. The Udâna, which evidently denotes gas regurgitating from a flatulent stomach, is an interesting counterpart to the Apâna, for while the latter is formally identified with death itself, the former carries away the soul from the body after death; the connection between them is naturally a close one, since they both represent intestinal gas, which may escape either upwards or downwards.[23]

It may seem strange that the child's or primitive's first concepts of breathing, or of any act of creation, should be the activities of the bowels. Yet, if for a moment we lay aside our adult prejudices and criticism, and put ourselves in place of the child, it is sufficiently comprehensible. For, to the child, its first creation is what comes from its body, whether feces or urine, the former being the more highly prized since it is solid, and does not run off like water. The noises, too, which often accompany elimination, greatly please the child before this pleasure is inhibited by its upbringing; they signify to it powerful and valorous deeds, traces of which singular pride may be observed in many individuals of primitive mentality.[24]

Yet the impressiveness of such noises is incalculably magnified when, like veritable *thunderings,* they issue from that dreaded, mighty being, the father. They then fill the child's soul with fear and awe, and are later readily transformed into the thunderbolts of Zeus or the rumble of Thor's hammer.

To this a last fact must be added which gives wind, breath, and breathing such prime importance; namely, that the small child is often present at the sex acts of adults, too heedless of its sensitiveness to such impressions. What it then sees leaves indelible traces in the unconscious—traces which later analysis reveals. Actually, the child already bears within it larval instinctual mechanisms which, strange though this seem to the thoughtless or ill-informed adult, make it particularly sensitive to, and observant of, similar instinctual manifestations in others.

Two senses in particular are concerned in the child's awareness of adult coitus and those the "noblest," sight and hearing; hearing, above all, since the sex act commonly takes place in darkness. And what, to the ear, most characterizes coitus, if not its panting breath, its sighs and moans and—even, at times, gross as it seems—the sound of the woman breaking wind, as a result of abdominal compression in the coital position. At such times, as analysis proves, the child habitually attributes such *thunderings* to the father; the omnipotent father he dreads and whom he imagines, in coitus, attacking the mother, since that is its earliest sadistic idea of the act. Many phobias in neurotics, of thunder as of loud noises and explosions, are found to derive from this association of anal noises with the dreaded father's genital activity. That the orgasm itself, though noiseless, is so frequently symbolized as an explosion doubtless, in part, also derives from the same cause.

This close proximity, in time and place, between the panting respiration of coitus and the flatus which at times accompanies it, serves to displace on the former the libidinal interest originally attached to the latter. Furthermore, the symbolizing of male potency as breath would solve many a problem for one who, like Poe, shrank from all that was frankly genital. It would, in effect, enable any reference to male potency to be expressed in seemingly innocent pregenital and even prephallic terms.

Jones has further demonstrated that the crocodile, the very image of impotence in its immobility and mutism, nevertheless, to the Egyptians, became the prime phallic symbol; a symbol as important as the legendary phoenix which, like the penis, is ever reborn from its ashes. Some such process seems to have determined the representing of virility by breath or wind, an essentially anal concept, giving us what we might call an *impotence symbol to symbolize potency,* which apparent contradiction gratifies both the desire to castrate and to exalt the father. In such a symbolic process one might, in fact, ignore the penis, for breath takes its place. But, owing to the consequent displacement, the omnipotence of the penis is attached to breath. By the blasts of trumpets the walls of Jericho fell—that Jericho, which, like "Samaria, Nineveh, Troy and Azoth," at last "opened her gates" after keeping them long closed. Finally, it is the displacement from below above (a frequent consequence of repression), which so effectively disguises the anal origin of the concept of the generative breath.

If, now, having passed in review the pneuma of the Greeks and the Vedic Prânas, we return from the generative and divine breath of Jehovah to that mislaid by our unfortunate hero, we shall see its anal origin betrayed in numerous details. We content ourselves with mentioning two. For instance, while hunting for his breath in his wife's chamber, Mr. Lacko'breath imagines it to be found when he overturns a bottle of Oil of Arch-angels—"which agreeable perfume" he, thereupon, permits himself to recommend to the reader. Now, after the word "bottle," Poe originally had a parenthesis, later suppressed, which makes his hero declare, "I had a remarkably sweet breath."[25]

As every analyst knows, however, and may frequently

verify from the patients he observes, predilections for scent
directly derive from anal erotism. The love of *pleasant* smells
derives from that of *bad*, which were originally the good
smells to the child before education repressed its pleasure in
them into its opposite, disgust. This pleasure in these first
odoriferous substances survives in animals, particularly in the
dog, while in many people original traces remain in the
predilection for strong cheeses, "high" meat and game. In
civilized man, however, this infantile pleasure in smells
produced by the bowels is largely transformed into pleasure
in scents which, though in supposedly contrary fashion,
equally titillate the nasal mucous membranes. The anal origin
of this predilection for scents we find further attested in the
popular belief that by-products of fecal matter largely enter
into their composition.

The fact that Poe suppressed just this brief sentence which
confesses the link between scent and breath ("I had a remarkably sweet breath"), is of some interest. The phrase
itself seems inoffensive and hardly to merit being banned:
it, in fact, barely affects the context. But it was doubtless
suppressed by Poe because of a vague feeling that it was too
open, too offensive an allusion.

Finally, we recall that the guttural and sepulchral utterance, like the croaking of frogs, forced on Mr. Lacko'breath
by his accident, reminds us—as we have already said—of
borborygms or intestinal noises which are denied issue.

We left Mr. Lacko'breath on the eve of his flight from
home and wife, about to set forth on his travels. Let us
follow this "fugue"—for such it was—and so comparable with
Poe's own repeated flights from the sex dangers associated,
for him, with women.

"Having at length put my affairs in order," our hero
continues,

I took my seat very early one morning in the mail stage for ———,
giving it to be understood, among my acquaintances, that business
of the last importance required my immediate personal attendance
in that city.

The coach was crammed to repletion; but in the uncertain twi-
light the features of my companions could not be distinguished.
Without making any effectual resistance, I suffered myself to be
placed between two gentlemen of colossal dimensions; while a

third, of a size larger, requesting pardon for the liberty he was about to take, threw himself upon my body at full length, and falling asleep in an instant, drowned all my guttural ejaculations for relief, in a snore which would have put to blush the roarings of the bull of Phalaris.

Thus, for the first time in this tale, in flesh and blood, the crushing image of the father appears, depicted as this passenger whose mighty breath at once conjures up the most potent of all animal symbols, the bull, though only in respect of its roars. This ill-mannered fellow, who seems to be traveling on business, to me seems strikingly to suggest John Allan, which appears confirmed by the manner in which he treats his victim. It is as though Poe were here telling that he himself had been *crushed* by John Allan. "Happily the state of my respiratory faculties rendered suffocation an accident entirely out of the question," which suggests that Poe seems unconsciously to have thought that, by sacrificing his virility, he might preserve his ego intact.

As, however, the day broke more distinctly in our approach to the outskirts of the city, my tormentor arising and adjusting his shirt-collar, thanked me in a very friendly manner for my civility. Seeing that I remained motionless (all my limbs were dislocated and my head twisted on one side), his apprehensions began to be excited; and arousing the rest of the passengers, he communicated in a very decided manner, his opinion that a dead man had been palmed upon them during the night for a living and responsible fellow-traveller; here giving me a thump on the right eye, by way of demonstrating the truth of his suggestion.

This eye motif we have met before, first in "The Gold-Bug" and, again, as our tale begins, when Mr. Lacko'breath finds a glass eye in his wife's drawer, together with false teeth and a pair of false hips. It represents symbolic castration and will find its completest expression in the gouged-out eye of *The Black Cat*. The thump on Mr. Lacko'breath's right eye, however, forms but the introduction to the multiple symbolic castrations that follow. For, when the other passengers, a mystic nine, have one by one "pulled his ear," a doctor among them eventually declares him dead after establishing that he lacks even breath to tarnish a mirror. Thereupon, with one accord, the passengers cast his "carcass" into the road.

I was . . . thrown out at the sign of the "Crow" (by which
tavern the coach happened to be passing) [continues our hero],
without meeting with any farther accident than the breaking of
both my arms, under the left hind wheel of the vehicle. I must
besides do the driver the justice to state that he did not forget
to throw after me the largest of my trunks, which, unfortunately
falling on my head, fractured my skull in a manner at once interesting and extraordinary.

Now another father figure appears, to emphasize the castration motif still more clearly. For, when the landlord of the
"Crow" has found enough in the trunk to reward his efforts,
he sends for a surgeon to whom he delivers our hero, with
fractured head and arms, against a receipt for ten dollars.

Follows a description of the surgeon's aid:

The purchaser took me to his apartment and commenced operations immediately. Having cut off my ears, however, he discovered signs of animation. He now rang the bell, and sent for
a neighboring apothecary with whom to consult in the emergency.
In case of his suspicions with regard to my existence proving
ultimately correct, he, in the meantime, made an incision in my
stomach, and removed several of my viscera for private dissection.

Symbolic castration could hardly go further. Nevertheless, our
hero remains alive, although the apothecary pronounces him
dead, for the victim's kicks and plunges, to prove his existence, are taken as a mere reflex to the apothecary's galvanic
shocks. It is as though we were already viewing Mr. Valde-
mar's convulsions, and even his sepulchral tones are anticipated in Mr. Lacko'breath's guttural voice. But now,
doubtless from the shock of these multiple castrations, he
loses such voice as he had, and cannot even make himself
heard.

As a result, the "practitioners," unable to reach a decision,
remand their victim "for further examination." The surgeon's
lady provides him with "drawers and stockings," and the
surgeon himself gags and binds and bolts him in a garret,
abandoned "to silence and to meditation."

The unfortunate hero now discovers that, but for the
handkerchief binding his jaws, he could resume his guttural
speech. Delighted by this discovery, he mentally begins to
repeat "passages of the 'Ominipresence of the Deity,' " (in
other words, of the father whom, indeed, he meets at every

turn: in the bulky passenger, in the castrating surgeon, and in others, as we shall see). At this point,

> two cats, of a greedy and vituperative turn, entering at a hole in the wall, leaped up with a flourish à la Catalani, and alighting opposite one another on my visage, betook themselves to indecorous contention for the paltry consideration of my nose.

But, as the loss of his ears proved the means of elevating to the throne of Cyrus, the Magian or Mige-Gush of Persia, and as the cutting off his nose gave Zopyrus possession of Babylon, so the loss of a few ounces of my countenance proved the salvation of my body.

So, too, the children of races which practice circumcision buy salvation of the rest of their beings. . . .

"Aroused by the pain, and burning with indignation," Mr. Lacko'breath bursts his bonds and, throwing open the window—to the "extreme horror and disappointment" of the belligerents—precipitates himself "very dexterously" into the street below.

Leaving for the moment the two cats, and what they may represent, let us follow our hero where his amazing destiny leads him:

> The mail-robber W——, to whom I bore a singular resemblance, was at this moment passing from the city jail to the scaffold erected for his execution in the suburbs. His extreme infirmity, and long continued ill health, had obtained him the privilege of remaining unmanacled; and habited in his gallows' costume—one very similar to my own—he lay at full length in the bottom on the hangman's cart (which happened to be under the windows of the surgeon at the moment of my precipitation) without any other guard than the driver who was asleep, and two recruits of the sixth infantry, who were drunk.

> As ill-luck would have it, I alit upon my feet within the vehicle. W——, who was an acute fellow, perceived his opportunity.

He leaps from the cart and, in a twinkling, disappears. The drunken recruits are somewhat muddled as to what has taken place but, seeing a man very similar to W—— on his feet, in the cart, they conclude that their captive is attempting to escape and, after another dram apiece, fell the poor wretch with the butts of their muskets.

Mr. Lacko'breath is thus turned over to the hangman, who slips the noose on his neck and lets fall the drop.

In the first version of this story the hanged man's sensations were now described in detail.[26] The following long and interesting passage is suppressed in the final *Broadway Journal* version and in Griswold.

"Die I certainly did not," it begins:

The sudden jerk given to my neck upon the falling of the drop, merely proved a corrective to the unfortunate twist afforded me by the gentlemen in the coach. Although my body certainly *was*, I had, alas! no breath *to be* suspended; and but for the skaking of the rope, the pressure of the knot under my ear, and the rapid determination of blood to the brain, should, I dare say, have experienced very little inconvenience.

The latter feeling, however, grew momentarily more painful. I heard my heart beating with violence—the veins in my hands and wrists swelled nearly to bursting—my temples throbbed tempestuously—and I felt that my eyes were starting from their sockets. Yet when I say that in spite of all this my sensations were not absolutely intolerable, I will not be believed.

Mr. Lacko'breath then describes the strange noises in his ears—bells toll, drums beat, and he hears the murmur of the sea. At the same time, his mental powers are strangely affected and permit him to analyze even his confused state, with paradoxical clarity and precision:

Memory, which, of all other faculties, should have first taken its departure, seemed on the contrary to have been endowed with quadrupled power. Each incident of my past life flitted before me like a shadow. There was not a brick in the building where I was born—not a dog-leaf in the primer I had thumbed over when a child—not a tree in the forest where I hunted when a boy—not a street in the cities I had traversed when a man—that I did not at that time most palpably behold. I could repeat to myself entire lines, passages, chapters, books, from the studies of my earliest days; and while, I dare say, the crowd around me were blind with horror, or aghast with awe, I was alternately with Æschylus, a demi-god, or with Aristophanes, a frog.

Where had Poe learned to describe such sensations? After a significant row of asterisks, he himself answers this question:

A dreamy delight now took hold upon my spirit, and I imagined that I had been eating opium, or feasting upon the Hashish of the old Assassins.

In these words Poe indirectly confesses his use of the drug, as much betrayed by Mr. Lacko'breath's fantasies and sensations as by those of the traveler in "The Oval Portrait," or Monos relating his experiences after death to Una.[27]

This drug, by the fevered visions it inspires, and the utter immobility it imposes, is admirably fitted to conjure up the fantasies of Life-in-Death that haunted Poe's unconscious. Now the hanged man experiences its effects: he has glimpses of "pure unadulterated reason," and blesses his stars as he looks out over the sea of waving heads round him: "In the intensity of my delight I eyed them with feelings of the deepest commiseration, and blessed, as I looked upon the haggard assembly, the superior benignity of *my* proper stars."

Meanwhile he continues to reason, in a sort of intoxication, on the most abstruse and varied metaphysical subjects, which include Coleridge, Kant, Fichte, and pantheism.

Here more asterisks herald a peak in his toxic delirium:

A rapid change was now taking place in my sensations. The last shadows of connection flitted away from my meditations. A storm—a tempest of ideas, vast, novel, and soul-stirring, bore my spirit like a feather afar off. Confusion crowded upon confusion like a wave upon a wave.

Whereupon Mr. Lacko'breath is shortly removed from the gallows. In his confusion he hardly knows what has happened, though he feels the concussion of his fall. It then appears that the real culprit has been caught, though somewhat late. Our hero, still alive, now seems quite dead, and since none claims his body, it is decided he be given a common burial next morning. Meanwhile, the supposititious corpse is laid out in a room, described as follows:

I was laid out in a chamber sufficiently small, and very much encumbered with furniture—yet to me it appeared of a size to contain the universe. I have never before or since, in body or in mind, suffered half so much agony as from that single idea. Strange! that the simple conception of abstract magnitude—of infinity—should have been accompanied with pain. Yet so it was. "With how vast a difference," said I, "in life as in death—in time and in eternity—here and hereafter, shall our merest sensations be embodied!"

Thus Mr. Lacko'breath relates the approach of death to the loss of the sense of time and space experienced in opium dreams, for, despite having lost his breath and most of his viscera, he still, and with reason, refuses to believe himself dead:

The day died away, and I was aware that it was growing dark— yet the same terrible conceit still overwhelmed me. Nor was it confined to the boundaries of the apartment—it extended, although in a more definite manner, to all objects, and, perhaps, I will not be understood in saying that it extended also to all *sentiments*. My fingers as they lay cold, clammy, stiff, and pressing helplessly one against another, were, in my imagination, swelled to a size according with the proportions of the Antæus. Every portion of my frame betook of their enormity. The pieces of money—I well remember—which, being placed upon my eyelids, failed to keep them effectually closed, seemed huge, interminable chariot-wheels of the Olympia, or of the Sun.

Yet it is very singular that I experienced no sense of weight—of gravity. On the contrary I was put to much inconvenience by the buoyancy—that tantalizing *difficulty of keeping down,* which is felt by the swimmer in deep water, Amid the tumult of my terrors I laughed with a hearty internal laugh to think what incongruity there would be—could I arise and walk—between the elasticity of my motion, and the mountain of my form.

This loss of sense of weight is also characteristic of the opium dream. Here we find it associated with the strange sensation of swelling, which, as we shall later see, derives from another different source.

Abandoning Mr. Lacko'breath, for the moment, to the torments and delights of his opium dream, we are now justified, as psychoanalysts, in asking why Poe should have elected that his burlesque hero be hanged and why, in place of resultant death, an opium dream should be substituted. If questions such as these seem idle to the reader, if to them these episodes are but the vagaries of a writer, they grossly underrate, as do so many, the power and extent of that deep psychic determinism which penetrates even the unconscious.

Hanging, it would appear, in all ages and climes, enjoys the same reputation of, so it is said, producing erection and ejaculation *in extremis.*[28] Whence, doubtless, the traditional association of the mandrake root, vaguely human in form and once so widely employed in magic, with the gallows. Even today, it is said, there are old men who resort to incomplete forms of hanging in hopes of increasing their erectile powers. And it is just when our hero has undergone his numerous visceral symbolic castrations at the surgeon's hands, that Poe's unconscious, as it were, protests and avenges itself by thus attaching a new penis to our hero. It is as though he here said: "No, I am not castrated; I still have my penis, as you very well see," as the onlooking multitude gazes astounded at the figure on the scaffold. But how sardonically this restitution is made! For though our hero feels himself "with Æschylus, a demi-god," and regards the crowd at his feet with the "deepest commiseration" while blessing the "superior benignity" of his fate, nevertheless, he himself is there hanging. Even the penis, so mock-heroically restored, with which he thus identifies himself with all his body,[29] is itself no better than a man hanged, in its flaccidity and limpness. Here too, then, as with wind and breath, we find an impotency symbol symbolizing potency.

The hanged man also reacts to his "rephallization" in a similar manner. He feels voluptuous pleasure, it is true, but it is the "chemo-toxic orgasm"[30] of opium, in which the libido, as it were, short circuits itself inside the body, owing to inability to reach out to an external love object The opium delirium, as that from all toxic substances, serves as a substitute for the masturbatory orgasm, a form of satisfaction derived from regression to the primal pregenital oral-erotic phase from which even trace of the child's penis-masturbation has vanished.

Glimpses of this past activity, however, appear in our hero's opium dream when he hangs, and after he is cut down. Yet, even as signs of this activity begin to work through into the preconscious, they are immediately charged with intense anxiety—that anxiety which, when he was a child, must have caused its own repression and thus doomed Poe to lifelong impotence.

What are Mr. Lacko'breathe's sensations at the moment he is hanged, that is, when his penis is thus restored?

I heard my heart beating with violence—the veins in my hands and wrists swelled nearly to bursting—my temples throbbed tempestuously—and I felt that my eyes were starting from their sockets.

Thus, once more, we find an unconscious allusion to erection,

in the form of an influx of blood into the bulbo-cavernous
tissues. By a reversal of affect, however—a classic mechanism
in neurotics—the sensation of swelling, as a result of repression, grows "momentarily more painful" and transforms the
pleasure into anxiety.

Even more transparent is the allusion to erection in the
victims's illusions after he is hanged, for the fingers, instru-
mental in masturbation, by a similar customary transference
from penis to hand, swell "to a size according with the
proportions of the Antæus," that giant whose strength was
drawn from contact with the Earth, his mother. So, too, with
the rest of our hero's body. Such sensations remind one of
certain nightmares. In one case I know, a little girl, later
analyzed, suffered from a recurrent nightmare which she
called the *screw dream*. She felt she was lying in bed, on her
back and that, from her abdomen, perpendicularly, in the
prevailing and sinister gloom, a huge wooden screw rose to
the ceiling. The screw, all slimy with glue, went on revolving
slowly and, as the child held the screw with her hands, they
would begin to swell, as in this story, until they filled the
whole room, whereupon the child awoke in a state of in-
describable anxiety. Later analysis enabled this nightmare to
be recognized as a substitute for infantile masturbation, once
the child had been broken of the habit by violence and
menaces that she would die. It was a dream of clitoris erection, accompanied by penis envy and genital pleasure, converted into anxiety. The "glue" represented both the moisture
of the genital mucosæ, and the real glue on flypapers hung
from the ceiling. The child had felt sorry for the poor
captured flies which died after touching the forbidden
(taboo) glue. Such was the final fate of people who loved
*vice*[31] and dared to induce their hands to swell, as substitutes
for another part of the body.

The feeling of flying, of being released from the laws of
gravity, which is characteristic not only of opium dreams,
but of dreams which represent erection, where gravity is also
overcome, need not, necessarily, have occurred in this nightmare, the erection itself being represented in a form thinly
disguised. In his delirium, however, Mr. Lacko'breath resorts
to it in the usual way, and is much inconvenienced by "the
buoyancy—that tantalising *difficulty in keeping down* which is
felt by the swimmer in deep water." From which we gather
that erectility must have seemed a veritable torment to the

profoundly inhibited, impotent Poe. The urge toward supremest pleasure had become the source of supreme anxiety.
Thus, he preferred the intoxications induced by alcohol and,
especially, opium—which do not importune the penis—that
he might remain "alive with the attributes of the dead and
dead, with the propensities of the living . . . very calm, yet
breathless." The rapid decline in virility, and loss of erectility,
in opium addicts, is well known.

Here we touch on a biological problem of some difficulty,
especially after the lapse of more than a century. What form
did Poe's impotence take? Was it a psychic impotence that
made the sex act impossible, owing to the dangers the
approach to women implied—although erection might occur
when he was away from them—or did erectility vanish at an
early age?

I incline to the view that it was the latter, more total, form
of impotence. If as appears, Poe, when twenty-two, that is in
1831 and at Baltimore, began to resort, probably inter-
mittently, to opium, it was no doubt because of the inner
prohibition which banned erection. The protracted, undiffer-
entiated, sensuous delights which opium induces, a pleasure
comparable with that of the torpid, replete babe, would
suit a necrophilist psyche, like Poe's, far better than the doing
of horrible acts, the very idea of which would strike him as
repellent. Yet he could indulge these ideas in his contem-
plative, gruesome, and aesthetic reveries, without fear of
remorse.

Unlike the depleted Mr. Lacko'breath of this story, it is
only in fiction that a hero, as in Poe's "Lionizing,"[32] can pride
himself on a huge nose—substitute for the penis—as the cause
of his social success. Yet, at the end of the tale, we find that
his triumphs are eclipsed by the Elector of Bluddennuff, from
whom, in a duel, he shoots off that same appendage. For, as
we have pointed out, the impotent often end, however they
may suffer, by priding themselves on that very impotence,
and considering it a mark of distinction which puts them
above the common run. Though "in Fum-Fudge the greatness
of a lion is in proportion to the size of his proboscis . . .
there is no competing with a lion who has no proboscis at
all."

But let us return to Mr. Lacko'breath, as he lies in the
chamber, so strangely encumbered with furniture, and waits
to be buried. He has spent all night meditating on his im-

minent death, in a state which he pictures as "motionless, yet
wishing for motion—powerless, yet longing for power." Now
morning arrives and, with the "misty and gloomy dawn" there
comes "in triple horror the paraphernalia of the grave."
Though still unable to move or speak, through half-closed lids
he sees the coffin appear, as also the undertaker "with attendants and a screw-driver." Again a "stout" man appears, who
grasps his feet, while another, out of sight, takes his head
and shoulders:

Together they placed me in the coffin, and drawing the shroud
up over my face proceeded to fasten down the lid. One of the
screws, missing its proper direction, was screwed by the carelessness of the undertaker deep—deep—down into my shoulder. A
convulsive shudder ran throughout my frame. With what horror,
with what sickening of heart did I reflect that one minute sooner
a similar manifestation of life would, in all probability, have
prevented my inhumation. But alas! it was now too late, and hope
died away within my bosom as I felt myself lifted upon the
shoulders of men—carried down the stairway—and thrust within
the hearse.

During the brief passage to the cemetery my sensations, which
for some time had been lethargic and dull, assumed, all at once,
a degree of intense and unnatural vivacity for which I can in no
manner account. I could distinctly hear the rustling of the
plumes—the whispers of the attendants—the solemn breathings
of the horses of death. Confused as I was in that narrow and
strict embrace, I could feel the quicker or slower movement of
the procession—the restlessness of the driver—the windings of the
road as it led us to the right or to the left. I could distinguish the
peculiar odor of the coffin—the sharp acid smell of the steel
screws. I could see the texture of the shroud as it lay close against
my face; and was even conscious of the rapid variations in light
and shade with the flapping to and fro of the sable hangings
occasioned within the body of the vehicle.

Thus our poor friend, with his "X-ray" eyes, even pierces
through the boards of his coffin. Yet, would there not be a
memory here, or fantasy rather, transferred to other hearses,
from some fantasy of having seen that of his mother? For a
child looking on could have seen the hearse, even if the man
in the coffin could not. Thus, the strange pomp of the hanged
man's funeral, the mourners and plumes and procession
through the city would be explained for, in his unconscious it

is, in fact, the hearse of Poe's mother that is here represented which, doubtless, was followed by admirers and fellow actors. In the same way, may not the small furniture-encumbered room where, to our surprise, the hanged man waits to be buried, be some reminiscence of the room in which the small Edgar first met Death: the humble "furnished room" rented from Mrs. Phillips, the milliner, where Elizabeth Arnold pined and died?

Be that as it may, the room, the coffin and, then, the hearse, all subserve an unconscious design in this story, by representing the places where our hero enacts each stage of *regression*, beginning with the "opium dream" which accompanies and follows his hanging. This dream replaces the pangs of death; the death which should have ensued being equated, in the unconscious, with a return to the womb. Given that the opium dream reproduces and augments the voluptuous pleasure of the satisfied babe, Mr. Lacko'breath, starting from the oral-erotic stage, regresses ever backward into the past. In this overfurnished room, doubtless reminiscent of the chance lodging in which Poe's mother died, the hero, entering his coffin, symbolically returns to the mother's womb. Then it is that the ubiquitous Father, like the God he is, now shown as an undertaker, pursues him to this final refuge and pierces his shoulder with a screw whose symbolic significance every analyst will understand. The screw, in the dream of the child we quoted earlier, had a similar phallic meaning; *screwing*, in vulgar parlance, denoting the sex act. There is here, too, an allusion to one of those unconscious fantasies which seem so strange to the layman; that of intra-uterine observation of coitus. We shall meet this fantasy again in its most transparent and most terrible form, in another famous tale by Poe which we shall analyze in due course.

Thus, restored to life by a penetrating screw, Mr. Lacko'-breath, in his coffin, is "lifted upon the shoulders of men," carried down the stairway—"and thrust within the hearse." Now, if the coffin represents the mother's womb, the hearse, following the common infantile symbolism attached to vehicles, would represent her whole body. The pregnant uterus, that is, the coffin with its contents, is thus borne along in the hearse, by "horses of death," whose "solemn breathings" he hears. In the same way, the little Edgar, then

Rosalie, were "carried" by a mother, breathless, consumptive, and bearing the stigma of death. In that "narrow and strict" placental embrace, the sensations of the fetus, nurtured by its mother's blood, suddenly and inexplicably assume an "intense and unnatural vivacity." So, too, might Poe's unconscious have pictured the vitality of the fetus toward the end of its intrauterine existence when, fully grown and rocked by the ponderous movements of its mother, it begins to move and demonstrate its existence. But this regression into the prenatal past extends yet further. Before this activity began, there was a time when the fetus experienced an utter immobility, a timeless sleep in the womb. So, too, our hero's coffin, when it reaches its place of sepulture, is laid in its grave in the earth's bowels, which then close on their tenant:

From what I overheard early in the morning . . . it was probable that many months might elapse before the doors of the tomb would be again unbarred—and even should I survive until that period, what means could I have more than at present, of making known my situation or of escaping from the coffin? I resigned myself, therefore, with much tranquillity to my fate, and fell, after many hours, into a deep and deathlike sleep.

The original limbo of prenatal existence being reached, regression can go no further:

How long I remained thus [in this prenatal sleep] is to me a mystery. When I awoke my limbs were no longer cramped with the cramp of death—I was no longer without the power of motion. A very slight exertion was sufficient to force the lid of my prison—for the dampness of the atmosphere had already occasioned decay in the woodwork around the screws.

He now, therefore, emerges from his womblike coffin and essays his first feeble, timid steps, with all the hesitation we might expect in one so newly born. Also, like a newborn child, he begins to feel the gnawing of hunger—and, above all, an "intolerable thirst." "Yet, as time passed away," he says,

it is strange that I experienced little uneasiness from these scourges of the earth, in comparison with the more terrible visitations of the fiend, *Ennui*. Stranger still were the resources by which I endeavoured to banish him from my presence.

For now he begins to speculate on the construction and dimensions of the many-dungeoned supulcher in which he is imprisoned, and counts and recounts its stones, as though afflicted with arithmomania:

But there were other methods by which I endeavored to lighten the tedium of my hours. Feeling my way among the numerous coffins ranged in order around, I lifted them down one by one, and breaking open their lids, busied myself in speculations about the mortality within.

We now return to the final version of this tale, in which Poe suppressed all our quotations from the time Mr. Lacko'-breath is hanged to the point we have reached. And here, we shall again note that in waking fantasies, as in dreams, the elements which are forgotten, or what amounts to the same thing, suppressed, are the most relevatory of the un-conscious meaning of the whole.

Mr. Lacko'breath, then, in his tedium, has just removed the lid from a coffin. "This!" he soliloquizes,

tumbling over a carcass, puffy, bloated, and rotund—"this has been, no doubt, in every sense of the word, an unhappy—an un-fortunate man. It has been his terrible lot not to walk, but to waddle—to pass through life not like a human being, but like an elephant—not like a man, but like a rhinocerous.

"His attempts at getting on have been mere abortions, and his circumgyratory proceedings a palpable failure. Taking a step for-ward, it has been his misfortune to take two towards the right, and three towards the left. His studies have been confined to the poetry of Crabbe. He can have had no idea of the wonder of a *pirouette*. To him a *pas de papillon* has been an abstract con-ception. He has never ascended the summit of a hill. He has never viewed from any steeple the glories of a metropolis. Heat has been his mortal enemy. In the dog-days his days have been the days of a dog. Therein, he has dreamed of flames and suffoca-tion—of mountains upon mountains—of Pelion upon Ossa. He was short of breath—to say all in a word, he was short of breath. He thought it extravagant to play upon wind instruments. He was the inventor of self-moving fans, wind-sails, and ventilators. He patronized Du Pont the bellows-maker, and died miserably in attempting to smoke a cigar. His was a case in which I feel a deep interest—a lot in which I sincerely sympathize!"

In our opinion, there is more in this "puffy, bloated, and rotund" carcass which Mr. Lacko'breath thus disinters, than

the mere reflection of his luckless self. Indeed, it reminds us
of other figures in his tales. The swollen corpse of Rogers in
*The Narrative of Arthur Gordon Pym,* for instance, and the
obese Queen Consort of "King Pest," whom he likens to a
beer keg, and who is "in the last stage of a dropsy." In Poe,
the lover of ethereal, of consumptive fragility in women, excess
of *embonpoint* always gave rise to especial derision. In "The
Thousand-and-Second Tale of Sheherazade,"[33] for example,
he expresses horror at the then fashionable bustle, which
made a "dromedary" of a woman. If all these general indications are put together and considered analytically, we are
struck by a new idea. In "King Pest," we see the royal pair as
an obese queen and an extraordinarily tall and emaciated
king. Similarly, in "Loss of Breath," we may anticipate somewhat by disclosing that the next coffin will yield a tall,
emaciated corpse, to partner the bloated corpse already revealed. Furthermore, we are told to satiety, even, that this
carcass cannot dance; not for it the *pirouette* or *pas de
papillon!* Can we not, then, in the reference to this bloated
carcass, see here a revenge taken by Poe on his mother, for
being so wicked as to produce a sister-rival when he was a
child? During her pregnancy, the once fragile, applauded
sylph would doubtless have been forced to abandon dancing,
and, ponderous, "short of breath" . . . "bloated and rotund,"
to remain at home with her son. Later, her movements about
the room would remind him of a duck's "waddle," and her
shape of an "elephant" or "rhinoceros." She, too, at night,
would have dreamed she was suffocating, of "mountains
upon mountains," and her "circumgyratory proceedings,"
had she wished to dance, would have ended in "palpable
failure" and possibly, even, in miscarriage.

The fact that the mother is here represented by someone
of the male sex need not trouble us greatly. When Elizabeth
Arnold was pregnant with Rosalie, Edgar, then under two,
was still too small to appreciate any difference in the sexes.
His mother, for him, still possessed a penis, and a carryover
from this time may, possibly, be detected in the fact that, in
his tales, Poe indifferently embodies his vision of the pregnant
mother as the bloated corpse of a woman, "King Pest," or as
those of men (*The Narrative of Arthur Gordon Pym* and
"Loss of Breath").

Nevertheless, it is not only the mother whom the tomb is
to deliver up to our hero, thus reborn, but those responsible

for the phenomenon of birth; the life-giving couple. Turning, therefore, from the bloated, rotund corpse, our hero passes to another:

"But here," said I, "here"—and I dragged spitefully from its receptacle a gaunt, tall, and peculiar-looking form, whose remarkable appearance struck me with a sense of unwelcome familiarity— "here is a wretch entitled to no earthly commiseration." Thus saying, in order to obtain a more distinct view of my subject, I applied my thumb and fore-finger to its nose, and causing it to assume a sitting position upon the ground, held it thus, at the length of my arm, while I continued my soliloquy.

—"Entitled," I repeated, "to no earthly commiseration. Who indeed would think of compassionating a shadow? Besides, has he not had his full share of the blessings of mortality? He was the originator of tall monuments—shot-towers—lightning-rods—lombardy poplars. His treatise upon 'Shades and Shadows' has immortalized him. He edited with distinguished ability the last edition of 'South on the Bones.'[34] He went early to college and studies pneumatics. He then came home, talked eternally, and played upon the French-horn. He patronized the bag-pipes. Captain Barclay, who walked against Time, would not walk against *him*. Windham[35] and Allbreath were his favorite writers—his favorite artist, Phiz.[36] He died gloriously while inhaling gas— *levique flatu corrumpitur*, like the *fama pudicitiæ* in Hieronymus. He was indubitably a—.'"

But here, Mr. Windenough—for he it is whom Lacko'breath thus holds by the nose—tears the bands from his jaws and hurls forth a spate of words. He complains that his jaws have been tied, for

"you *must* know—if you know anything—how vast a superfluity of breath I have to dispose of! . . . In my situation it is really a great relief to be able to open one's mouth. . . . How the devil, sir, did you get into this place?—not a word I beseech you—been here some time myself—terrible accident!—heard of it, I suppose— awful calamity!—walking under your windows—some short while ago—about the time you were stage-struck—horrible occurrence!— heard of 'catching one's breath,' eh?—hold your tongue I tell you! —I caught somebody else's!—had always too much of my own— met Blab at the corner of the street—wouldn't give me a chance for a word—couldn't get in a syllable edgeways—attacked, consequently, with epilepsis—Blab made his escape—damn all fools!— they took me up for dead, and put me in this place. . . ."

Thus all is explained, and Mr. Lacko'breath at last knows what became of his breath.

It is impossible [he says] to conceive . . . the joy with which I became gradually convinced that the breath so fortunately caught by the gentleman (whom I soon recognized as my neighbour Windenough) was, in fact, the identical expiration mislaid by myself in the conversation with my wife.

Mr. Lacko'breath, however, is prudent and circumspect, not to say cunning, and therefore carefully conceals his design from his adversary, for "in displaying anxiety for the breath of which he was at present so anxious to get rid, might I not lay myself open to the exactions of his avarice?"—in other words, blackmail! Accordingly, still grasping his enemy's nose, he cries,

"Monster! . . . and double-winded idiot—dost *thou*, whom for thine iniquities, it has pleased heaven to accurse with a two-fold respiration—dost *thou*, I say, presume to address me in the familiar language of an old acquaintance?—'I lie,' forsooth! and 'hold my tongue,' to be sure!—pretty conversation indeed, to a gentleman with a single breath!—all this, too, when I have it in my power to relieve the calamity under which thou dost so justly suffer—to curtail the superfluities of thine unhappy respiration."

Lacko'breath's tactics succeed. Windenough capitulates without even asking how our hero, who has not revealed his infirmity, proposes to help:

Preliminaries being at length arranged, my acquaintance delivered me the respiration; for which (having carefully examined it) I gave him afterwards a receipt.

I am aware that by many I shall be held to blame for speaking, in a manner so cursory, of a transaction so impalpable. It will be thought that I should have entered more minutely into the details of an occurrence by which—and this is very true—much new light might be thrown upon a highly interesting branch of physical philosophy.

To all this I am sorry that I cannot reply. A hint is the only answer which I am permitted to make. There were *circumstances* —but I think it much safer upon consideration to say as little as possible about an affair so delicate—*so delicate*, I repeat, and at the time involving the interests of a third party whose sulphurous resentment I have not the least desire, at this moment, of incurring.

Though we are not told the identity of this third party, the Devil is clearly designed, that classic representative of the wicked Father and, here, Mr. Windenough's double. As to the "delicacy" of the transaction, a transaction involving a branch of "physical philosophy," this is too obvious to need comment.

We then learn how the two characters, who thus restore each other to normality, escape from their tomb: "The united strength of our resuscitated voices was soon sufficiently apparent. Scissors, the Whig Editor, republished a treatise upon 'the nature and origin of subterranean noises' . . ." (so that, again, voice is equated with flatus). The opening of the vault, and the discovery of the two men, brings the tale to an end.

Mr. Lacko'breath concludes by directing the readers' attention to

the merits of that indiscriminate philosophy which is a sure and ready shield against those shafts of calamity which can neither be seen, felt, nor fully understood. It was in the spirit of this wisdom that, among the Ancient Hebrews, it was believed the gates of Heaven [like the besieged cities which symbolized women in the preamble], would be inevitably opened to that sinner, or saint, who, with good lungs and implicit confidence, should vociferate the word "*Amen!*" It was in the spirit of this wisdom that, when a great plague raged at Athens, and every means had been in vain attempted for its removal, Epimenides . . . advised the erection of a shrine and temple "to the proper God."

The "proper" God is here, doubtless, the real father; he to whose erection the child was, in fact, due, whatever might be its legitimacy. Can Poe, in his unconscious, have doubted not only Rosalie's but his own legitimacy? We shall never know. But we are here brought back to the first tragedy of his childhood, the protagonists then being his legitimate parents and, possibly, another male; a tragedy whose shadows are thrown on the walls of the tomb in which Lacko'-breath and Windenough at last meet.

Perhaps it is not only because he has robbed his less fortunate rival that Mr. Windenough has double breath. May we not here have an unconscious memory of the little Edgar seeing his mother in the possession of two men? Even if we omit this hypothetical lover, there was surely a time when Edgar knew that before becoming Mrs. Poe, his mother was Mrs. Hopkins. A further and unmistakable clue to such a memory seems to have crept into this tale for, in fact, it is

the morning after his marriage that Lacko'breath discovers
a whole packet of love letters from Windenough, his neighbor,
to his wife. These letters, then, could only have been written,
sent, and received before the marriage. Elizabeth Arnold's
son knew his mother to have been another man's wife before
her remarriage. Indeed, the event took place in a "suprisingly
short time,"[37] for it was only three months after Hopkins'
death that she married David Poe, a fellow actor.

Thus, vestiges of real memories seem to have crept into
this tale from all directions, their autobiographical nature
being further confirmed by the fact that Poe, for some unknown reason, as though in disclaim, signed it *Lyttleton
Barry*.

All in all, this story, "Loss of Breath," might be summed
up thus: a man loses his breath, the morning after his marriage, for trying to shout too loudly into his wife's ear. The
lost breath is caught by his neighbor, Windenough, who
happens to pass by. Mrs. Lacko'breath already loves the
latter, before this accident, because of his mighty breath,
and now we see him doubly endowed. Nevertheless, Lacko'-
breath, after various mishaps, such as being crushed in a
coach by a huge fellow passenger, dissection by a surgeon,
and hanging by an executioner, rediscovers his luckier rival
in the tomb, harassed by his theft, and his double endow-
ment of breath. Whereupon Lacko'breath persuades Windenough to restore his stolen respiration.

Breath, as we saw, is here the symbol of male potency. The
tale would thus appear to be both a confession of the truth,
and a wish fantasy in which Poe admits himself impotent:
it also indirectly conveys that the potency stolen, as it were,
by the father, is restored when, at the end of the tale, he
rediscovers that same father. Such is the gist of this tale
which, rearranged as fiction, relates the infantile and pre-
adolescent vicissitudes which beset the development of Poe's
sexual potency and the path which, but for them, it might
have taken. For having too urgently, at the sadistic-anal
stage, desired sole possession of the mother, manifested by
yelling and general aggression, his sado-erotic trends were
forced into repression by the father, or one in his position.
But at what point in his childhood did the actual repression
of his instinctual urges take place? These urges the child

might have rediscovered and reactivated, as happens at the end of the tale, had this repression been less severe, less early imposed. What happened however, was that from his parents, he went to live with the Allans. There the discipline was equally stern—the coach in the tale—but under a far more crushing father figure than the skinny Mr. Windenough: whether David Poe or another. The huge and casual traveler surely represents John Allan, while the two other passengers who wedge Lacko'breath between them seem also, as it were, to be buried under his weight: for we do not find them mentioned again. Flung into the road with broken limbs, Lacko'breath then finds himself under the knife of the castrator-surgeon who, like John Allan, "for his own good," tortures and mutilates him. The dour merchant, given the stern upbringing he impressed on the child, and the filial respect he whipped into him, must have seemed the very fount of morals, and their inculcation, to the charity orphan he fostered. Rich, honored, and lord of several women, John Allan, like the patriarchs of old or their prehistoric ancestor, the father of the primal horde, allowed himself what he denied the young, and was far better suited to enact the part ordained by fate—that which consisted in subduing the childish soul to the moral code imposed by society—than the indifferent actor David Poe, himself a son in revolt, or the unknown lover of Elizabeth Arnold. Moreover, Edgar's age when he found himself in John Allan's power contributed to the disciplinarian, repressive part the latter was to play, for, only after three and, above all, in the latency period which generally begins after five or six—when the first outburst of the child's sexuality subsides—is it ready to receive the repressions imposed by education and morality.

This is not to say that John Allan actually eviscerated his ward like the surgeon in our story. But all physical violence inflicted on the child by the father, in the child's unconscious, is interpreted as a kind of castration, the fear of which archaic retribution finally submerges the Oedipus complex in the unconscious of the small boy.[38] The symbolic evisceration of the unfortunate Mr. Lacko'breath by the well-meaning surgeon may perhaps be read as displaced from the real punishment inflicted on Edgar, "for his own good," by his benefactor's fatherly hand. Colonel Ellis, son of John Allan's partner—with whose parents, in 1820, the Allans spent several months after their return from England—testifies in his memoirs that, during this period, Edgar, though almost adolescent, was still whipped by his guardian:

The only whipping I ever knew Mr. Allan to give him was for carrying me into the fields and woods beyond "Belvidere" adjacent to what is now Hollywood Cemetery, one Saturday, and keeping me there all day and until after dark, without anybody at home knowing where we were; and for shooting a lot of domestic fowls belonging to the proprietor of "Belvidere" who was at that time, I think, Judge Bushrod Washington.[39]

Now, when a father whips a twelve-year-old boy, we may safely conclude that it is not for the first time. Corporal punishment was also the general thing at the time and, had John Allan not occasionally thrashed his ward, despite the tears of the tender-hearted Frances—as happened, for instance, when Edgar pulled away the old lady's chair[40]—he would have thought to have failed in his duty.

Be that as it may, it is clear that John Allan represented the male and awe-inspiring "father" through whom Poe's Oedipus complex was so drastically repressed by the physical and moral violence which the child interpreted as castration. It was John Allan who castrated Poe and condemned him to impotence by inflicting, and inculcating, moral standards incompatible with the sado-necrophilist trends of his primary sexual make-up. As a result, these were repressed deep into his unconscious, and were never again to emerge save in the harmless imaginative form of literary production.

It must never be forgotten, for the true understanding of Poe's psyche, that his unconscious included two distinct forms of the Oedipus complex. For first, to the child, the parental pair had comprised his true father and mother; both actors, both consumptive, David and Elizabeth. Suddenly, at eighteen months old, that is, in July, 1810, that father, David, vanished in New York. One cannot say, therefore, that David Poe, before his disappearance, played any real Oedipal part in the life of his son, since he was then too young and still too immersed in the pre-Oedipal, pregenital stages of libido development. Later, however, when Edgar lived with John Allan and when the latter, to the child in the Oedipal stage, had acquired the awe-inspiring proportions of the Oedipal father, the real father David Poe, by projection into the past, was doubtless "Oedipalized" in the son's unconscious. It is to this first and, retrospective, Oedipus complex in Poe—which, we must remember, was never experienced on the true Oedipal plane—that the presumptive lover of Elizabeth Arnold, Rosalie's rumored father, also belongs.

But Edgar, when three, was taken by the Allans. There, a new parental pair took him in charge: the gentle Frances and the dour John Allan. Doubtless, for a time, his pregenital, infantile, and presumably phallic sexuality continued to develop, with its accompanying infantile masturbation, and soon led him, given his mental and concomitant sexual precocity, to the true Oedipal phase. Ever more ardently would he covet the mother's caresses, and ever more fiercely hate the father, his rival, who kept them ineluctably apart. The large and awe-inspiring figure of the father, as every child, more or less, sees it, thus for Edgar assumed John Allan's dour and hostile characteristics. Frances, his foster mother, however, had many of the characteristics of his true but vanished mother and, even, the same ill-health. It was at this time, when repression began under the dour, whipping father, a time when his infantile masturbation was doubtless checked and replaced by anxiety, that indelible memory traces of the first parental pair—or pairs, if we accept the theory of Elizabeth's adultery—must have been Oedipalized and, so, reactivated in his unconscious.

For there is something else we should not forget; namely, that as a babe, Edgar's infantile libido had derived far greater satisfactions from his mother than from anything Frances Allan could provide, given his age at their meeting and the obstacle of John Allan. It is, therefore, no wonder that Poe's libido, then undergoing repression, should remain fixated on the vanished mother; that first mother whose possession no violent father disputed and from whose breast he had fed. In his pregenital, oral, and anal phases she had been wholly his as, doubtless, he had been her only tiny companion, in the six months before Rosalie was born.

Frances Allan could never be all this to him; and, besides, there was always the dour John Allan with his whip, and harsh reproofs, to remind him that Frances was not his true mother. Thus, in his mind, he would unconsciously revert to that vanished time as to a paradise lost, a time when he had a real mother. So it was the dead Elizabeth, whom he could

freely love who, in her avatars, always returned to dwell in
his fearful and deathless stories. Another factor, too, must
have encouraged this fixation. Poe's precocity as a child,
which would result in his ego development doubtless ante-
dating the development of his libido, thus contributing to
keep him fixated at that pregenital stage where his true
mother reigned supreme.

Thus, if in the first parental pair the dominant figure for
Poe was a loved mother, in the second it was the awe-
inspiring father. And indeed, for most men, this is the order
of the parent's successive importance in time. First the small
boy is drawn to the mother who satisfies every wish. Then
the father appears, with his moral bans, sunders them, and
so shuts the gates on the small son's paradise. But because
Edgar was passed from the first parents to the second, the
two figures which, for him, embodied the essential qualities of
father and mother were split and recomposed from each
couple.

For Poe, the mother, in all her avatars, was ever and always Elizabeth Arnold. The father, even when retrojected
into the past on David Poe or another was, always, more
or less, John Allan. Thus we find Mr. Windenough, who
so clearly embodies the adventurer David Poe, or his substitute Elizabeth's lover, taxed with avarice as though he were
John Allan.

These considerations singularly illumine the conclusion of
"Loss of Breath." From the moment the hero is shorn of
breath and symbolically castrated and, yet again, when he
is eviscerated, Poe's Unconscious cries halt, and rebels. "No!"
he seems to cry: "I refuse to be castrated by this wicked
Father!" Whereupon his hero is hanged, which amounts to
reendowing him with the penis, symbolically and ironically
expressed. Follows a prolonged opium stupor, in which he
relives the replete babe's pregenital, oral phases at the
breast, with all their ancient delights. Then, once more he
imagines himself in the womb pursued, for the last time,
by the father's penis as an undertaker's screw. Then he is
reborn. There, in the sepulchral vault where he has been
preceded by both, he rediscovers the mother (pregnant) and
the harmless father—David Poe or that other—whom he had
known in the pregenital phase when a child. That father is

the inventor of Lombardy poplars and other phallic emblems, as well as Doctor of Pneumatics, and happens to have the "breath" which was stolen from him by John Allan. Yet in the story—reversing reality—the father returns his breath and potency to the son so that it is as though Poe were saying: had it been possible, by some sort of retroactive magic, to wipe out the time when he was crushed and mutilated "for his own good" by John Allan, the Oedipal father, he would have retained his potency and never been doomed to lifelong impotence. That potency, however, was buried with the dead; there only, by their contact, could it be restored to life. But the gates of Heaven, which would open without fail to "that sinner or saint who, with good lungs and implicit confidence, should vociferate the word 'Amen,' " were ever to remain, for him, the massive portals of the vault of Ulalume: portals he would never open because of the sternness of his upbringing by John Allan.

Thus, this tale, in manifest content a kind of burlesque, reveals its latent content, on analysis, as profoundly tragic. Not without reason does Poe's humor here appear—as ever, for that matter—wearing a gruesome grin. Force himself as he may to ridicule or depreciate the envied potency of the father, by showing him choked by his double breath, or manipulating Mr. Lacko'breath like a puppet, these antics are still funereal and there is something sinister in his sarcasm. Force himself to laugh as he may, to keep back the tears, Poe's laughter is never wholehearted. For, to the impotent, loss of potency is no laughing matter.

## NOTES

### I. "Berenice

[1] The reference to opium was suppressed by Poe in a later edition.

[2] This sentence is omitted from Poe's last versions of the tale. (See *Virginia Edition*, II, 314.)

[3] "Her lips were red, her looks were free,
Her locks were yellow as gold:
Her skin was as white as leprosy,
The Night-mare Life-in-Death was she,
Who thicks man's blood with cold.

(*The Rime of the Ancient Mariner*, Part III.)

[4] *Virginia Edition*, Vol. 7, p. 54.

[5] *Virginia Edition*, II, 314.

[6] K. Abraham, "A Short Study of the Development of the Libido" in *Selected Papers of Karl Abraham, M.D.*, London, Institute of Psychoanalysis and Hogarth Press, 1927. Translated from *Versuch einer Entwicklungsgeschichte der Libido* (Internationaler Psychoanalytischer Verlag, 1924).

[7] I owe this interesting and just observation, which links the apparently fantastic concept of the *vagina dentata* with actual experience, to a remark made by Freud.

[8] Reported by Dr. Géza Róheim, on his return from Australia, 1931. (Cf. *International Journal of Psycho-analysis, Róheim Australasian Research Number*, London, January–April, 1932; Vol. XIII, Parts 1 and 2.)

## II. "Loss of Breath"

[1] Braggart, bully, hector.

[2] *Israfel*, p. 20. Cf. *op. cit.*, pp. 13, 24, 141, and 727.

[3] *Israfel*, p. 125.

[4] Poe to William Poe, Richmond, August 20, 1835 (*Virginia Edition*, XVII, 15).

[5] Cf. the fine study by L. Jekels, "Der Wendepunkt im Leben Napoleons I," *Imago*, IV, 1914 (abstract in English, *The Psychoanalytic Review*, VII, 278–295).

[6] *Israfel*, pp. 14–15.

[7] E. Jones, *The Madonna's Conception Through the Ear*, first published in German (*Die Empfängnis der Jungfrau Maria durch das Ohr*) in *Jahrbuch der Psychoanalyse*, 1914, Vol. VI. Quotations and references from *Essays in Applied Psycho-Analysis*, 1923, London, Hogarth Press and Institute of Psycho-Analysis, p. 261.

[8] *Sermo de tempore*, XXII.

[9] Bodley MS Latin Liturgy, Fol. X, Vol. 91.

[10] Langlois, *Essai sur la peinture sur verre*, 1832, p. 157.

[11] St. Eleutherius Tornacensis, *Serm. in Annunt. Fest.*, Tome 65, p. 96.

[12] Genesis 2:7.

[13] Psalms 33:6.

[14] Strehlow, *Die Aranda-und Loritja-Stämme in Zentralaustralien*, 1907, p. 14.

[15] *Leonardo da Vinci: A Psycho-Sexual Study of an Infantile Reminiscence*, London, Kegan Paul, 1922. *Eine Kindheitserinnerung des Leonardo da Vinci*, 1910, *Ges. Werke*, Band VIII.

[16] Sierich, "Samoanische Märchen," *Int. Arch. für Ethnographie*, XVI, 90.

[17] *Civ. Dei*, XXI, 5.

[18] *Georgics*, III, 266–276.

[19] *Hist. nat.*, VIII, 67.

²⁰ *Hist. anim.*, V, 4.

²¹ *Op. cit.*, X, 51. This and previous references from Jones, *op. cit.*, p. 380.

²² This, and the preceding quotations, from Jones, *op. cit.*, pp. 296–298, after Brett, *A History of Psychology, Ancient and Patristic*, 1912, pp. 118, 291.

²³ Jones, *op. cit.*, pps. 299-300, based on the Upanishads and other Vedic literature (Müller).

²⁴ Like the "Jesus-Christ" of Zola's *La Terre:* by no means unique.

²⁵ *Virginia Edition*, II, 357.

²⁶ *Virginia Edition*, II, 357-364.

²⁷ "The Colloquy of Monos and Una," *Graham's Magazine*, August, 1841; 1845.

²⁸ Doubtless, in part, this belief derives from the fact that, as suicide statistics show, suicides by hanging (always a numerous class) are almost invariably men. In France especially, during the last thirty years, suicide by hanging represents 30 to 40 per cent of all suicides and includes practically no women (from figures communicated by Prof. René Piédelièvre in 1933). (See also Balthazard, *Précis de Médecine légale*, Paris, Baillière, 1928, p. 185.)

As to whether or no hanging really produces erection and ejaculation *in extremis*, L. Thoinot, in his *Précis de Médecine légale* (Paris, Octave Doin et fils, 1913), writes as follows (I, 638–639):

"A very disputed problem in the past concerns *erection* and *ejaculation* during hanging.

"In most cases semen is found in the urethra of men hanged and, often, spots of semen on the clothing.

"Is this presence of semen a common phenomenon of death equally observed in the hanged as in all corpses, owing to the relaxation of the sphincter muscles, or does it result from a vital activity: true erection and ejaculation?

"Guyon, a French naval doctor who, in 1822, witnessed the hanging of fourteen negroes, observed concurrently with strangulation, powerful erections in all: an hour later, in nine corpses, the member was semi-erect and the urethra full of seminal fluid. This semen was therefore produced by a real ejaculation (after Brouardel).

"Guyon's story was considered a fable. Devergie was almost the only nineteenth-century writer to accept erection and ejaculation occurring in the hanged.

"Orfila found that when corpses were suspended even three or four hours after death, marked congestion of the genital organs occurred with descent of spermatozoa into the urethra.

"Tardieu, in a lively controversy with Davergie on this point, maintained that seminal fluid in the urethra resulted from mechanical causes due to the body's position.

"Pellereau, in Mauritius, with ample opportunities to witness hangings, never observed actual ejaculation in any criminals he saw hanged.

"The classic German writers Casper, Maschka, and Hofmann also opposed the idea that ejaculation precedes death in the hanged. As a result, the belief arose, now universally adopted, that the presence of semen in the urethra of the hanged has neither more nor less significance than in other corpses.

"To-day it would seem necessary somewhat to modify this extreme view and admit that, in certain cases, exceptional no doubt but authenticated, erection and true ejaculation do take place during hanging."

Feld, Ebertz, Pellier, Baslini, Caprara, Ziemke, Hansen, Puppe, and Götz are all then cited as having observed erection and even ejaculation in the hanged.

Whether, however, erection and/or ejaculation take place, any accompanying pleasurable sensations must be extremely slight, since all the accounts of those cut down agree that after a first phase in which there is "a feeling of warmth in the head and a ringing and whistling in the ears, with sensations of bright light, sparks, flashes, etc. . . . ," the legs grow heavy, all feeling disappears, and loss of consciousness ensues, painlessly and without any feeling of suffocation. (*loc. cit.*, p. 637.)

It is only later that the convulsions occur which habitually precede the death of the hanged.

Nevertheless, the reality of these facts has no bearing on the universal symbolism of hanging. The psychoanalyst may indeed ask whether this very divergence of opinion as to erection and ejaculation in the hanged may not, more or less, be due to the degree to which its symbolism, with which we shall now deal, is repressed in the observer.

[29] I owe to Freud this observation on the phallic meaning of the bodies of the hanged.

[30] Cf. Sándor Rado, "The Psychic Effects of Intoxicants: An Attempt to Evolve a Psycho-Analytical Theory of Morbid Cravings," *International Journal of Psycho-Analysis*, VII, 396–413, translated from *Die psychischen Wirkungen des Rauschgifte. Versuch eines psychoanalytischen Theorie des Suchte, Int. Zeitschrift für Psychoanalyse*, XII, 1926, Heft. 3. Rado's argument may be summarized as follows: The orgasm is characterized by its extension to the whole body and the general discharge of excitation which it affords. This is true of the orgasm of pharmacological origin, as of the genital orgasm, although in the former the discharge is nonexplosive in character and, as it were, in slow motion. The original form of this orgasm, which is always oral in origin, would be the "alimentary orgasm" of the nursling, a feeling

of euphoria and general relief from tension experienced during the ingestion and digestion of food, which constitute the nursling's intensest sensations at this oral phase. The drug addict regresses to this primitive oral phase to which he has remained fixated, losing his genitality in the process and gradually withdrawing his libidinal attachments from all external objects. Finally, his libido becomes entirely concentrated on the poison which brings him pleasure, this obtaining of the drug constituting his only aim in life, in the same way that the absorption of milk and the subsequent alimentary orgasm, form the sole vital objective of the nursling.

[31] The little girl was French, and in French the word *vis*, meaning screw, is pronounced like the word *vice*.

[32] "Some Passages in the Life of a Lion (Lionizing)": *Southern Literary Messenger*, May, 1835; 1840; 1845; *Broadway Journal*, I, 2.

[33] "The Thousand-and-Second Tale of Sheherazade," *Godey's Lady's Book*, February, 1845; *Broadway Journal*, II, 16.

[34] John F. South (1797–1882), *Short Description of the Bones* (1st Ed., 1825).

[35] William Windham (1750–1810), English orator and statesman. I have been unable to identify Allbreath.

[36] Phiz: pseudonym of Hablot Knight Browne (1815–1882), illustrator of Dickens, and occasionally of *Punch*.

[37] *Israfel*, p. 10. Three months, according to Woodberry (I, 9).

[38] Cf Freud, *The Passing of the Oedipus-Complex*, *Collected Papers*, II, 269, trans. from *Der Untergang des Oedipuskomplexes*, 1924, *Ges. Werke*, Band XIII.

[39] *Virginia Edition*, I, 24.

[40] *Israfel*, pp. 54 and 57.

# TALES OF THE FATHER

## 3. "THE TELL-TALE HEART"*

"TRUE!—nervous—very, very dreadfully nervous I had been and am; but why *will* you say that I am mad?" begins the hero of "The Tell-Tale Heart" who, like his fellows in "The Black Cat" and "The Imp of the Perverse," writes from behind prison bars, where his crime has consigned him:

The disease had sharpened my senses—not destroyed—not dulled them. Above all was the sense of hearing acute. I heard all things in the heaven and in the earth. I heard many things

* "The Tell-Tale Heart," *The Pioneer*, January, 1843; *Broadway Journal*, II, 7.

in hell. How, then, am I mad? Hearken! and observe how healthily
—how calmly I can tell you the whole story.

Thus the narrator—whom Poe evidently wishes to show as
mad or, at least, the victim of the Imp of the Perverse—
begins by denying his madness like the "logical" lunatic he is.
"It is impossible to say how first the idea entered my brain;
but once conceived, it haunted me day and night." The
nature of this obsessional thought will soon appear.

> Object there was none. Passion there was none. I loved the old
> man. He had never wronged me. He had never given me insult.
> For his gold I had no desire.

This strangely resembles the representation, by its opposite,
of Poe's own relation to his foster father John Allan! But let
us see the *motive* our narrator assigns for his deed:

> I think it was his eye! yes, it was this! One of his eyes re-
> sembled that of a vulture—a pale blue eye, with a film over it.
> Whenever it fell upon me, my blood ran cold; and so by degrees—
> very gradually—I made up my mind to take the life of the old
> man, and thus rid myself of the eye forever.

This eye, filmed over, if only in part, permitting of dim or
oblique vision, corresponds to an excised eye and so brings
us back to the main motif in "The Black Cat." All in all, the
old man must be killed for the same reason as the cats. Here,
however, the murder is premeditated, as in "The Imp of the
Perverse" where, again, the victim is the father; there, it was
for gold but, here, to annihilate the filmed eye: "You should
have seen how wisely I proceeded—with what caution—
with what foresight—with what dissimulation I went to work!"
For the father, indeed, is to be feared and needs a cautious
approach!

> I was never kinder to the old man than during the whole week
> before I killed him. And every night, about midnight, I turned the
> latch of his door and opened it—oh so gently! And then, when I
> had made an opening sufficient for my head, I put in a dark
> lantern, all closed, closed, so that no light shone out, and then I
> thrust in my head. . . . I moved it slowly—very, very slowly, so
> that I might not disturb the old man's sleep. It took me an hour
> to place my whole head within the opening so far that I could
> see him as he lay upon his bed. . . . And then, when my head was
> well in the room, I undid the lantern cautiously—oh, so cautiously

—cautiously (for the hinges creaked)—I undid it just so much that a single thin ray fell upon the vulture eye. And this I did for seven long nights . . . but I found the eye always closed; and so it was impossible to do the work; for it was not the old man who vexed me, but his Evil Eye. And every morning, when the day broke, I went boldly into the chamber, and spoke courageously to him, calling him by name in a hearty tone, and inquiring how he had passed the night. So you see he would have been a very profound old man, indeed, to suspect that every night, just at twelve, I looked in upon him while he slept.

Here we see the son clearly outwitting the father in caution and astuteness! Even as we watch him enter the room, each morn, with friendly greeting, we seem to see the small Edgar as he visited his waking "Pa," calling him by "name" and asking had he "passed the night well?" For so children must often do, compelled as they are to be affectionate and behave, though recent punishments may inspire quite different feelings.

Upon the eighth night I was more than usually cautious in opening the door. A watch's minute hand moves more quickly than did mine. Never before that night, had I *felt* the extent of my own powers—of my sagacity. I could scarcely contain my feelings of triumph. To thank that there I was, opening the door, little by little, and he not even to dream of my secret deeds or thoughts. I fairly chuckled at the idea; and perhaps he heard me; for he moved on the bed suddenly, as if startled. Now you may think that I drew back—but no. His room was as black as pitch with the thick darkness, (for the shutters were close fastened, through fear of robbers), and so I knew that he could not see the opening of the door, and I kept pushing it on steadily, steadily.

I had my head in, and was about to open the lantern, when my thumb slipped upon the tin fastening, and the old man sprang up in bed, crying out—"Who's there?"

Thus the adversaries are opposed; the eyes of the son, in the dark, being fixed on the menaced father:

I kept quite still and said nothing. For a whole hour I did not move a muscle, and in the meantime I did not hear him lie down. He was still sitting up in the bed, listening;—just as I have done, night after night, hearkening to the death watches in the wall.

The old man's increasing terror is then described, and the tale continues:

When I had waited a long time, very patiently, without hearing
him lie down, I resolved to open a little—a very, very little
crevice in the lantern . . . until, at length, a simple dim ray, like
the thread of the spider, shot from out the crevice and fell full
upon the vulture eye.

It was open—wide, wide open—and I grew furious as I gazed
upon it. I saw it with perfect distinctness—all a dull blue, with a
hideous veil over it that chilled the very marrow in my bones;
but I could see nothing else of the old man's face or person: for
I had directed the ray as if by instinct, precisely upon the damned
spot.

We are not told whether it is with his good or clouded eye
that the old man perceives the ray which shoots into the dark
room, nor is it ever made clear exactly how much he sees
with his "vulture eye." Whatever the case, the ray, thin as a
spider's thread, striking the offending eye, is responsible for
an amazing reaction: ". . . have I not told you that what you
mistake for madness is but over acuteness of the senses?" he
says, almost as though a paranoiac justifying his auditory
hallucinations—and, continuing:

. . . now, I say, there came to my ears a low, dull, quick sound,
such as a watch makes when enveloped in cotton. I knew *that*
sound well, too. It was the beating of the old man's heart. It
increased my fury, as the beating of a drum stimulates the soldier
into courage.

The murderer, however, restrains himself and remains
motionless, his ray still fixed on that eye, while the "hellish
tattoo" of the old man's heart goes on increasing. Meanwhile,
his own terror rises to "uncontrollable" heights, as

. . . the beating grew louder, louder! I thought the heart must
burst. And now a new anxiety seized me—the sound would be
heard by a neighbour! The old man's hour had come! With a
loud yell, I threw open the lantern and leaped into the room. He
shrieked once—once only. In an instant I dragged him to the
floor, and pulled the heavy bed over him. I then smiled gaily, to
find the deed so far done. But, for many minutes, the heart beat
on with a muffled sound. This, however, did not vex me; it
would not be heard through the wall. At length it ceased. The
old man was dead. I removed the bed and examined the corpse.
Yes, he was stone, stone dead. I placed my hand upon the heart
and held it there many minutes. There was no pulsation. He was
stone dead. His eye would trouble me no more.

The murderer then describes his "wise precautions" to conceal the body, as giving proof of his sound reason:

> The night waned, and I worked hastily, but in silence. First of all I dismembered the corpse. I cut off the head and the arms and the legs.
>
> I then took up three planks from the flooring of the chamber, and deposited all between the scantlings. I then replaced the boards so cleverly, so cunningly, that no human eye—not even *his* —could have detected anything wrong. There was nothing to wash out—no stain of any kind—no blood-spot whatever. I had been too wary for that. A tub had caught all—ha! ha!"

Now, however, it is 4:00 A.M., and knocks are heard at the street door. "A shriek had been heard by a neighbour," and the police have appeared, to investigate.

The murderer, nevertheless, is wholly at ease. "The shriek," he said, was his own in a dream. "The old man . . . was absent in the country. . . ." And now, worthy precursor of the murderer in "The Black Cat" (evidently written after "The Tell-Tale Heart"), he leads his visitors through the house and bids them search, and search well:

> I led them, at length, to *his* chamber. I showed them his treasures, secure, undisturbed. In the enthusiasm of my confidence, I brought chairs into the room, and desired them *here* to rest from their fatigues, while I myself, in the wild audacity of my perfect triumph, placed my own seat upon the very spot beneath which reposed the corpse of the victim.

This anticipates the murderer in "The Black Cat," who raps on the cellar wall, both being reminiscent of those murderers who haunt the scene of their crime.

As might be expected, the victim, from the depths of his tomb, takes up the challenge. The statue on the Commander's tomb accepts the invitation of Don Juan and turns up at his feast. The walled-in cat shrieks out. And now the old man, whose heart beats so hellishly, *also* responds in his way:

> The officers were satisfied. . . . They sat, and while I answered cheerily, they chatted of familiar things. But, ere long, I felt myself getting pale and wished them gone. My head ached, and I fancied a ringing in my ears. . . .

The ringing increases "—until, at length, I found that the

noise was *not* within my ears." The auditory hallucination is thus re-established.

No doubt I now grew *very* pale—but I talked more fluently, and with a heightened voice. Yet the sound increased—and what could I do? It was *a low, dull quick sound—much such a sound as a watch makes when enveloped in cotton.* I gasped for breath—and yet the officers heard it not. I talked more quickly—more vehemently; but the noise steadily increased. I arose . . .

And now the poor wretch makes ever more desperate efforts to drown the increasing noise. In vain he paces heavily to and fro, or grates his chair on the boards: the sound

grew louder—louder—*louder!* And still the men chatted pleasantly, and smiled. Was it possible they heard not? Almighty God!—no, no! They heard!—they suspected!—they *knew!*—they were making a mockery of my horror!

Whereupon, possessed by this illusion and no longer able to bear their derision, the murderer cries:

Villains! . . . dissemble no more! I admit the deed!—tear up the planks! here, here!—it is the beating of his hideous heart!

Such is "The Tell-Tale Heart," possibly the most shorn of trimmings of Poe's tales and thus, possibly, one that is nearest to our "modern" taste. Among Poe's works, it stands like a faint precursor of that great parricidal epic which is Dostoevski's opus.[1]

It has been said[2] that the composition of "The Tell-Tale Heart," to which Poe refers in a letter dated December, 1842,[3] was doubtless stimulated by his severe heart attack, toward the summer of that year, after returning from Saratoga Springs. Possibly, it was this—according to Hervey Allen, Poe's third serious heart attack since the first, in 1834-1835[4] —which furnished the adventitious cause for Poe's choice of just these anguished heartbeats to express the deep and buried complexes with which we shall now deal. The same device, also, was to serve him later, when his heart condition grew still worse, to express the weariness of living, in his poem "For Annie."[5] This explanation, however, far from exhausts all that "The Tell-Tale Heart" reveals.

Actually, we know, difficult as it may be for our conscious

mental processes to grasp, that the functions of organs are not represented, in the unconscious, in a manner proportionate to the vital importance of each. The heartbeat, for instance, is so vitally important that, if it stops, death ensues. One might, therefore, imagine that the heart's activity would be extensively reflected in the psyche. This is not, however, the case; the beating of the heart no more disturbs the unconscious than do the rhythmic movements of the thorax. Both belong to those vegetative activities of organic functions which ordinarily do not concern the psychic unconscious.

Should, however, some organic disturbance suddenly disturb one or other of these important organs—or a conversion neurosis of hysterical or hypochondriac origin—we are likely to find them become a main source of anxiety. When this happens, however, it is never due to the organ as such and its function, but to the libidinal charge which invests it. Such organs then represent, apart from their proper function, that of the whole organism's libidinal function, now largely "displaced" upon them. In psychoneurotic disturbances less severe than the complete narcissistic regression that determines hypochondria, the libidinally hypercathected and disturbed organ may even serve to express the subjects' object relations to other beings.

So with Poe's story of "The Tell-Tale Heart." As already noted, the murdered old man resembles John Allan in several ways, even to the symptom of the thudding heart. Did not his first attack of dropsy occur in England, in 1820: which illness, worsening with age, in 1834, ended his life? The reader will recall Edgar's last meeting with his foster father and the cane—attribute of his disease—which the latter brandished against this intruder into his once home. His fear of the pounding heart in the murdered old man's breast thus, doubtless, directly derives from the oppressed, laboring, and dropsical heart of the Scotch merchant. With that heart, as a result of buried complexes we shall study—and by that identification with the father habitual with sons—Poe later, and unconsciously, identified his own neurotic, alcoholic heart.

Yet the mere fact that John Allan suffered from dropsy does not account for the whole content of this anxiety-fraught tale. To understand the deeper motives which inspire man to dream or artists to create, we must grasp, in their plenitude, all the primitive, vital instincts which throng the unconscious. We already saw, as regards "The Murders in the Rue

Morgue," and "The Man of the Crowd," that the child's
sexual instincts awake much earlier than is deemed by adults.
At an unbelievably early age, the child already possesses
larval instinctual mechanisms which allow it to store up
impressions of adult sex acts performed in its presence. That
Poe, as a child, was present at such times, when sharing the
room of his actress mother, the crime of the ape is almost
certain testimony. For that very same crime, shrouded in
London fog, those fogs among which Frances Aïlan acquired
her mysterious illness, the Man of the Crowd is described as
"type and genius of deep crime." For, to the child, at a time
when coitus seems purely sadistic, the sex attack on the
mother is the prototype of all crime.

Even though, when the child is small, adults do not always
conceal themselves in the sex act, a time comes when they
protect themselves from its eyes by what they imagine the
impenetrable barrier of dark, so vividly described in "The
Tell-Tale Heart" as, "pitch"-like. This darkness is indeed
the preferred setting for the coitus of civilized man, as
though it were something disapproved by society.

Nevertheless, alert as they are, the child's sex instincts
continue to perceive and record, though in the dark. What it
saw earlier may contribute to this but, even without sight,
hearing would suffice. For, in effect, coitus has its own sounds,
rhythmic movements and precipitate breath, combined with
an accelerated heartbeat. And even though these heartbeats
may be imperceptible from a distance, the panting which
accompanies them and characterizes the sex act is strangely
audible to infant ears, straining to every sound in the still
darkness.

Thus, it need not surprise us to find, in "The Tell-Tale
Heart," reference to an almost supernatural acuteness of
hearing. Doubtless, we have here the unconscious memory of
nocturnal eavesdroppings when, in the night, "hellish" things
were heard by the child:[6] in other words, the father's sex
attack on the mother. Similar unconscious memories are found
at the root of many auditory hallucinations of paranoia.

The old man's heartbeat, that "hellish tattoo" which grew
"quicker and quicker, and louder and louder," would thus
be the heart's fanfare for the sex act: its assault on the
woman and supremest pleasure. Whence, doubtless, in the
tale, the furious crescendo of the heartbeats, twice repeated,
which culminate first in the old man's death and, next, in the

murderer's seizure and eventual death also. Thus, the talion law is satisfied twice; first by punishment of the mother's *murderer* and, then, by punishment of the slayer of that murderer.

In the last analysis, therefore, it is the Man of the Crowd— in this tale lying in the old man's bed—who thus receives just punishment. In the same way that, in neurotic symptoms, the repressed material finally emerges from the repressing process itself so, here, the sign of the crime, the clamoring heart in the sex act, reappears in this retributive punishment of the heart that thuds with the anguish of death.

Also, it is under the *bed*, in which his crime—the sex attack —was enacted, that the old man is stifled to death. Thus, the instrument of his crime becomes that of his destruction.

The darkness again, black as pitch, where the old man— or the beating heart—sleeps, into which the hero spies and which is pierced by his lantern beam must, evidently, be interpreted as an echo of the intensity with which the child once wished to see through the dark. I knew a young man whose memories of spying on his parents' sex acts reappeared, in analysis, in the shape of a dream where he saw himself, as a child, observing them through the diaphragm of his camera lens instead of eyes. Photography was very young in Poe's time and here, in "The Tell-Tale Heart," the lantern, instead, symbolizes viewing. We know, in primitive concepts of vision, that it is not the illuminated object which sends rays to the eye, but the eye which projects its rays on the object. This primitive concept reappears here, implicit in this way of viewing through darkness by half-opening a lantern shutter as though an eyelid. Juxtaposing this element in the tale with its main motif, the heartbeat, we get some idea how much yearning, both visual and aural, must have remained in the child Poe, all through his life with the Allans, to go on responding to the sex scene as he once knew it with his mother.

Nevertheless, our tale gives quite another reason why this father figure must be destroyed by the son figure. The narrator declares that he "loves the old man," who never had "wronged" him or "given him insult," while, as for his "gold," for that he had no desire: all which, in fact, represent the opposites, as we showed, of Edgar's relation to his "Pa," John Allan.[7] There is a certain hypocrisy here, and this tale, in

which we might expect the son's ambivalence to the father
to appear is, primarily, a tale of hate. The reason alleged,
however, for this hate, is remarkable: the old man is hated
for his eye: "I think it was his eye! Yes, it was this! He had
the eye of a vulture—a pale blue eye, with a film over it." We
shall not presume to affirm that, in this mention of the vulture,
there is an incontestable allusion to the mother, though the
vulture was a classic mother symbol of the ancient Egyptians
and though we find it, later, in the vulture fantasy of the
child Leonardo da Vinci.[8] But what cannot be denied is
that the old man's eye establishes a direct connection with
the eyes of the mother totem cats in "The Black Cat." True,
a film over the eye does not invariably imply a total loss of
vision, but in general it does or, at least, suggests it. In other
words, like Wotan in Germanic mythology, the father in "The
Tell-Tale Heart" is represented as blind in one eye, which is
equivalent to being castrated.[9]

Clearly, also, castrated for his crimes! For, as regards the
mother, the father was indeed the prototype of all crime, as
to the son. Was it not he who kept the son from the mother
by wielding the threat of castration? Here, however, lies the
rub! For, if it is the mother who, by her body, manifests to
the son that the dread possibility of deprivation of the penis
exists, in the last analysis it is the father—by whom or in
whose interests the Oedipal prohibitions were instituted—
who, from remotest time and the depths of the unconscious,
threatens to castrate the son for his guilty desires. It is because
the father has committed this crime against the son that the
latter repays him by castration in retribution of the crime
for which the son would have been castrated: that of possessing the mother. Thus Zeus, when grown, castrated his father
Kronos, who himself had castrated Uranos, *his* father.

These are the two great, eternally human themes which
underlie Poe's tale and confer such sovereign power on it.
The two prime complexes, through which all humanity and
every child must pass, are its marrow and substance. Here,
the son's Oedipus wish for his father's death becomes effective; the father is struck down for the crime of possessing the
mother and for inventing the curse of castration, first as a
threat to the son, but more for effecting it. For it is the father
whom the son generally considers responsible for the woman's
castration, when he discovers she lacks the penis. Secure in

memories of the parents' coitus, the child imagines that though the mother did not succumb to the father's sadistic attacks, nevertheless it cost her a wound which, like Amfortas' hurt, would go on eternally *bleeding.* The menstruation, of which the child, sooner or later, becomes aware, is the proof. Thus, for the great crime of bringing castration into the world when, without it, all created beings would be whole and entire, each of the parents, in his or her way, is responsible; the mother for having undergone the castration and the father for having inflicted it. That is why both must be punished. The cats are hanged or immured and the old man is stifled under his mattress. Both flaunt the emblem of their common crime: the cats have a gouged-out eye and the old man's eye has a film over it.

Here it seems pertinent to ask whether the old man in "The Tell-Tale Heart" is, in fact, blind in that eye? Poe does not say: he even seems to imply that, in spite of its covering film, it still retains sight, for, as he says at the start of the tale, "Whenever it fell upon me, my blood ran cold." Later, after the murder, when the dismembered body is buried under the floor, he once more tells us: "no human eye—not even *his*—could have detected any thing wrong." Thus, extreme acuity of vision is now attributed to that eye. There is some contradiction here, for, if in Poe's unconscious the eye, though filmed, retained its vision, nevertheless it continued a *blind* eye, as in the Norse myth of Father Wotan.

We know, however, that contradictions in the manifest content of dreams or myths represent other, perfectly coherent thoughts, in the latent content. This contradiction then, as regards the eye, an eye that can see so well in spite of its blindness, must derive from the fact that, in this story, the father receives punishment for two distinct crimes; first, that of coitus with the mother, and, second, for its result, which led to castration, as the mother reveals. Yet, to effect castration, a weapon was needed, and this was the penis, so that, to enact his deed, the father must still possess the penis, though he will later be punished by castration for it. The old man's eye that sees and is sightless would, thus, in this apparent contradiction, condense two successive aspects of the criminal father; first, when with his weapon the crime is committed and, then, when as punishment that weapon is cut off.[10]

There is a somewhat earlier tale by Poe where the father-castration motif appears far purer and death in not concomitant with castration. In "The Man That Was Used Up,"[11] Brigadier John A. B. C. Smith, in full possession of his strength and faculties, while engaged in a more than epic campaign against the savage Kickapoos and Bugaboos, is captured and submitted to almost every kind of mutilation. The narrator, meeting the general at a social gathering, is at first dazzled by his fine presence, beautiful voice, and assured manner. The general, in particular, passes for a very lion with women. Nevertheless, it is whispered that some mystery surrounds him, the nature of which the narrator cannot discover. At his wits' ends, he seeks the truth at its source and, one fine morning, calls on our hero. Though the general is at his toilet, the visitor is shown in. As he enters, he stumbles over a nondescript bundle which emits the ghost of a voice. It is the general, in the state to which he is reduced when without the artificial limbs, organs, and muscles, prodigies of modern invention, which remedy his many mutilations. The cardinal mutilation, however, is not mentioned, but we may well imagine it included, for the Kickapoos and Bugaboos who so generously relieved him of leg, arm, shoulders, pectoral muscles, scalp, teeth, eye, palate and seven-eighths tongue, would surely not have left him the penis! The castration of prisoners, moreover, holds high place among tribes quite as savage as were the Kickapoos and Bugaboos!

Though the murderer in "The Tell-Tale Heart" also mutilated his victim by removing head, arms, and legs before depositing him under the floor, what he "castrated" was but a corpse, whereas the treatment to which General Smith is subjected is castration, in its pure symbolic form, and does not include death. For, though the castration motif (deprivation of the penis) is related to that of death (deprivation of existence), the two are not identical, as this tale of "The Man That Was Used Up" shows.

Moreover, in this tale, we find echoes of Poe's army life and a time when his military superiors stood, for him, in the place of the father he had left, in fleeing from John Allan.

Before we close this study of "The Tell-Tale Heart," let us seek to discern those features of the murdered old man which would relate him to the child Edgar's successive fathers.

Poe's unconscious memories, as we saw, of the parents' coitus, dated from the time when, as an infant, he shared his mother's room on her tours with Mr. Placide. At that time his father was David Poe whom, doubtless, a lover was soon to replace; that mysterious unknown, Rosalie's father. Probably it was this lover from whom, primarily, derived the motif of the increasingly violent heartbeats. And the fact that, at last, when the man with the lantern bursts into the old man's room, he reveals himself by yelling and opening his lantern—slips which imply the wish to be revealed—may well re-echo another frequent occurrence; namely, when the childish, jealous eavesdropper, with his cries or need to urinate, sought to interrupt the parents' intercourse because of the excietment communicated or for other reasons.

All these impressions, however, so precociously stored up, after Edgar's adoption were transferred *en bloc* to John Allan, a far more imposing father whose harshness laid an indelible mark on the growing child. It was certainly in this respectable middle-class household that the repression of his precociously early sexuality was forced upon Poe. This was the time when he was scourged by the castration complex, whence our morality derives. Thus, the old man's film-clouded, vulture-like eye belongs, in fact, to John Allan. It was on him that the full force of the child's Oedipal rage and resentment must have been concentrated, given the fact that, dour and forbidding, he stood in the father's position to Poe, in addition to owning and martyrizing his new mother. To us, the old man's heartbeats appear, at least, triply determined. If first they represent the panting of coitus, overheard in the dark of fortuitous lodgings during his mother's life, its cardiac transposition must be determined by memories of the heart attacks experienced by his dropsical father John Allan which again, in reality, were echoed by the neurotic, alcoholic heart of the son Edgar. Yet these hearts ail because they are guilty of one and the same sin: that of desiring the mother. Their disease, like their precipitate heartbeats, to Poe's unconscious, expresses both the crime and the punishment.

The compulsion of the man with the lantern to open the old man's door, night after night, that he may watch him asleep and alone, in bed, surely also re-echoes some precise reminiscence of Poe's, as a child. And indeed, it is unlikely that John Allan, who disliked his wife's love of the orphan,

would have permitted him to sleep in their room, even if ill,
to please her. Besides, the Allans had a large, comfortable
house and slaves. It was to one of these, his black "mammy,"
that Edgar would be entrusted and, with her, he would have
slept.[12]

Perhaps through this Negress, in "pitch"-black nights, nights
as dark as her skin, the listening child may have re-experi-
enced its responses to the parents' coitus—which he could hear
only in the dark—as the man with the lantern listens to the
old man's heart. Nevertheless, the libido of this child, as
Poe's life and tales both testify—for in neither do Negresses
play any part—was by then fixated on his foster mother, as
white and pretty as his own, in accordance with the classic
mechanism of the compulsion to repetition. It was on her
room that, falling asleep, his childish desires must have
converged at night, because he so loved and desired her,
and because of his jealousy, too; all his yearning, in fact, to
see what another was doing there.

That "other" was John Allan, whom the child would certainly suspect as guilty of attacks similar to those he remembered being made on his mother. When the man with the
lantern, night after night, feels urged to go and spy on the
old man's bedroom, he doubtless enacts only what the child,
kept by his nurse in his crib was, in his helplessness, prevented from doing. Though the image of the mother is here
suppressed, as in "The Man of the Crowd," it is nevertheless
for her that the father has one eye blinded and then is killed.

It is the old man's death that is at stake in this Oedipal
battle where the mother is the prize. But the mother is
eliminated from the story, and the old man appears alone in
bed, as the small Edgar would doubtless have wished John
Allan always to be. Apparently, the old man's solitary sleep
re-echoes one of the fantasy wishes of the small Edgar.

Yet, though the old man sleeps alone, his heart beats in
crescendos. Thus, he condenses in one being both the negation and affirmation of the father's coital activity, in the
same way that his eye suggests both the presence and absence
of the penis. Such modes of representation are natural to the
unconscious, in which opposites exist side by side. Though
conscious logic disapprove, they none the less continue buried
in our depths, as the dreams of the normal and the neurotic
testify, as well as the myths to which humanity has given
birth.

### 4. "THE PIT AND THE PENDULUM"*

DOOMED by the Inquisition, victim of sadist Fathers, the narrator in this tale does not bother to tell us what heretical deed led to his condemnation, and thus begins the tale:

> I was sick—sick unto death with that long agony; and when they at length unbound me, and I was permitted to sit, I felt that my senses were leaving me. The sentence—the dread sentence of death—was the last of distinct accentuation which reached my ears. After that, the sound of the inquisitorial voices seemed merged in one dreamy, indeterminate hum. . . .

He swoons:

> Then silence, and stillness, and night were the universe.
> I had swooned; but still will not say that all of consciousness was lost. What of it there remained I will not attempt to define, or even to describe; yet all was not lost. In the deepest slumber—no! In delirium—no! In a swoon—no! In death—no! even in the grave all *is not* lost. Else there is no immortality for man. Arousing from the most profound of slumbers, we break the gossamer web of *some dream*. Yet in a second afterwards, (so frail may that web have been) we remember not that we have dreamed. In the return to life from the swoon there are two stages; first, that of the sense of mental or spiritual; secondly, that of the sense of physical, existence. It seems probable that if, upon reaching the second stage, we could recall the impressions of the first, we should find these impressions eloquent in memories of the gulf beyond. And that gulf is—what? How at least shall we distinguish its shadows from those of the tomb? But if the impressions of what I have termed the first stage, are not, at will, recalled, yet, after long interval, do they not come unbidden, while we marvel whence they come? . . .

We have quoted in its entirety this dissertation on "the gulf beyond," for there could be no more appropriate introduction —more appropriate indeed than Poe himself knew—to the narrative that follows. The states which Poe groups with delirium (in which the unconscious is in complete control)— sleep, the swoon, death, the grave—are, to the unconscious, so many regressions to a prenatal condition. That immortality of which all men dream and which would be incapable of realization were "all" indeed "lost in the grave" is, primarily,

* "The Pit and the Pendulum," *The Gift*, 1843; *Broadway Journal*, I, 20.

the projection beyond death of that sense of immortality proper to all living beings which itself doubtless expresses the fact that the psychic or biological memory of the living can deal only with periods of existence. But, before life, as we know it, began, the life we entered upon with our first breath, there was a time when, though in one sense not *alive*, we nevertheless did live, though *buried* and sheltered deep in the mother's body. And since, in the unconscious, neither annihilation nor nothingness exists, the moment we learn of this first abode (a recognition helped by some dim instinct or biological "mneme"), our psyche builds on this knowledge to deny the annihilation we fear in our conscious minds. Our idea of life after death then becomes, as it were, a tracing of life before birth, so that eternal life is conceived on the pattern of embryonic existence. Before we were yet of this world, we lived a sort of mysterious, timeless, spaceless, hidden life of our own in the mother's body, and such we consider will be our ultimate survival. Thus, primitive and ancient religions placed the abode of the dead underground; in a giant womb, as it were. The Elysian fields, like Tartarus, were caverns beyond the Styx. The projection of heaven to the skies, leaving the grave and hell to earth, results from a secondary elaboration of this theme.

To return, however, to this tale, Now, it is a veritable descent into Hell that the doomed man describes after his swoon which, as it were, has cast him back into a semi-embryonic condition:

Amid frequent and thoughtful endeavours to remember; amid earnest struggles to regather some token of the state of seeming nothingness into which my soul had lapsed, there have been moments when I have dreamed of success; there have been brief, very brief periods when I have conjured up remembrances which the lucid reason of a later epoch assures me could have had reference only to that condition of seeming unconsciousness. These shadows of memory tell, indistinctly, of tall figures that lifted and bore me in silence down—down—still down—till a hideous dizziness oppressed me at the mere idea of the interminableness of the descent. They tell also of a vague horror at my heart, on account of that heart's unnatural stillness. Then comes a sense of sudden motionlessness throughout all things; as if those who bore me (a ghastly train!) had outrun, in their descent, the limits of the limitless, and paused from the wearisomeness of their toil. After this I call to mind flatness and

dampness; and then all is *madness*—the madness of a memory
which busies itself among forbidden things.

He now awakes; his heart begins to beat tumultuously, and
he recovers "the mere consciousness of existence"; then—but
with what terror—the power of *thought:*

So far, I had not opened my eyes. I felt that I lay upon my back,
unbound. I reached out my hand, and it fell heavily upon something damp and hard. There I suffered it to remain for many
minutes, while I strove to imagine where and *what* I could be. I
longed, yet dared not to employ my vision. I dreaded the first
glance at objects around me. It was not that I feared to look
upon things horrible, but that I grew aghast lest there should be
*nothing* to see. At length, with a wild desperation at heart, I
quickly unclosed my eyes. My worst thoughts, then, were confirmed. The blackness of eternal night encompassed me. I struggled
for breath. The intensity of the darkness seemed to oppress and
stifle me. The atmosphere was intolerably close. . . .

What better description of claustrophobia—certainly justified here—could be given? Infantile fear of the dark, suffoca-
tion, dampness, solitude, and the sense of being closely imprisoned combine to make this Inquisitor's cell a perfect
anxiety-determined womb fantasy. To bear out our interpretation, let us here note the absence, throughout the account of
his various tortures, of any reference whatever to feelings of
cold, though we are told that the cell is damp, deep underground, and that the prisoner, weak with pain and fasting,
wears only a "wrapper of coarse serge." We may also note
the constant recurrence of references to sleeping.

The unhappy man, after remaining motionless for a while,
seeks to exercise his reason: ". . . not for a moment did I
suppose myself actually dead." He knows, however, that,
though of rare occurrence, there was held an auto-da-fé the
previous night. Why, then, was he spared?

A fearful idea now suddenly drove the blood in torrents upon
my heart, and for a brief period, I once more relapsed into insensibility. Upon recovering, I at once started to my feet, trembling
convulsively in every fibre. I thrust my arms wildly above and
around me in all directions. I felt nothing; yet dreaded to move
a step, lest I should be impeded by the walls of a *tomb*. . . .
I proceeded for many paces; but still all was blackness and

vacancy. I breathed more freely. It seemed evident that mine was
not, at least, the most hideous of fates.

Thus, with movements as of a child in the womb, the prisoner assures himself he is not buried alive. This terror, so intense in Poe, directly derives, as analysis always shows, from
the unconscious wish to return to the womb, expressed in
negative form as anxiety. From this torment our prisoner is
to find no escape:

And now, as I still continued to step cautiously onward, there
came thronging upon my recollection a thousand vague rumors
of the horrors of Toledo. . . . Was I left to perish of starvation
in this subterranean world of darkness; or what fate, perhaps
even more fearful, awaited me? That the result would be death,
and a death of more than customary bitterness, I knew too well
the character of my judges to doubt. The mode and the hour were
all that occupied or distracted me.

The prisoner now explores his cell by groping along the
walls. He feels for his knife, with the idea of driving the
blade into a crevice to mark his point of departure, but finds
that his clothes are exchanged for "a wrapper of coarse
serge." From this he tears part of the hem and places it on the
ground.

. . . but I had not counted upon the extent of my dungeon, or
upon my own weakness. The ground was moist and slippery. I
staggered onward for some time, when I stumbled and fell. My
excessive fatigue induced me to remain prostrate; and sleep soon
overtook me as I lay.
Upon awaking, and stretching forth an arm, I found beside me
a loaf and a pitcher with water. I was too much exhausted to
reflect upon this circumstance, but ate and drank with avidity.

Thus our prisoner, like the embryo in its "cell," is fed by
an invisible Providence, though with less loving intent.
Somewhat refreshed, he soon resumes exploring his prison,
and concludes that in circuit, though broken by many angles,
it measures some fifty yards.
He now resolves to "cross the area of the enclosure." The
floor is slippery, and he trips on the torn hem of his robe,
and violently falls on his face.

In the confusion attending my fall, I did not immediately apprehend a somewhat startling circumstance, which yet, in a few seconds afterward, and while I still lay prostrate, arrested my attention. It was this—my chin rested upon the floor of the prison, but my lips and the upper portion of my head, although seemingly at a less elevation than the chin, touched nothing. At the same time my forehead seemed bathed in a clammy vapor, and the peculiar smell of decayed fungus arose to my nostrils. I put forward my arm, and shuddered to find that I had fallen at the very brink of a circular pit, whose extent, of course, I had no means of ascertaining at the moment. Groping about the masonry just below the margin, I succeeded in dislodging a small fragment, and let it fall into the abyss. For many seconds I hearkened to its reverberations as it dashed against the sides of the chasm in its descent; at length, there was a sullen plunge into water, succeeded by loud echoes.

The prisoner thus discovers the only exit from his prison to be this dreadful *pit* or abyss, whose symbolic meaning we shall see more clearly as we proceed.

At the same moment, a sudden opening and shutting, as of a door overhead, reveals how closely he is watched:

Shaking in every limb, I groped my way back to the wall; resolving there to perish rather than risk the terrors of the wells, of which my imagination now pictured many in various positions about the dungeon. In other conditions of mind I might have had courage to end my misery at once by a plunge into one of these abysses; but now I was the veriest of cowards. Neither could I forget what I had read of these pits—that the *sudden* extinction of life formed no part of their most horrible plan.

After long hours of agitation and terror, the unfortunate wretch slumbers again. Again, on waking, he finds a loaf and pitcher of water at his side. Burning with thirst, he empties the vessel at a draught (again the horrors of thirst described, as in *The Narrative of Arthur Gordon Pym*). But the water must have been drugged, for

scarcely had I drunk, before I became irresistibly drowsy. A deep sleep fell upon me—a sleep like that of death. How long it lasted of course, I know not; but when, once again, I unclosed my eyes, the objects around me were visible. By a wild sulphurous lustre, the origin of which I could not at first determine, I was enabled to see the extent and aspect of the prison.

He then discovers that his cell is only about half the size he supposed. This detail troubles him at first for, in his condition, his soul takes "a wild interest in trifles." Eventually, it occurs to him that, after his sleep, when exploring the vault, he must have retraced his steps and so covered a double distance.

"I had been deceived, too, in respect to the shape of the enclosure." It is less irregular that he imagined, while the angles felt in his circuit of the walls

were simply those of a few slight depressions, or niches, at odd intervals. The general shape of the prison was square. What I had taken for masonry, seemed now to be iron, or some other metal, in huge plates, whose sutures or joints occasioned the depression. The entire surface of this metallic enclosure was rudely daubed in all the hideous and repulsive devices to which the charnel superstition of the monks has given rise. The figures of fiends in aspects of menace, with skeleton forms, and other more really fearful images, overspread and disfigured the walls. . . .

Though the outlines were distinct, the colors seemed faded and blurred. The floor was of stone, and

in the centre yawned the circular pit from whose jaws I had escaped.

All this I saw distinctly and by much effort: for my personal condition had been greatly changed during slumber. I now lay upon my back, and at full length, on a species of low framework of wood. To this I was securely bound by a long strap resembling a surcingle. It passed in many convolutions about my limbs and body, leaving at liberty only my head and my left arm to such extent that I could, by dint of much exertion, supply myself with food from an earthen dish which lay by my side on the floor.

His pitcher has been removed, and the prisoner, "consumed with intolerable thirst," is offered nothing but "meat pungently seasoned."

Looking upward, I surveyed the ceiling of my prison. It was some thirty or forty feet overhead, and constructed much as the side walls. In one of its panels a very singular figure riveted my whole attention. It was the painted figure of Time as he is commonly represented, save that, in lieu of a scythe, he held what, at a casual glance, I supposed to be the pictured image of a huge pendulum such as we see on antique clocks. There was something, however, in the appearance of this machine which caused me to regard it more attentively. While I gazed directly upward at it (for its position was immediately over my own) I fancied that I saw it in motion. . . . Its sweep was brief, and of course slow.

Wearied with watching "its dull movement," he turns his eyes and now sees several enormous rats issue from the well, allured by the scent of the meat. For some time the prisoner's attention is distracted by efforts to scare them away.

It might have been half an hour, perhaps even an hour . . . before I again cast my eyes upward. . . . The sweep of the pendulum had increased in extent by nearly a yard. As a natural consequence, its velocity was also much greater. But what mainly disturbed me was the idea that it had perceptibly *descended*. I now observed—with what horror it is needless to say—that its nether extremity was formed of a crescent of glittering steel, about a foot in length from horn to horn; the horns upward, and the under edge evidently as keen as that of a razor. Like a razor also, it seemed massy and heavy, tapering from the edge into a solid and broad structure above. It was appended to a weighty rod of brass, and the whole *hissed* as it swung through the air.
I could no longer doubt the doom prepared for me by monkish ingenuity in torture.

The wretch has escaped the pit, image of hell, only to become the prey of "a different and milder destruction." For the moment, let us keep to the simple lines of the narrative and postpone discussion of its latent symbolic meaning:

What boots it to tell of the long, long hours of horror more than mortal, during which I counted the rushing vibrations of the steel?

He has no means of judging passing time, and the pendulum goes on descending with tormenting deliberation:

. . . it might have been that many days passed—ere it swept so closely over me as to fan me with its acrid breath. The odor of the sharp steel forced itself into my nostrils. . . . I grew frantically mad, and struggled to force myself upward against the sweep of the fearful scimitar. And then I fell suddenly calm, and lay smiling at the glittering death, as a child at some rare bauble.

The sufferer swoons into "utter insensibility." But soon, awakening, despite the agonies he has experienced, feels a

craving for food. As he puts what the rats have left to his
lips, "a half-formed thought of joy—of hope"—rushes to his
mind and is as immediately forgotten:

The vibration of the pendulum was at right angles to my
length. I saw that the crescent was designed to cross the region
of the heart. It would fray the serge of my robe—it would return
and repeat its operations—again—and again. Notwithstanding its
terrifically wide sweep (some thirty feet or more) and the hissing
vigor of its descent, sufficient to sunder these very walls of iron,
still the fraying of my robe would be all that, for several minutes,
it would accomplish.

Meanwhile, the pendulum creeps steadily down:

I saw that some ten or twelve vibrations would bring the steel
in actual contact with my robe, and with this observation there
suddenly came over my spirit all the keen, collected calmness of
despair. For the first time during many hours—or perhaps days—
I *thought*. It now occurred to me that the bandage, or surcingle,
which enveloped me was unique. I was tied by no separate cord.
The first stroke of the razor-like crescent athwart any portion of
the band, would so detach it that it might be unwound from my
person by means of my left hand.

Vain hope! The victim lifts his head and sees that the thong
encircles his body "in all directions—*save in the path of the
destroying crescent.*" Yet the vague hope, revived in him by
food, returns once more:

For many hours the immediate vicinity of the low framework
upon which I lay, had been literally swarming with rats. They
were wild, bold, ravenous. . . . With the particles of the oily
and spicy viand which now remained, I thoroughly rubbed the
bandage wherever I could reach it; then, raising my hand from
the floor, I lay breathlessly still.

Now the rats, with others from the pit, swarm over the
prisoner's body. And though he feels an unspeakable disgust,
his hopes are proved not in vain:

I at length felt that I was *free*. The surcingle hung in ribands from
my body. But the stroke of the pendulum already pressed upon
my bosom. It had divided the serge of the robe. It had cut
through the linen beneath. Twice again it swung, and a sharp

sense of pain shot through every nerve. But the moment of escape had arrived.

With a steady sidelong movement the victim slides "from the embrace of the bandage and beyond the reach of the scimitar. For the moment, at least, *I was free.*" He is still under the eyes of the Inquisition, however: "I had scarcely stepped from my wooden bed of horror upon the stone floor of the prison, when the motion of the hellish machine ceased and I beheld it drawn up, by some invisible force, through the ceiling."

What new torture is in store, he wonders? "Something unusual—some change which, at first, I could not appreciate distinctly—it was obvious, had taken place in the apartment," and, for the first time, the prisoner becomes aware that there is an interval of about half an inch between the base of the walls and the floor of his cell. Through this fissure a sulphurous light enters and ". . . the mystery of the alteration in the chamber broke at once upon my understanding." The colored figures on the walls, formerly blurred, now assume

a startling and most intense brilliancy. . . . Demon eyes . . . gleamed with the lurid lustre of a fire that I could not force my imagination to regard as unreal.

*Unreal!*—Even while I breathed there came to my nostrils the breath of the vapour of heated iron! A suffocating odour pervaded the prison! . . . A richer tint of crimson diffused itself over the pictured horrors of blood. I panted! I gasped for breath! There could be no doubt of the design of my tormentors. . . . I shrank from the glowing metal to the centre of the cell. Amid the thought of the fiery destruction that impended, the idea of the coolness of the well came over my soul like balm. I rushed to its deadly brink. I threw my straining vision below. The glare from the enkindled roof illumined its inmost recesses. Yet, for a wild moment, did my spirit refuse to comprehend the meaning of what I saw. At length it forced—it wrestled its way into my soul. . . . Oh, any horror but this! With a shriek, I rushed from the margin, and buried my face in my hands—weeping bitterly.

Such to our victim, though doomed to die by fire, was the horror the pit inspired!

The heat rapidly increased, and once again I looked up, shuddering as with a fit of the ague. There had been a second change in the cell—and now the change was obviously in the *form.* . . .

The room had been square. I saw that two of its iron angles were now acute—two, consequently, obtuse. The fearful difference quickly increased with a low rumbling or moaning sound. In an instant the apartment had shifted its form into that of a lozenge. But the alteration stopped not here—I neither hoped nor desired it to stop. I could have grasped the red walls to my bosom as a garment of eternal peace. "Death," I said, "any death but that of the pit!" Fool! might not I have known that *into the pit* it was the object of the burning iron to urge me? . . . And now, flatter and flatter grew the lozenge, with a rapidity that left me no time for contemplation. Its centre, and of course, its greatest width, came just over the yawning gulf. I shrank back—but the closing walls pressed me resistlessly onward. At length for my seared and writhing body there was no longer an inch of foothold on the firm floor of the prison. I struggled no more, but the agony of my soul found vent in one loud, long, and final scream of despair. I felt that I tottered upon the brink—I averted my eyes—

There was a discordant hum of human voices! There was a loud blast as of many trumpets! There was a harsh grating as of a thousand thunders! The fiery walls rushed back! An outstretched arm caught my own as I fell, fainting, into the abyss. It was that of General Lasalle. The French army had entered Toledo. The Inquisition was in the hands of its enemies.

So this tale ends, on a sort of Cæsarean operation, performed by the general himself, to free our victim; the general embodying the *good* father in contrast to the *bad* fathers of the Inquisition.

Certain readers will doubtless opine it idle, after this résumé, to seek a "latent," complicated, involved significance beneath the manifest content. Poe's mind, they will say, clearly sadistic—a point we concede—evidently enjoyed imagining torments and horrors and excelled in their invention. Why introduce such absurd fantasies as that of returning to the womb, such as you mentioned earlier and others, doubtless as shocking, to come?

Nevertheless, "The Pit and the Pendulum," like our dreams or reveries, is a kind of two-part song. True, exquisitely cruel torturers might indeed construct a cell with such walls of heated metal, a yawning pit, a descending, hissing pendulum, to end their agonizing victim's days. None of this is impossible, and the very *plausibility* of these terrors accounts, in part, for the horror the tale inspires. But none of this explains

why Poe should choose, of all possible anxiety themes, particularly these: nor, above all, why these piled-up horrors
should make us shudder, when many a similar invention
leaves us cold.

To bring this about, these atrocites, for Poe, must have
been charged with that libido which wells up from the
deepest unconscious sources and communicates conviction
through works of art: only thus, by ways unknown to
consciousness, can the author's unconscious speak to that of
his readers. And though the terror theme of the torture cell
seems superficially self-explanatory, our analytic task is to
reveal the anxiety theme on which it is built, which alone
gives this fearful tale its poignant and enduring impressiveness.

Two great underlying themes, latent in Poe's unconscious,
seem to have inspired "The Pit and the Pendulum"; one, the
fantasy of the return to the womb, already mentioned, now,
though not always, conceived in terms of anxiety; the other,
ignored in our résumé of this tale, the son's homosexual and
masochistic passivity to the father, similarly conceived in
anxiety terms.

Yet a third theme will confront us in "The Pit and the
Pendulum"; the vast, primary problem of the origin of
anxiety, as yet far from biologically or analytically resolved.

Reverting to the first of these themes, the victim's im-
prisonment in his torture cell was, as we said, to be seen as
a womb fantasy. Fantasies of the sort are the common
heritage of man. They figure in the dreams and other unconscious constructions of adults, as in the activities and
behavior of children. They should not, however, be confused
with biological tendencies to regress to the fetal condition, a
tendency doubtless common to all creatures which have
experienced an amniotic existence.[1] This tendency reveals
itself most clearly in their periodic need to sleep in darkness
and at rest and often, even, in the prenatal position, another
manifestation of which would be coitus, that partial return
into the female body—complete return being only effected
by one sperm cell. The penis achieves only a semi- and
temporary return to our prenatal bliss, and the body, totally
and as it were by proxy, attains it in voluptuous pleasure.

Apart from these biological aspects, however, and returning to our specific theme, *fantasies* of a return to the womb,
these psychic edifices—true, biologically based, as in general

is everything pertaining to the psyche—begin to be raised as soon as the child suspects an earlier existence inside the mother's body.

But contrary, however, to what Rank advances in his *The Trauma of Birth*,[2] to which we shall later revert, the womb fantasies of the adult or child, are not *necessarily* anxiety cathected. Many are exceedingly pleasurable. I knew, for example, a small girl whose favorite game was "playing houses." Drawing chairs and tables together, she would cover them with shawls, thus making a dark little airless enclosure into which she would creep and remain for hours, ecstatically contented. No amount of persuasion or efforts to make her play in the air and sunlight could wean her from this game, which she always reluctantly abandoned. The analysis of this girl, in afterlife, showed that her childish game was a typical womb fantasy. There only, in these symbolic play "houses," could she recover the shelter and peace of the womb—for she had prematurely lost her mother. The fantasies she thus acted out, true in this instance to their origin, always remained a source of deepest pleasure, exempt from all anxiety. The same will be found true for many fantasies of this type, both in children and adults.

And now we must ask why this womb fantasy which, given its origins, should be encompassed by calm, gentleness, and blissful well-being, is, in effect, so often anxiety-cathected, and so much so as to become the anxiety fantasm in excelsis. This it is, too, which lies at the roots of various claustrophobias and which, again, is expressed in that most fearful of all instances of morbid anxiety, fear of premature burial. It was this fear, in particular, which haunted Poe and inspired the terrible and epic vision described in "The Premature Burial,"[3] a vision in which all mankind's graves open to reveal the corpses feebly struggling in the faint phosphorescence of decay.

Rank has tried to answer this question in his book *The Trauma of Birth*. In it, he says, we all strive to return to that state of primal pleasure (*Urlust*) of the fetus in the womb; a condition in which we, as yet, know nought of painful or disturbing stimuli from without, and bathe in paradisal calm. But, in regressing to this point, we strike an obstacle in our path: the memory of the event which catastrophically ended that period and expelled us from this paradise; namely, birth with its concomitant affect, the earliest of our anxiety conditions (*Urangst*). Thus, whenever we are beset by memories of or yearnings for the lost paradise of the mother's body, the memory of that obstacle at once recurs and regressively opposes such return. Thus, these womb memories, at every recurrence, are automatically reinvested with anxiety and the anxiety aroused by the menacing *pit,* as being the way the prisoner *must* issue, is attached to the *cell* that was once paradisal.

At first sight, this would seem well to apply to our victim whose horror of the pit is such that, when the red-hot walls contract about him, as though a womb, any death seems preferable—even fire and its "red walls"—to the depths of the pit which, rationally, may seem surprising to us.

Nevertheless, the possibility that such *psychological* memories of birth anxiety exist admits of some doubt and, in *Inhibitions, Symptoms and Anxiety,*[4] Freud critically evaluates this venturesome, simple, and possibly ingenuous theory of Rank's.

The concept that physiological phenomena of birth, such as disturbed heartbeat and even asphyxia, are the prototypes of every later anxiety condition, was first formulated by Freud. It is expounded in the chapter on anxiety in his *Introductory Lectures on Psycho-Analysis* and elsewhere.

Rank, however, differs from Freud in maintaining that birth anxiety is a *psychic memory* which never deserts us and not one that is merely *physiological.* Where, as Freud said to me, it is impossible to follow Rank is when he claims that the embryo so distinctly *remembers* its passage through the vagina that the female genitals thereafter remain, for all mankind, anxiety-cathected. As a result, the cardinal castration anxiety is pushed into the background, though responsible, far more often than birth anxiety, for the fears associated, in the unconscious, with that forever gaping "wound," the vagina.

Furthermore, in womb fantasies anxiety-cathected (which we must remember is not always the case), there enter anxiety factors other than those which originate in the "memory" of birth. Such fantasies in adults and, even, children do not exist alone, and other anxieties have been or will be experienced, as Freud chronologically systematizes in *Inhibitions, Symptoms and Anxiety.* Birth anxiety, for instance, is succeeded by separation anxiety, whenever the

mother absents herself from the child. Later, there appear
castration fears, inspired by our upbringers, linked with the
repression of our infantile sexuality. Follows the anxiety
derived from conscience, issuing from the introjection of the
menaces of these same upbringers and, lastly, fear of death
which derives from the ego narcissistically fearful for its
survival, once it has learned that death exists: that death
which the unconscious never admits. All these forms of
anxiety may, through regression, fuse with womb fantasies
and that, so closely, that often it is difficult to separate them
at first sight.

To return, however, to our analysis of "The Pit and the
Pendulum."

By the villainy of the Inquisitors (who, a sort of royal
"we," represent the infinitely multiplied Father), a poor
wretch is doomed to a terrible punishment, certain to end
in death. His crime was that he did not believe in them
blindly, or submit, utterly, to their will; in short, he is guilty
of heresy against the Father. But death and its approaches,
here, take the form—one constant in the unconscious—of the
return to the womb and that primal fetal condition on which
imagination models our future state. This wretch is immured
in a deep underground cell, dark and damp, though, strangely
enough, he appears to have no sensation of cold. And indeed,
toward the end of the tale, the then *red* walls will throw out
a burning heat and, like a giant womb, begin to contract, as
though to force the embryo toward the cloacal abyss.

Let us not anticipate, however. First, the doomed man
miraculously escapes the pit, or premature birth, as it were.
He nevertheless remains imprisoned, hidden, and protected in
the anxiety-causing womb of his grim cell. These events and
their accompanying emotions are interrupted, from time to
time, by periods of semireturn to a fetal condition; sudden
lapses into deep, dreamless slumbers from which the prisoner
always awakes starving but, mostly, dying of thirst. Possibly
here, too, we find a memory, as in *The Narrative of Arthur
Gordon Pym*, of what the little undernourished Edgar
suffered, as a result of his mother's inadequate milk?

Now, after his first escape from the cloacal birth gulf, the
prisoner wakes to find himself surrounded by sulphurous
figures which cover his cell walls: hideous demons that recall
the animal totems which represent the Father in primitive

minds. And when the victim lifts his eyes what, in fact, he discovers is, indeed, the castrating Father in excelsis: Time with his scythe. Yet though, in his prison, our victim is alone and desperately far from help and, though, to a certain extent, his horror of the dark corresponds to what Freud so well expresses as regards the child's fear of dark—separation from the mother and loss of her protection[5]—our victim is not, in fact, alone, for the dread eyes of invisible Fathers, from their hiding place, watch his every movement, while over and above him is the castrating Father, Time with his scythe.

But this theme of a pendulum, a huge clock, and a murderous weapon of steel does not now appear, in Poe's work, for the first time. In "A Predicament: The Scythe of Time,"[6] the eyes of Signora Psyche Zenobia are forced from their sockets, and her head is cut off, by the minute hand of a cathedral clock. Thus, two classic castration symbols are here juxtaposed and applied to a woman, as in "The Black Cat." In "The Masque of the Red Death," the great melanchcholy clock, with its sinister chime and weighty pendulum, the double of the specter of doom at its side, was the father symbol heralding the son's overthrow. Nowhere, however, does the son appear so defenseless, so masochistically delivered up to the father, as in this pendulum torture in the Inquisition cell. Here is the son garroted, swaddled like a newborn babe, lying on his low wood cradle. Around are the walls of his cell, substituting the womb of the mother. Above, triumphant, is Father Time, with his pendulum-scythe.

And now what does this fantasy recall? Many, in fact, often met in clinical analysis, whether of men or women. These, strange as it may seem to those unfamiliar with the fantasy world of the unconscious, all reproduce a certain imaginary situation: that of the child imagining itself still in the womb and—thence—witnessing the parents' coitus. This fantasy, analytically expressed, is termed *intrauterine observation of coitus.* Obviously, the word "memory" cannot be used here. What we have before us is clearly a fantasy, generally built up after the child has observed the coitus of adults and then, by regression, retrojected on the past.

But what instinctual stimulus, what unconscious wish can have engendered this fantasy, for fantasies are no more fortuitous than dreams? We shall find, as might be expected, that the unconscious wish, thus expressed, is sexually determined and specific to the individual's libido. A child which has observed adult coitus, in effect, by virtue of latent and responsive instinctual mechanisms, identifies itself with each of the partners in the act, though such identification tends to be made with male or female in proportion as female or male elements are dominant in the child. Biologically, no individual is wholly male of female, and all creatures, more or less, would seem bisexual, males presenting feminine features and females male: a fact confirmed by embryology, anatomy, and physiology. Similar testimony from psychoanalysis and depth psychology might be added, pending endocrinology's last and, possibly, conclusive word.[7]

Nevertheless, in each of us, male and female are variously embodied. In men, a prime condition of health is the possession of maximum physical virility. But, in Poe, that condition seems to have been vitiated, for we know how poorly he defended that virility and what a psychically inhibited, impotent individual he was. This, indeed, the fantasy of the tortured victim under the pendulum-scythe now, once more, indicates.

This first of Poe's great tales, derived from the theme of passivity to the father, must have been written at a time when his paranoiac attacks were beginning to be persecutory;[8] as Freud has shown, these are always rooted in homosexuality.

The homosexual nature of this pendulum fantasy is sufficiently clear: the pendulum, here, replaces the father's penis and its movements in coitus. Simultaneously with the mother, the child within is possessed and entered—or will be—by the father's penis and, given its bisexuality, can identify itself with the mother and, in imagination, possess the father's penis woman-fashion. All this in Poe, however, was associated with powerful regressive trends as well as strong moral disapproval. Poe thus, for the most part, remained fixated at the anal-sadistic stage reached when he lost his mother, that is, before three. Also, his upbringing had made him puritanical about sex. As a result, the father's act of possession is manifested in masochistically cruel and destructive forms, and the father's penis is equated with a murderous steel crescent which will enter and castrate the son, as it were, of his heart, whose throbbing, to Poe, as we saw in other tales, symbolized those forbidden sexual and phallic activities which inevitaby entailed punishment. Libidinal passivity to the father and sex guilt are both, therefore, magnificently gratified in this tale.

Here, once again, we return to the problem of anxiety. What is the origin of the anxiety, of which this tale, as it were, is compacted? Birth anxiety, alone, cannot altogether account for it, despite the overpowering horror of the pit. Nor could separation anxiety, either, despite the victim's solitude and abandon to the dark. To me, it seems that the primordial anxiety in this tale is castration anxiety from which, more or less, stems both conscience- and death anxiety. What menaces the victim, in the crescent of shining steel, is the slow castration destruction of the heart—or substitute phallus. And the horror of the pit, too, may well be largely fear of castration, since, to Poe, the female genitals were banned, terrifying, dentated, and castrating.

All this tale, in fact, evidences Poe's invincible reluctance, dominated as he was by the castration threat, to accept the incest fantasies of his infancy and subsequent sexuality. There is a page in Freud's *Inhibitions, Symptoms and Anxiety*[9] which throws so much light on this anxiety story we are analyzing that we must quote it in its entirety. After showing how anxiety, neurotic or "real," always arises from the perception of some *real* danger, whether this be internal and emanates from instinctual menaces to the ego (neurotic anxiety), or external, arising from without ("real" anxiety); he goes on to say, with special reference to castration anxiety:

Ferenczi[10] has traced, quite correctly, I think, a clear line of connection between this fear and the fears contained in the earlier situations of danger. According to him the high degree of narcissistic value which the penis possesses is due to the fact that this organ is a guarantee to its owner that he can be once more united to his mother—*i.e.*, to a substitute for her—in the act of copulation. Being deprived of it amounts to a renewed separation from her and this in its turn means being helplessly exposed to an unpleasurable tension due to instinctual need, as was the case in birth. But this need whose increase is feared is now a specific one belonging to the genital libido and is no longer an indeterminate one, as in the period of infancy. It may be added that for a man who is impotent (that is, who is inhibited by the threat of castration) the substitute for copulation is a fantasy of returning into his mother's womb. Following out Ferenczi's line of thought, one might say that such a man, while endeavouring to return to his mother's womb vicariously—by means of his

genital organ, proceeds to replace that organ regressively by his
body as a whole.

Now, if ever anyone was "inhibited by the castration
threat," it was surely Poe! It need not therefore surprise us
that his whole opus abounds in instances of the womb fantasy,
those "substitutes for coitus to the impotent," nor that they
reach their zenith in "The Pit and the Pendulum," that most
significant and impressive of them all.

As we have seen, however, this tale does not merely tell
of a return to the womb in the symbol of the underground
cell, its cloacal pit, and contracting walls. True, part of the
tale is invested with the anxiety attached to repressed incest
desires—the genital danger represented by the mother, or
wife, here being expressed in typical impotency fashion,
that is, in terms of fetal existence. And this face of the tale,
aspected, so to speak to the mother is, at least, as anxiety-
cathected—the pit being the victim's main horror—as the face
aspected to the father. None the less, the father also plays
an enormous part in this tale, as source of anxiety.

Doubtless, it was fear of the forbidden mother, and thus
woman, which helped, libidinally, to turn Poe back to the
father, a process facilitated by his marked bisexuality. In
life, as in fiction, Poe escaped the pit only to be garroted
under the pendulum. But neither there could he escape
the castration threat that had made him stumble and recoil
from the pit. Thus, all through life, the velleities of his
ill-starred sexuality doomed him to oscillate between these
dual forces, the pit and the pendulum, each luring him on
but each, also, the castrator. For, to find erotic pleasure in
woman he would have had to brave the pit which, however,
was so constructed, following the Inquisitors' (Father, God,
Creator) "most horrible plan," that there no "sudden extinction of life" would be possible. There seems a distinct suggestion, here, that the pit was lined with sharp blades or cutting
edges on which the victim would be torn and hung—in
short, the pit was a "cloaca dentata." To find erotic pleasure
in men, he would have, however, to behave as a castrated
being, woman, and let the scimitar enter and split his heart—
the scimitar replacing the phallus—but, against this, his male
narcissism rebelled. Thus, the two forms of erotic satisfaction
Poe's unconscious could accept—to one like him inhibited by
castration anxiety and given his marked bisexuality—were

each charged with anxiety, castration anxiety, in fact. The apparent invention, therefore, of "The Pit and the Pendulum," but faithfully and biographically records Poe's bisexual oscillations between his male and female trends, trends which always encountered the castration threat as an insurmountable obstacle.

The victim escapes the pit only to be ligatured under the pendulum, and escapes that only to be redelivered, inescapably, to the pit, owing to the cell's womblike contracting walls. Only General Lasalle (possibly, to Poe's unconscious, a surrogate of the good General Lafayette, in contrast to the bad John Allan); only the good father, a *deus ex machina*, by a kind of Cæsarean operation, slits open the contracting walls and rescues his victim *in extremis*. This was the supreme wish fantasy of Poe, for, in effect, he was always to be tossed between these poles of his bisexuality with never a hope of escape.

In his life, Poe, who passed for the adorer of woman, thanks to his verse and ardent utterances, was, in the depths of his soul, always flung back from his ecstatic attraction toward them to libidinal subjection to the male and, against this, the male in him constantly rebelled. The chaste and tender husband of the dying Virginia would leave her bedside for sudden and, at times, long drinking "fugues" with bosom cronies. More significant still, Poe, paranoiac and persecuted, as usually happens, remained attached to his persecutors and, oddly, wished always to renew his friendship with them. His lamentable visit to Thomas Dunn English to ask him to act as his second will be recalled, nor should we forget that it was his most treacherous and persistent enemy, Rufus Griswold, a man he had every reason to distrust, whom he desired to be his "executor," a term one is tempted to take in its most literal sense!

Such, then, was the passivity retained by Poe, the adult, to father figures: such was the mold he had acquired in childhood under John Allan's roof, by contact with a rigid, powerful father whom he feared, hated, admired and, also, loved. His libido (markedly bisexual from the outset), must have oscillated continuously between Frances Allan the gentle foster mother, and the dour husband; hatred, like love, creates libidinal fixation, and Poe's inveterate hatred of John Allan, as, later, of all father figures, was, on a deeper level, a confession of indissoluble attachment.

Notes

III. "The Tell-Tale Heart"

[1] Freud, "Dostoevski and Parricide," *International Journal of Psycho-analysis*, 1945, 1–8; *Dostojewski und die Vatertötung*, 1928, *Ges. Werke*, Band XIV.

[2] *Israfel*, p. 567.

[3] Lowell to Poe, Boston, December 17, 1842, *Virginia Edition*, XVII, 125.

[4] *Israfel*, p. 540.

[5] "The moaning and groaning,
     The sighing and sobbing,
     Are quieted now,
     With that horrible throbbing
     At heart:—ah that horrible,
     Horrible throbbing!

[6] Cf. Henri Barbusse, *L'Enfer* (Paris, Librairie Mondiale, 1908), where sexuality in general is equated with "hell."

[7] Similarly, in "Thou Art the Man," (*Godey's Lady's Book*, November, 1844), the poor hack-writer, so appropriately named Mr. Pennifeather, is as innocent as the newborn babe of the murder of his rich uncle, Mr. Shuttleworthy, whose heir he is. Only a double of the latter, a rogue ironically called Old Charley Goodfellow, who likewise belongs to the series of "fathers," or hypocritical John Allans, could have been capable of so heinous a deed! Goodfellow succeeds in having the innocent nephew arrested and condemned to the gallows but, by a device typically Poe's (the corpse of the victim rises to denounce his murderer from a case of wine), he is exposed and brought to justice. The murderer falls dead, while Pennifeather, released from prison, in all innocence enjoys the murdered man's fortune.

[8] Freud, *Leonardo da Vinci: A Psycho-Sexual Study of an Infantile Reminiscence, op. cit.*, page 35, Note 15.

[9] The *Encyclopaedia Britannica* article "Odin" tells us that, among ancient peoples, prisoners taken in war were often sacrificed to the "one-eyed old man." "The commonest method of sacrifice was by hanging the victim on a tree; and in the poem, *Hávamál*, the god himself is represented as sacrificed in this way." There must be something more than coincidence in the fact that Wotan, the castrated father, should be hanged or, in other words, have his penis mockingly restored, in the same way as the Black Cat, a one-eyed monster like Wotan.

[10] Yet another contradiction may be noted. The sound of the old man's heartbeats is likened to the ticking of a watch: a watch "enveloped in cotton," even. Now, watches or the ticking of a watch (in contrast, as we shall see, with the imposing swing of a

clock pendulum) are classic symbols, in the unconscious, for the female organ and the throbbings, in sexual excitement, of the tiny clitoris it conceals. Before the old man's heartbeats have swollen to the "hellish tattoo" of truly virile character, they thus begin to beat twice, muted as it were, and in *feminine* fashion. We therefore may have here another instance of a dualism similar to that of the film-covered eye which both sees and does not see or, in other words, which is at the same time ultravirile and castrated.

[11] "The Man That Was Used Up, A Tale of the Late Bugaboo and Kickapoo Campaign." *Burton's Gentleman's Magazine,* August, 1839; 1840; 1843; *Broadway Journal,* II, 5.

[12] Cf. *Israfel,* p. 61, for a reference to this "mammy."

## IV. "The Pit and the Pendulum"

[1] In this connection and for what follows, see Ferenczi's excellent essay "Thalassa: A Theory of Genitality," *The Psychoanalytic Quarterly,* II (1933), 361–403; III (1934), 1–29, 200–222; trans. from *Versuch Einer Genitaltheorie, Internationaler Psychoanalytischer Verlag,* 1921.

[2] O. Rank, *The Trauma of Birth,* London, Kegan Paul, Trench, Trubner & Co., 1929; trans. from *Das Traum der Geburt, Internationaler Psychoanalytischer Verlag,* 1924.

[3] "The Premature Burial" appeared in August, 1844, in an unknown Philadelphia periodical; *Broadway Journal,* I, 24.

[4] *Inhibitions, Symptoms and Anxiety.*

[5] Cf. *Introductory Lectures on Pyscho-Analysis,* p. 340. A child is afraid in the dark and asks its aunt to speak to it: "If someone talks, it gets lighter." London, Allen & Unwin, 2nd Ed., 1933; trans. from *Vorlesungen zur Einführung in die Psychoanalyse,* 1916–1917, *Ges. Werke,* Band XI.

[6] "A Predicament: The Scythe of Time," *The American Museum,* December, 1838; 1840; *Broadway Journal,* II, 18.

[7] Cf. Marañon, *The Evolution of Sex and Intersexual Conditions,* London, George Allen & Unwin, Ltd., 1932; trans. by W. B. Wells, with new appendix from *La Evolución de la Sexualidad y los Estados Intersexuales,* Morata, Madrid, 1930.

[8] Cf. *Israfel,* p. 569; Poe's letter to Tomlin, August 28, 1843, in which he libelously attacks Wilmer for maligning him.

[9] *Op. cit.*

[10] Referring to *Thalassa: A Theory of Genitality (op. cit.* page 91, Note 1).

*Clarence P. Oberndorf**

# PSYCHOANALYSIS IN LITERATURE AND ITS THERAPEUTIC VALUE

No original writing can be either entirely subjective or objective, and even strictly scientific writing, which is theoretically objective, is influenced by the author's subjective atttitudes. In purely technical writing this subjectivity may be so slight that it can be detected only in the frequency with which the author chooses to express himself in the active or passive tense or in his use of the personal pronoun. In the fields of narrative, dramatic, fictional, or poetic composition the writer is in the possession of the medium of words through which he may unconsciously reflect his deepest emotions; and the more freely he allows his pen to follow his fantasy, the more apt he is to reveal unconsciously in his literary creations that which he has often painstakingly sought to conceal in his more deliberate expressions.

One of the purposes of psychoanalysis is to uncover unconscious drives which cause disturbing conflicts in patients. Therefore the practicing psychoanalyst necessarily devotes great attention to fantasies, dreams, diaries, pet phrases, and other unconscious verbal productions, such as slips of the tongue, in the course of his daily therapeutic sessions. Freud was the first to apply his own method originally introduced for the treatment of psychic disturbances, to the interpretation of literary productions, choosing for his subject *Delusion and Dream in W. Jensen's Gradiva* (1907). Later, in 1910, he undertook the analysis of the character of a man of extraordinary genius, Leonardo da Vinci, through a study of his dreams and memories. Indeed, Freud's last book, *Moses and Monotheism,* written shortly before his death in London in 1939, in which he seeks to prove that Moses was an Egyptian, is an outstanding example of this type of delving into some of the enigmas of the past through the application of psychoanalysis.

* CLARENCE P. OBERNDORF was one of the pioneers of modern psychoanalysis in America. He is the author of *A History of Psychoanalysis in America* and also of *The Psychiatric Novels of Oliver Wendell Holmes.*

The little group of analysts around Freud in Vienna in the first decade of this century faced violently hostile reactions from both psychiatrists and psychologists. They regarded as a corroboration of their science the discoveries of descriptions and interpretations of soul conflicts by writers the world over, so similar to those which they postulated as responsible for the mental difficulties of their patients.[1] Thus it soon became a pleasant recreation—a busman's holiday—for medical analysts to hunt for specimens among the writings of great authors that reflected Freud's theories and to undertake studies of famous personalities through the application of psychoanalytic criteria to their works and character traits. Both these types of investigation we may in turn interpret as the analyst's own escape from the challenge, worry, and resistance of patients in clinical practice to academic analyses of persons long dead. These unconsulted characters can neither contradict his subjective deductions nor desert him in case they do not approve what he asserts—to which this excursion of the present writer is no exception.

Many of these character analyses are fascinating because it is always interesting and sometimes valuable to reappraise the work of minds that have molded our culture at one time in the light of the standards of other times. Certainly such psychoanalytic studies are frequently more enlightening and plausible in their explanation of the paradoxes of character found in some of the most beloved authors and artists than had been possible with descriptive approaches used before the advent of psychoanalysis. The range of these observations in the first volume of the first psychoanalytic periodical ever published[2] is astonishing, including significant excepts from Bulwer Lytton's *A Strange Story*, Wagner's *Die Meistersinger*, Anatole France, and quotations from Nietzsche, Shakespeare, and Schopenhauer illustrating elements in their thinking which, needless to say, preceded Freud's formulations. Similar reports have continued to appear in the foremost psychoanalytic journals up to the present time, most recent examples of which are Hitschmann's explanation of Samuel Johnson's contradictory characteristics,[3] and the study of so circumscribed and incidental a pathological symptom as *déjà vu* in the works of Proust and Tolstoi.[4]

The most common formula in these analyses is to demonstrate or sometimes assume the existence of strong instinctual drives in the author and their fixations at various levels, such as the anal or oral, and to show how in his writing he reveals them either by overcompensation, by his unconscious choice of symbols, or occasionally by permitting them to break through in tender or violent passages.

On the other hand, as the psychoanalytic mechanisms and the theories of the unconscious gradually became more generally known throughout the world (after 1910), many writers deliberately or through their indirect assimilation of the subject introduced psychoanalytic concepts into their biographic, romantic, or detective stories to illuminate or explain the motives of their characters, or to serve as the bases for their plots. Because of the intentional, almost clinical nature of the introduction of these psychoanalytic mechanisms into the theme of the story, they are seldom as convincing to the reader or as effective as when they appear as the unconscious manifestation of the writer's deeper feelings.

One analytic theory[5] maintains that the writer under the pressure of unconscious guilt feelings gives expression in his writing to the defenses he has developed against his forbidden wishes and fantasies and that while writing is exhibitionistic, the primary tendencies in the writer are voyeuristic and the writing is a defense against deeply repressed voyeurism (early interest in sexual observation). Some studies in this field of the analysis of literature even attempt to place the type of writing on a particular pregenital level. For example, Brill[6] states "that some poets do not advance much beyond the earliest and later oral phases," and he believes that in the case of the artist "the preoedipal phase has been the most significant one for his development."

From the earliest times man has recognized that in dreams he often found himself in situations about which he dared not allow himself to think in waking life or in possession of prized objectives which he had never hoped to attain. He has also been aware that fantasy has been an escape from the bitter hardships and stern demands of reality's daily needs. Thus, for example, a patient, a young woman of twenty-seven, suffering from feelings of unreality, reported the following dream:

She came rushing into a room where several of her friends were seated. Someone asked her why she had been running. She replied: "I am running because I am cold." Immediately thereafter her friend, Mary, came running into the room in a similar manner and again someone asked Mary the same question. She responded: "I am running away from my thoughts." In her dream my patient thought: "Why can't I tell the truth like Mary because I am really running away from my thoughts."

While still in the dream it also occurred to her that the whole idea of running away from thoughts must be her own because she had furnished Mary's answer in the dream. In this particular instance the dream tells the story of the patient's neurosis which consisted of a fear of insanity, inability to unbend in society, conscious indifference to men and awkwardness in their presence. She had entered psychoanalytic treatment with great reluctance and misgiving because she knew that eventually it would bring her to face certain thoughts which were deeply buried and which she had avoided and also to acknowledge the existence of certain physical reactions which she correctly surmised to be sexual. The dream reflects the method by which she tried to escape from these unwelcome manifestations but is also indicative of her unconscious wish now to meet them.

Sometimes the neurotic character traits that the analyst detects in the novels or the characters of an author parallel closely those with which he is very familiar in his patients. Similarly these reactions, attitudes, and preoccupations can be demonstrated to repeat themselves over and over again in books written years apart. Occasionally the writer unconsciously seems to be attempting to cure his neurotic conflicts by writing, as we sometimes find patients who either write or talk endlessly about them. In most cases, however, the attempt of the author to free himself of the neurosis by writing it out is unsuccessful. Possibly the feeling which occurs to many authors from time to time, that they have written themselves out, may be dependent upon the unconscious appretiation that relief from some personal neurotic conflict through their writing has not been satisfactory and therefore no incentive remains for them to continue their literary efforts.

Writing out or writing off by an author may equate itself with the confessional or cathartic elements of the clinical analytic procedure, but such self-revelation as a rule does not suffice to relieve permanently the essential conflicts of the writer any more than it does the troubled mind of the neurotic patient. The cathartic material must be appraised by the interpretative comment of the analyst which eventually brings to the attention of the patient what unconscious motives his productions signify and which drives he is attempting to express or avoid. Such critical, objective influence is ordinarily not brought to bear on the work of the novelist, dramatist, or poet either by himself or by the observations of his friends or of professional reviewers whose interest focuses on other aspects of literary composition.

Many of the most distraught and unhappy great writers found little permanent relief, although there may have been temporary satisfaction, in their literary productions, and lived with their difficulties fundamentally unaltered until their death. De Quincey, Coleridge, Poe, and Baudelaire may be mentioned as outstanding examples of the failure of creative writing to liberate them from their prolonged and physically destructive emotional suffering.

Nathaniel Hawthorne, the recluse of Salem and later of Concord, Massachusetts, may also be included, it seems to me, in the type of writer who labored under a repetitive compulsion to expose his own feelings of self-reproach and criminality, such as he portrayed so dramatically in the character of the culpable minister, Arthur Dimmesdale, in *The Scarlet Letter*. He was fully aware that his subjective writing was self-revealing for he remarks in one of his prefaces: "You must look through the range of his (the author of the psychological romance) fictitious characters, good and evil, in order to detect his essential traits." Most of Hawthorne's many critics have seen him and his family reflected in his work more frequently and more patently than is usual with imaginative authors.

Nearly a century after Hawthorne's death biographies of this obscure, dissonant man continue to be published, and all his biographers agree upon the psychopathological background of his life which may have been responsible for many of his frustrations and perplexities. Especially emphasized are his difficulties with reality, his flight into the past, the traits he had in common with his abnormal mother, and the influence of his older sister, Elizabeth.[7] These latter form the basis of his feminine identifications and of many of his conflicts.

Hawthorne was of the clearest Puritan strain. One of his ancestors, William Hathorne, was among the harshest persecutors of those who ventured to disagree with the religious or political proscriptions of the Puritan colony at Salem. His grandfather, John Hathorne, made himself conspicuous by his zeal in persecuting witches, and Nathaniel in early boyhood took to himself the shame and guilt that he felt his forefathers should have endured for their cruelties in punishing every evidence of social and religious nonconformity and deviation, no matter how slight a sin it might be.

Hawthorne's father died in Surinam when the boy was four years old. He grew up with two older sisters in a dismal household where his mother after her husband's death seldom left her room until Hawthorne had grown to manhood. His was a solitary and forlorn childhood and as a very young man he became moody of temperament, very uneasy when in groups of people, with a reservation in his manner which prevented him from making friends. After his return from college at Bowdoin to the gloomy household in Salem, Hawthorne wrote that like his mother he was "surrounding himself with shadows which bewildered him and had drawn him aside from the beaten path of life" and "had made a captive of himself and put him in a dungeon."

The feeling of attachment to and rejection of his mother did not change from boyhood until her death some seven years after his marriage, when Hawthorne himself was forty-five. "A sort of coldness of intercourse existed between us such as is apt to come between persons of strong feelings if they are not managed rightly," he wrote in his notebook just before she died. But at her deathbed he found "tears gathering in his eyes and he sobbed."[8] His withdrawal from life, so like his mother's, and his feeling of inadequacy to cope with reality were accompanied by almost continuous depression and feelings of guilt. He was given to punitive self-denials for minor self-indulgences, such as refusing to drink tea because he liked it, a characteristic so typical of neurotic patients.

When he was thirty-four, the determined Miss Elizabeth Peabody, who had known him from childhood, succeeded in overcoming his diffidence, dragged him away from his somber surroundings, and induced him to visit at the Peabody home. There he met her sister, Sophia, an invalid who like his mother had been confined to her room for years, and immediately fell in love with her. They married four years later despite the opposition of his older sister, Elizabeth, and after an engagement which he had felt necessary to conceal for several years from his mother. Sophia Peabody, like Hawthorne, was also a person of delicate sensitivity, and their marriage, notwithstanding some financial stringency and severe illness, is considered to have been a singularly happy and tranquil one. However, in many respects it developed into a solitude and isolation *à deux,* comparable to the psychiatric situation known as a *folie à deux,* when two persons, closely related, develop the same pathological traits.

Perhaps the periods of his life when Hawthorne's despondency reached its depth were at the age of thirty-two when he thought seriously of suicide and again at forty-two shortly before he published *The Scarlet Letter,* and then after his return from Europe in 1860 until his death in 1864 at the age of fifty-nine. His wife as early as July, 1861, had become greatly distressed and alarmed to see him "so apathetic, so indifferent, so hopeless, so unstrung." No organic disease has been established as the cause of his lingering final illness which had all the characteristics of his previous depressions.

It is not the primary purpose of this paper to interpret Hawthorne's life and writings psychoanalytically, though few authors provide a more tempting material and setting, but to show the inadequacy of his almost compulsive concern in his works with wrongdoing and moral guilt to alter his feelings of his own criminal responsibility. He not only possessed an extraordinary insight into the problems that beset him but also sensed the psychological method by which they might be reached and solved. For example, in *The Scarlet Letter,* in several places, he has described accurately and vividly the approach made by old Dr. Roger Chillingworth in his attempt to cure the guilty minister's, Mr. Dimmesdale's, alarming physical illness. This is so anticipatory of the psychoanalytic method developed by Freud that a quotation seems worth while:

Chillingworth scrutinized his patient carefully, both as he saw him in his ordinary life, keeping an accustomed pathway in the range of thoughts familiar to him, and as he appeared when thrown amidst other moral scenery, the novelty of which might call out something new to the surface of his character. He deemed it essential, it would seem, to know the man, before attempting to do him good. Wherever there is a heart and an intellect, the diseases of the physical frame are tinged with the peculiarities of these. In Arthur Dimmesdale, thought and imagination were so

active, and sensibility so intense, that the bodily infirmity would
be likely to have its groundwork there.

So Roger Chillingworth—the man of skill, the kind and friendly
physician—strove to go deep into his patient's bosom, delving
among his principles, prying into his recollections, and probing
everything with a cautious touch, like a treasure-seeker in a dark
cavern. Few secrets escape an investigator, who has opportunity
and license to undertake such a quest, and the skill to follow it up.

Hawthorne, however, like other neurotics, including those
who today are fully acquainted with modern psychoanalytic
methods, found them of little use in the psychological disturbances from which he suffered and which he described so
fully in his first literary efforts. Many psychoanalysts believe
that the first dream that the patient reports after beginning
treatment epitomizes his entire life's conflict. So, too, perhaps
the earliest writings of an author are more apt to reflect those
difficulties by which he is most troubled and with which he is
most familiar.

In Hawthorne's case, we find an uncommonly frank, if
romanticized, autobiographical picture in his immature and
boyish novel, *Fanshawe*, which he published anonymously
and at his own expense at the age of twenty-four. So mortified
was he at its lack of success that he recalled all the copies
he could lay his hands on and burned them. Possibly his
discouragement and distress may also have been influenced
by a sense of shame when he saw some of his own frustrations exposed in cold print, for Hawthorne relates that Fanshawe, from an early age "had spent years in solitary study,
in conversation with the dead, while he scorned to mingle
with the living world or to be actuated by any of its motives,"
Fanshawe, like his creator, also "deemed himself unconcerned,
unconnected with the world's feelings."

Fanshawe dies at the end of the novel, and of him Hawthorne says: "There were many who felt an interest in
Fanshawe; but the influence of none could prevail upon him
to lay aside the habits, mental and physical, by which he was
bringing himself to the grave." The inscription which his
fellow students selected for Fanshawe's tombstone was borrowed from the grave of Nathaniel Mather—"whom in his
almost insane eagerness for knowledge Fanshawe resembled."

The theme of the consequences of withdrawal from reality
and denial of emotion is found in many of Hawthorne's short
stories but nowhere is it more dramatically pictured than in

Ethan Brand, the bleak, mysterious, terribly lonely lime
burner who sought and discovered The Unpardonable Sin.
This is the sin of allowing the heart to wither and contract
while the intellect develops at its expense.

Hawthorne continued to deal with the consciousness of sin
and similar retributions for hundreds of pages, and his
greatest success, *The Scarlet Letter* (1849), is a pitiful tale
of self-torture and expiation. And so, too, from his second
popular novel, *The House of Seven Gables*, which immediately followed the timeless story of adultery in the Puritan
colony, to *The Marble Faun* (1860), his last complete novel,
the same morbid ruminations recur. In *The Blithedale
Romance* (1852) he continues his lugubrious musings concerning retribution, and as pointed out by Ruth Morris[9] "is
still obsessed with guilt and expiation as if he had not written
his earlier works." This comment seems to refute the main
thesis of Morris' article that the author who "works from an
emotional need heals himself through the process." Certainly
Hawthorne, with his masses of unpublished material, with
utter disregard for attuning his material to the tastes and
demands of his public, is a striking example of a writer who
benefited little through disclosing his fears and irresolution.

Some of Hawthorne's notebooks show simple attitudes and
childlike traits, but his untiring preoccupation with questions
of conscience led a French critic, Monsieur Montegut,[10] to
remark: "This habit of seeing sin everywhere; this dusky gaze
bent always upon a damned world, and a nature draped in
mourning; these lonely conversations of the imagination with
the conscience; this pitiless analysis resulting from a per-
petual examination of one's self, all these elements of the
Puritan character have passed into Mr. Hawthorne, or, to
speak more justily, have filtered into him, through a long
succession of generations."

To the above Henry James, sometimes regarded by literary
critics as strongly influenced by Hawthorne's psychological
analyses, comments as follows: "Hawthorne was all that
Monsieur Montegut says minus the conviction. These things
have been lodged in the mind of a man whose fancy had
straightway begun to take liberties and play tricks with
them." And yet subsequently James in commenting upon the
character of Hilda in *The Marble Faun*, remarks:

She had done no wrong, and yet wrong-doing has become a
part of her experience, and she carries the weight of her detested

knowledge upon her heart. Finding herself in St. Peter's, she enters a confessional, strenuous daughter of the Puritans as she is, and pours out her dark knowledge into the bosom of the church—then comes away with her conscience lightened, not a whit the less a Puritan than before.

Hawthorne's efforts to adapt himself to a realistic world seem to have been aided very little by his repeated descriptions, beginning with Fanshawe, of situations and figures involved in retreat from actualities. As late as 1856 he records with great detail and emotion a personal experience of *déja vu* while in England. He had previously described this phenomenon in his fictional characters, both in *The Scarlet Letter* and *The House of the Seven Gables* from which latter the following is quoted.

He was evidently trying to grapple with the present scene, and bring it home to his mind with a more satisfactory distinctness. He desired to be certain, at least, that he was here, in the low-studded, cross-beamed parlor, and not in some other spot, which had stereotyped itself into his senses. But the effort was too great to be sustained with more than a fragmentary success. Continually, as we may express it, he faded away out of his place; or, in other words, his mind and consciousness took their departure, leaving his wasted, gray, and melancholy figure—a substantial emptiness, a material ghost—to occupy his seat at table.

In the *déjà vu* phenomenon the person still distinguishes fantasy from reality but it is also closely akin to the feeling of unreality and depersonalization. Most psychiatrists interpret these symptoms as an involuntary reaction which permits the person escape from some actual situation which he feels himself unable to meet, and as closely associated with difficulties in thinking.[11]

Hawthorne's wretched final four years, from fifty-five to fifty-nine, found him in a depressed state of mind which cannot be directly attributed to worry about the Civil War or the unfavorable criticisms of his last books or even the illness of his daughter, Una, to whom he was intensely attached. He suffered from "something preternatural" in his reluctance to begin to write, although in financial need and frequently urged by his sympathetic friend and admiring publisher, Mr. Fields. He wrote: "I linger at the threshold, and have a perception of very disagreeable phantoms to be encountered if I enter," and seemed to be desperately weary of life and to wish to die.

The sensitive, self-critical Puritan, whose dreams and fantasy life were far more real to him than actualities, had perhaps partially attained the absolution he sought in his profuse and relentless confessional writing but it had not touched the source of his need for atonement. His unhappiness, his reserve, his isolation persisted notwithstanding the most propitious external circumstances after the age of thirty-four, namely, the love of a tender woman who adored and idolized him, parenthood to three children whom he cherished, and acclaim, somewhat late in life to be sure, by the most eminent literary men of his time as the first great novelist America had produced.

Yet, with all these blessings, when Hawthorne died on May 18, 1864, Ralph Waldo Emerson,[12] returning from the funeral which was attended by the notables of the Boston intellectual group, wrote in his journal: "Clarke in the church said that Hawthorne had shown a sympathy with the crime in our nature, and, like Jesus was the friend of sinners. I thought there was a tragic element in the event—in the painful solitude of the man, which, I suppose, could not longer be endured and he died of it. I have felt sure of him in his neighborhood and in his necessities of sympathy and intelligence—that I could well wait for time, his unwillingness and caprice, and might one day conquer his friendship."

These lines are indeed reminiscent of the final words which Hawthorne had selected for his prototypic hero, Fanshawe, a quarter of a century before.

At the outset of this article I pointed out that most of the large number of psychoanalytic studies of the literary compositions of famous authors have sought to trace the libidinal drives reflecting the character of the author and their conversion into various sublimated interests. They stress unconscious symbolization and the consonance of the poet's productions with the experiences of psychiatric patients. These studies have not considered what effect, if any, such creative production and artistic efforts have had in altering the writer's underlying, poorly tolerated instinctual urges which so often have shown themselves in inebriety, drug addiction, debauchery, sexual perversions, compulsion neuroses or psychoses.

Taking Nathaniel Hawthorne's writings as a basis, I have attempted to demonstrate the general inadequacy of confessional writing, in his case as in others, to change his tyrannical conscience or to lessen his characterological difficulties. Just before his death he was still longing to write a "sunshiny book," but his legendary curses, his sinister phantoms and haunting ghosts continued to smolder in the profundity of his exhausted mind until the end came to him gently in his sleep.

## NOTES

[1] Sandor Ferenczi, "Anatole France als Analytiker," *Ztrbl. Psa.* 1, 1911, p. 467.

[2] *Ztrbl. Psa.*, 1–2, 1911.

[3] Edward Hitschmann, "Samuel Johnson's Character," *Psa. Rev.*, 32, 1945.

[4] R. W. Pickford, "Déjà Vu in Proust and Tolstoi," *Int. J. Psa.*, 25, 1944, p. 152.

[5] Edmund Bergler, "A Clinical Approach to the Psychoanalysis of Writers," *Psa. Rev.*, 31 (1944), p. 70.

[6] A. A. Brill, "Poetry as an Oral Outlet," *Psa. Rev.*, 18, 1931.

[7] Edward Mather, *Nathaniel Hawthorne, A Modest Man*, New York, Thomas Y. Crowell Co., 1940, p. 47. Also (see Footnote 12) Lloyd Morris, who is psychoanalytically oriented.

[8] Julian Hawthorne, *Nathaniel Hawthorne and his Wife*. University Press, Cambridge, 1884, I, 347.

[9] Ruth Morris, "The Novel as Catharsis," *Psa. Rev.*, 31, p. 99.

[10] Henry James, Jr., *Nathaniel Hawthorne*, New York, Harper and Brothers, 1880, p. 60.

[11] C. P. Oberndorf, "Depersonalization in Relation to Erotization of Thought," *Int. J. Psa.*, 15 (1934), p. 27.

[12] Lloyd Morris, *The Rebellious Puritan*, New York, Harcourt, Brace, 1937, p. 361.

Kenneth Burke*

# FREUD—AND THE ANALYSIS OF POETRY

ABSTRACT

There is an important margin of overlap in the aesthetic and the neurotic, in that the act of both the poet and the neurotic are symbolic acts. In so far as this margin prevails, co-ordinates developed for the charting of the one field may be taken over for the charting of the other. There are also important divergencies between the two fields. And in so far as the aesthetic and neurotic fields diverge, there must be a corresponding difference in co-ordinates. Freud's perspective, developed primarily for the charting of neurosis, is better suited to the margin of overlap than to the area of divergency. As regards the margin of overlap, two modifications of Freudian co-ordinates are offered: (1) A poem's structure should be discussed as a recipe or synthesis of several motives rather than in terms of one essential motive with all others treated as derivatives from it; (2) Freud's overly patriarchal emphasis obscures the matriarchal factors operating in literary works that symbolize a change of lineage or identity. As regards the area of divergency, Freud's co-ordinates, in stressing the poem as dream, understress the poem as a communicative structure and as a realistic gauging of human situations. Communication, rather than wish fulfillment, is the key term for literary analysis.

The reading of Freud I find suggestive almost to the point of bewilderment. Accordingly, what I should like most to do would be simply to take representative excepts from his work, copy them out, and write glosses upon them. Very often these glosses would be straight extensions of his own thinking. At other times they would be attempts to characterize his strategy of presentation with reference to interpretative method in general. And, finally, the Freudian perspective was developed primarily to chart a psychiatric field rather

* KENNETH BURKE is an outstanding poet and literary critic, author of such books as *A Grammar of Motives* and *A Rhetoric of Motives*.

than an aesthetic one; but since we are here considering the analogous features of these two fields rather than their important differences, there would be glosses attempting to suggest how far the literary critic should go along with Freud and what extra-Freudian material he would have to add. Such a desire to write an article on Freud in the margins of his books must for practical reasons here remain a frustrated desire. An article such as this must condense by generalization, which requires me to slight the most stimulating factor of all—the detailed articulacy in which he embodies his extraordinary frankness.

Freud's frankness is no less remarkable by reason of the fact that he had perfected a method for being frank. He could say humble, even humiliating, things about himself and us because he had changed the rules somewhat and could make capital of observations that others, with vested interests of a different sort, would feel called upon to suppress by dictatorial decree. Or we might say that what for him could fall within the benign category of observation could for them fall only within its malign counterpart, spying.

Yet though honesty is, in Freud, methodologically made easier, it is by no means honesty made easy. And Freud's own accounts of his own dreams show how poignantly he felt at times the "disgrace" of his occupation. There are doubtless many thinkers whose strange device might be *ecclesia super cloacam*. What more fitting place to erect one's church than above a sewer! One might even say that sewers are what churches are for. But usually this is done by laying all the stress upon the ecclesia and its beauty. So that, even when the man's work fails to be completed for him as a social act, by the approval of his group, he has the conviction of its intrinsic beauty to give him courage and solace.

But to think of Freud, during the formative years of his doctrines, confronting something like repugnance among his colleagues, and even, as his dreams show, in his own eyes, is to think of such heroism as Unamuno found in Don Quixote; and if Don Quixote risked the social judgment of ridicule, he still had the consolatory thought that his imaginings were beautiful, stressing the ecclesia aspect, whereas Freud's theories bound him to a more drastic self-ostracizing act— the charting of the relations between ecclesia and cloaca that forced him to analyze the cloaca itself. Hence, his work was with the confessional as cathartic, as purgative; this haruspicy required an inspection of the entrails; it was, bluntly, an interpretative sculpting of excrement, with beauty replaced by a science of the grotesque.

Confronting this, Freud does none the less advance to erect a structure which, if it lacks beauty, has astounding ingeniousness and fancy. It is full of paradoxes, of leaps across gaps, of vistas—much more so than the work of many a modern poet who sought for nothing else but these and had no search for accuracy to motivate his work. These qualities alone would make it unlikely that readers literarily inclined could fail to be attracted, even while repelled. Nor can one miss in it the profound charitableness that is missing in so many modern writers who, likewise concerned with the cloaca, become efficiently concerned with nothing else, and make of their work pure indictment, pure oath, pure striking-down, pure spitting-upon, pure kill. True, this man, who taught us so much about father-rejection and who ironically became himself so frequently the rejected father in the works of his schismatic disciples, does finally descend to quarrelsomeness, despite himself, when recounting the history of the psychoanalytic movement. But, over the great course of his work, it is the matter of human rescue that he is concerned with—not the matter of vengeance. On a few occasions, let us say, he is surprised into vengefulness. But the very essence of his studies, even at their most forbidding moments (in fact, precisely at those moments) is its charitableness, its concern with salvation. To borrow an excellent meaningful pun from Trigant Burrow, this salvation is approached not in terms of religious hospitality but rather in terms of secular hospitalization. Yet it is the spirit of Freud; it is what Freud's courage is for.

Perhaps, therefore, the most fitting thing for a writer to do, particularly in view of the fact that Freud is now among the highly honored class—the exiles from Nazi Germany (how accurate those fellows are! how they seem, with almost 100 percent efficiency, to have weeded out their greatest citizens!) —perhaps the most fitting thing to do would be simply to attempt an article of the "homage to Freud" sort and call it a day.

However, my job here cannot be confined to that. I have been commissioned to consider the bearing of Freud's theories upon literary criticism. And these theories were not designed primarily for literary criticism at all but were rather a perspective that, developed for the charting of a nonaesthetic field, was able (by reason of its scope) to migrate into the aesthetic field. The margin of overlap was this: The acts of the neurotic are symbolic acts. Hence, in so far as both the neurotic act and the poetic act share this property in common, they may share a terminological chart in common. But in so far as they deviate, terminology likewise must deviate. And this deviation is a fact that literary criticism must explicitly consider.

As for the glosses on the interpretative strategy in general, they would be of this sort: For one thing, they would concern a distinction between what I should call an essentializing mode of interpretation and a mode that stresses proportion of ingredients. The tendency in Freud is toward the first of these. That is, if one found a complex of, let us say, seven ingredients in a man's motivation, the Freudian tendency would be to take one of these as the essence of the motivation and to consider the other six as sublimated variants. We could imagine, for instance, manifestations of sexual impotence accompanying a conflict in one's relations with his familiars and one's relations at the office. The proportional strategy would involve the study of these three as a cluster. The motivation would be synonymous with the interrelationships among them. But the essentializing startegy would, in Freud's case, place the emphasis upon the sexual manifestation, as causal ancestor of the other two.

This essentializing strategy is linked with a normal ideal of science: to "explain the complex in terms of the simple." This ideal almost makes one vow to select one or another motive from a cluster and interpret the others in terms of it. The naïve proponent of economic determinism, for instance, would select the quarrel at the office as the essential motive, and would treat the quarrel with familiars and the sexual impotence as mere results of this. Now, I don't see how you can possibly explain the complex in terms of the simple without having your very success used as a charge against you. When you get through, all that your opponent need say is: "But you have explained the complex in terms of the simple—and the simple is precisely what the complex is not."

Perhaps the faith philosophers, as against the reason philosophers, did not have to encounter a paradox at this point. Not that they avoided paradoxes, for I think they must always cheat when trying to explain how evil can exist in a world created by an all-powerful and wholly good Creator. But at least they did not have to confront the complexity-simplicity difficulty, since their theological reductions referred to a ground in God, who was simultaneously the ultimately complex and the ultimately simple. Naturalistic strategies lack this convenient "out"—hence their explanations are simplifications, and every simplification is an oversimplification.[1]

It is possible that the literary critic, taking communication as his basic category, may avoid this particular paradox (communication thereby being a kind of attenuated God term). You can reduce everything to communication—yet communication is extremely complex. But, in any case, communication is by no means the basic category of Freud. The sexual wish, or libido, is the basic category; and the complex forms of communication that we see in a highly alembicated philosophy would be mere sublimations of this.

A writer deprived of Freud's clinical experience would be a fool to question the value of his category as a way of analyzing the motives of the class of neurotics Freud encountered. There is a pronouncedly individualistic element in any technique of salvation (my toothache being, alas! my private property), and even those beset by a pandemic of sin or microbes will enter heaven or get discharged from the hospital one by one; and the especially elaborate process of diagnosis involved in Freudian analysis even to this day makes it more available to those suffering from the ills of preoccupation and leisure than to those suffering from the ills of occupation and unemployment (with people generally tending to be only as mentally sick as they can afford to be). This state of affairs makes it all the more likely that the typical psychoanalytic patient would have primarily private sexual motivations behind his difficulties. (Did not Henry James say that sex is something about which we think a great deal when we are not thinking about anything else?)[2] Furthermore, I believe that studies of artistic imagery, outside the strict pale of psychoanalytic emphasis, will bear out Freud's brilliant speculations as to the sexual puns, the double entendres, lurking behind the most unlikely façades. If a man acquires a method of thinking about everything else, for instance, during the sexual deprivations and rigors of adolescence, this cure may well take on the qualities of the disease; and in so far as he continues with this same method in adult years, though his life has since become sexually less exacting, such modes as incipient homosexuality or masturbation may very well be informatively interwoven in the strands of his thought and be discoverable by inspection of the underlying imagery or patterns in this thought.

Indeed, there are only a few fundamental bodily idioms—and why should it not be likely that an attitude, no matter how complex its ideational expression, could be completed only by a channelization within its corresponding gestures? That is, the details of experience behind A's dejection may be vastly different from the details of experience behind B's dejection, yet both A and B may fall into the same bodily posture in expressing their dejection. And in an era like ours, coming at the end of a long individualistic emphasis, where we frequently find expressed an attitude of complete independence, of total, uncompromising self-reliance, this expression would not reach its fulfillment in choreography except in the act of "practical narcissism" (that is, the only wholly independent person would be the one who practiced self-abuse and really meant it).

But it may be noticed that we have here tended to consider mind-body relations from an interactive point of view rather than a materialistic one (which would take the body as the essence of the act and the mentation as the sublimation).

Freud himself, interestingly enough, was originally nearer to this view (necessary, as I hope to show later, for specifically literary purposes) than he later became. Freud explicitly resisted the study of motivation by way of symbols. He distinguished his own mode of analysis from the symbolic by laying the stress upon free association. That is, he would begin the analysis of a neurosis without any preconceived notion as to the absolute meaning of any image that the patient might reveal in the account of a dream. His procedure involved the breaking down of the dream into a set of fragments, with the analyst then inducing the patient to improvise associations on each of these fragments in turn. And afterward, by charting recurrent themes, he would arrive at the crux of the patient's conflict.

Others (particularly Stekel), however, proposed a great short cut here. They offered an absolute content for various items of imagery. For instance, in Stekel's dictionary of symbols, which has the absoluteness of an old-fashioned dreambook, the right-hand path equals the road to righteousness, the left-hand path equals the road to crime, in anybody's dreams (in Lenin's presumably, as well as the Pope's). Sisters are breasts and brothers are buttocks. "The luggage of a traveller is the burden of sin by which one is oppressed," and so on. Freud criticizes these on the basis of his own clinical experiences—and whereas he had reservations against specific equations, and rightly treats the method as antithetical to his own contribution, he decides that a high percentage of Stekel's purely intuitive hunches were corroborated. And after warning that such a gift as Stekel's is often evidence of paranoia, he decides that normal persons may also occasionally be capable of it.

Its lure as efficiency is understandable. And, indeed, if we revert to the matter of luggage, for instance, does it not immediately give us insight into a remark of André Gide, who is a specialist in the portrayal of scrupulous criminals, who has developed a stylistic trick for calling to seduction in the accents of evangelism, and who advises that one should learn to "travel light"?

But the trouble with short cuts is that they deny us a chance to take longer routes. With them, the essentializing strategy takes a momentous step forward. You have next but to essentialize your short cuts in turn (a short cut atop a short cut), and you get the sexual emphasis of Freud, the all-embracing ego compensation of Adler, or Rank's master emphasis upon the birth trauma, and so on.

Freud himself fluctuates in his search for essence. At some places you find him proclaiming the all-importance of the sexual, at other places you find him indignantly denying that his psychology is a pansexual one at all, and at still other places you get something halfway between the two, via the concept of the libido, which embraces a spectrum from phallus to philanthropy.

The important matter for our purposes is to suggest that the examination of a poetic work's internal organization would bring us nearer to a variant of the typically Freudian free-association method than to the purely symbolic method toward which he subsequently gravitated.[3]

The critic should adopt a variant of the free-association method. One obviously cannot invite an author, especially a dead author, to oblige him by telling what the author thinks of when the critic isolates some detail or other for improvisation. But what he can do is to note the context of imagery and ideas in which an image takes its place. He can also note, by such analysis, the kinds of evaluations surrounding this image of a crossing; for instance, is it an escape from or a return to an evil or a good, and so on? Until finally, by noting the ways in which this crossing behaves, what subsidiary imagery accompanies it, what kind of event it grows out of, what kind of event grows out of it, what altered rhythmic and tonal effects characterize it, and so on, one grasps its significance as motivation. And there is no essential motive offered here. The motive of the work is equated with the structure of interrelationships within the work itself.

"But there is more to a work of art than that." I hear this objection being raised. And I agree with it. And I wonder whether we could properly consider the matter in this wise:

For convenience, using the word "poem" to cover any complete artistic product, let us divide this artifact (the invention, creation, formation, poetic construct) in accordance with three modes of analysis: dream, prayer, chart.

The psychoanalysis of Freud and of the schools stemming from Freud has brought forward an astoundingly fertile range of observations that give us insight into the poem as dream. There is opened up before us a sometimes almost terrifying glimpse into the ways in which we may, while overtly doing one thing, be covertly doing another. Yet, there is nothing mystical or even unusual about this. I may, for instance, consciously place my elbow upon the table. Yet at the same time I am clearly unconscious of the exact distance between my elbow and my nose. Or, if that analogy seems like cheating, let us try another: I may be unconscious of the way in which a painter friend, observant of my postures, would find the particular position of my arm characteristic of me.

Or let us similarly try to take the terror out of infantile regression. In so far as I speak the same language that I learned as a child, every time I speak there is, within my speech, an ingredient of regression to the infantile level. Regression, we might say, is a function of progression. Where the progression has been a development by evolution or continuity of growth (as were one to have learned to speak and think in English as a child, and still spoke and thought

in English) rather than by revolution or discontinuity of
growth (as were one to have learned German in childhood, to
have moved elsewhere at an early age, and since become
so at home in English that he could not even understand a
mature conversation in the language of his childhood), the
archaic and the now would be identical. You could say, indifferently, either that the speech is regression or that it
is not regression. But were the man who had forgot the
language of his childhood to begin speaking nothing but this
early language (under a sudden agitation or as the result
of some steady pressure), we should have the kind of regression that goes formally by this name in psychoanalytic nomen-
clature.

The ideal growth, I suppose—the growth without elements
of alienation, discontinuity, homelessness—is that wherein
regression is natural. We might sloganize it as "the adult a
child matured." Growth has here been simply a successive
adding of cells—the growth of the chambered nautilus. But
there is also the growth of the adult who, "when he became
a man, put away childish things." This is the growth of the
crab, that grows by abandoning one room and taking on
another. It produces moments of crisis. It makes for philos-
ophies of emancipation and enlightenment, where one gets a
jolt and is "awakened from the sleep of dogma" (and, alas!
in leaving his profound "Asiatic slumber," he risks getting
in exchange more than mere wakefulness, more than the
eternal vigilance that is the price of liberty—he may get
wakefulness plus, that is, insomnia).

There are, in short, critical points (or, in the Hegel-Marx
vocabulary, changes of quantity leading to changes of
quality) where the process of growth or change converts
a previous circle of protection into a circle of confinement.
The first such revolution may well be, for the human individual, a purely biological one—the change at birth when the
fetus, heretofore enjoying a larval existence in the womb,
being fed on manna from the placenta, so outgrows this circle
of protection that the benign protection becomes a malign circle of confinement, whereat it must burst forth into a different
kind of world—a world of locomotion, aggression, competition, hunt. The mother, it is true, may have already been
living in such a world; but the fetus was in a world within
this world—in a monastery—a world such as is lived in by

"coupon clippers," who get their dividends as the result of sharp economic combat but who may, so long as the payments are regular, devote themselves to thoughts and diseases far "above" these harsh material operations.

In the private life of the individual there may be many subsequent jolts of a less purely biological nature, as with the death of some one person who had become pivotal to this individual's mental economy. But whatever these unique variants may be, there is again a universal variant at adolescence, when radical changes in the glandular structure of the body make this body a correspondingly altered environment for the mind, requiring a corresponding change in our perspective, our structure of interpretations, meanings, values, purposes, and inhibitions, if we are to take it properly into account.

In the informative period of childhood our experiences are strongly personalized. Our attitudes take shape with respect to distinct people who have roles, even animals and objects being vessels of character. Increasingly, however, we begin to glimpse a world of abstract relationships, of functions understood solely through the medium of symbols in books. Even such real things as Tibet and Eskimos and Napoleon are for us, who have not been to Tibet, or lived with Eskimos, or fought under Napoleon, but a structure of signs. In a sense, it could be said that we learn these signs flat. We must start from scratch. There is no tradition in them; they are pure present. For though they have been handed down by tradition, we can read meaning into them only in so far as we can project or extend them out of our own experience. We may, through being burned a little, understand the signs for being burned a lot—it is in this sense that the coaching of interpretation could be called traditional. But we cannot understand the signs for being burned a lot until we have in our own flat experience, here and now, been burned a little.

Out of what can these extensions possibly be drawn? Only out of the informative years of childhood. Psychoanalysis talks of purposive forgetting. Yet purposive forgetting is the only way of remembering. One learns the meaning of "table," "book," "father," "mother," "musn't," by forgetting the contexts in which these words were used. The Darwinian ancestry (locating the individual in his feudal line of descent from the ape) is matched in Freud by a still more striking causal ancestry that we might sloganize as "The child is father to the man."[4]

As we grow up, new meanings must either be engrafted upon old meanings (being to that extent double entendres) or they must be new starts (hence, involving problems of dissociation).

It is in the study of the poem as dream that we find revealed the ways in which the poetic organization takes shape under these necessities. Revise Freud's terms, if you will. But nothing is done by simply trying to refute them or to tie them into knots. One may complain at this procedure, for instance: Freud characterizes the dream as the fulfillment of a wish; an opponent shows him a dream of frustration, and he answers, "But the dreamer wishes to be frustrated." You may demur at that, pointing out that Freud has developed a "Heads I win, tails you lose" mode of discourse here. But I maintain that, in doing so, you have contributed nothing. For there are people whose values are askew, for whom frustration itself is a kind of grotesque ambition. If you would, accordingly, propose to chart this field by offering better terms, by all means do so. But better terms are the only kind of refutation here that is worth the trouble. Similarly, one may be unhappy with the concept of ambivalence, which allows pretty much of an open season on explanations (though the specific filling-out may provide a better case for the explanation than appears in this key term itself). But, again, nothing but an alternative explanation is worth the effort of discussion here. Freud's terminology is a dictionary, a lexicon for charting a vastly complex and hitherto largely unchartered field. You can't refute a dictionary. The only profitable answer to a dictionary is another one.

A profitable answer to Freud's treatment of the Oedipus complex, for instance, was Malinowski's study of its variants in a matriarchal society.[5] Here we get at once a corroboration and a refutation of the Freudian doctrine. It is corroborated in that the same general patterns of enmity are revealed; it is refuted in that these patterns are shown not to be innate but to take shape with relation to the difference in family structure itself, with corresponding difference in roles.

Freud's overemphasis upon the patriarchal pattern (an assumption of its absoluteness that is responsible for the

Freudian tendency to underrate greatly the economic factors influencing the relationships of persons or roles) is a prejudicial factor that must be discounted, in Freud, even when treating the poem as dream. Though totemistic religion, for instance, flourished with matriarchal patterns, Freud treats even this in patriarchal terms. And I submit that this emphasis will conceal from us, to a large degree, what is going on in art (still confining ourselves to the dream level—the level at which Freudian co-ordinates come closest to the charting of the logic of poetic structure).

In the literature of transitional eras, for instance, we find an especial profusion of rebirth rituals, where the poet is making the symbolic passes that will endow him with a new identity. Now, imagine him trying to do a very thorough job of this reidentification. To be completely reborn, he would have to change his very lineage itself. He would have to revise not only his present but also his past. (Ancestry and cause are forever becoming intermingled—the thing is that from which it came—cause is *Ur-sache*, and so on.) And could a personalized past be properly confined to a descent through the father, when it is the *mater* that is *semper certa?* Totemism, when not interpreted with Freud's patriarchal bias, may possibly provide us with the necessary cue here. Totemism, as Freud himself reminds us, was a magical device whereby the members of a group were identified with one another by the sharing of the same substance (a process often completed by the ritualistic eating of this substance, though it might, for this very reason, be prohibited on less festive occasions). And it is to the mother that the basic informative experiences of eating are related.

So, all told, even in strongly patriarchal societies (and much more so in a society like ours, where theories of sexual equality, with a corresponding confusion in sexual differentiation along occupational lines, have radically broken the symmetry of pure patriarchalism), would there not be a tendency for rebirth rituals to be completed by symbolizations of matricide and without derivation from competitive, monopolistic ingredients at all?[6]

To consider explicitly a bit of political dreaming, is not Hitler's doctrine of Aryanism something analogous to the adoption of a new totemic line? Has he not voted himself a new identity and, in keeping with a bastardized variant of the strategy of materialistic science, rounded this out by laying claim to a distinct bloodstream? What the Pope is saying, benignly, in proclaiming the Hebrew prophets as the spiritual ancestors of Catholicism, Hitler is saying malignly in proclaiming for himself a lineage totally distinct.

Freud, working within the patriarchal perspective, has explained how such thinking becomes tied up with persecution. The paranoid, he says, assigns his imagined persecutor the role of rejected father. This persecutor is all-powerful, as the father seems to the child. He is responsible for every imagined machination (as the Jews, in Hitler's scheme, become the universal devil function, the leading brains behind every "plot"). Advancing from this brilliant insight, it is not hard to understand why, once Hitler's fantasies are implemented by the vast resources of a nation, the "persecutor" becomes the persecuted.

The point I am trying to bring out is that this assigning of a new lineage to one's self (as would be necessary, in assigning one's self a new identity) could not be complete were it confined to symbolic patricide. There must also be ingredients of symbolic matricide intermingled here (with the phenomena of totemism giving cause to believe that the ritualistic slaying of the maternal relationship may draw upon an even deeper level than the ritualistic slaying of the paternal relationship). Lineage itself is charted after the metaphor of the family tree, which is, to be sure, patriarchalized in Western heraldry, though we get a different quality in the tree of life. Mac-Leish, in his period of aesthetic negativism, likens the sound of good verse to the ring of the ax in the tree, and if I may mention an early story of my own, *In Quest of Olympus*, a rebirth of fantasy, it begins by the felling of a tree, followed by the quick change from child to adult, or, within the conventions of the fiction, the change from tiny "Treep" to gigantic "Arjk"; and though, for a long time, under the influence of the Freudian patriarchal emphasis, I tended to consider such trees as fathers, I later felt compelled to make them ambiguously parents. The symbolic structure of Peter Blume's painting, "The Eternal City," almost forces me to assign the tree, in that instance, to a purely maternal category, since the rejected father is pictured in the repellant phallus-like figure of Mussolini, leaving only the feminine role for the luxuriant tree that, by my interpretation of the picture, rounds out the lineage (with the dishonored Christ and the beggarwoman as vessels of the past lineage, and the lewd

Mussolini and the impersonal tree as vessels of the new lineage, which I should interpret on the nonpolitical level as saying that sexuality is welcomed, but as a problem, while home is relegated to the world of the impersonal, abstract, observed).

From another point of view we may consider the sacrifice of gods, or of kings, as stylistic modes for dignifying human concerns (a kind of neo-euhemerism). In his stimulating study of the ritual drama, *The Hero*, Lord Raglan over-stresses, it seems to me, the notion that these dramas appealed purely as spectacles. Would it not be more likely that the fate of the sacrificial king was also the fate of the audience, in stylized form, dignified, "writ large"? Thus, their engross-ment in the drama would not be merely that of watching a parade, or the utilitarian belief that the ritual would ensure rainfall, crops, fertility, a good year, and so on; but, also, the stages of the hero's journey would chart the stages of their journey (as an Elizabethan play about royalty was not merely an opportunity for the pit to get a glimpse of high life, a living newspaper on the doings of society, but a digni-fication or memoralizing of their own concerns, translated into the idiom then currently accepted as the proper lan-guage of magnification).[7]

But though we may want to introduce minor revisions in the Freudian perspective here, I submit that we should take Freud's key terms, "condensation" and "displacement," as the over-all categories for the analysis of the poem as dream. The terms are really two different approaches to the same phenom-enon. Condensation, we might say, deals with the respects in which house in a dream may be more than house, or house plus. And displacement deals with the way in which house may be other than house, or house minus. (Perhaps we should say, more accurately, minus house.)

One can understand the resistance to both of these empha-ses. It leaves no opportunity for a house to be purely and simply a house—and whatever we may feel about it as regards dreams, it is a very disturbing state of affairs when transferred to the realm of art. We must acknowledge, however, that the house in a poem is, when judged purely and simply as a house, a very flimsy structure for protection against wind and rain. So there seems to be some justice in retaining the Freudian terms when trying to decide what is going on in poetry. As Freud fills them out, the justification becomes stronger. The ways in which grammatical rules are violated, for instance; the dream's ways of enacting conjunctions, of solving arguments by club offers of mutually contradictory assertions; the importance of both concomitances and discontinuities for interpretative purposes (the phenomena of either association or dissociation, as you prefer, revealed with greatest clarity in the *lapsus linguae*); the conversion of an expression into its corresponding act (as were one, at a time when "over the fence is out" was an expression in vogue, to apply this comment upon some act by following the dream of this act by a dreamed incident of a ball going over a fence); and, above all, the notion that the optative is in dreams, as often in poetry and essay, presented in the indicative (a Freudian observation fertile to the neopositivists' critique of language)—the pliancy and ingenuity of Freud's researches here make entrancing reading, and continually provide insights that can be carried over, *mutatis mutandis*, to the operations of poetry. Perhaps we might sloganize the point thus: In so far as art contains a surrealist ingredient (and all art contains some of this ingredient), psychoanalytic co-ordinates are required to explain the logic of its structure.

Perhaps we might take some of the pain from the notions of condensation and displacement (with the tendency of one event to become the synecdochic representative of some other event in the same cluster) by imagining a hypothetical case of authorship. A novelist, let us say, is trying to build up for us a sense of secrecy. He is picturing a conspiracy, yet he was never himself quite this kind of conspirator. Might not this novelist draw upon whatever kinds of conspiracy he himself had experientially known (as for instance were he to draft for this purpose memories of his participation in some childhood *Bund*)? If this were so, an objective breakdown of the imagery with which he surrounded the conspiratorial events in his novel would reveal this contributory ingredient. You would not have to read your interpretation into it. It would be objectively, structurally, there, and could be pointed to by scissor work. For instance, the novelist might explicitly state that, when joining the conspiracy, the hero recalled some incident of his childhood. Or the adult conspirators would, at strategic points, be explicitly likened by the novelist to children, and so on. A statement about the ingredients of the work's motivation would thus be identical with a statement about the work's structure—a statement as to what goes with what in the work itself. Thus, in Coleridge's "The Eolian Harp," you do not have to interpret the poet's communion with the universe as an affront to his wife; the poet himself explicitly apologizes to her for it. Also, it is an objectively citable fact that imagery of noon goes with this apology. If, then, we look at other poems by Coleridge, noting the part played by the sun at noon in the punishments of the guilt-laden Ancient Mariner, along with the fact that the situation of the narrator's confession involves the detention of a wedding guest from the marriage feast, plus the fact that a preference for church as against marriage is explicitly stated at the end of the poem, we begin to see a motivational cluster emerging. It is obvious that such structural interrelationships cannot be wholly conscious, since they are generalizations about acts that can be made only inductively and statistically after the acts have been accumulated. (This applies as much to the acts of a single poem as to the acts of many poems. We may find a theme emerging in one work that attains fruition in that same work—the ambiguities of its implications where it first emerges attaining explication in the same integer. Or its full character may not be developed until a later work. In its ambiguous emergent form it is a synecdochic representative of the form it later assumes when it comes to fruition in either the same work or in another one.)

However, though the synecdochic process (whereby something does service for the other members of its same cluster or as the foreshadowing of itself in a later development) cannot be wholly conscious, the dream is not all dream. We might say, in fact, that the Freudian analysis of art was handicapped by the aesthetic of the period—an aesthetic shared even by those who would have considered themselves greatly at odds with Freud and who were, in contrast with his delving into the unbeautiful, concerned with beauty only. This was the aesthetic that placed the emphasis wholly upon the function of self-expression. The artist had a number—some unique character or identity—and his art was the externalizing of this inwardness. The general Schopenhauerian trend contributed to this. Von Hartmann's *Philosophy of the Unconscious* has reinforced the same pattern. This version of voluntaristic processes, as connected with current theories of emancipation, resulted in a picture of the dark, unconscious drive calling for the artist to "out with it." The necessary function of the

Freudian secular confessional, as a preparatory step to
redemption, gave further strength to the same picture. Add
the "complex in terms of the simple" strategy (with its
variants—higher in terms of lower, normal as a mere attenua-
tion of the abnormal, civilized as the primitive sublimated);
add the war of the generations (which was considered as a
kind of absolute rather than as a by-product of other factors,
as those who hated the idea of class war took in its stead
either the war of the generations or the war of the sexes)—
and you get a picture that almost automatically places the
emphasis upon art as utterance, as the naming of one's number, as a blurting out, as catharsis by secretion.

I suggested two other broad categories for the analysis of
poetic organization: prayer and chart.

Prayer would enter the Freudian picture in so far as it
concerns the optative. But prayer does not stop at that. Prayer
is also an act of communion. Hence, the concept of prayer,
as extended to cover also secular forms of petition, moves us
into the corresponding area of communication in general. We
might say that, whereas the expressionistic emphasis reveals
the ways in which the poet, with an attitude, embodies it in
appropriate gesture, communication deals with the choice of
gesture for the inducement of corresponding attitudes.
Sensory imagery has this same communicative function, in-
viting the reader, within the limits of the fiction as least, to
make himself over in the image of the imagery.

Considering the poem from this point of view, we begin
with the incantatory elements in art, the ways of leading in
or leading on the hypothetical audience X to which the poem,
as a medium, is addressed (though this hypothetical audience
X be nothing more concrete, as regards social relations, than
a critical aspect of the poet's own personality). Even Freud's
dream had a censor; but the poet's censor is still more exacting, as his shapings and revisions are made for the purpose
of forestalling resistances (be those an essay reader's resistances to arguments and evidence or the novel reader's resistance to developments of narrative or character). We
move here into the sphere of rhetoric (reader-writer relationships, an aspect of art that Freud explicitly impinges upon
only to a degree in his analysis of wit), with the notion of
address being most evident in oration and letter, less so
in drama, and least in the lyric. Roughly, I should say that the
slightest presence of revision is per se indication of a poet's

feeling that his work is addressed (if only, as Mead might say, the address of an "I" to its "me").

Here would enter consideration of formal devices, ways of pointing up and fulfilling expectations, of living up to a contract with the reader (as Wordsworth and Coleridge might put it), of easing by transition or sharpening by ellipsis; in short, all that falls within the sphere of incantation, imprecation, exhortation, inducement, weaving and releasing of spells; matters of style and form, of meter and rhythm, as contributing to these results; and thence to the conventions and social values that the poet draws upon in forming the appropriate recipes for the roles of protagonist and antagonist, into which the total agon is analytically broken down, with subsidiary roles polarized about one or the other of the two agonists tapering off to form a region of overlap between the two principles—the ground of the agon. Here, as the reverse of player, would come also invective, indictment, oath. And the gestures might well be traced down eventually to choices far closer to bodily pantomime than is revealed on the level of social evaluation alone (as were a poet, seeking the gestures appropriate for the conveying of a social negativeness, to draw finally upon imagery of disgust, and perhaps even, at felicitous moments, to select his speech by playing up the very consonants that come nearest to the enacting of repulsion).

As to the poem as chart: the Freudian emphasis upon the pun brings it about that something can only be in so far as it is something else. But, aside from these ambiguities, there is also a statement's value as being exactly what is. Perhaps we could best indicate what we mean by speaking of the poem as chart if we called it the poet's contribution to an informal dictionary. As with proverbs, he finds some experience or relationship typical, or recurrent, or significant enough for him to need a word for it. Except that his way of defining the word is not to use purely conceptual terms, as in a formal dictionary, but to show how his vision behaves, with appropriate attitudes. In this, again, it is like the proverb that does not merely name but names vindictively, or plaintively, or promisingly, or consolingly, and so on. His namings need not be new ones. Often they are but memorializings of an experience long recognized.

But, essentially, they are enactments, with every form of expression being capable of treatment as the efficient extension of one aspect or another of ritual drama (so that even the scientific essay would have its measure of choreography, its pedestrian pace itself being analyzed as gesture or incantation, its polysyllables being as style the mimetics of a distinct monasticism, and so on). And this observation, whereby we have willy-nilly slipped back into the former subject, the symbolic act as prayer, leads us to observe that the three aspects of the poem, here proposed, are not elements that can be isolated in the poem itself, with one line revealing the "dream," another the "prayer," and a third the "chart." They merely suggest three convenient modes in which to approach the task of analysis.[8]

The primary category, for the explicit purposes of literary criticism, would thus seem to me to be that of communication rather than that of wish, with its disguises, frustrations, and fulfillments. Wishes themselves, in fact, become from this point of view analyzable as purposes that get their shape from the poet's perspective in general (while this perspective is in turn shaped by the collective medium of communication). The choice of communication also has the advantage, from the sociological point of view, that it resists the Freudian tendency to overplay the psychological factor (as the total medium of communication is not merely that of words, colors, forms, and so on, or of the values and conventions with which these are endowed, but also the productive materials, co-operative resources, property rights, authorities, and their various bottlenecks, which figure in the total act of human conversation).

Hence, to sum up: I should say that, for the explicit purposes of literary criticism, we should require more emphasis than the Freudian structure gives, (1) to the proportional strategy as against the essentializing one, (2) to matriarchal symbolizations as against the Freudian patriarchal bias, (3) to poem as prayer and chart, as against simply the poem as dream.

But I fully recognize that, once the ingenious and complex structure has been erected, nearly anyone can turn up with proposals that it be given a little more of this, a little less of that, a pinch of so-and-so, and so on. And I recognize that, above all, we owe an enormous debt of gratitude to the man who, by his insight, his energy, and his remarkably keen powers of articulation, made such tinkering possible. It is almost fabulous to think that, after so many centuries of the family, it is only now that this central factor in our social organization has attained its counterpart in an organized critique of the family and of the ways in which the informative experience with familiar roles may be carried over, or "metaphored," into the experience with extrafamiliar roles, giving these latter, in so far as they are, or are felt to be, analogous with the former, a structure of interpretations and attitudes borrowed from the former. And in so far as poets, like everyone else, are regularly involved in such informative familiar relationships, long before any but a few rudimentary bodily gestures are available for communicative use (with their first use unquestionably being the purely self-expressive one), the child is indeed the adult poet's father, as he is the father of us all (if not so in essence, then at least as regards an important predisposing factor "to look out for"). Thence we get to "like father like son." And thence we get to Freud's brilliant documentation of this ancestry, as it affects the maintenance of a continuity in the growing personality.

Only if we eliminate biography entirely as a relevant fact about poetic organization can we eliminate the importance of the psychoanalyst's search for universal patterns of biography (as revealed in the search for basic myths which recur in new guises as a theme with variations); and we can eliminate biography as a relevant fact about poetic organization only if we consider the work of art as if it were written neither by people nor for people, involving neither inducements nor resistances.[9] Such can be done, but the cost is tremendous in so far as the critic considers it his task to disclose the poem's eventfulness.

However, this is decidedly not the same thing as saying that "we cannot appreciate the poem without knowing about its relation to the poet's life as an individual." Rather, it is equivalent to saying: "We cannot understand a poem's structure without understanding the function of that structure. And to understand its function we must understand its purpose." To be sure, there are respects in which the poem, as purpose, is doing things for the poet that it is doing for no one else. For instance, I think it can be shown by analysis of the imagery in Coleridge's "Mystery Poems" that one of the battles being fought there is an attempt to get self-redemption by the poet's striving for the vicarious or ritualistic redemption of his drug. It is obvious that this aspect of the equational structure is private and would best merit discussion when one is discussing the strategy of one man in its particularities. Readers in general will respond only to the sense of guilt, which was sharpened for Coleridge by his particular burden of addiction, but which may be sharpened for each reader by totally different particularities of experience. But if you do not discuss the poem's structure as a function of symbolic redemption at all (as a kind of private-enterprise Mass, with important ingredients of a black Mass), the observations you make about its structure are much more likely to be gratuitous and arbitrary (quite as only the most felicitous of observers could relevantly describe the distribution of men and postures in a football game if he had no knowledge of the game's purpose and did not discuss its formations as oppositional tactics for the carrying out of this purpose, but treated the spectacle simply as the manifestation of a desire to instruct and amuse).

Thus, in the case of *The Ancient Mariner*, knowledge of Coleridge's personal problems may enlighten us as to the particular burdens that the Pilot's boy ("who now doth crazy go") took upon himself as scapegoat for the poet alone. But his appearance in the poem cannot be understood at all, except in superficial terms of the interesting or the picturesque, if we do not grasp his function as a scapegoat of some sort—a victimized vessel for drawing off the most malign aspects of the curse that afflicts the "greybeard loon" whose cure had been effected under the dubious aegis of moonlight. And I believe that such a functional approach is the only one that can lead into a profitable analysis of a poem's structure even on the purely technical level. I remember how, for instance, I had pondered for years the reference to the "silly buckets" filled with curative rain. I noted the epithet as surprising, picturesque, and interesting. I knew that it was doing something, but I wasn't quite sure what. But as soon as I looked upon the Pilot's boy as a scapegoat, I saw that the word "silly" was a technical foreshadowing of the fate that befell this figure in the poem. The structure itself became more apparent: the "loon"-atic Mariner begins his cure from drought under the aegis of a moon that causes a silly rain, thence by synecdoche to silly buckets, and the most malignant features of this problematic cure are transferred to the Pilot's boy who now doth crazy go.

Now, if you want to confine your observations to the one

poem, you have a structural-functional-technical analysis of some important relationships within the poem itself. If you wish to trail the matter farther afield, into the equational structure of other work by Coleridge, you can back your interpretation of the moon by such reference as that to "moon-blasted madness," which gives you increased authority to discern lunatic ingredients in the lunar. His letters, where he talks of his addiction in imagery like that of the "Mystery Poems" and contemplates entering an insane asylum for a cure, entitle you to begin looking for traces of the drug as an ingredient in the redemptive problem. His letters also explicitly place the drug in the same cluster with the serpent; hence, we begin to discern what is going on when the Mariner transubstantiates the water snakes, in removing them from the category of the loathsome and accursed to the category of the blessed and beautiful. So much should be enough for the moment. Since the poem is constructed about an opposition between punishments under the aegis of the sun and cure under the aegis of the moon, one could proceed in other works to disclose the two sets of equations clustered about these two principles. Indeed, even in *The Ancient Mariner* itself we get a momentous cue, as the sun is explicitly said to be "like God's own head." But, for the moment, all I would maintain is that, if we had but this one poem by Coleridge, and knew not one other thing about him, we could not get an insight into its structure until we began with an awareness of its function as a symbolic redemptive process.

I can imagine a time when the psychological picture will be so well known and taken into account—when we shall have gone so far beyond Freud's initial concerns—that a reference to the polymorphous perverse of the infantile, for instance, will seem far too general—a mere first approximation. Everyone provides an instance of the polymorphous perverse, in attenuated form, at a moment of hesitancy; caught in the trackless maze of an unresolved, and even undefined, conflict, he regresses along this channel and that, in a formless experimentation that "tries anything and everything, somewhat." And in so far as his puzzle is resolved into pace, and steady rhythms of a progressive way out are established, there is always the likelihood that this solution will maintain continuity with the past of the poet's personality by a covert drawing upon analogies with this past. Hence the poet or speculator, no matter how new the characters with which he is now concerned, will give them somewhat the roles of past characters; whereat I see nothing unusual about the thought that a mature and highly complex philosophy might be so organized as to be surrogate for, let us say, a kind of adult breast-feeding—or, in those more concerned with alienation, a kind of adult weaning). Such categories do not by any means encompass the totality of a communicative structure; but they are part of it, and the imagery and transitions of the poem itself cannot disclose their full logic until such factors are taken into account.

However, I have spoken of pace. And perhaps I might conclude with some words on the bearing that the Freudian technique has upon the matter of pace. The Freudian procedure is primarily designed to break down a rhythm grown obsessive, to confront the systematic pieties of the patient's misery with systematic impieties of the clinic.[10] But the emphasis here is more upon the breaking of a malign rhythm than upon the upbuilding of a benign one. There is no place in this technique for examining the available resources whereby the adoption of total dramatic enactment may lead to correspondingly proper attitude. There is no talk of games, of dance, of manual and physical actions, of historical role, as a "way in" to this new upbuilding. The sedentary patient is given a sedentary cure. The theory of rhythms—work rhythms, dance rhythms, march rhythms—is no explicit part of this scheme, which is primarily designed to break old rhythms rather than to establish new ones.

The establishing of a new pace, beyond the smashing of the old puzzle, would involve in the end a rounded philosophy of the drama. Freud, since his subject is conflict, hovers continually about the edges of such a philosophy; yet it is not dialectical enough. For this reason Marxists properly resent his theories, even though one could, by culling incidental sentences from his works, fit him comfortably into the Marxist perspective. But the Marxists are wrong, I think, in resenting him as an irrationalist, for there is nothing more rational than the systematic recognition of irrational and nonrational factors. And I should say that both Freudians and Marxists are wrong in so far as they cannot put their theories together, by an over-all theory of drama itself (as they should be able to do, since Freud gives us the material of the closet drama, and Marx the material of the problem play, the one worked out in terms of personal conflicts, the other in terms of public conflicts).

The approach would require explicitly the analysis of role: salvation via change or purification of identity (purification in either the moral or chemical sense); different typical relationships between individual and group (as charted attitudinally in proverbs, and in complex works treated as sophisticated variants); modes of acceptance, rejection, self-acceptance, rejection of rejection[11] ("The enemies of my enemies are my friends"); transitional disembodiment as intermediate step between old self and new self (the spirituality of Shelley and of the Freudian cure itself); monasticism in the development of methods that fix a transitional or otherworldly stage, thereby making the evanescent itself into a kind of permanency—with all these modes of enactment finally employing, as part of the gesture idiom, the responses of the body itself as actor. (If one sought to employ Freud, as is, for the analysis of the poem, one would find almost nothing on poetic posture or pantomime, tonality, the significance of different styles and rhythmic patterns, nothing of this behaviorism.) Such, it seems to me, would be necessary, and much more in that direction, before we could so extend Freud's perspective that it revealed the major events going on in art.

But such revisions would by no means be anti-Freudian. They would be the kind of extensions required by reason of the fact that the symbolic act of art, whatever its analogies with the symbolic act of neurosis, also has important divergencies from the symbolic act of neurosis. They would be extensions designed to take into account the full play of communicative and realistic ingredients that comprise so large an aspect of poetic structure.

NOTES

[1] The essentializing strategy has its function when dealing with classes of items; the proportional one is for dealing with an item in its uniquesness. By isolating the matter of voluntarism, we put Freud in a line or class with Augustine. By isolating the matter of his concern with a distinction between unconscious and conscious, we may put him in a line with Leibniz's distinction between perception and apperception. Or we could link him with the Spinozistic *conatus* and the Schopenhauerian will. Or, as a rationalist, he falls into the bin with Aquinas (who is himself

most conveniently isolated as a rationalist if you employ the essentializing as against the proportional strategy, stressing what he added rather than what he retained). Many arguments seem to hinge about the fact that there is an unverbalized disagreement as to the choice between these strategies. The same man, for instance, who might employ the essentializing strategy in proclaiming Aquinas as a rationalist, taking as the significant factor in Aquinas' philosophy his additions to rationalism rather than considering this as an ingredient in a faith philosophy, might object to the bracketing of Aquinas and Freud (here shifting to the proportional strategy, as he pointed out the totally different materials with which Aquinas surrounded his rational principle).

² We may distinguish between a public and universal motive. In so far as one acts in a certain way because of his connection with a business or party, he would act from a public motive. His need of response to a new glandular stimulation at adolescence, on the other hand, would arise regardless of social values, and in that sense would be at once private and universal. The particular forms in which he expressed this need would, of course, be channelized in accordance with public or social factors.

³ Perhaps, to avoid confusion, I should call attention to the fact that "symbolic" in this context is being used differently by me from its use in the expression "symbolic action." If a man crosses a street, it is a practical act. If he writes a book about crossings—crossing streets, bridges, oceans, etc.—that is a symbolic act. Symbolic, as used in the restricted sense (in contrast with free association) would refer to the imputation of an absolute meaning to a crossing, a meaning that I might impute even before reading the book in question. Against this, I should maintain: One can never know what a crossing means, in a specific book, until he has studied its tie-up with other imagery in that particular book.

⁴ Maybe the kind of forgetting that is revealed by psychoanalysis could, within this frame, be better characterized as an incomplete forgetting. That is, whereas table, for instance, acquires an absolute and emotionally neutral meaning, as a name merely for a class of objects, by a merging of all the contexts involving the presence of a table, a table becomes symbolic, or a double entendre, or more than table, when some particular informative context is more important than the others. That is, when table, as used by the poet, has overtones of, let us say, *one* table at which his mother worked when he was a child. In this way the table, its food, and the cloth may become surrogates for the mother, her breasts, and her apron. And incest awe may become merged with "mustn't touch" injunctions, stemming from attempts to keep the child from meddling with the objects on the table. In a dream play by Edmund Wilson, *The Crime in the Whistler Room*, there are two worlds of plot, with the characters

belonging in the one world looking upon those in the other as dead, and the hero of this living world taking a dream shape as werewolf. The worlds switch back and forth, depending upon the presence or removal of a gate-leg table. In this instance I think we should not be far wrong in attributing some such content as the above to the table when considering it as a fulcrum upon which the structure of the plot is swung.

5 It is wrong, I think, to consider Freud's general picture as that of an individual psychology. Adler's start from the concept of ego compensation fits this description par excellence. But Freud's is a family psychology. He has offered a critique of the family, though it is the family of a neopatriarch. It is interesting to watch Freud, in his *Group Psychology and the Analysis of the Ego* frankly shifting between the primacy of group psychology and the primacy of individual psychology, changing his mind as he debates with himself in public and leaves in his pages the record of his fluctuations, frankly stated as such. Finally, he compromises by leaving both, drawing individual psychology from the role of the monopolistic father, and group psychology from the roles of the sons, deprived of sexual gratification by the monopolistic father, and banded together for their mutual benefit. But note that the whole picture is that of a family, albeit of a family in which the woman is a mere passive object of male wealth.

6 Or you might put it this way: Rebirth would require a killing of the old self. Such symbolic suicide, to be complete, would require a snapping of the total ancestral line (as being an integral aspect of one's identity). Hence, a tendency for the emancipatory crime to become sexually ambivalent. Freud's patriarchal emphasis leads to an overstress upon father rejection as a basic cause rather than as a by-product of conversion (the Kierkegaard earthquake, that was accompanied by a changed attitude toward his father). Suicide, to be thorough, would have to go further, and the phenomena of identity revealed in totemism might require the introduction of matricidal ingredients also. Freud himself, toward the end of *Totem and Taboo,* gives us an opening wedge by stating frankly, "In this evolution I am at a loss to indicate the place of the great maternal deities who perhaps everywhere preceded the paternal deities. . . ." This same patriarchal emphasis also reinforces the Freudian tendency to treat social love as a mere sublimation of balked male sexual appetite, whereas a more matriarchal concern, with the Madonna and Child relationship, would suggest a place for affection as a primary biological motivation. Not even a naturalistic account of motivation would necessarily require reinforcement from the debunking strategy (in accordance with which the real motives would be incipient perversions, and social motives as we know them would be but their appearances, or censored disguise).

7 Might not the sacrificial figure (as parent, king, or god) also

at times derive from no resistance or vindictiveness whatsoever, but be the recipient of the burden simply through "having stronger shoulders, better able to bear it?" And might the choice of guilty scapegoats (such as a bad father) be but a secondary development for accommodating this socialization of a loss to the patterns of legality?

8 Dream has its opposite, nightmare; prayer has is opposite, oath. Charts merely vary—in scope and relevance. In *Kubla Khan*, automatically composed during an opium dream, the dream ingredient is uppermost. In *The Ancient Mariner*, the prayer ingredient is uppermost. In *Dejection* and *The Pains of Sleep*, the chart ingredient is uppermost: here Coleridge is explicitly discussing his situation.

9 Those who stress form of this sort, as against content, usually feel that they are concerned with judgments of excellence as against judgments of the merely representative. Yet, just as a content category such as the Oedipus complex is neutral, i.e., includes both good and bad examples of its kind, so does a form category, such as sonnet or iambic pentameter, include both good and bad examples of its kind. In fact, though categories or classifications may be employed for evaluative purposes, they should be of themselves nonevaluative. Apples is a neutral, nonevaluative class, including firm apples and rotten ones. Categories that are in themselves evaluative are merely circular arguments—disguised ways of saying "This is good because it is good." The orthodox strategy of disguise is to break the statement into two parts, such as: "This is good because it has form; and form is good." The lure behind the feeling that the miracle of evaluation can be replaced by a codified scientific routine of evaluation seems to get its backing from the hope that a concept of quality can be matched by a number. The terms missing may be revealed by a diagram, thus:

| | |
|---|---|
| Quantity | Number |
| Weight | Pound |
| Length | Foot |
| Duration | Hour |
| | |
| Quality | ( ) |
| Excellence | ( ) |
| Inferiority | ( ) |

Often the strategy of concealment is accomplished by an ambiguity, as the critic sometimes uses the term "poetry" to designate good poetry, and sometimes uses it to designate "poetry, any poetry, good, bad, or indifferent." I do, however, strongly sympathize with the formalists, as against the sociologists, when the sociologist treats poetry simply as a kind of haphazard sociological survey—a report about world conditions that often shows commendable intuitive insight but is handicapped by a poor methodology of research and controls.

[10] There are styles of cure, shifting from age to age, because each novelty becomes a commonplace, so that the patient integrates his conflict with the ingredients of the old cure itself, thus making them part of his obsession. Hence, the need for a new method of jolting. Thus, I should imagine that a patient who had got into difficulties after mastering the Freudian technique would present the most obstinate problems for a Freudian cure. He would require some step beyond Freud. The same observation would apply to shifting styles in a poetry and philosophy, when considered as cures, as the filling of a need.

[11] I am indebted to Norbert Gutermann for the term "self-acceptance," and to William S. Knickerbocker for the term "rejection of rejection."

*Ludwig Jekels*

# THE RIDDLE OF
# SHAKESPEARE'S "MACBETH"

The problem of this paper is suggested in a remark of the distinguished Shakespearean scholar Gervinus. In one of his studies, he urges that a bridge be thrown between Shakespeare's inner life and his poetry "with a few speaking touches, and a connection pointed out, which may show *that with Shakespeare,* as with every rich poetic nature, *no outer routine and poetic propriety, but inner experiences and emotions of the mind were the deep springs of his poetry*—then for the first time we should have reached a point which would bring us near the poet; we should gain a complete idea of his personal existence, and obtain a full picture, a living view of his mental stature."[1]

Perhaps interpretations of *Macbeth* differ so widely because few scholars have adopted this plan, which seems to be the only correct one. Ulrici, for instance, while underestimating the ambition motif, interprets the drama as based on the relation between the external world and man's will power and energy.[2] Other authors conceive the plot of the tragedy and the character development of its heroes as arising, for the most part, from the conflict between ambition and conscience. From none of these comments could we infer any of Shakespeare's *"inner experiences."*

This need not imply that the poet's emotional keyboard lacked ambition. On the contrary, a thorough analysis should also disclose this psychic element, which, by the way, is so obviously stressed by the words of Macbeth and his Lady. But we do deny that ambition has the central position generally assumed for it in the psychological structure of the plot. When he wrote *Macbeth,* Shakespeare was already at

---

* Ludwig Jekels was analyzed by Sigmund Freud and became a renowned psychoanalyst. He is the author of many professional articles, and he translated Freud's *Psychopathology of Everyday Life* into Polish.

the peak of his successes. It seems unlikely, therefore, that his ambition should have had the tremendously high tension one would expect from the powerful impact of the play. To be sure, Macbeth's ambition might be sufficient reason for the murder of Duncan, and even for the persecution of Macduff (although the two deeds are only indirectly connected with each other). But it is wholly inadequate to explain the murder of Banquo or to elucidate a number of important side issues and countless enigmatic details of the drama.

Small wonder, therefore, that Bodenstedt, Gervinus, Ulrici, Brandes, and others have reached such contradictory opinions concerning the heroes—although all of them consider ambition the motive causing the conflicts. Bodenstedt's admission that "Macbeth and his Lady are among those characters on whose interpretation scholars have not been able to agree,"[3] exposes the utter inadequacy, if not incorrectness, of the stress on ambition.

A reconsideration of the problem of *Macbeth*, though it has been discussed so much already, would therefore seem perfectly justified. The reader will have to decide whether or not the author has obeyed Gervinus's admonition to avoid producing a poem of the historian instead of a history of the poet.

I

As with most of Shakespeare's plays, the date of the origin of *Macbeth* has not been established exactly. But we do know that it could not have been written before 1604 or after 1610.[4] The later date is fixed by the first known performance of the tragedy. The earlier date, however, is derived from an important historical event: in 1604, the Scottish king, James, was crowned King of Great Britain and Ireland; the play contains an unmistakable allusion to this event.[5]

There are still other indications that the play was composed with the king in mind. For instance, the healing power of Edward the Confessor is mentioned. As Edward himself had prophesied, this power was supposedly passed on to his descendants, including, of course, King James. The allusion is unanimously characterized by scholars as "dragged in by the hair," and is definitely out of place.

Shakespeare, moreover, elaborated the witch motif in very great detail, devoting whole scenes to a factor which is made very little of in his source (Holinshed's *Chronicle*). This procedure is obviously connected with James's interest in witchery, a preoccupation which was exceptional even in a time submerged in the belief in witchcraft. James had only recently composed a *Demonology*, and had personally interrogated an alleged witch.

The most striking evidence of the poet's concern with the king is his choice of subject. At this time, all England was familiar with the Macbeth legend. In 1605, when the king had visited Oxford, students had greeted him with a rhapsody containing elements of the legend. It seemed to be particularly well suited as an ovation for the king. Having come to Scotland and its throne only by way of wedlock, the Stuarts were particularly eager to deny their Gallic origin, and to affirm their "Scottish" ancestry by referring it to Banquo and Fleance, although both are now considered purely legendary.

The dramatist's intention to pay homage to his king is further revealed by another modification of the original material. As already noted, Shakespeare took the plot of his play from Raphael Holinshed's *Chronicle of Scottish History*. There, Banquo is depicted as an accomplice to the murder of the king, while Shakespeare shows him to be completely outside it. He did this—according to general opinion—precisely because it would have been impossible to present the king's ancestor as a bloody assassin (all the more so since the play was probably performed in James's presence). In the face of this data, it is difficult to avoid the conclusion that *Macbeth* really represented an apotheosis of James upon his accession to the throne.

Our first problem, therefore, is why the dramatist offered this homage: From what inner urge did it arise?

This question may conceal a much deeper problem than appears at first. In any case, we are fully justified in putting it, since such flattery is altogether incompatible with Shakespeare's usual habits. He had, on the contrary, been extremely chary of praise for James's predecessor, the great Elizabeth. Yet, in the course of more than ten years, she had frequently attended performances of his play; Shakespeare had himself repeatedly appeared before her as an actor; and the playwright had achieved acknowledgment and wealth under her reign—even receiving a grant of arms. Still, as Brandes points out, "Shakespeare was the only poet of the period who absolutely refused to comply with this demand" of the queen for "incessant homage."[6]

For this very reason we consider most unsatisfactory the analysis which some authors give of Shakespeare's attitude toward James. Wagner[7] and W. A. Schegel, for example, believe that in writing this play the dramatist had intended "to please the King particularly." And Brandes thinks that "if the unobtrusive, mildly flattering allusions to James . . . [had been] in the slightest degree deferential, [they] would have been gratuitously and indefensibly churlish, in view of the favour which James had made haste to extend to Shakespeare's company."[8]

Opposing all these explanations stands the dramatist's entirely different behavior toward Queen Elizabeth. Just why the poet was so anxious to ingratiate himself with the new king, or even to avoid any appearance of a demonstration against him, is still not clear when we recall that the queen, who had done so much for him, had received no such consideration.

This contrast between James and Elizabeth, and its intimate relation to the plot of the tragedy, has already been emphasized by Freud in his essay on *Macbeth*.[9] Despite its cursoriness, this essay is of prime importance; careful study of it was indispensable for the present paper. Not only does it throw light on the particular question raised here; it also clears the way for a general understanding of the play.

According to Freud, the tragedy is basically concerned with the contrast between sterility and fecundity. This follows from the fact that the weird sisters assure Macbeth "that he shall indeed be king, but to Banquo they promise that *his* children shall obtain possession of the crown.[10] In Freud's opinion, the plot is developed in accordance with this prophecy.

Furthermore, Freud points out that the same contrast between sterility and fecundity is illustrated by the historical succession to the English throne which took place, as it were, before the very eyes of the dramatist, shortly before the play was written.

"The 'virginal Elizabeth,' of whom it was rumored that she had never been capable of childbearing and who had once described herself as 'a barren stock,' in an anguished outcry at the news of James's birth, was obliged by this very childlessness of hers to let the Scottish king become her successor. And he was the son of that Mary Stuart whose execution she,

though reluctantly, had decreed, and who, despite the cloud-
ing of their relations by political concerns, was yet of her
blood and might be called her guest."[11]

In order to make more obvious this parallel to the historical
situation which he discovered, Freud refers to Macbeth's
words:

> Upon my head they plac'd a fruitless crown
> And put a barren sceptre in my gripe,
> Thence to be wrench'd with an unlineal hand,
> *No son of mine succeeding.* [III, i, 61–64][12]

These words repeat Elizabeth's outcry almost literally.

The mythological content of the Scottish legend of Macbeth, which is the foundation of the play, seems also to
corroborate Freud's conception of the basic motif. Although
he dealt with the subject only in passing, he probably came
very close to the psychological problem concealed in it. Even
a superficial examination of the legend reveals the contrast
between fertility and its opposite as the core.

According to Simrock's comments,[13] there can be hardly
any doubt that the legend symbolizes the processes of vegetation, that it is in reality a vegetation myth. There are actually
considerable analogies with the legend of the Hessian King
Grunewald as well as with that of the Giant King of Saxo
Grammaticus (VII, 132). From these parallels, Simrock concludes that Macbeth, like these legendary characters, is a
hibernal giant, whose reign comes to an end when the May
festival begins and the green wood comes marching.

What Simrock says about the meaning of the second
prophecy (". . . none of woman born/Shall harm Macbeth,"
IV, i, 80-81), however, is less specific. He sees in Macduff an
analogy to mythical characters like Rogdai, Rusten, Woelsung,
and others, men or demigods, who have supposedly been
"ripped" from their mothers' wombs, in token of their strength
and power.

This explanation of the second prophecy need not conflict
with that of the Birnam Wood prophecy, if we recall Simrock's
hint that being "ripped from one's mother's womb" is a
sign of the demigod. It would be an expression of deep reverence for the fructifying power of nature that spring—in
contrast to Winter, which is personified as purely human—be

endowed with divine attributes and thus implicitly represented as victorious.

Since, however, we expect to reach a thorough explanation of this special problem in the course of our investigation, let us conclude these preliminary remarks by merely repeating that the myth of *Macbeth* somehow contains the contrast between sterility and generative power.

Although this theme recurs in so many aspects of the drama, it is inadequate as a basic motif—as the readers of Freud's essay will remember. It does not explain in what sense the problem of fertility or its opposite may have been meant by Shakespeare; it cannot be related to the further development of the drama; above all, it cannot elucidate the crucial psychological problem.

In the first place, this conception of the basic problem of the tragedy is remarkably weak historically. Its relation to the external historical situation, which Freud revealed in so promising a way, is only slight. It cannot establish any profound and revealing parallel.

On the other hand, Freud attempts to explain the transformation of Macbeth into a raving murderer and of his Lady into a distracted penitent by the couple's childlessness. They are understood to have conceived their disappointed hopes of children as a punishment for their crimes. This interpretation, however, failed—as will be remembered—because Shakespeare, by reducing to eight days the ten-year period which Holinshed had described between the murder of Duncan and the subsequent crimes of Macbeth (particularly the murder of Banquo), had left "no time for a long-drawn disappointment of their hopes of offspring to enervate the woman and rive the man to an insane defiance."[14] Freud is forced to conclude:

> What, however, these motives can have been which in so short a space of time could turn the hesitating, ambitious man into an unbridled tyrant, and his steely-hearted instigator into a sick woman gnawed by remorse, it is, in my view, impossible to divine. I think we must renounce the hope of penetrating the triple obscurity of the bad preservation of the text, the unknown intention of the dramatist, and the hidden purport of the legend.[15]

We shall therefore attempt to gain a deeper understanding of the problems discussed by a more detailed psychological analysis of the characters of the tragedy, of their grouping, and of their interrelations.

## II

The psychological structure of the tragedy, which seems so bewildering at first, becomes clearer if we conceive the king as a father symbol—a conception revealed and confirmed again and again by psychoanalysis.

We should then conclude that Macbeth's psychic function is twofold. First, like Banquo and Macduff, he is son to the father (King), Duncan. Second, however, when he himself has become king, he is father to Banquo and Macduff: these two come to be seen as his sons, just as they are originally conceived as Duncan's sons. Macbeth's first phase thus concerns the relationship of son to father; his second phase involves the opposite relationship, that of father to son.

In order to facilitate orientation, let us first investigate the son-father relationship. Needless to say, the murder of Duncan cannot be classified, analytically, as other than parricide.[16]

As a son, Macbeth is therefore parricidal, or—to put it less strongly—hostile, rebellious; Hecate calls him the "wayward son" (III, v, 11).

The motive of the parricide, the reason for the hostility against the father, is personified in Lady Macbeth. She is the "demon-woman," who creates the abyss between father and son. We can prove the correctness of this interpretation by a number of instances. To begin with, Lady Macbeth is accomplice only to the crime Macbeth commits as son, that is, before he had become king (father). From the moment he obtains the throne, she has no part at all in his criminal deeds: apparently she is not privy to his murderous plans against either Banquo or Macduff.

Shakespearean scholars seem scarcely to have been startled by this fact. Supported by psychoanalytic insight, however, we gain the most important corroboration of our conception of Lady Macbeth from the following dialogue. (In the great seventh scene of the first act, in which she finally induces the still reluctant Macbeth to murder, the Lady refers to the past):

What beast was't then
That made you break this enterprise to me?

. . . Nor time nor place
Did then adhere, and yet you would make both. [I, vii, 47–48,
51–52.]

Since the discussion referred to in these words is not in the
text as we have it, Brandes and others conclude that much has
been omitted from that text. We, however, think that these
lines nicely illustrate Darmesteter's judicious words: "Dans
nombre de cas où le texte semble corrompu, il est probable
qu'il n'est qu'obscur et que nous devons accuser notre mala-
dresse de commentateur plutôt que l'incurie des premiers
éditeurs." (In a number of places where the text seems to be
corrupted, it is probably only obscure, and *we should rather
hold our ineptitude as commentators responsible than the
inaccuracy of the first publishers.*) [17] For the words quoted
point to abysmal psychic depths. Lady Macbeth, the "demon-
woman," refers Macbeth to the past—indeed, "woman," in
the guise of the three witches, had already stepped between
him and the father.

A good deal has been written and argued about the witches
in *Macbeth;* the most select minds of Germany, such as
Goethe, Schiller, Grillparzer, as well as Schlegel, Vischer,
Ludwig, and others, have been concerned with this question.
However, Holinshed tells us plainly who these "weitches" (as
he called them) are, and the dramatist himself has them name
themselves the "weird sisters" (I, iii, 32). "Weird" means
destiny, fate; Holinshed also speaks of the witches as "goddesses of destiny." [18]

Schiller is doubtless right in concluding that the three
witches represent the three Fatal Sisters, the Norns of the
Edda, the Parcae of the Romans, the Moires of the Greeks.
According to an essay by Freud, the same is true of Lear's
three daughters, Cordelia, Regan, and Goneril, and of the
three caskets in *The Merchant of Venice.* [19]

To the same engrossing essay by Freud, we owe the insight
that the motif of the three sisters, which is customarily conceived as an allegory of the past, the present, and the future,
also means "the three inevitable relations man has with
woman," the three forms into which the image of the mother
is cast for man in the course of his life: "the mother herself,
the beloved who is chosen after her pattern, and finally the
Mother Earth. . . ." [20] Lady Macbeth's vague allusion to the
past refers in reality to the mother as the origin and the

deepest source of hostility against the father.

That is why the poet has the three witches meet the hero on a "blasted heath" with the prophecy that he will become Thane of Cawdor. The title of Thane of Cawdor does not mean an elevation in rank; it is rather a symbol of treason. For Ross calls the Thane a "most disloyal traitor" (I, ii, 52), and Angus reports that "treasons capital, confess'd and prov'd,/Have overthrown him" (I, iii, 115-116). By this detail Shakespeare implies that, through his mother, the son turns traitor to his father: Lady Macbeth, through the image of the mother, symbolizes the abyss separating father and son.

Finally, this conception of Lady Macbeth is corroborated by the character of Banquo. Having no part at all in the murder, he stands for the exact opposite of the bad son, Macbeth, and must represent the good son.[21]

In connection with the immediate subject, however, two peculiarities of Banquo are important contrasts with Macbeth: no wife is mentioned for him, and he appears to have no contact with Lady Macbeth. When the Lady exclaims:

> Had he not resembled
> My father as he slept, I had done it. [II, ii, 13-14.]

she is telling us that the genii of the sexes disarm each other. At the same time, she teaches that man is urged by woman to fight his own sex, and she thus embodies the "other" sex, victorious over one's "own" sex. She stands for heterosexuality, which overpowers homosexuality.

In short, the woman—Lady Macbeth—makes Macbeth turn into a bad son, and thus the woman is the son's doom.

In his second psychic phase, Macbeth is the "father." As such, he has one son, Banquo, murdered, and also seeks the life of his other son, Macduff; consequently, he is the bad father, hostile to his sons and ready to kill them.

The validity of this interpretation is established by the great emphasis with which Macbeth orders the hired assassins not to kill Banquo alone, but also to kill his son, Fleance. When the murderers talk, after Fleance's successful flight, their stress is obviously on "son":

Third Murderer:    There's but one down; the son is fled.
Second Murderer:   We have lost
                   Best half of our affair. (III, iii, 19-21.)

This problem of hostility against the son becomes even clearer when Macduff's little son is murdered; though we are repeatedly told that Macduff has lost *all his kith and kin,* yet the son is emphatically singled out; it is the fate of the son that Shakespeare puts into the foreground.

What is the motif of this hostility against the son?

Suffice it that we hint at the famous vision of Banquo's ghost—often interpreted and as often misunderstood—which Macbeth sees taking his, the father's, seat, just as formerly he himself had dislodged Duncan from his seat. And let us recall Macbeth's words at this moment:

> Ay, and a bold one, that dare look on that
> Which might appal the devil. [III, iv, 59–60]

Here the poet dramatizes, with wonderful clarity, the fear of the son, now a father, upon confronting, in his own son, the same hostility he had himself harbored against his father —a motif Rank has also disclosed in Hamlet.

This *fear of requital,* a fear nourished and maintained by consciousness of the wrong committed against the father, explains Macbeth's desperate outcry at the news that although Banquo is dead, his son, Fleance, has succeeded in escaping:

> Then comes my fit again. I had else been perfect;
> Whole as the marble, founded as the rock,
> As broad and general as the casing air.
> But now I am cabin'd, cribb'd, confin'd, bound in
> To saucy doubts and fears. [III, iv, 21–25]

It is the father within Macbeth, the never-silenced memories of hatred against his father and of the injury inflicted on that father in his thoughts, that nourishes suspicions of the very same feelings in the son; it is the father surviving within him that demands the death of the son. Malcolm, the cautious son, therefore speaks of

> . . . wisdom
> To offer up a weak, poor, innocent lamb
> T'appease an angry God. [IV, iii, 15–17]

Obviously, the relation to one's son appears to the poet as strictly conditioned by the relation to one's father; one will be, as a father, as one was as a son. *Macbeth demonstrates the fact that a bad son will make a bad father.*

The same close connection of the psychical functions of son and father is revealed in other characters of the tragedy, especially in Macduff and Banquo.

We are not absolutely alone in this supposition of a repetition of motif; a few Shakespearean scholars seem to have observed something similar. Ulrici finds it "an undeniable defect of the tragedy that the fundamental motive of the action represented, is not fully carried out in the personal character, life and fate of the hero, but, in part, merely in his outward surroundings." He also asserts that "the fundamental idea of the drama . . . is not merely reflected in the character, the fortunes and fate of the chief bearers of the action, but is also reflected in various degrees of light and shade in all the other figures," and that "the effect of the tragic pathos . . . is not only found in the history of the hero and his consort, but appears, as it were, halved and assigned to two different sides."[22]

For Macduff must be called a bad, obstinate son, quite as much as Macbeth. Despite his love for his father (amply demonstrated for Duncan, and hinted at even for Macbeth),[23] Macduff rebels against Macbeth. He does not attend the coronation at Scone; he uses "broad words," according to Lennox (III, vi, 21); and, unlike the submissive son, Banquo, who accepts unhesitatingly, Macduff refuses the invitation to the banquet offhand.

Why does he act thus?—because Macbeth has murdered Duncan, committed parricide, shown the traditional hostility against the father.

It is Macduff's rebellion against the father, however, which destroys all his kin. Persecuted by the father, he is forced to abandon them to the murderous hand, especially his son, who is stabbed to death before our very eyes. That is why he wails:

> Sinful Macduff,
> They were all struck for thee! Naught that I am,
> Not for their own demerits, but for mine,
> Fell slaughter on their souls. [IV, iii, 224–227]

Here is the same motif as in the story of Macbeth; Macduff, too, demonstrates the fact that a bad son is also a bad father.

This identical content is communicated to us, however, in two distinct dialects. Macduff's fate proclaims in an undisguised, direct manner what the character of Macbeth expresses in a veiled and therefore indirect form; the latter seems to be a symbolic presentation of the former. Analysis of Macbeth should, then, disclose a technique similar to that which is frequently used in dreams. Everyone familiar with Freud's *theory of dreams* knows that they discard nuances and tints and instead adopt a lapidary brevity and a violent imagery. Almost every negative emotional relation is expressed by death, for example. Macbeth's murder of the king thus corresponds to Macduff's mere unconcern about him.[24]

The same insight is even more accurate for the female characters.

Is not Lady Macduff in her little scene (IV, ii) but reproducing Lady Macbeth's actions in the first two acts? Macduff's wife incites her little son against his father, calling her husband a traitor who swears and does not keep his word, a man who should be hanged. She deeply degrades the child's father before him by saying how easily he could be replaced by another father. Schiller, in his translation, thought this scene so irrelevant that he left it out. But can Lady Macduff's words be symbolized more adequately than by Lady Macbeth's daggers? Hamlet, reproaching his mother with her sins, says: "I will speak daggers to her but use none" (III, ii); even in colloquial language, "words like daggers" is a familiar figure.[25]

What could have led Shakespeare to the double presentation of this motif? We shall not answer this question fully at this stage of our investigation. We may, however, venture the surmise that the character of Macduff, so poorly outlined in the legend, has been endowed so richly by Shakespeare because he saw in it a more concrete, more cleanly cut, more specific formulation of the motif which Macbeth's character expresses in a much more general way. This may explain why he developed the Macduff nucleus of the legend, treated it separately and paralled it to Macbeth, almost pointing out that in this case Macbeth should be understood as practically identical with Macduff.

Combining these elements, we reach a conclusion essential for the understanding of the tragedy: that *not Macbeth, but Macduff, is the true hero.* Similarly, the further development of the basic idea of the drama—the concatenation of the father function with that of the son—proceeds, not in Macbeth, but in Macduff, who becomes, as it were, the continuation of Macbeth.

Banquo is, so to speak, the positive of the picture of which Macduff is the negative. In saving himself from Macbeth's persecutions, Macduff disregards his son and sacrifices him; when Banquo is attacked by murderers, however, he gives his last thought to his son. "Fly, good Fleance, fly!" are his dying words (III, iii, 17). His fate therefore symbolizes the idea treated in the play, that one's conduct as father is conditioned by one's attitude as son; here, the meaning is reversed, however, and the implication is that only a good son can become a good father.

Our original interpretation of Banquo as, notwithstanding his inner contradictions, a tractable son, is borne out if we interpret the allegory as meaning that while such a son may fall victim to his father, he will safeguard his own son. Furthermore, the apparition of the infinitely long line of Stuart kings (IV, i) shows that by saving his child a good son may expect further reward, since this action guarantees the undisturbed succession of generations: the House of Stuart originates from that same Fleance.

Applying this insight to Macbeth, *the basic idea is* discovered to be *that a bad son not only sacrifices his son, but, in so doing, also forfeits the blessing of continuous descent.*

This complex, we believe, this worry about the preservation of the clan, bears the main emphasis of the drama. The son is regarded primarily as a means to this end, that is, as the firstborn male descendant. Although Banquo is represented in the procession of kings, therefore, Fleance is missing.

The historical incident to which the drama can be traced also supports the supposition that the author aims principally at the problem of preservation of the line of descent. When Elizabeth died, and the Tudor dynasty was ended, the transference of the crown to the Stuarts offered an analogy with the contrasting fates of Banquo and Macduff in the tragedy. The same disappointment at the disruption of the line of descent can also be inferred from Macduff's reaction to Ross's report of the murder of

> Wife, children, servants, all
> That could be found. [IV, iii, 212–213]

In his desperate outcry, what he bemoans is the loss of *all* his children:

> He has no children. All my pretty ones?
> Did you say all? O hell-kite! All?
> What, all my pretty chickens . . . [IV, iii, 216–218]

This grief is not directed to the children as such, but to their function as links in the chain of generations. Macduff's exclamation, "He has no children," which has so often been reinterpreted, may favor this interpretation. It refers to Macbeth, and, keeping the congruity of the two figures, could be replaced by a resigned, "And so I have no children." That these words, in so general a form, and in the specific situation, can only reflect on the lost prospect of continuous descent can hardly be denied. What else, moreover, could Macbeth mean when he tells his wife:

> Bring forth men-children only;
> For thy undaunted mettle should compose
> Nothing but males. [I, vii, 72-74]

Some doubt may be aroused, however, by the unexplained distinction with which Macduff's son, among all his kin, has been treated. The individual treatment of this character's fate has proved very useful for our understanding of the drama: perhaps this son, even more than his counterpart, Fleance, has shown how the tragedy is built around the son problem. The question is why Shakespeare so fully displayed this part of the problem, "the son," when he wrapped the other part, "the father," in so foggy a symbolic darkness? What was his purpose? What did he want to express? Holinshed cannot answer; he does not mention Macduff's son. Could the character be elucidated from another viewpoint, from reality? Shakespeare's biographers may answer that question.

### III

Among their meager data, his biographers include the fact that when he was twenty-one, Shakespeare left his home town, Stratford, his wife and his children, and moved to London. The biographers agree that this serious step, this separation from all that should be dearest to him, was mainly and almost exclusively due to his conflict with the wealthy squire, Sir Thomas Lucy. Caught while poaching, William Shakespeare was punished somewhat severely by Lucy. His revenge was a satiric ballad on the latter. The effect of this, however, was that the squire now "redoubled the persecution against him to that degree that he was obliged to leave his business and family . . . and shelter himself in London."[26]

The biographers, however, have no more to offer than a mere "probability"—despite the preserved first stanza of the ballad, and despite the reference to the incident in *The Merry Wives of Windsor* and the consistency of both. With rare conformity, they conclude their discussions with some such remark as Kellner's: ". . . even without this conflict with Lucy, Shakespeare would have been driven out into the world by an inner spirit."[27]

And what if we suggested that Shakespeare's relationship to his father might also have been one of the motives prompting his departure? This conjecture gains considerable support from a hint that the conflict between father and son became more marked at this time. Shortly before Shakespeare's departure, the woman, Lady Macbeth, had stepped between father and son. Not quite three years earlier, William, then eighteen, had married a farmer's daughter, much older than himself. She was of socially inferior parentage, and the marriage was contracted under unusual circumstances, without the father's consent, though this, for minors, was indispensable. "It is absolutely understandable that the clever John Shakespeare was not asked for his consent—he would never have given it,"[28] Kellner remarks. With these facts before us, do not Lady Macduff's words sound almost like a spontaneous confession of the dramatist's? (She reproaches her husband, who has fled before the king's wrath:)

> . . . to leave his wife, to leave his babes,
> His mansion and his titles, in a place
> From whence himself does fly? He loves us not,
> He wants the natural touch. [IV, ii, 6–9]

The certainty of this supposition is particularly strengthened by another fact. It is not easy to discover why Shakespeare has Macduff's son stabbed *after* the escape of the father instead of *before*. If the stabbing took place first, not only would there be sufficient motivation for that base deed (especially when compared with the causes of Banquo's fate), but there would be much better reasons for Macduff's flight—which otherwise lacks the added incentive of retaliation. As it is, the irrationality of Macduff's action leads his wife to exclaim, "What had he done to make him fly the land?" and, "His flight was madness" (IV, ii, 1, 3). Some commentators seem to agree with her. Gervinus actually slights the fact that the sequence of events is reversed in this way, and says that Macduff was not prepared to oppose Macbeth until after the murder of his family.[29] And Ulrici calls the flight of Macduff unmanly and unfatherly.[30]

This incongrity, however, also disappears once we understand the allegory, and realize that a personal experience of Shakespeare's has been transposed into the drama. Exactly as in the tragedy, Shakespeare, while living far from his family and unconcerned about them for several years, lost his eleven-year-old son, Hamnet. Surely Macduff embodies this intimate personal experience of the dramatist.

In 1601, Shakespeare is said to have entered a period of great depression, which darkened a long span of his life, but to which an admiring world apparently owes such master-works as *Julius Caesar, Hamlet, Othello, King Lear,* and *Macbeth.* For this depression, various reasons have been given: the doom of Lords Essex and Southampton, with both of whom the dramatist had close contact; the crisis in his and Lord Pembroke's relations with the "Dark Lady" of the sonnets; and finally the fact that the year 1601 was the year his father died. Freud aligned these motives in order of importance; he correctly placed one factor which was neglected before him, the death of Shakespeare's father, and he showed its significance for the striking metamorphosis in the author— who had previously been so very sunny and merry. How right he was is proved by Macbeth when, after the murder of the king is discovered, he exclaims, with ostensible hypocrisy:

> Had I but died an hour before this chance,
> I had liv'd a blessed time; for from this instant
> There's nothing serious in mortality;
> All is but toys; renown and grace is dead;
> The wine of life is drawn, and the mere lees
> Is left this vault to brag of. [II, iii, 96–101]

What Freud has disclosed in *Hamlet,* consequently, is also true for *Macbeth;* this tragedy, as well as *Hamlet,* was created by Shakespeare under the impression of his father's death and "during a revival . . . of his own childish feelings in respect of his father."[31] Since *Macbeth* was written several years after

*Hamlet,* however, the reaction formations against those infantile emotions were much more advanced; by this time,
the psychic situation of the poet had gone through a definite
change.

Rank, in his instructive essay on *Hamlet,* stresses this
attitude of love toward the father, which is present latently,
and is fed by feelings of guilt and repentance.[32] In *Macbeth,*
this positive feeling of fatherhood appears by far to out-
balance the negative feelings of the son in the poet.

Father feelings predominate in the heart of the dramatist,
because his repressions have now reached a deeper level.
Earlier works of this period had shown a feeling of guilt
toward his father as the reaction to infantile hatred for him;
now this reaction has become a feeling in the author that his
own attitude toward his son is menaced. It is when the self-
reproaches and feelings of guilt derived from this menace
are bound up with the fate of the neglected and (supposedly)
sacrificed son, that they appear most intensely:

> Sinful Macduff,
> They were all struck for thee! Naught that I am,
> Not for their own demerits, but for mine
> Fell slaughter on their souls. [IV, iii, 224–227]

## IV

Similarly, through Macduff's stirring lament on the shatter-
ing of his hope for the preservation of his clan, Shakespeare's
own pain can be sensed. During the years following the death
of his father, two historical events occurred which harmon-
ized with the despondency of his psychic disposition: the
death of Queen Elizabeth and the accession of King James.

It seems psychologically consistent that the fate of the old,
unmarried, "virginal" Elizabeth should start a powerful echo
in the heart of the dramatist. Dying without offspring, the
last of her line, Elizabeth was forced to bequeath her crown
to an alien family. The demonstration that even such grandeur
was transitory could not help turning the poet's mourning for
his son into grief about his endangered descent. Biographers
agree that he had little in common with the two daughters
who were left, if he was not actually estranged from them.
Suzanne, the elder, moreover, was either married or engaged,
and Judith, the younger, was also eligible. Not a loved one

was left to receive his inheritance, and there was nobody at all to continue his name and fame. No wonder Macbeth despairs!

> Upon my head they plac'd a fruitless crown
> And put a barren sceptre in my gripe,
> Thence to be wrench'd with an unlineal hand,
> No son of mine succeeding. [III, i, 61–64]

It really does credit to Brandes' intuition that he so accurately estimated the significance of Hamnet's death for the dramatist's psyche. "We cannot doubt that this loss was a grievous one to a man of Shakespeare's deep feeling; doubly grevious, it would seem, because it was his constant ambition to restore the fallen fortunes of his family, and he was now left without an heir to his name."[33] The sensitive critic felt what we could only laborously decipher.

Granting Elizabeth so prominently a role in the conception of the tragedy may seem arbitrary and high-handed. Nevertheless, we are prepared to suggest that the queen's influence on the composition was even greater than we have yet intimated. With the royal life which had just ended, Shakespeare may have had a sympathy of unsuspected depth. Had not Elizabeth, like himself, been a bad child?

The relation of the young princess to her fostermother, Katherine Parr, the last wife of Henry VIII, was a troubled one, especially after Katherine remarried. Yet Elizabeth herself wrote that Katherine had bestowed "manifold kindnesses"[34] upon her.

Shakespeare's imagination must indeed have been active to recognize Elizabeth's attitude toward Mary Tudor—the half-sister who preceded her on the throne—as mother hatred. Elizabeth had been able to attract not only the Earl of Devonshire, whom Mary had loved deeply, but also Mary's husband, Philip II.[35] She had actually played the part of a rebellious daughter toward Mary, being intimately implicated in the conspiracy of Wyatt and his confederates against the queen in 1554. Elizabeth's very life was then imperiled, and it was thanks only to extremely cautious maneuvering that she received no more severe punishment that detention in the Tower, followed by banishment to Hatfield.

And surely Shakespeare unconsciously sensed Elizabeth's

hostility toward her mother in her treatment of Mary Stuart, Queen of Scots. How else can the many irrational details of that behavior be explained? Elizabeth brought no charge against Mary Stuart, and failed to have her sentenced, though she imprisoned her for eighteen years; nor was she ever unaware of Mary's political conspiracies and intrigues. Besides that, she confirmed the death sentence of the Scottish queen and yet appeared alarmed and disconcerted at the news of the execution. These inconsistencies lead one to suspect unconscious influences. Elizabeth was probably repeating the girlhood situation already described, and thereby ridding herself of those affects which she had had to suppress toward Mary Tudor.[36] She identified the Scottish queen with Mary Tudor—an easy process, since both, unlike Protestant, "bastard" Elizabeth, were legitimate, Catholic, and named "Mary." Philip II, moreover, assisted Mary Stuart in her troubles, just as he had once assisted Princess Elizabeth. With so many correspondences, it is only natural to conclude that the mother-daughter relationship was also carried over in Elizabeth's attitude toward the Queen of Scots.

In addition to the "bad child" character, Elizabeth displays a still closer accord with Shakespeare's experience. Like himself, she had murdered her own son: as recently as 1601, she had ordered the execution of her lover, Robert Devereux, Earl of Essex, who had been very close to the dramatist. Nor should Shakespeare have had any trouble in unconsciously interpreting Elizabeth's relationship to Essex as a mother-son relationship, since the Earl was thirty-one years younger than the queen, and was the stepson of Leicester, her lover of many years standing.

Although Elizabeth was, therefore, Shakespeare's model when he wrote this tragedy, we do not find her in one character of the play, but in two. Analysis of *The Merchant of Venice* led me to understand that Shakespeare—and perhaps other playwrights—often use, as a means of disguising an event, the technique of splitting a psychic personality, distributing it to two or more characters of the drama. Each of these is, of course, only fragmentary, and therefore not easily interpreted: they must be pieced together in order to form a psychic whole. Freud accepts this opinion, and continues:

It might be thus with Macbeth and the Lady; and then it

would of course be futile to regard her as an independent personage and seek to discover her motivation without considering the
Macbeth who completes her. I shall not follow this hint any
further, but I would add, nevertheless, a remark which strikingly
confirms the idea—namely, that the stirrings of fear which arise
in Macbeth on the night of the murder, do not develop further
in him, but in the Lady. It is he who has the hallucination of
the dagger before the deed, but it is she who later succumbs to
mental disorder; he, after the murder, hears the cry from the
house: "Sleep no more! Macbeth does murder sleep . . . ," and
so "Macbeth shall sleep no more," but we never hear that King
Macbeth could not sleep, while we see that the Queen rises from
her bed and betrays her guilt in somnambulistic wanderings. He
stands helpless with bloody hands, lamenting that not great
Neptune's ocean can wash them clean again, while she comforts
him: "a little water clears us of this deed"; but later it is she who
washes her hands for a quarter of an hour and cannot get rid of
the bloodstains. "All the perfumes of Arabia will not sweeten
this little hand." Thus is fulfilled in her what his pangs of conscience had apprehended; she is incarnate remorse after the deed,
he incarnate defiance—together they exhaust the possibilities of
reaction to the crime, like two disunited parts of the mind of a
single individuality, and perhaps they are the divided images of
a single prototype.[37]

As the model of the two leading characters, however,
hardly anybody could have been in Freud's mind but Elizabeth—for we have seen how, with his unequaled intuition, he
guessed from the beginning the part of the queen in the
conception of the drama.

Thus it was Elizabeth whom Shakespeare molded into the
forms of Macbeth and his Lady. For his ability to do so, and
in such eternal magnificance, we are indebted to that fantasy
which made it possible for him to identify himself with the
queen in his innermost experience. It was thus a kind of
identification, almost an interchange of personalities, which
permitted him to use the Macbeth saga in celebrating the
succession of James to the English throne, since that story was
so essentially in accordance with the historical event. The
sterile queen seemed to him to be the murderer of her son,
just as he felt himself, having murdered his son, to be sterile.
To quote a sociologist, "Indeed, both queen and poet stand
inseparable on the peak of their world."[38]

But was it not also on account of this identification that
Shakespeare's feelings for the queen were, as Brandes says,

so cool that he did not even write a few lines of praise at her
death—despite Chettle's request?[39]

# V

It should be no surprise to find, therefore, that James and
his accession to the throne are also merged with the dramatist's own fate. While the queen's death, however, wrought
only despair and remorse in the author because of his self-
inflicted grief, he drew expiation and wish fulfillment from the
character of James. James is the cue for the effervescent wish
symphony now surrounding the sadness in his heart: it is
merely an expression of wish fulfillment that Macduff is "none
of woman born."

This unnatural birth is, first of all, a contrast to the impotence and inadequacy of "mortal" man, especially since
Macbeth is incited, by the prophecy, to "laugh to scorn/The
pow'r of man" (IV, i, 79-80), thereby pointing, as it were, to
a god as his successor. As this sharp contrast between god and
man does not appear in Holinshed,[40] it would seem to have
originated in Shakespeare. We may therefore conclude that
he conceives Macduff as a deity with the attribute, "none
of woman born."

However, have we not already met with almost the same
contention? Does not Simrock, refering to Macduff's other
attribute, his being "ripped from his mother's womb," say
this usually betokens the demi-god?[41]

We can even guess which god the author meant. This dark
"none of woman born" has two possible contents: first, the
stress may lie on "born," and imply "ripped from the womb";
second, it may lie on "woman," and imply the opposite, that
is, "one born of a man." The god would then be one who
had been both "ripped from his mother's womb" and born
of his father. There is only one such figure in the ancient
pantheon: the Greek god Dionysus.

According to the best known so-called Theban saga, this
god is the son of Semele, daughter of Cadmus, King of
Thebes. She conceived him from Zeus, with whom she had
secret intercourse in her palace in Thebes. Betrayed by
treacherous advice from jealous Hera, Semele urges Zeus
to visit her in his full celestial majesty, after she has wheedled
the oath from him that he will fulfill any wish. As Zeus then
appears in his true character with thunder and lightning,
Semele dies, struck by the lightning. By order of Zeus, Hermes

opens Semele's body, which is enveloped in flames, and wrests her child from the fire. Zeus takes the unripe fruit, sews it into his thigh, and in due time gives birth to the child.

Of course, Dionysus is par excellence the god of nature's blessings, of "the growth of nature, god of all fecundity and procreation."[42]

This is truly a magnificent achievement of Shakespearean fantasy: transforming the "barrenness" of which he had despaired into its immense antinomy!

As we know, the time the play was written is uncertain. Yet we dare set the year 1606 as the precise date:[43] ten years after he has become father (king), Holinshed's Macbeth murders his son (Banquo); and ten years after he has murdered his son, Shakespeare revives him—in Malcolm. While it is James who entices this magic tune from the poet's lyre, the author's love encompasses both sons equally, both the living king and his reflection in the play. James was the son of a murdered mother, as Malcolm was the son of a murdered father. And James is more than son; he is also a distant offspring of the clan. Banquo finds his continuation, even after many centuries, in James; Malcolm, for the dramatist, likewise represents a desired future descendant. For now the son is, like Banquo, a good son. Malcolm has

> Great Birnam Wood to high Dunsinane Hill
> . . . come against him [that is, Macbeth]. [IV, i, 93–94]

What is more, however, Macduff stamps out Macbeth—the hatred against the father. As the "motherless" Dionysus, Macduff does not even know the mother, Lady Macbeth, who is the doom of the son: only the father is his procreator, and that is God, nay, the King of the Gods.

But in his trouble the poet also seeks refuge in self-assertion. Since the early birth of Dionysus from Semele took place at Thebes, this was taken as the god's original home and became the most famous sanctuary for his worship. As, however, the second birth, from the thigh of Zeus, took place at Nysa in Thrace, Dionysus was generally considered the victorious god who, coming from abroad, had enforced his worship there. Had not the poet also to fight hard for acknowledgment and fame in his native Stratford? Had he not left it, years before, poor and humiliated, with the determination that "the little town which had witnessed this disgrace should also witness the rehabilitation?"[44]

At the risk of pressing the analogy too far, may we close, at last, with a figurative tribute, by suggesting that William Shakespeare in his own lifetime and ever since, has been the god of comedy and tragedy, of which Dionysus was the father.[45]

## NOTES

[1] Georg Gottfried Gervinus, *Shakespeare Commentaries*, trans. F. E. Bunnètt, New York, Scribner, Welford & Armstrong, 1875, p. 22.

[2] Hermann Ulrici, *Shakespeare's Dramatic Art*, trans. by L. D. Schmitz, London, George Bell & Sons, 1876, I, 460–461.

[3] Friedrich Bodenstedt, *Shakespeare's Frauencharaktere*, Berlin, A. Hofmann & Co., 1874, p. 303.

[4] Recent investigations, however, have restricted this period to three years, 1604, 1605, and 1606.

[5] ". . . and some I see
That twofold balls and treble scepters carry."
—IV, i, 120–121. Kittredge edition.

[6] Georg Brandes, *William Shakespeare . . .*, trans. William Archer, Mary Morison, and Diana White, London, William Heinemann, 1905, p. 41.

[7] Wilhelm Wagner, *Macbeth von William Shakespeare*, Leipzig, Teubner, 1872.

[8] Brandes, *op. cit.*, p. 418.

[9] Sigmund Freud, "Some Character Types Met with in Psycho-Analytic Work" 1915), *Collected Papers*, London, The Hogarth Press, 1924–1925, IV, 318–344.

[10] *Ibid.*, p. 329.

[11] *Ibid.*, p. 328.

[12] Except when within other quotations, the text of *Macbeth* is quoted from the edition of George Lyman Kittredge, Boston, Ginn & Company, 1939. (Italics have been added in the last line of the passage quoted above.)

[13] Karl Simrock, *Die Quellen des Shakespeare . . .*, Bonn, Marcus, 1872, pp. 255–260.

[14] Freud, *op. cit.*, p. 331.

[15] *Ibid.*

[16] There are lines of the text which corrobrate the nature of Duncan's murder as we conceive it. Because of the basic importance of this conception for the content of the tragedy as we intend to develop it here, and because such psychoanalytic statements still meet with incredulity in many places, we quote Lennox's short speech in which parricide is mentioned repeatedly, though with ironic intent:

> *Who cannot want the thought* how monstrous
> It was for Malcolm and for Donalbain
> To kill their gracious father? [III, vi, 8–10]

This quotation actually contains two negations. One is in "want," which is of rather indefinite nature, and means basically: not-to-have, to miss, to feel the lack of; this passage should therefore read: "Who can want . . ."

Curiously enough, a second negation, "not," is appended to "want"—and this double negation leads to the affirmation and approval of the parricide.

Naturally, commentators have noticed the contradiction in this significant passage. I quote Darmesteter (*Macbeth,* Édition classique par James Darmesteter, Paris, 1881, Librairie Delagrave): "La negation est de trop dans *cannot* et ferais dire la phrase tout le contraire de ce qu'elle signifie—si le sens n'était trop claire de lui-même." (*The negation in "cannot" is superflous and would make the phrase mean the opposite of what it should*—if the sense in itself were not perfectly clear.)

This speech of Lennox is very well known among the commentators on account of its ironic content. Darmesteter calls it "un modèle d' ironie voilée" (a model of veiled irony); the remark refers particularly to Lennox's words when he says Banquo was killed because he went out late. Actually, however, the irony here does not lie in this ambiguity of motivation, but rather in the fact that the poet is telling us the truth about Macbeth's crime —doing so, however, in such a way that we do not notice it. By proposing the ridiculous motive of Banquo's going out late, the poet creates an atmosphere of absolute incredibility, into which the information about the real fact is thrown. The essential irony is that the audience is duped by receiving the truth in such a way as to be further than ever from recognizing it.

17 Darmesteter, *op. cit.*

18 *Holinshed's Chronicles* . . . , London, J. Johnson . . . , 1808, V, 269.

19 Freud, "The Theme of the Three Caskets" (1913), *op. cit.,* IV, 244–256.

20 Freud, *op. cit.,* p. 256.

21 Our designation of Banquo as the "good son" is a summary one, bound to rouse certain doubts, since the character does not entirely tally with it. As characterized by Shakespeare, Banquo shows a certain incompleteness, at least some indistinctness. This has been noted by several of the more serious scholars. Gervinus, arguing that imprudence causes the downfall of the minor characters, adduces the character of Banquo as another example of such poetic justice: "The same want of foresight ruins Banquo. He had been initiated into the secret of the weird sisters; pledged to openness towards Macbeth, he had opportunity of convincing

himself of his obduracy and secrecy; he guesses at, and strongly
suspects, Macbeth's deed; yet he does nothing against him or in
self-defence" (Gervinus, *op. cit.*, p. 605–606). Ulrici also describes
Banquo as one who, "in self-complacent conceit, believes in the
promises for his future good fortune, and thus brings destruction
upon his own head" (Ulrici, *op. cit.*, p. 474). Bodenstedt objects
to Banquo's kindness, which is commonly taken for granted:
Banquo has long discovered all about Macbeth but has done nothing to warn or protect old King Duncan against him" (Bodenstedt,
*op. cit.*, p. 315). We are inclined to take this vague and com-
promising characterization of Banquo as simply another way of
expressing psychological insight. The dramatist seems to mean that
it was, after all, only the woman (the mother) who opened an
unbridgeable abyss between father and son, and drove the latter
into extreme hostility. All other reasons—e.g. unequal reward for
equal merits (so often noticed by scholars)—could only result in
vexation or indifference toward the father (Banquo confesses to
"cursed thoughts" [II, i, 8] against Duncan) but they could never
produce the sudden turn into explicit hostility.

Still, Banquo can hardly be considered a "good" son. In reply
to the king's scanty words of gratitude, he assures him, "There if
I grow, The harvest is your own" (I, iv, 33–34), and yet, in the
next act, harbors "cursed thoughts" against him. Both suspecting
and envying King Macbeth, he nevertheless submissively states,
"Let your Highness command upon me, to the which my duties
Are with a most indissoluble tie for ever knit" (III, i, 15–17).
Considering that Banquo thus, though wrathful in his heart, always
shows himself devoted to his father, we shall find the conception
of him as the "submissive son" to be much more conclusive than
that of the "good son." At the same time, this analysis fully retains
the contrast to the "wayward" Macbeth.

²² Ulrici, *op. cit.*, pp. 476, 475.

²³ Malcolm to Macduff: "You have lov'd him well . . ." (IV,
iii, 13).

²⁴ It is beyond the framework of this investigation to decide
whether, or to what extent, such simultaneous use of the veiled
and the direct manners of presenting a leading motif can be considered a basic phenomenon of dramatic composition. This problem will be examined more thoroughly elsewhere.

²⁵ The common external fate of the two ladies seems to confirm
the correspondence stated here: although the poet does not usually
refrain from having murders acted out, both ladies die offstage.

²⁶ Brandes, *op. cit.*, p. 10 (quoting from another source).

²⁷ Leon Kellner, *Shakespeare*, Leipzig . . . , E. A. Seemann . . . ,
1900, p. 7. (The quotation given has been reworded in translation.)

²⁸ *Ibid.*, p. 6.

²⁹ Gervinus, *op. cit.*, p. 606.

[30] Ulrici, *op. cit.*, p. 474.

[31] Sigmund Freud, *The Interpretation of Dreams*, trans. A. A. Brill, London, Geo. Allen & Unwin, Ltd., pp. 258–259.

[32] Otto Rank, *Das Inzest-Motiv in Dichtung und Sage . . .*, Leipzig und Wien, Franz Deuticke, 1912, pp. 44–45 *et passim*.

[33] Brandes, *op. cit.*, p. 140.

[34] Agnes Strickland, *The Life of Queen Elizabeth*, London, J. M. Dent (Everyman's Library), 1910, p. 22.

[35] J. E. Neale, *Queen Elizabeth*, New York, Harcourt, Brace, 1934, pp. 45–52.

[36] When she was told that Mary Stuart had been beheaded, Elizabeth behaved like "a guilty child . . . self-convicted and terrified at the prospect of disgrace and punishment . . ." (Strickland, *op. cit.*, pp. 500–501).

[37] Freud, *Collected Papers*, IV., 332–333.

[38] Erich Marcks, *Konigen Elisabeth von England . . .* (Monographien Velhagen & Klasing, zur *Weltgeschichte*, II), Bielefeld und Leipzig, 1897, p. 114.

[39] Brandes, *op. cit.*, p. 250.

[40] Holinshed reduces the whole scene (IV, i) to a sentence: "A certeine weitche, whome hee had in great trust, had told him he should never be slaine with man borne of anie woman . . ." (*op. cit.*, p. 274).

[41] Simrock, *op. cit.*, p. 259.

[42] Dionysus also represents "the symbol of elementary creation in nature, a half-chthonic character, since, according to the creative power of nature symbolised by him in wood and field, he is submerged in sleep and death by the rough storms of winter, and later awakens to life again." All this harmonizes perfectly with the myth of vegetation—as does no other mythological character (a fact, curiously enough, which has received little attention).

[43] Other signs, too, point to this date: the porter's reference to "plenty" (II, 3), the equivocator, and the change of men's fashions. It is further supported by the fact that Shakespeare's *Macbeth* is alluded to only in such works as we know had not come into existence before 1607. (Since the time this note was originally written, we have learned *that* 1606 *is* now the accepted date for the composition of *Macbeth*. See Kittredge, *op. cit.*, p. ix, or Lilian Winstanley, *Macbeth, King Lear & Contemporary History*, Cambridge, The University Press, 1922, p. 37.)

[44] Brandes, *op. cit.*, p. 152.

[45] Thus Francis Meres wrote in *Palladis Tamia*, in 1598: "As Plautus and Seneca are accounted the best for Comedy and Tragedy among the Latines: so Shakespeare among the English . . . " (C. Gregory Smith, *Elizabethan Critical Essays*, Oxford, Clarendon Press, 1904, II, 317–318).

*George Devereux**

# WHY OEDIPUS KILLED LAIUS

## A Note on the Complementary
## Oedipus Complex in Greek Drama

It is striking to note that psychoanalytic theory pays
exceedingly little attention to certain complexes which, in a
very genuine sense, complement the Oedipus complex. In
particular, even though occasionally reference is made (13)
to the tender and even to the erotic components of what may
be called the Laius complex and the Jocasta complex, the
sadistic (and homosexual) components of these complexes
are, generally speaking, ignored by psychoanalytic writers.[1]
Indeed, there exist certain Greek traditions regarding Laius
which suggest that the complementary Oedipus complex, even
in its homosexual and sadistic phases, was close enough to the
threshold of consciousness to receive at least a mythological
expression. Yet even Rank (20), who specifically discusses
these traditions, fails to stress that they provide us with a
highly specific and "historical," rather than only with a
general and "paleopsychological," explanation of Laius' behavior toward the infant Oedipus.

It must be assumed that this continued scotomization of
the complementary Oedipus complex is rooted in the adult's
deep-seated need to place all responsibility for the Oedipus
complex upon the child, and to ignore, wherever possible,
certain parental attitudes which actually stimulate the infant's
Oedipal tendencies. This deliberate scotoma is probably
rooted in the authoritarian atmosphere characteristic of nineteenth century family life. This interpretation is supported
by the history of Freud's thoughts on the subject of the
etiology of hysteria. At first, Freud accepted as genuine the
seduction stories narrated by his patients. When he discovered
that these tales merely expressed certain fantasies and wishes,

* GEORGE DEVEREUX is Professor of Research in Ethnopsychia-
try at the Temple University School of Medicine in Philadelphia.
He is the author of many articles in the fields of psychiatry and
anthropology. Within this article, numbers in parentheses indicate
references at the end of the essay.

he made the necessary revisions in his theory of the etiology of the neuroses. Unfortunately, from that time onward he also began to ignore fairly consistently the very genuinely seductive behavior of parents,[2] perhaps because the concept of the Laius and Jocasta complexes was even more egodystonic and culturally objectionable than was the theory of the Oedipus complex, which, in a sense, merely confirmed the nineteenth-century adult's low opinion of children in general.[3] In certain later writers the scotomization of the Laius and Jocasta complexes appears to have led to the need to develop an elaborate, and not overconvincing, theory of a phylogenetically determined infantile fantasy life. This theory predicates that, regardless of how loving and humane the father may be, the infant will none the less view him primarily as a monster, because of instinctually determined and phylogenetically anchored fantasies of its own.

The trend away from the recognition of the seductive behavior of adults, which was bolstered up not only by Freud's genius and prestige but also by social pressure and by the analyst's own need to scotomize this anxiety-arousing idea, was too strong to be reversed even by the findings of Ferenczi (13) and of certain of his students, who stressed that, presumably by means of the "dialogue of the unconscious," children recognize the true instinctual roots of the tenderness which adults display toward them (23).

Actually, it is a matter of common experience that in sexual relations between adults and children—which are far less uncommon than one would like to believe—it is usually the adult who takes the initiative. Only in rare instances are the children the actual seducers (8).

The great popularity of Sophocles' Oedipus trilogy also tends to support this interpretation. It must be assumed that many members of the Greek audience found the play of absorbing interest precisely because they successfully—though perhaps unconsciously—identified themselves with the problems of certain major characters.[4] Alice Balint's analysis of the irrational and primitive aspects of the mother-child relationship (1) also lends plausibility to our inference that the women in Sophocles' audience must have had at least an unconscious empathy with Jocasta's problems. By extension, the male audience must likewise have felt a certain carefully repressed kinship with Laius, who, as we propose to show, was not a mere puppet of fate, but a psychologically consist-

ent and plausible person, whose character structure provides
us with the true explanation of his destiny.

## THE CHARACTER OF LAIUS

Laius' early life is vaguely reminiscent of that of Oedipus.
King Labdakos of Thebes died when Laius was but a year
old. A nobleman named Lykos (Wolf) usurped the throne,
and grievously wronged his niece Antiope. Later on, Antiope's
sons conquered Thebes, slew Lykos, and banished Laius, who
regained his throne only after the death of Antiope's sons. At
the time of his restoration to the throne Laius was already
burdened with a curse, which he had brought on himself
through an act of homosexual rape. It was this curse which
eventually culminated in the Oedipus tragedy (22).

Numerous Greek sources and fragments[5] reveal that Laius
was deemed to have been the inventor of pederasty. In his
early manhood, long before he married Jocasta and fathered
Oedipus, Laius fell violently in love with Chrysippus, son
of King Pelops. Instead of courting and winning the hand-
some youth, in a manner which the latter-day Greeks would
have deemed proper, he chose to kidnap him during the
sacred Nemean games, without seeking to obtain the consent
of King Pelops, which, Licht intimates, would probably have
been forthcoming. The enraged Pelops therefore laid upon
Laius the curse that his own son should slay him and then
marry his own mother. According to a later version it is the
Delphic oracle which informs Laius of Zeus's decision that
Laius' son would kill him in retribution for the rape of
Chrysippus. This curse seems to suggest that the Greek mind
linked Oedipus with Chrysippus—an inference which is
further substantiated by still another version of this myth,
according to which Hera was so greatly angered by the rape
of Chrysippus that she sent the Sphinx to ravage Thebes, in
order to punish the Thebans for having tolerated Laius'
homosexual escapade (20). The *Oidipodeia* is even more
specific in conjoining the fates of Chrysippus and of Oedipus.
According to this epic, Oedipus was exposed as a propitiatory
sacrifice, in order to appease Hera's wrath over the Chrysippus
incident (20). In other words, Hera caused Laius to lose
not only his youthful bedfellow Chrysippus but also his son
Oedipus.[6]

In this context it cannot be stressed strongly enough that
after the imposition of the curse, and especially after the

birth of Oedipus, almost nothing further is heard of Chrysippus, until the moment of the fatal encounter between Laius and Oedipus. At that point several sources once more bring Chrysippus into the plot, it being alleged that Laius and Oedipus fought each other because they were rivals for the love of Chrysippus. Yet, significantly, Chrysippus himself was not present during this combat, while, according to some sources, Jocasta did witness the death of Laius. Be that as it may, various versions of this myth clearly represent this combat as a homosexually motivated encounter. After this episode Chrysippus once more disappears, for all practical purposes, from the rest of the Oedipus myth. The over-all impression created by these various accounts is that, psychologically at least, Chrysippus is, in a sense, the representative of Oedipus' own passive homosexual characteristics, which were brought into being, or were at least aroused, by Laius' aggressive and homosexual impulses toward his son.

Regardless of whether this curse was uttered by Pelops in person, or by the Delphic oracle, it made a considerable impression upon even so impulsive a man as Laius. According to sources cited by Rank, Laius (self-castratively) refrained from cohabiting with Jocasta for several years, in order to avoid the risk of procreating a son.[7] However, on a certain occasion, when Laius was either drunk or else unable to resist Jocasta's seductiveness he succumbed to temptation and knowingly procreated a son, even though he well knew what calamities the birth of an heir would entail for him. Thus, after a period of self-restraint, Laius' self-destructive impulsiveness once more got out of hand, only to be followed by another futile (self-castrative) attempt to ward off the consequences of his second hasty sexual act by exposing the infant Oedipus.

Laius appears to have retained throughout life a propensity for unconsidered violence. This is clearly shown by his wanton aggression against the wayfarer Oedipus, which caused the latter to slay him.

This, however, is not the whole story. Indeed, there exist several versions of this incident, the best known being the story that Oedipus and Laius quarreled over the right to *pass first* over a certain *narrow road*. This incident appears to be a somewhat bowdlerized and symbolic version of certain far more explicit accounts of Laius' death. Rank quotes a series of sources, according to which Oedipus and Laius did

not quarrel over even so symbolic a trifle as the right to pass
first over a narrow road. Indeed, *Praxilla* affirms that not only
Laius but Oedipus himself was also in love with Chrysippus,
and the scholium to Euripides' *Phoenissae* is even more
explicit, in that it states outright that Oedipus killed Laius in
a quarrel over Chrysippus.

In apparent contradiction to this homosexual motive,
various sources quoted by Rank allege that the combat took
place in the presence of Jocasta. For example, Nikolaos
Damaskenos stated that incest between Oedipus and his
mother occurred immediately after the combat, while still
another source stresses that Oedipus *knowingly* raped his
mother. Furthermore, the *Oidipodeia* specifies that, after killing Laius, Oedipus deprived him both of his sword (castration) and of his belt. The latter deed suggests the feminization
of Laius, since, in ancient Greece, the undoing of a woman's
belt was a preliminary to intercourse. If this inference is
correct, Oedipus did more than kill his father and marry his
mother, in token of his heterosexual maturity. He also turned
the tables on his homosexual father, by castrating (sword)
and feminizing him (belt), as he himself had once been
castrated and feminized (pierced ankles) by Laius. If this be
so, then cohabitation with Jocasta was not only cohabitation
with the mother as a woman but also with the mother as the
representative of the now feminized homosexual paternal
ogre.

This latter inference gives added meaning to Gruppe's
opinion (16), cited by Rank, that Oedipus originally bested
the Sphinx—who, according to Rank, is a phallic mother—
in physical combat.[8] If Rank's inference is correct, then
Oedipus' triumph over the phallic mother—whose phallus,
needless to say, was derived from the father—represents both
a heterosexual and a homosexual victory and gesture of
triumph. Since this latter meaning of incest with the phallic
mother—that is, the combination of heterosexual relations with
the mother and of symbolic active homosexual relations with
the father—is a relatively novel inference, it is offered here
only as a tentative conclusion, and as a problem which may
well deserve further study.[9]

The important point in all these considerations is the fact
that our sources emphasize primarily the homosexual element
in the causation of Laius' death, and bring in the incest with
Jocasta only more or less as an afterthought, for example, as

the link which couples the tragedy of Laius with the latter fate of Oedipus Rex. Thus, it may not be too farfetched to suggest that cohabitation with Jocasta should be viewed primarily as a homosexual, and only epiphenomenally as a heterosexual, act, Oedipus' true love-hate object being the now feminized homosexual ogre Laius.

In this context it is important to remember that Greek mythology, which, after all, is our real authority in regard to the problem of Oedipus, did not derive Oedipus' hostility to Laius from heterosexual, but from homosexual, sources. Indeed, Oedipus is not even described as having been particularly fond of his foster mother, Queen Merope, while all accounts of his early life emphasize his devotion to his savior and foster father, King Polybus, who apparently represented the "good father" in Oedipus' unconscious. What we do find in Greek accounts is an explanation of Oedipus' aggression against Laius in terms of Laius' character structure: his propensity for homosexual rape, and for unconsidered, injudicious violence and overbearingness ("hubris").[10] Indeed, Laius is presented to us as a pederastic ogre—as a homosexual rapist rather than as a seducer—even before Oedipus was born. Licht also adds that when Laius married Jocasta he was deprived both of his real love object, Chrysippus, and of the hope of an heir (17). After the birth of Oedipus, Laius made himself guilty first of attempted infanticide, and, later on, of an attempt to kill his adult son in the course of a quarrel which the overbearing old man had wantonly started with the peaceful wayfarer Oedipus.

Be that as it may, Laius' character, as depicted by Greek mythology and tragedy alike, is not an attractive one, and corresponds rather closely to what clinical psychoanalysis found to be the small boy's conception of his father. Indeed, unlike many other tragic figures of Greek drama, Laius is not presented to us as a good man caught in the toils of fate, and having "an Appointment in Samarra" with death, but as a violator of good manners, which the Greeks deemed more important than good morals. In brief—and despite Oedipus' possible rivalry with Laius for the love of Chrysippus— Laius' death was not caused primarily by Oedipus' own incestuous impulses, but by Laius' character, which included both "hubris" and a tendency toward homosexual and other violence.

Despite the rivalry over Chrysippus, it is not asserted that

Oedipus himself was not partially motivated also by the
violent impulses connected with the normal Oedipus complex.
We simply suggest that, according to Greek data, Oedipus'
murderous and incestuous wishes were neither purely heterosexual nor truly spontaneous ones, but were induced by the
behavior of his father, Laius. In fact, it may even be
tentatively suggested that Oedipus' partly heterosexual attraction to Jocasta was to a certain extent motivated by his
desire both to escape and to gratify indirectly his own sado-
masochistic and homosexual wishes which had been stimulated by his father's behavior. At the same time, Oedipus'
marriage to Jocasta may also represent an unconscious attempt
at restitution, since he took Laius' place at Jocasta's side,[11]
and provided further heirs for the Kingdom of Thebes.[12]
Conversely, it may be permissible to suggest, at least tentatively, that aggressively homosexual paternal attitudes toward
the child may represent—in part at least—a defense against
murderous impulses elicited by the sight of the nursing
infant, whose very existence interferes with the formerly close
relationship between husband and wife.[13]

Our central thesis—that Oedipus' own impulses were stimulated by the behavior of his father—appears at least plausible
in the light of the preceding considerations. However, in order
to render this thesis even more convincing, and worthy of
being taken into account in actual clinical work, it is necessary
to examine rather closely the real, albeit unconscious, causes
of King Pelop's extreme wrath, and the motives which impelled him to utter *precisely* and *specifically* the rather
unusual curse that Laius' son should kill his father and wed
his mother.

## PELOPS, OEDIPUS, AND ELECTRA

Accoring to Licht, Pelops' wrath over the abduction of
Chrysippus should be understood as follows:

> The father [Pelops] is not driven to the curse because Laius
> loved a boy and was intimate with him, consequently not by the
> "unnatural nature" of his passion . . . but simply and solely
> because Laius steals the boy, and abducts him against his father's
> wish: it is not the perverted direction of the impulse that makes
> Laius guilty, but the violence employed by him. . . . Laius be-
> comes a curse-laden man in consequence of an offense against
> conventional form; he thought he might be allowed to abduct

the boy, when he could have sued for the beautiful prize freely and openly [17].

In other words, Laius is guilty of a breach of manners, rather than of morals, in a context—pedophilia—in which the Greeks manifested that "poetic chivalrousness" which the knights of the feudal period manifested toward women. Laius' behavior toward Chrysippus is, thus, an unusually clear-cut expression of "hubris"—excess and overbearingness—which, in Greek tragedy, is the cause of man's ultimate downfall.

These considerations refer, however, only to the conscious causes of Pelops' reaction to the rape of Chrysippus. On a deeper level the psychological problem of Pelops' wrath has an even more significant connection with the fate of Laius and of Oedipus.

More even than Oedipus himself, Pelops was familiar with the potential cruelty of fathers and father figures. Pelops was the son of the evil King Tantalus, who, from sheer overbearingness, wished to test the omniscience of the Immortals whom he presumed to invite to his palace as his guests. He therefore had young Pelops slain and served to the Immortals as the *pièce de résistance* of the feast he gave in their honor. Fortunately the Gods discovered the deed, but not before Demeter, still distressed by Persephone's loss, had absentmindedly eaten the dismembered Pelops' shoulder. At the request of the Immortals, either Rhea or else Clotho, one of the Fates, cast Pelops' remains into a caldron, from which he re-emerged alive, but with an ivory shoulder. The cannibalistic impulses of Tantalus are further underscored by the fact that his eternal punishment in Hades consisted of being "tantalized" by food and drink, and in his being in constant fear of death. Despite these evil deeds, Greek legends stress that Pelops honored his deceased cannibalistic father devoutly.

If we take into account only the best-known version of *The Feast of Tantalus*, it is hard to understand why Pelops should display such filial piety toward his brutally egotistical and cannibalistic father. Indeed, such devotion would be understandable only if, by some twist in his unconscious fantasy life, Pelops managed to construe this cannibalistic act as a token of love. This startling inference is strikingly confirmed by Pindar's *First Olympian Ode*, which Bunker (3) interprets *primarily* as a bowdlerized version of the original cannibalistic feast. According to Pindar, the Feast of Tantalus never took place at all. He assures us, instead, that the story of that feast was hollow gossip and that, in reality, Poseidon had abducted Pelops, with whom he was in love, and had taken him to the abode of the Immortals, just as Zeus brought Ganymede to Olympus. On the basis of the contrast between the original myth of the Feast of Tantalus and Pindar's version of Pelops' disappearance, Bunker concludes that *The Feast of Tantalus* is a disguised description of initiation ceremonies.

However, Pindar's version is not *simply* a bowdlerization of a cannibalistic myth which originated in ruder days. Rather does it enunciate the selfsame theme as the original myth, but in a language and by means of symbols which pertain to a *different stage* of psychosexual development. Specifically, the fate of Pelops which, in the earlier version, is told in the language of the oral stage, and represents the anxiety-laden and yet pleasurable fantasy experience of being devoured, appears in Pindar's version as an experience pertaining to the second phase of the Oedipus complex, and is presented to us as erotized submission to a divine homosexual father figure, Poseidon.

When seen in this light, Pelops' filial piety toward his ogre-like father Tantalus no longer appears to us as a paradox, but only as the one-sided—and highly erotized—expression of the positive component of Pelops' ambivalence toward his father, whose idealized representative is Pelops' homosexual divine lover Poseidon.

Yet Pelops could not have accepted without ambivalence his passive role either in the Feast of Tantalus or in his abduction by Poseidon, which so startlingly duplicates the abduction of his son Chrysippus by Laius. We must examine, therefore, also the manner in which Pelops expressed the hostile component of his ambivalence toward Tantalus. This was accomplished by means of a displacement of his hostility from its initial object Tantalus to Pelops' murderous father-in-law, King Oenomaus, ruler of Elis. Oenomaus had a daughter, Hippodamia, of whom it was prophesied that she would be married on the day her suitor slew her father.[14] Being cognizant of this prophecy, Oenomaus tried to fend off his daughter's suitors by proposing to them a chariot race. If the suitors lost, the king was at liberty to slay them, and, until Pelops arrived to sue for Hippodamia's hand, the king had

always succeeded in his designs. However, Pelops asked
Oenomaus' coachman Myrtilus, son of Hermes, to replace
the linchpin of his master's chariot with a waxen one. To
pay for this treachery, he promised that Myrtilus would be
permitted to share Hippodamia's favor (22).[15] The king
pursued Pelops and Hippodamia, and almost won the race,
when his sabotaged chariot disintegrated and he was killed.
Then, in order not to have to pay Myrtilus the promised
bribe, Pelops drowned his accomplice.

From the sociological point of view, this peculiar courtship
episode is understandable in terms of Frazer's discussion of
the transmission of kingly powers in early Greek society (14).
Apparently such powers were transmitted from the present
king to the king's son-in-law. Hence, in permitting his daughter to marry, the king automatically created a rival for his
throne, exactly as Laius provided a future king for Thebes
by fathering Oedipus. In this system, in which power was
transmitted from mother to daughter, although the exercise
of power was delegated to the spouse—a mechanism characteristic of matri*liny* as distinct from matri*archy*—the same
effect could be achieved by marrying either the mother or the
daughter. Thus, Oedipus married Jocasta, as Pelops married
Hippodamia, in order to be elevated to the throne. The fact
that Oedipus obtains Jocasta after mortal combat, while
Pelops obtains Hippodamia by means of a (murderous)
race, is fully explained by Frazer's proof that athletic competi-
tions for the bride were but attenuated latter-day representations of earlier mortal combats. The fact that Hippodamia
rode in Pelops' chariot is reminiscent of the practice of bride
theft.

From the psychoanalytic point of view, even if we disregard
the obvious symbolism of the chariot race, the sexual bribe
offered to Myrtilus, and the fact that he was killed so that the
bribe (*ius primae noctis?*) need not be paid, clearly suggests
that—psychologically speaking—King Oenomaus and his unfaithful coachman Myrtilus are one and the same person in
the eyes of Pelops, and that Oenomaus' murder was Oedipally
motivated. At the same time Myrtilus is perhaps also a part of
Pelops himself, who, after profiting by the treachery, kills his
accomplice. These deeds caused a blood guilt which gave
rise to the tragedy of Pelops' sons and also to that of
Electra.[16]

Indeed, Tantalus seems to have been psychologically

reincarnated in Pelops' vicious sons, Atreus and Thyestes. The latter seduced his brother's wife Aerope, and stole a marvelous golden ram given to Atreus by the gods, in token of sovereignity over Mycenae.[17] Atreus first banished Thyestes, then feigned to be reconciled with him, and set before him *a dish made of the flesh of Thyestes' own children*. Thyestes then departed, but first placed a curse upon his brother Atreus. This curse eventually caused the tragedy of Electra, precisely as the curse of Pelops caused the tragedy of Oedipus. Indeed, Thyestes soon discovered that he could be avenged on his brother *by cohabiting with his own daughter, Pelopia*.[18] The son born of this union, Aegisthus, is the killer of Agamemnon and the lover of Clytaemnestra, who is then slain by Orestes and Electra—a deed which, to psychoanalysts, is the prototypal expression of the Electra complex. These events confirm the validity of our thesis that the legend of the Pelopids is intimately connected with that of the house of Laius. It will be sufficient, however, if, in this context, we summarize only King Pelops' connections with the death of Laius.

The legend of Pelops—who was both cannibalized and homosexually raped by his father, respectively by the father figure Poseidon, and who nonetheless devoutly revered his father even though he slew his father-in-law—explains precisely why Pelops was so enraged by Chrysippus' abduction, and why he chose to curse Laius in so highly distinctive a manner. The chief features of Pelops' conflict may be summarized as follows:

1. Pelops behaves toward Chrysippus as a fond father should behave. In doing so he performs a highly complex action, since, on the one hand, he shows Tantalus how he *should* have treated him, and, on the other hand, shows Poseidon how he should *not* have treated him.

2. Laius' deed enraged Pelops beyond all measure, probably because Laius, in raping Chrysippus, acted out one of Pelops' own most severely repressed impulses, and at the same time reawakened Pelops' own passive homosexual conflicts.

3. The curse which Pelops laid on Laius is quite clearly rooted in Pelops' own conflicts: Oedipus is to slay his father Laius and then marry his mother Jocasta. This curse gives us the true unconscious meaning of Pelops' killing his father-in-law on the very day on which he married Hippodamia, these

deeds reflecting the displacement of his Oedipal homosexual hostility from Tantalus and Poseidon to Oenomaus and Myrtilus.

## Character and Fate in Greek Drama

The analysis of Laius' character, and of the character and curse of Pelops' casts a great deal of doubt upon the validity of the traditional conception of Greek tragedy as an account of man's helplessness in the face of undeserved fate. Laius' death at the hands of Oedipus is not the trigger event which sets in motion the millstones of the gods. Rather it is a rigidly determined consequence of Laius' own character structure, just as the nature of the curse laid upon him is an unavoidable consequence of Pelops' own passive homosexual conflicts and of his repressed murderous hatred of his father Tantalus, which was displaced to, and then acted out in, the killing of Oenomaus and of Myrtilus. Thus, in a very genuine sense, we must credit the Greek poets and dramatists with more psychological acumen than we have so far done. What they called "Fate" was merely the personification of man's character structure and of his need to act out those of his intrapsychic conflicts which determine the course of his life. The role which the Greek tragedians assigned to the character trait "hubris," as a determinant of man's tragic fate, at once confirms this view, and casts a vivid light upon the social psychology or Greek society, in which a character structure involving hubris was the one least well adapted to the demands of society. At the same time the need to manifest overbearingness and excess must have been very strong indeed in a society which professed to follow the path of the "golden mean" (which is the true meaning of the constantly misused term *aurea mediocritas*). This subjective need to escape the bounds of the golden mean explains why the Greek dramatists not merely condemned but also admired and pitied those whose hubris brought about their downfall.[19]

In brief, Greek drama is not a tragedy set in motion by a fate external to man, but by man's character structure and latent conflicts, witness the adage that whom the gods wish to destroy they first render mad. If we replace "the Gods" with parental figures, this adage confirms our interpretation of the characterological and conflictual sources of Greek tragic destinies. This fact was simply obscured by the Greeks' habit of personifying character structure as "Fate," and also by the fact that the dramatist dealt with well-known mythical personages, whose background and early history were expected to be familiar to the audience. In other words, it is very much to be doubted whether the intelligent Greek attending the representation of Sophocles' *Oedipus Trilogy* was unaware of Laius' character and early history, and accepted the thesis that Laius' death was predetermined by fate in the literal sense. It must be presumed that he accepted this thesis simply as a poetically appropriate allegorical reference to Laius' personality, since at that time—and until very recently—explicit "psychologizing" was not considered to be a poetical or even a literary device. The dramatist was therefore compelled to achieve plausibility—both psychological and other—by means which the society from which his audience was recruited was culturally conditioned to accept as "literary plausibility."[20] It might also be added that these considerations further justify the psychological and psychoanalytic interpretation of nominally nonpsychologically formulated narratives and myths.

## CONCLUDING HYPOTHESES

The following remarks, and in particular the remarks which pertain to clinical problems, are offered in a very tentative manner. They should be viewed, not as conclusions in the strict sense of this term, but as attempts to indicate the location of certain problem areas in psychoanalytic theory, which deserve to be explored further. The fact that they have been expressed in the form of simple declarative sentences should not be taken as an indication that they represent statements of fact or time-tested theoretical insights. We have used simple declarative statements solely because we did not wish to encumber our statements with monotonous and repetitive warnings that all our remarks are highly tentative and stand in need of a great deal of further confirmation.

This being said, the material presented in the preceding pages suggests that the following hypotheses stand in need of further study:

### (1) HISTORY OF PSYCHOANALYSIS

Culturally determined scotomata may be responsible for the tendency to minimize the significance of the Laius complex and of the Jocasta complex, which complement the Oedipus complex.

## (2) METAPSYCHOLOGY

An analysis of the Oedipus myth does not seem to support
the thesis that biological and/or phylogenetic factors are
*primarily* responsible for the Oedipus complex. The notion
that the child's psyche is a "chamber of horrors" for *biological*
reasons is also contradicted by Freud's thesis (15), further
elaborated by the writer (11), that instincts become luxuriant
and monstrous *only as a result of repression*. As suggested
elsewhere (10, 12) it may be necessary to assume that the
child's sensitiveness even to minimal aggression may be
epiphenomenal to its sensitiveness to minimal tokens of love,
since the latter appears to be one of the child's chief psychic
homeostatic mechanisms.

## (3) PSYCHOSEXUAL DEVELOPMENT

The Oedipus complex appears to be a consequence of the
child's sensitiveness to its parents' sexual and aggressive
impulses. Homosexual conflicts may play a greater role in the
genesis and development of the Oedipus complex than has
hitherto been suspected.

## (4) CLINICAL IMPLICATIONS

It may be worth while to investigate to what extent heterosexual impulses directed to the parent of the opposite sex
include and/or disguise also homosexual impulses directed to
the parent of the same sex. Genitality seems to mean more
than the attainment of heterosexuality pure and simple. In
the case of males it also seems to require a shift from sublimated passive to sublimated active homosexuality, and, in
the case of women, a shift from sublimated active to sublimated passive homosexuality. It may even be possible to
assume that "activity" and "passivity" in the sexual sphere
may be derived from homosexual rather than from heterosexual sources, since these attitudes are closely related to
aggression, which belongs to the pregenital stage of psycho-
sexual development.

## (5) APPLIED PSYCHOANALYSIS

(*a*) *The Oedipus Myth.* The early history of Laius seems
to provide us with data which are fundamental for the
understanding of the entire Oedipus myth. These data appear
to express the Greeks' insight into the external and realistic
sources of the male child's tendency to view his father as

a homosexual ogre, and of his desire to exchange roles with
the father also in this respect.

(b) *Greek Literature.* A study of the problem of Laius
suggests that, especially in Greek drama, "Fate" is actually
a personification of character structure.

(c) *Mythology.* We found that whenever there exist
divergent and even seemingly contradictory versions of a
given mythical episode, these variants not only do not contradict each other psychologically but actually supplement each
other, and help us obtain a deeper insight into the latent
nuclear meaning of the basic theme, motif, or plot element.
For example, we found that the bowdlerized explanation of
the causes of the quarrel between Laius and Oedipus not only
repeats in a symbolic form (narrow road) the sexual theme
which is explicitly mentioned in other sources but also helps
us obtain a deeper insight into Laius' character structure,
which is of paramount importance for the understanding of
the entire Oedipus myth.[21] Furthermore, the various unexpurgated versions, some of which highlight the role of
Jocasta, while others highlight that of Chrysippus, enable us
in turn to discover the combined heterosexual and homosexual
undercurrent in the male child's struggle against his father and
in his love for his mother. As regards the legend of Pelops,
the striking contrast between the traditional version of *The
Feast of Tantalus* and Pindar's theory that Pelops was abducted by Poseidon amounts to little more than the presentation of the basic theme—erotized passivity in the face of
aggression—in oral, respectively in homosexual-Oedipal,
terms. This suggests that a given theme has an inherent and
specific latent significance, which no amount of voluntary or
involuntary, or else conscious or unconscious, distortion can
obliterate. In fact, such distortions serve only to highlight
certain additional psychological implications of the basic
theme. Thus in mythology, as in dream work, we seem to be
constantly confronted with the basic fact that *plus ça change,
plus c'est la même chose.* This finding may have an important
bearing not only upon the study of dreams, fantasies, and
mythology but also upon such everyday matters as false
perception, the embellished and distorted rumor, deliberate
lying, false evidence in courts of law, and so on, all of which,
though being distortions of the manifest content, probably
adhere rather closely to the latent content. Finally, this
inference also has a bearing upon those clinical psychological

tests in which the subject is expected to repeat a story told to him, as well as upon such partially structured projective tests as the Rorschach, the TAT, and probably also the Draw-a-Man Test.[22] Needless to say, these suppositions are fully compatible with classical psychoanalytic theory.

The one conclusion which we can offer with any degree of confidence is that, as long as there are human beings, the task of psychoanalytic research will never be finished.

## NOTES

[1] Offhand, the writer can think of only one author who devoted considerable attention to the Jocasta complex, and that author was not a psychoanalyst but an anthropologist (19).

[2] This development led to a shift toward greater conservativeness in matters pertaining to the ethics of sexual acts, and also to the theory of the death instinct, or primary self-aggression, which psychoanalytically well-informed theologians have sometimes compared to the doctrine of original sin.

[3] This outlook—represented, e.g., by such attitudes as "spare the rod and spoil the child," or "children should be seen and not heard"—had as its complement the conception of the "angelic" nature of children. Similar institutionalizations of ambivalence toward children also occur in primitive society (5).

[4] Licht records that a rather cynical and hedonistic defense of incest—in terms of the thesis that whatever gives pleasure is good —occurring in one of Euripides' plays was hooted by the audience so violently that the line had to be changed to an admission that whatever is dishonorable *is* dishonorable, regardless of how pleasant it may be. Of course, in this instance, the incest enacted on the stage was that of a brother and a sister, which was both psychologically and economically unacceptable to parents in the audience (17).

[5] According to Licht, these sources include: the epic *Oidipodeia*, *Praxilla*, a fragmentary play by Euripides, a fragmentary play by Aeschylus, and some other fragments (17).

[6] Hera's anger over this incident is, in itself, a problem of some magnitude, which can be only partially understood in terms of her position as the custodian of family life and in terms of her own experiences with Zeus's various heterosexual and homosexual loves. Her choice of the Sphinx—whom Rank (20) views as a phallic woman—as the special instrument of her further retribution is equally perplexing. Unfortunately, lack of space prevents us from discussing this matter in detail, and forces us to content ourselves with pointing out the existence of this interesting mythological problem.

[7] Some aspects of the problem of chastity in marriage were discussed in another essay (9) in connection with certain ancient

Indian traditions regarding two kings, each of whom killed a
father figure at the very moment when the latter was engaging
in marital relations.

⁸ If the Sphinx was killed in a physical combat, then its death
was, in a sense, similar to the death which Laius brought upon
himself. If the Sphinx killed itself after Oedipus guessed its riddle,
the suicide of the Sphinx approximates that of Jocasta. These
seemingly divergent versions of the same plot element therefore
actually converge and further support the thesis that Jocasta, when
"raped" by Oedipus, represented both herself and the castrated
and feminized Laius.

⁹ A Hungarian military joke specifically describes an incident in
which adultery with the wife is at the same time represented as
anal cohabitation with the woman's husband, thus further sub-
stantiating well-known theories of paranoid jealousy.

¹⁰ Only rarely—and then primarily in those versions which attribute Laius' death to a quarrel over the right of way—is there
any mention of Oedipus' own proneness to violence, which it is
specified, *is similar to that of Laius*. In other words, even where
impulsiveness is attributed also to Oedipus, this character trait
of the son is derived from, or correlated with, the father's character structure.

¹¹ In certain primitive societies the murderer is adopted as a
replacement for the murdered kinsman (6).

¹² The providing of heirs is analyzed elsewhere (9).

¹³ In many primitive societies cohabitation is prohibited during
the long period of lactation. This situation, as it pertains, e.g., to
the Sioux Indians, has been discussed elsewhere (11).

¹⁴ In this connection, too, Pelops' fate is similar to that of a
personage in the Oedipus myth. Just as Laius had to protect his
life against his son Oedipus, so Oenomaus stood in danger of
death from his daughter's suitor Pelops.

¹⁵ According to another version Pelops' victory was due to the
direct intervention of Pelops' erstwhile lover Poseidon who, at the
crucial moment, caused the wheel of Oenomaus' chariot to become
detached (24).

¹⁶ A note on unconscious insight may not be out of place in this
context. Rose, whose style is usually of exemplary clarity, at this
particular point failed to make it clear whether the blood guilt
which Pelops had to shoulder was for the death of Oenomaus or
for that of Myrtilus (22). Since Rose was not an analyst, his
slip is of special interest, in that it reveals his unconscious insight
into the identity of Oenomaus and Myrtilus. Correctly stated, the
myth records that the blood guilt fell upon Pelops as a result of
the murder of Myrtilus.

¹⁷ Compare here the story that Tantalus concealed a golden
dog, sacred to Zeus, which had been stolen by a thief from
Zeus's shrine.

[18] In one of the Bantu tribes a man setting out to hunt a dangerous beast first commits incest, so that his terribleness shall match that of the hunted beast.

[19] The psychological situation obtaining in Pueblo Indian society is very much the same. These tribes profess to follow a way of life which Ruth Benedict has characterized as Apollonian (2). Yet, we do know that underneath this peaceful façade there bubbles a witch's caldron of hate, which finds expression in constant panicky preoccupation with witchcraft (25, 11). As regards the tendency to condemn with admiration those guilty of violating the social norm, we learn that in Central Australia those guilty of incest are "condemned with admiration" (21). The same attitude also prevails in at least one of the Moi tribes of French Indochina (4).

[20] The problems of the cultural and psychological formulation of the criteria of literary plausibility are discussed elsewhere (7).

[21] It is of considerable interest that Laius' character structure, i.e., his proneness to unconsidered violence, is put in relief more strikingly in the bowdlerized than in those unexpurgated versions of this incident in which the grosser instinctual elements are more prominent. This is not surprising, since character formation results from attempts to cope with the instincts and with unmanageable external stimulation.

[22] These considerations seem to provide a theoretical basis for an interesting idea advanced by Linton in a private conversation (18). He suggested that divergent versions of primitive tales may represent a kind of cultural Thematic Apperception Test, in which the basic plot—corresponding to a TAT picture—is subjectively elaborated by various tellers of tales.

## References

1. Balint, A., Liebe zur Mutter und Mutterliebe," *Int. Ztschr. f. Psa. u. Imago*, XXIV (1939), pp. 33–48.

2. Benedict, R., *Patterns of Culture*, Routledge, London, 1934.

3. Bunker, H. A., "The Feast of Tantalus," *Psa. Quart.*, XXI (1952), pp. 355–372.

4. Devereux, G., *Moi Field Notes*, Manuscript.

5. Devereux, G., "Mohave Beliefs Concerning Twins," *Am. Anthropologist*, XLIII (1941), pp. 573–592.

6. Devereux, G., "Social Structure and the Economy of Affective Bonds," *Psa. Rev.*, XXIX (1942), pp. 303–314.

7. Devereux, G., "Mohave Coyote Tales," *J. Am. Folklore*, LXI (1948), pp. 233–255.

8. Devereux, G., "Status, Socialization and Interpersonal Relations of Mohave Children," *Psychiatry*, XIII (1950), pp. 489–502.

9. Devereux, G., "The Oedipal Situation and Its Consequences in the Epics of Ancient India," *Samiksa*, V (1951), pp. 5–13.

10. Devereux, G., "Cultural and Characterological Traits of the Mohave Related to the Anal Stage of Psychosexual Development," *Psa. Quart.*, XX (1951), pp. 398–422.

11. Devereux, G., *Reality and Dream: The Psychotherapy of a Plains Indian*, International Universities Press, New York, 1951.

12. Devereux, G., "The Technique of Analyzing Occult Occurrences in Analysis," in *Psychoanalysis and the Occult*, International Universities Press, New York, 1953.

13. Ferenczi, S., "Confession of Tongues Between the Adult and the Child," *Int. J. Psa.*, XXX (1949), pp. 225–230.

14. Frazer, Sir J. G., "The Succession to the Kingdom of Ancient Latium," in *The Magic Art, The Golden Bough*, Macmillan, London, 1951.

15. Freud, S. (1915), "Repression," *Collected Papers*, IV, Hogarth Press, London, 1925.

16. Gruppe, O., *Griechische Mythologie und Religionsgeschichte*, Beck, München, 1897–1906.

17. Licht, H., *Sexual Life in Ancient Greece*, Routledge, London, 1932.

18. Linton, R., Personal Communication.

19. Raglan, L., *Jocasta's Crime*, Methuen, London, 1933.

20. Rank, O., *Das Inzestmotiv in Dichtung und Sage*, Deuticke, Leipzig, 1912.

21. Róheim, G., "Psycho-Analysis of Primitive Cultural Types," *Int. J. Psa.*, XIII (1932), pp. 1–224.

22. Rose, H. J., *A Handbook of Greek Mythology*, Methuen, London, 1928.

23. Rotter, L. K., "A Nöi Genitalitas Pzichológiájáról," in *Lélekelemzési Tanulmáyok* (Ferenczi Memorial Volume), Somlo, Budapest, 1933.

24. Schwab, G., *Gods and Heroes*, Pantheon, New York, 1946.

25. Simmons, L. W., Ed., *Sun Chief*, Yale University Press, New Haven, 1942.

*Simon O. Lesser**

# THE SOURCE OF GUILT
# AND THE SENSE OF GUILT

## KAFKA'S "THE TRIAL"

### I

There are two miraculous things about *The Trial* and the
other stories of Franz Kafka. Such fantasies could occur only
to an exceptionally rare kind of person: one disturbed almost
to the point of psychosis and yet sufficiently integrated,
sufficiently courageous, to face, indeed to want to capture,
precisely the most unpleasant truths about himself and his
world—to be willing "to cross the supersonic thresholds of
the mind"[1] in quest of them. The second miracle is that the
fantasies were not only faced, permitted to register on the
mind, but worked out to completion or virtual completion
and written down. It is not surprising that Kafka left some
of his works unfinished and wanted most of them destroyed
after his death. The marvel is that he accomplished as much
as he did. This frail, shortlived man, who did not feel free
to give his whole time to writing and dealt with material
from which most writers would recoil, produced three novels,
two of them of the very first rank, and many short stories,
fables, meditations, and parables, some of them indubitably
great. Kafka was a dedicated man. At a cost in loneliness
and suffering which if it were not for some of his own stories,
such as "A Hunger Artist," we could perhaps not even
comprehend, he made explorations in terrifying realms. His
discoveries have enormously enlarged the world of experience
open to us through prose fiction.

The plot of *The Trial* has become well known. The novel
opens with a sentence at once as colloquial and as captivating
as a good news-story lead: "Someone must have been telling
lies about Joseph K., for without having done anything wrong
he was arrested one fine morning."[2] K. is a bank official and
a bachelor. The arrest takes place on his thirtieth birthday in
his room at the boardinghouse of Frau Grubach. A preliminary hearing is held in an adjacent room, which has recently

* SIMON O. LESSER is the author of *Fiction and the Unconscious*.
He studied at the University of Chicago and Columbia University
and at the Chicago and New York Psychoanalytic Institutes.

been occupied by a Fräulein Bürstner, a typist to whom K. is attracted. K. has a fugitive desire to dismiss the whole business as a practical joke; he blusters a good deal, and protests his innocence. He seeks—in vain—to find out just what authority it is which is arresting him and the nature of the crime with which he is charged. He is destined never to learn the answer to these questions or to acquire an understanding of the laws, procedures, and ultimate meaning of the mysterious Court before which he is summoned to appear. K. becomes progressively more absorbed in his case until practically all his time and energies are devoted to it; he becomes less and less able to give his attention to his work at the bank. He retains an advocate, and exerts himself to prove his innocence or at any rate reach some sort of understanding with the merciless tribunal by which he is being judged. Yet, for all his efforts, he becomes increasingly convinced of his own guilt and reconciled to the need for being punished. When on the eve of his thirty-first birthday two men in frock coats come to his lodgings, K.—though he has not been informed of their coming—is waiting for them. He is also dressed in black. He goes with the men, not seeking help, indeed pulling his companions away from a policeman who, it seemed, was about to question them. In a deserted stone quarry on the outskirts of the town, the group comes to a halt. While one of the partners holds K., the other thrusts a knife into his heart.

Even in broad outline the story seems at once meaningful and baffling, and the outline gives no sense of the richness of the novel. Each detail of *The Trial*, and not simply, as with some other novels, the legend as a whole, seems charged with meaning. The immense literature which has grown up about *The Trial* since its posthumous publication in German in 1925 and in English in 1937 is proof of the significance the book possesses for at least the present generation of readers. A sampling of this literature may help both to illuminate this particular work and to enlarge our understanding of the kind of communication which may occur in reading any moving and meaningful story.

## II

Among the many interpretations of *The Trial* which might have been considered, I have tried to select a few which seem to me to be representative of the *kinds* of response the novel has provoked. There are difficulties in dealing with even this handful of interpretations adequately, for most of them are elaborately developed. Since I shall have to indicate what I regard as acceptable and what mistaken about each of these interpretations, perhaps the best procedure is to start by indicating what *The Trial* means to me. Some circularity, however, may be unavoidable: my own reading of the novel may have been shaped in part by the natural tendency to extend, qualify, or quarrel with the points made by other critics.

On the deepest level, *The Trial* seems to me a quasi-abstract story of a man's mental and spiritual collapse—of what is sometimes loosely called a nervous breakdown, but can be more accurately described as a psychotic episode.[3] More schematically, it is the story of the disintegration of an initially none too strong ego under the onslaught of a suddenly angry and implacable superego. This onslaught is caused by certain instinctual impulses which are unacceptable and which reactivate the emotional turmoil, the tabooed desires, and, above all, the fears and guilt feelings associated with the Oedipus conflict.

Though they sometimes fuse, there are two distinct strands to the story of *The Trial*. There is, first, the story of certain *specific* conflicts faced by Joseph K., in the present and in the past. It is to be noted, however, that—quite deliberately, I think—this phase of the story is only lightly and incompletely developed. For Kafka is simultaneously telling the story of another struggle which is in some ways even more bitter than the Oedipal conflicts which are recalled and relived, in memory and in terms of actual experiences, in the course of *The Trial*. This is the struggle against generalized authority, generalized guilt—in short, against the superego, the "Court" whose jurisdiction can never be escaped this side of death or madness because it is part of our personality itself.

The fact that *The Trial* has at once this specific and abstract reference accounts for its perculiar power and appeal. If Kafka had patterned the novel more closely and exclusively on his own love for F. (who is undoubtedly the prototype of Fräulein Bürstner in *The Trial*),[4] he could still have produced a moving story, for this love, which he could never consummate by marriage, threw him into agonizing conflict and, as one can see more clearly in "The Judgment," mobilized the whole cluster of feelings associated with the Oedipal

situation. But in *The Trial* Kafka goes further than he did in
"The Judgment" in disguising the autobiographical material.
The father, *in propria persona,* is omitted, and Fräulein
Bürstner and K.'s feeling for her are only lightly sketched
in, so that the abstract strand of reference can receive
simultaneous development. Though by itself this stand might
have been less compelling than the first, it is also fertile
material for a novel. As indicated, it too has a significant
"objective correlative" in the world of our emotional experience: it mirrors the never-ceasing struggle with the superego.

We regard *The Trial* as a masterpiece because it fuses and
permits us to deal simultaneously and economically with
these two basic emotional preoccupations. Many of the
characters and incidents in the novel are overdetermined; in
responding to them we simultaneously act out our feelings
toward individual authority figures and toward authority in
the abstract. Besides the obvious contribution this makes to
the richness and intensity of our response, this double strand
of reference heightens our reaction in a more subtle way: it
cues two different, and complementary, *kinds* of response.
The specific strand encourages us to identify with K.; the
abstract strand, to project ourself into the novel in our own
person, to "analogize."[5] Since, for example, the causes of K.'s
guilt are only faintly indicated, we tend to supply the explanation for it out of our own knowledge and experience. We fill in
the blank spaces with reminiscences of the things which cause
us guilt; we evoke our own conflicts, our own "trial." *The
Trial* furnishes an unexcelled example of the kind of story
which permits us to deal with our own problems while
ostensibly (and so far as we ourselves know) we are "just
reading."

One final point: the degree of abstractness in *The Trial*
corresponds to the situation which usually prevails in life
itself. Like Joseph K., most of us know our own suffering, but
we know ourselves less well. Though we may be aware of
some of the weaknesses in ourselves against which we must
struggle, we can seldom track down the original weaknesses,
the more remote failures, which may have burdened us with
such an abiding sense of guilt that even hard-won victories
over temptation in the present can relieve it only temporarily.
Nor are we any more successful in identifying the institutional
arrangements which oppress and thwart us so cleverly that,
except in occasional flashes of lucidity, we tend to believe

that in some mysterious way we rather than they are responsible for all the deprivations and sufferings to which we are subjected.

Of the fact that *The Trial* is concerned with internal conflicts there is more evidence than can or need be cited. The point receives continuous stress. During his first interrogation K. says: "You may object that it is not a trial at all; you are quite right, for it is only a trial if I recognize it as such" (page 51). In the cathedral scene, toward the end of the book, the priest reminds K. of the same thing: ". . . the Court makes no claim upon you. It receives you when you come and relinquishes you when you go" (page 279).

Whole scenes of the novel bear the mark of being born of K.'s wishes and fears, of being dramatizations of half-desired, half-dreaded events. The arrest scene which opens the novel and the execution scene which closes it are the most conspicuous examples, but in between there are many others: the whipping scene (which perhaps because of its peculiar vividness seems almost like a dream within a dream), the arrival of K.'s uncle, and the meeting and discussion with Block. Though not always so obviously as in these instances, the entire novel may be said to be composed of such scenes: it is a series of objectified dreams mirroring K.'s thought processes at particular times and tracing his gradual disintegration.

In the same way, most if not all of the characters in *The Trial* can be regarded as projections—as evocations of the father, the mother, siblings, splinters of K. himself. At the same time they have sufficient objective validity, as have the dramatized representations of K.'s thoughts and problems. In form *The Trial* is always a story, not an interior monologue.

Kafka's capacity to write objectively without ever losing sight of the essentially subjective nature of his material is most triumphantly shown in the way he dramatizes K.'s struggle with his superego. Critics have seen the "Court" as a symbol of social convention, the bureaucratic or Fascistic state, capitalism, even God. It is each of these and all of these; and, because it is, on one level *The Trial* is a tale of man versus oppressive and inadequately understood external authority. But beyond any question the Court is also a projection of the persecuting superego. The whole novel bears witness to the psychical validity of this, and in Kafka's depiction of the Law-Court offices, the only fixed and visible locus of the Court's authority, the superego may even be said to

receive physical representation. The offices occupy an indefinite number of (one feels) mostly small cubicles; they are
invariably situated in low-lying attics; they are poorly lighted
so that whatever people happen to be present and whatever
activities are taking place are usually perceived, if at all,
in a confused, ambiguous way. Kafka's description seems
to echo an archetypal way of imagining an institution of the
mind. Rounding out the representation, the qualities attributed to the Court mirror, in condensed fashion, both the
functions of the superego of which K. is most painfully aware
and his own defensive reactions, past and present, toward
it and toward the parental figures whose aspirations and
decrees it inherited: the Court is stern, judicial, punitive—
and unwarrantedly so because it itself is irrational, lustful, and
corrupt. With a kind of knowledge almost too comprehensive
and systematic to be called intuitive, Kafka lets us know that,
whatever else it was, K.'s trial was an internal struggle also.

Before exploring the meaning of *The Trial* in greater detail,
we must take cognizance of two important aspects of Kafka's
art which are closely related but distinguishable: his exploitation of ambivalence and of ambiguity. The qualities are never
stressed, as in some of Kafka's imitators, for decorative effect.
They are an integral part of the understanding of human
behavior and the human predicament Kafka is seeking to
convey, and they have important narrative functions.

K.'s ambivalence is stressed either to explain his behavior
in full or to account for what might otherwise seem an excessive or inadequate response. It is K.'s compulsive desire
for Fräulein Bürstner which precipitates the superego onslaught that in the end demolishes his ego. Since the desire
reactivates such deep guilt feelings and fears that it cannot
be faced, it is not surprising that it has devastating effects.
Nevertheless, for it to destroy K. as it does, it must be
assumed that in a sense he wants to be destroyed. From
the very beginning he feels a desire to submit to some strong
and protective, albeit castrating, authority; his ego is looking
for an opportunity to abdicate its precarious sovereignty. This
desire might be regarded as K.'s tragic flaw, the weakness
which leads ultimately to his defeat and death. The central
conflict of the novel is whether this desire or the integrative
forces of the ego will prevail.

The dependency wishes manifest themselves very early in
the novel; they gradually gain complete sway. When Franz,

one of the warders who arrest K., shouts that the inspector wants to see him, K. finds that "the command . . . was actually welcome to him" (page 13). K. is summoned to his first interrogation, but the following Sunday he reports to the Court without having been summoned. While in the empty interrogation chambers, he gets so weak that he practically has to be carried out. Finally he hears a voice saying, "First he wants to go, then you tell him a hundred times that the door is in front of him and he makes no move to go" (page 90). In the Cathedral scene, K. hears himself called. He wavers: he knows that he is still free, but that "if he were to turn round he would be caught, for that would amount to an admission . . . that he was really the person addressed, and that he was ready to obey" (page 264).

In addition to securing representation in such ways as these, at various points the dependency wishes express themselves through self-defeating tendencies, for example, by some form of defiance which at once masks and reveals the wish to be overcome. In every major episode of the novel K. vacillates between submissiveness and the protection of his own autonomy. Thus ambivalence lies at the very heart of *The Trail*. The book is a legend of our confused feelings toward ourselves, our own impulses, authority figures, and social institutions.

More consistently perhaps than any other prose writer, Kafka also exploits the ambiguity characteristic of our experience. The ambiguity is related to the ambivalence: in a sense is its intellectual analogue. Compulsives[6]—and among other things, Joseph K., like his creator, is a compulsive—develop alternative explanations of events to express their ambivalence and to avoid decisions; their thinking is a mechanism of defense. Thus it is not surprising that ambiguity rules in Kafka's world, where the meaning of everyone and everything—the Court, the whipping continually going on in the lumber room at the Bank—seems ultimately lost in mist. Sometimes the ambiguity is a direct expression of emotional ambivalence. "Was the Advocate seeking to comfort him or to drive him to despair?" (page 158). Later, K. wavers among various explanations of the Advocate's conduct. Two of these are hostile, but one would suggest the desirability of retaining the Advocate, the second of giving him up: "Was it personal affection for K.'s uncle, or did he really regard the case as so extraordinary that he hoped to win prestige

either from defending K. or—a possibility not to be excluded—
from pandering to his friends in the Court?" (page 235).

At other times the ambiguity simply reflects K.'s inability
to determine the real meaning of something. "The Inspector
was possibly of the same mind, K. fancied, as far as he could
tell from a hasty side glance. But it was equally possible that
the Inspector had not even been listening . . ." (p. 19). And
there is the moment of tremulous hope before his execution:

His glance fell on the top storey of the house adjoining the
quarry. With a flicker as of a light going up, the casements of a
window there suddenly flew open; a human figure, faint and in-
substantial at that distance and that height, leaned abruptly far
forward and stretched both arms still farther. Who was it? A
friend? A good man? Someone who sympathized? Someone who
wanted to help? Was it one person only? Or were they all there?
Was help at hand? Were there some arguments in his favor that
had been overlooked? [pages 287–288]

A moment's reflection will convince us that this sort of
ambiguity, like the kind which expresses our ambivalence, is a
pervasive if neglected characteristic of our everyday life.
Whether we are trying to understand the ultimate source of
authority, the laws which govern human life, or the basis of
our friends' actions, we can arrive at absolutely unequivocal
explanations only if we are fools. Kafka is the dramatist of
the inescapable uncertainty of our experience.

### III

"Ever since I can remember," wrote Kafka in his famous
Letter to his Father, "a deep anxiety about safeguarding my
mental existence has made me indifferent to everything
else."[7] There is evidence that Joseph K., like his creator,
expended a great deal of psychic energy in preventing just
such mental crisis as he goes through in *The Trial:*

If immediately on wakening I had got up without troubling my
head about Anna's absence [he explains to Frau Grubach] . . .
all this would have been nipped in the bud. But one is so un-
prepared. In the Bank, for instance, I am always prepared, nothing
of that kind could possibly happen to me there, I have my own
attendant, the general telephone and the office telephone stand
before me on my desk, people keep coming in to see me, clients
and clerks, and above all my mind is always on my work and
so kept on the alert. [pages 26–27]

But one cannot always keep busy, and those last minutes in bed are a natural time for daydreaming and, on the morning of one's thirtieth birthday, for stocktaking.

A natural time, too, for thinking of the typist in a nearby room, whose appearance and actions may have suggested to K. that she was not inaccessible.[8] The fact that K. is "called" to her room may have more than one meaning. Though he can never acknowledge his desire for Fräulein Bürstner, it is made unmistakably clear. K. feels compelled to discuss his "case" with her and waits up for her until half-past eleven, in his fear of missing her postponing his dinner and a visit to Elsa, a prostitute whom he is accustomed to seeing once a week. His talk with Fräulein Bürstner ends up with compulsive love-making. " 'I'm just coming,' K. said, rushed out, seized her, and kissed her first on the lips, then all over the face, like some thirsty animal lapping greedily at a spring of long-sought fresh water" (page 38).

Fräulein Bürstner's connection with K.'s "case" is made clear to us in many other ways—for example, by K.'s hostile feelings toward the other male boarder, Captain Lanz, and by his asking for someone by that name on his first visit to the Interrogation Commission. When K. tells his Uncle about his case, he mentions the Fräulein only once, because, he assures himself, she has no connection with it. One does not need to be aware of Freud's observation that in situations like this the negative can be disregarded to realize that Kafka has introduced the denial only to remind us of the connection.

The most dramatic evidence of the connection is the reappearance of Fräulein Bürstner in the concluding scene of the novel. K. has a momentary impulse to resist and escape from the men who are leading him to his death:

And then before them Fräulein Bürstner appeared, mounting a small flight of steps leading into the square from a low-lying side-street. It was not quite certain that it was she, but the resemblance was close enough. Whether it was really Fräulein Bürstner or not, however, did not matter to K.; the important thing was that he suddenly realized the futility of resistance. [page 284]

He is reminded, that is to say, of his own guilt. Perhaps Fräulein Bürstner resembled his mother. But for anyone as inhibited as K. that would not have to be the case. It would be enough that, for whatever reason, he felt strongly attracted to her, so that he dreamed, however fugitively, of winning her for himself—of marriage or at any rate of something better than his relationship with Elsa. Ironically, a desire K. tried to deny was powerful enough to mobilize the whole cluster of Oedipal feelings: envy and hatred of the father, guilt, and talion fears.

*The Trial* moves simultaneously forward and backward in time. The story of K.'s struggle to remain sane, to resist the onslaught of his punitive superego, carries us forward. We see how a paranoid fantasy which K. at first feels he can throw off at will gradually gains control of him until all his energies are absorbed in a losing struggle against it, until he can think of nothing else even at the Bank, where he had once felt so secure. This strand of the story ends in K.'s execution, which may be taken literally or regarded as a symbol of his mental collapse—it does not matter, for in any case the execution means the death of his ego. But at the same time that K.'s struggle against abstract authority carries us forward, he is regressing to childhood, recalling and reliving the original experiences which account for his desire for Fräulein Bürstner being so laden with guilt. And here the execution stands for the final submission to the strong and castrating father, a submission K. has struggled against but longed for from the first.

This two-way movement is another source of *The Trial's* richness and strange, half-realistic, half-dreamlike quality. Many of the incidents, like the execution, have a place both in K.'s "trial" and in his unconscious evocation of his past. But there is no attempt to work out this double movement of the story in complete detail; in particular, K.'s unconscious recall of the infantile source of his conflict is only lightly sketched in. Any attempt to give each element in the story dual significance would almost certainly have interfered with the narrative flow and given *The Trial* a mechanical quality. It would have been psychologically wrong as well: the recapture of the past is neither an orderly process nor one that can ordinarily aspire to completeness.

Nevertheless, there is copious evidence of regression, of "the return of the repressed." Twice, for example, K. struggles with a father figure—and to a lesser extent with a brother—for the favor of a woman. There is, first of all, the scene with the wife of the Law-Court Attendant. She finds K. attractive, and K. finally overcomes his fears and begins to dream of winning her: ". . . some night the Examining Magistrate . . .

might come to the woman's bed and find it empty. Empty because she had gone off with K., because the woman now standing in the window, that supple, voluptuous warm body under the dark dress of rough material, belonged to K. and to K. alone" (page 70). But in the end K. loses out both to the Examining Magistrate and to the student Bertold. The fear of the father is so great that even in dreams K. cannot at this point permit himself a victory. We begin to understand why K. is so frightened by his feeling for Fräulein Bürstner and why, at thirty, he has not achieved a satisfactory heterosexual adjustment.

In this scene, as in the previous one ("First Interrogation") K. is also searching for evidence of the sexuality of adults. This is the significance, for example, of his discovery that the "lawbooks" contain indecent pictures and erotic stories. It is the *tu quoque* defiance of the child for the adults who judge him though they are no better than he is. But the very fact that he feels compelled to reassure himself in this fashion shows how guilty he feels.

K. also relives his Oedipus conflict in his fight with the Advocate for Leni's favors, and this series of scenes provides a brilliant illustration of the way Kafka handles the two-way progression of his plot. On one level the scenes advance the story of the trial, of K.'s effort to defend himself against his punitive superego. It is a losing fight: K.'s position steadily deteriorates. He defeats himself, and a second level of the story reveals the infantile source of this tendency. Most of the people and incidents in these scenes have a two-edged reference. For example, the Advocate has a realistic place in the trial story and reveals K.'s attitude toward authority in general. K. vacillates between leaning on the Advocate and dispensing with his services altogether, just as in his appearance before the Court he alternates between self-defense and defiance. At the same time, the Advocate is a father figure, with whom K. relives all his infantile struggles. His castrative tendencies toward the old man are revealed by his effort to persuade himself that the Advocate is ineffectual and, above all, by the constant emphasis on his age, illness, and weakness. In the meetings with the Advocate which are dramatized, the old man is in bed—just as in "The Judgment" the son puts his father to bed, symbolically murdering him. But there is the same fear which reveals itself in that story that the aggressive act is, after all, unsuccessful. The Advo-

cate, like the father, asserts his superior strength at the
critical moment.

The compulsive sexual episode with Leni is a defiance and
momentary triumph over three authority figures: the Advocate, the Chief Clerk of the Court who is visiting him at the
time of K.'s first call, and K's uncle. But of course the episode
also reveals K.'s self-defeating tendencies: it confirms his
guilt and immeasurably weakens his position.

Leni is clearly a mother figure; more specifically, she is
the "bad" mother; the connecting web of skin between the
two middle fingers of her right hand symbolizes her animality.
"What a pretty little paw!" exclaims K. (page 139). His
experience with Leni reflects the small boy's distorted belief
that he is taking the mother away from the father and enjoying some sort of guilty intimacy when he is alone with her.
One penalty of the distortion is sibling jealousy—thus K.'s
immediate suspicion that Block is also enjoying Leni's favors.
Block is a brother figure and at the same time a projection of
what K. fears he will become if he gives in to his dependency
wishes.[9]

While the specific anxieties which trouble K. have their
roots in the past they cause him to recall and re-experience,
and are triggered by his lust for Fräulein Bürstner, they are
probably fed also by dissatisfaction with the way he is living
at the time the story opens and by fears about the future. It
is not without significance that the onset of his illness occurs
on his thirtieth birthday. The thirties are a critical period for
most men. It is a time when one may feel compelled to face
the fact that one has not built a satisfactory life for oneself—
and the terrifying possibility that this may be because of
some inner weakness, not easily to be overcome. At thirty
a man is no longer young; it is not enough simply to be
promising. About this time most men begin quite soberly
to take stock of their goals and their resources for reaching
them, of external obstacles and the competition one faces
not only from those on about the same level but from younger
men fighting their way up. (This may be one of the explanations for the appearance of the three clerks on the morning
of K.'s arrest.) We may begin to worry about our health,
about old age, and even death. The will to live may become
less keen.

At about this time, too, we begin to realize that other
people are taking our measure, professionally and personally,

that we are being judged not only by friends but also by people whom we do not even know. We have grown accustomed to talking about others, not always without malice. Suddenly we realize that others have been talking about *us,* that without our knowledge we have acquired that frightening thing, a reputation. We may fear, not without reason, that we have been judged too harshly—dismissed as cold when we feel ourselves to be warm, held guilty for failures for which we feel others are primarily responsible. Particularly if something happens to upset our lives, we may begin to feel that we are on trial and be as puzzled as K. was about who is trying us and how to conduct our defense.

IV

In order to round out the interpretation which has been offered, and to define certain facets of it more clearly, I should like to turn now to Paul Goodman's psychoanalytic study of *The Trial* in his *Kafka's Prayer.*[10]

Though I believe that at times Goodman searches too hard for specific symbolic meanings, he is well aware of the abstract quality of *The Trial.* He errs, however, it seems to me, in accounting for it. "Psychologically the abstraction indicates the withdrawal of affect, anesthetizing the perceptions of ordinary experience" (page 149). This is good psychological theory, but does not seem to me to have relevance for *The Trial,* where there is relatively little withdrawal of affect. The affect is admitted to consciousness, but disassociated from what occasions it; it is this which is repressed. K. is aware of his turbulent feelings but not of what causes them.

The point is unimportant in itself, but worth mentioning because it is typical: most of what few errors Goodman makes are due to his getting outside the framework of the novel. Repressed homosexuality is clinically associated with paranoia, and as I have suggested is present in *The Trial,* but not, in my judgment, to anywhere near the extent Goodman maintains. Similarly, when (perhaps simply out of carelessness) Goodman refers to K.'s "falling in love" with Fräulein Bürstner, I feel sure that he is thinking, not of *The Trial,* but of Kafka's feeling for F. A final, and more important, error comes from considering the novel in terms of an extrinsic philosophical standard. Goodman begins his book by assessing Kafka's thought, particularly as it reveals itself in his

aphorisms. But, unlike an aphorism or an essay, a novel cannot be profitably dealt with in terms of its truth or falsity;
it is not so much a statement of the writer's beliefs as it is
a projection, by means of character and situation, of his
wishes and fears. When Goodman talks of the importance of
the "willful ego [relaxing] to the instincts," and of "The
right use of the ego: open to the soul and the world . . ."
(page 173), I believe that he is once again thinking of Kafka,
or of Kafka's thought, rather than of *The Trial*. There is
never any chance that K. will use his ego in this desirable
fashion. The question—if there is *any* question; the falling
action of the novel starts almost at once—is whether K. will
be able to maintain the weak ego organization he has to begin
with or whether he will go to pieces completely.

These errors do not loom large in comparison with the
many insights Goodman offers us. For example, there is the
brilliant surmise that the two warders who arrest K. are
brother figures—the two younger brothers of Kafka who
died in infancy. "He hated them. They die. He is guilty of
it" (page 157). This seems to me an example of the legitimate
use of biographical material. Whatever prompted the surmise, the evidence for its accuracy is in the novel. The
warders eat K.'s breakfast and take his body linen. The
brothers turn up again, Goodman points out, as K.'s executioners. Witness the "fat double chins . . . painful cleanliness
of their faces. One could literally see that the cleansing hand
had been at work in the corners of the eyes. . . ." (*The Trial*,
page 283).

Goodman is particularly persuasive when he writes of the
novel in social terms. Here is his interpretation of the abstractness of the Court:

. . . these traits accurately describe the atomization of natural
groups into mass-men alien to each other; the loss of meaningful
productive work in the subdivision of labor; the impersonality of
exchange value and bourgeois financial relations; the loss of function of the family; the distant, indirect, but all-pervasive coercion
of centralized states; the lapse of individual responsibility in
corporate action; the puzzlement of the little man when his life
is ruled by powers he knows only by name, never face to face;
the sterilization of city life from all biological experience; the
discouragement of initiative by remote planning; the substitution
of actuarial probabilities for proximate causes. The anonymity
and mystery of the Court is little deeper than the annoymity and

remoteness of every part of our economy, politics, pedagogy, entertainment—*and nevertheless the blow falls*. [page 176]

## V

A number of interpretations of *The Trial* are too superficial or confused to reward analysis. Of those which seek to probe the meaning of the book and possess internal consistency we shall consider three more, one religious, one ethical, one socioeconomic. Besides giving us new perspectives for understanding *The Trial*, a glance at these interpretations may shed light on the general question of multiple response to fiction. To what extent should we accept different glosses of the same story? When are we justified in dismissing an interpretation as mistaken?

John Kelly offers a religious interpretation of *The Trial*.[11] It is an eschatological novel, he argues, as indebted to Kierkegaard's theology of crisis as is the religious thought of Karl Barth. There is an infinite distance, an incommensurability between God and man. "God is transcendent and absolute. . . . Any quest for Him on the part of man is pointless, for there is no way up to Him" (page 157). At his moment of crisis, Joseph K. accepts his trial. From that moment, "Bit by bit, the continuity of his life is broken down, and all his reliance, habits, and safeguards cease to operate" (page 158). He is in the grip of the Law:

What is the Law? What must a man do to be saved? Kafka works out his hero's problem by basing his allegory on the prophetic writings of the Old Testament, and on Calvin's Pauline Christianity, absorbed through Kierkegaard. The most bewildering problem which confronts Joseph K. after his arrest is that of his "guilt." In the court offices, K. encounters some other "claimed" men. "They did not stand quite erect, their backs remained bowed, their knees bent, they stood like street beggars. K. waited for the Law-Court Attendant, who kept slightly behind him, and said: 'How humbled they must be!' 'Yes,' said the Law-Court Attendant, 'these are accused men, all of them are accused of guilt.' 'Indeed!' said K. 'Then they're colleagues of mine.' " Thus sarcastically, humorously, tentatively, K. fumbles with the notion of his own "guilt" for a time; but, in the end, he is so convinced of it that he wills his own destruction in expiation. He evolves into a Pauline Christian. [pp. 158-159]

"Guilt," it is to be noted, is a key word in this interpretation, and Kelly tends to accept guilt as an absolute. But

Kafka does not simply describe K.'s guilt; he explains it, albeit in symbolic and elliptical fashion. The analytically oriented critic cannot fail to feel that his first task is to decode and piece out the explanation. K.'s guilt is to be understood, not taken for granted. Nevertheless, I can see no basis for rejecting Kelly's interpretation. Though he makes one or two mistakes—for example, "Women cease to concern [K.]" —he provides a key by which most of the major happenings in *The Trial* can be explained. The key leads to some beautiful insights: "The final scene is . . . conceived in an atmosphere of ritual: the ceremonial attitude of the executioners, the questions of precedence that arise between them, the pains taken to find a suitable sacrificial stone" (page 169).

In *Man for Himself*[12] Erich Fromm offers a superficially psychological but basically ethical interpretation of *The Trial*, which is further elaborated in *The Forgotten Language*.[13] Fromm's interpretation rests upon the belief that there are two consciences. The first, the authoritarian, conscience is the same as the Freudian superego: it is "the internalized voice of an authority whom we are eager to please and afraid of displeasing."[14] There is also a humanistic conscience. It is "the reaction of our total personality to its proper functioning or disfunctioning . . . knowledge of our . . . success or failure in the art of living."[15] K.'s guilt feeling, Fromm maintains, is to a considerable extent a reaction of his humanistic conscience. It expresses his dissatisfaction with his sterile and unproductive life.

Now, there is no doubt that K.'s life was sterile and unproductive, if judged from the perspective of someone poignantly aware of the potentialities of an ideal and ideally adjusted human being. Nor is there any doubt that K. himself felt some degree of dissatisfaction about his life and some anxiety about the future and that these contributed to his collapse. But there is no evidence that his dissatisfaction was so acute as to have precipitated his collapse, or that his work was an important source of such dissatisfaction as he felt. In picturing K. as a person who had creative abilities and impulses which he felt were being thwarted, Fromm seems to me to be using *The Trial* to substantiate certain of his own theories. Judged in K.'s own terms, or in the terms of his immediate associates, he was not unproductive. A paragraph Fromm quotes to demonstrate the opposite tells us that K.

was usually at his office until nine and that the Manager of the Bank "highly valued his diligence and ability." To be sure, one of the reasons K. worked as long and as hard as he did may have been to ward off anxiety. But until the Bürstner affair the device served its purpose; indeed, the security he felt at the Bank was one of the last of his defenses to crumble. In the area of work, it can be maintained, K. had found an adjustment which enabled him to make the most of his meager psychological resourses.

It was a reaching out of an altogether different sort, not for greater productiveness, or increased autonomy, but simply for a more satisfactory love object, that was responsible for K.'s collapse. In terms of his psychosexual organization, Fräulein Bürstner satisfied "higher," that is, more mature, needs than the prostitute Elsa. Ironically, that is why K.'s desire for her aroused deep guilt and an ultimately over-powering need for punishment. I cannot refrain from adding that I believe this is something Fromm would have seen at an earlier stage of his career, before his zeal for grafting ethical tenets upon psychoanalysis caused him to slight more primitive drives and conflicts.

Hannah Arendt sees *The Trial* as the legend of a man's forced submission to a world "of necessity and injustice and lying."[16] His feelings of guilt are exploited to make him adapt himself to existing conditions. On one level, the novel is a critique of the bureaucratic regime of the prewar Austrian government, from whose "senseless automatism" no man might expect justice. More broadly, it is a critique of an entire society "which has established itself as a sub-stitute for God," a world in which the laws of men are looked upon as though they were divine laws. According to Miss Arendt, behind all of Kafka's work there is an ideal image of the man of goodwill, the (Hegelian-Marxian) *fabricator mundi*, a man who wants to remake the world "in accordance with human needs and dignities, [to create] a world where man's actions are determined by himself and which is ruled by his laws and not by mysterious forces emanating from above or from below" (p. 421). K. dies like a dog, feeling that the shame of his death will outlive him, because he submits instead of attempting to build such a world.

There is much in *The Trial* which Miss Arendt's interpreta-tion leaves unexplained. She does not tell us, for example, why K. was suddenly overcome by guilt, or attempt to ac-

count for the novel's sexual episodes and imagery. But she
enriches our understanding of the abstract objective meaning
of the novel. It is certainly possible to include the state and
capitalism among the anonymous forces against which K.
struggles.

## VI

It is not, however, *necessary* to include them. Miss Arendt
makes the opposite assumption—that her reading of *The Trial*
is the only correct one. She expresses impatience in particular
with religious and psychoanalytic interpretations. Now, the
belief that one reading of a literary work invalidates all others
is certainly not unusual. What amounts to a theoretical
defense of the belief appears in *Theory of Literature* by René
Wellek and Austin Warren:[17] "The real poem," they maintain, "must be conceived as a structure of norms, realized
only partially in the actual experience of its many readers"—
a *complex* system of norms, to be sure, "made up of several
strata," but nevertheless a single fixed thing. Wellek and
Warren compare a work of art to a system of language. Just
as a language has a "fundamental coherence and identity,"
even though this is realized only imperfectly in any individual
speech act, so, they argue, a work of art has one correct
meaning which no individual experience of it can hope to
realize completely.

What makes Miss Arendt's position interesting is that she
seems on the verge of discovering another possibility. The
search for religious significance in *The Trial* began, she feels,
because "to the public of the twenties, bureaucracy did not
seem an evil great enough to explain the horror and terror
in the novel."[18] If she had asked herself why it *did* seem
great enough to explain the horror in the novel to her, she
would have discovered, I believe, that it was because of her
particular political orientation—an orientation which is clearly
grounded on deep feelings as well as intellectual convictions.
She might then have made the still more significant discovery
that other people, with different backgrounds, might have
read the novel in different, but perhaps equally valid, ways.

In fact, a great work of narrative art, quite unlike a system
of language, can never be reduced to a single "correct"
meaning; it is a symbolical structure admitting of many
different interpretations. Some of these, to be sure, may be
superficial or otherwise inadequate, incomplete, or altogether

erroneous. But others may be of approximately equal validity and worth—as incommensurate as different imaginative works of relatively equal stature.

A corollary of the fact that a story says different things to different readers is that its meaning does not remain fixed: it changes with the experience readers bring to bear upon it, and that experience includes the broad historical developments which affect our lives. Many readers of *The Trial* have been struck by the resemblance between the Court which persecuted K. and the fascist state. The resemblance does not mean that Kafka was a prophet. It is simply a striking example of the fact that upon completion a story acquires an autonomous existence and through time may gain levels of meaning and reference its author could not have anticipated.

## NOTES

[1] *Time*, XLIX (April 28, 1947), 106.

[2] *The Trial*, trans. Willa and Edwin Muir, New York, Knopf, 1945, p. 3. All subsequent references to *The Trial* are taken from this edition.

[3] Paul Goodman is more specific still. In *Kafka's Prayer*, New York, Vanguard, 1947, p. 142, he describes *The Trial* as "a paranoic dream."

[4] See Max Brod, *Franz Kafka*, New York, Schocken Books, 1947, especially p. 146.

[5] See my book *Fiction and the Unconscious*, Boston, Beacon, 1957, pp. 241–247 *et passim*, for a discussion of this seldom-noted but highly valued component of reader response.

[6] The most important features of the compulsive character are "inflexibility . . . , the inability to abandon or alter a course of action or thought in order to avoid suffering, and excessive indecisiveness."—Ives Hendrick, *Facts and Theories of Psychoanalysis*, New York, Knopf, 1939, pp. 346–347.

[7] Quoted in *Kafka's Prayer*, p. 134.

[8] She regularly comes home late. Note also Frau Grubach's report on Fräulein Bürstner and K.'s overindignant reaction to it, pp. 28–29.

[9] Chapter VIII contains many amusing indications that the Advocate, Leni, K., and Block comprise a family in which Block is the less-favored son. "Yes, one becomes very dependent on one's Advocate in the course of time," he says (p. 228). "He's just pretending to complain," Leni puts in, "for he likes sleeping here, as he has often told me." She shows K. his bedroom, which is a small, low-roofed chamber off the kitchen. After a time K. can no longer stand the sight of Block. "Put him to bed," he cries to

Leni (p. 229). Later the Advocate asks for a report of Block as though he were a child: "How has he been behaving today?" Leni gives a favorable report: "He has been quiet and industrious" (pp. 242–243).

10 Charles Neider has also written a psychoanalytic study of Kafka, *The Frozen Sea*, New York, Oxford, 1948. But Neider scants the abstract quality of *The Trial* and makes a number of basic errors. For example, he constantly tends to equate the unconscious with the id, overlooking the superego, though in *The Trial* it plays the more immediately important role. He assumes that Kafka "applied Freud's dream findings deliberately" (p. vii). In general his study is less valuable than Goodman's.

11 "*The Trial* and the Theology of Crisis," in Angel Flores, ed., *The Kafka Problem*, New York, New Directions, 1946, pp. 151–171.

12 *Man for Himself, An Inquiry into the Psychology of Ethics,* New York, Rinehart, 1947, pp. 167–171.

13 New York, Rinehart, 1951, pp. 249–263.

14 *Man for Himself*, p. 158.

15 *Man for Himself*, p. 158.

16 "Franz Kafka: A Revaluation," *Partisan Review* XI (Fall, 1944), p. 413.

17 New York, Harcourt, Brace, 1949. The quotations are from pages 151, 152, and 153.

18 "Franz Kafka: A Revaluation," p. 414.

*Norman N. Holland**

# SHAKESPEAREAN TRAGEDY
# AND THE THREE WAYS
# OF PSYCHOANALYTIC CRITICISM

"Shakespeare," said Buck Mulligan's friend, "is the happy hunting ground of all minds that have lost their balance." Be that as it may, Shakespeare's tragedies seem to be a favorite preserve of psychoanalytic critics and, therefore, a convenient place to peer at the three basic kinds of psychoanalytic criticism. Alas, there is a fourth kind—you might call it the here-a-phallic-symbol-there-a-phallic-symbol school—which is the only one working or classroom Shakespeareans usually encounter. It erupts when a class comes across a remark like Othello's:

> Behold, I haue a weapon:
> A better neuer did it selfe sustaine
> Vpon a Soldiers Thigh.

Invariably, a student puts up his hand and says, "Professor Weltschmerz, isn't that a phallic symbol?" and faces light up, mental sirens sound, and the class goes "Oo-o-o-h," as though something very profound had been said. Actually, nothing very profound has been said because the student has abandoned the basic procedure of psychoanalytic criticism.

Any statement in psychoanalytic criticism involves two steps. First, the critic must establish a congruity between something in the work of literature and some general psychoanalytic proposition. Second, the critic must relate the psychoanalytic proposition about the mind in general to some mind in particular. It is this second step that our phallicly-minded student, like most critics, forgot. Psychoanalysis, like

* NORMAN N. HOLLAND is Associate Professor of English at the Massachusetts Institute of Technology and the author of many professional articles.

any psychology, deals not with literature as such, but with minds, and there is absolutely no justification for bringing psychoanalysis into literary criticism at all except to relate the work of literature to somebody's mind. In the case of a tragedy, there are three minds handy: the author's, a character's, and the audience's, and these three minds lead in turn to the three basic methods of psychoanalytic criticism (that is, working psychoanalytic criticism, not the psychoanalytic metacriticism of, say, Lionel Trilling, which is another matter entirely).

The most obvious mind to which the psychoanalytic critic turns is the author's. Freud's essay "Creative Writers and Day-Dreaming" (1908) supplies the theoretical link, the comparison of literary creations to daydreams (and for that matter to night dreams), all of them being projections of the fulfillment of wishes. If, in a dream, one character emerges as the "central character," such a character would represent the dreamer himself. So, Freud said, in a work of literature: where one character seems to stand out, that character must represent the poet himself. Thus, the two Shakespearean tragedies which most psychoanalytic critics have singled out as expressions of Shakespeare himself are *Hamlet* and *Coriolanus*. *Hamlet*, they say, shows the death of John Shakespeare in 1601 reactivating the poet's childhood attitudes toward his father, and *Coriolanus* is supposed to show the death of Mary Shakespeare in 1608 reactivating the poet's childhood feelings toward his mother.

According to psychoanalytic theory, the death of a loved one produces a period in which the bereaved person gradually accustoms himself to the idea that the deceased now lives on only in his own mind. A deceased parent becomes, as it were, incorporated into the mind of his surviving child, often as an accusing voice reminding the child of all the ways in which he has wronged or failed the dead parent. Thus, both *Hamlet* and *Coriolanus* are tragedies in which the hero (the poet) is made to suffer. In both tragedies, the heroes fail to live up to the demands their parent makes of them. And in both tragedies the hero identifies with or incorporates the parent in question. Coriolanus seems to identify with his mother in such passages as:

> My throat of Warre be turn'd,
> Which quier'd with my Drumme into a Pipe,

Small as an Eunuch, or the Virgin voyce
That Babies lull a-sleepe.

Hamlet inscribes his father's command on the tables of his memory, a singularly apt and graphic image for the incorporating process the theory posits.

But there are problems. First of all, the date of *Hamlet* is not nearly so clear as the psychoanalytic critics would have us believe; in fact, *Hamlet* was probably written before the death of John Shakespeare rather than after, and about the date of *Coriolanus*, the less said, the better. Second, anything we say about Shakespeare's life properly belongs to biography, not literary criticism. Finally, and most important, there is no possibility of verifying these ingenious deductions about Shakespeare's emotional life. Entertaining as they may be, even, as Leon Edel suggests, helpful to the critic, they will always remain mere speculations.

By far the greatest part of psychoanalytic criticism of Shakespearean tragedy relates the play to the second mind available, the mind of one or another of the characters. The classic example, of course, is Freud's "brainstorm" (as one orthodox Shakespearean has called it) that Hamlet delays because he has Oedipal feelings about his father. Freud argued that Hamlet could not punish Claudius for getting rid of his father and marrying his mother because that is exactly what Hamlet wanted to do as a child and, in his unconscious, still wants to do. To punish Claudius would be to punish himself. In another famous psychoanalytic reading, Freud compared Lady Macbeth to a patient who had a compulsion to wash her hands all the time. In both cases, he said, the washing is a symbolic attempt to restore a moral cleanliness which the patient—or character—thinks she has lost. In *King Lear*, Freud (and others) have suggested that the real reason Lear goes mad is that he cannot admit to himself that there is a sexual tinge in his feelings toward his daughters. Other critics have argued that Iago wreaks his terrible revenge because, unconsciously, he is himself in love with Othello and jealous of Desdemona. And so on. One could add examples almost indefinitely, some by Freud, some by other analysts, some sane and some zany.

In all of them, however, the psychoanalytic critic treats the character as a living human being, and all these readings, therefore, present the same theoretical problem. After all, a literary character is really only a tissue of words. To what extent are we entitled to assume that this conglomeration of syllables has a past and a future, a Freudian childhood that reaches back before the opening of the play? Ernest Jones, in the introduction to his *Hamlet and Oedipus,* discusses this problem and decides that it is all right for the psychoanalyst to treat Hamlet as living human being, because this is what the literary critics themselves do. And recently, Professor Louis Fraiberg has argued that literary critics should treat Hamlet as a living person because the psychoanalysts do.

This critical do-se-do is not final, of course. There is still the third of the three minds to which psychoanalytic critics have referred Shakespearean tragedy, the mind of the audience or at least some average member of it, maybe even the critic himself. To this mind (as to the author's) the *whole* play appears as a total configuration or *Gestalt,* not as just a single character. The first two psychoanalytic approaches represent the "older" view, the third, the "newer" view. My description of these approaches as "older" and "newer" is, however, a gross oversimplification. You can find the so-called newer view in some of the earliest psychoanalytic criticism, and the older view goes about yet like the snake scotched but not killed. The theoretical justification for the newer view, considering the whole play in relation to the audience's mind, occurs in the same essay, "Creative Writers and Day-Dreaming," that gives rise to the biographical approach. Freud suggested that it was only in crude literature that a single character gratifies a simple wish of the author. In more sophisticated writings, he said, the author gets split up among several characters, and he made several analyses of audience reaction on this basis in his much-neglected essay "The 'Uncanny.' "

Basically, then, in calling these views "older" and "newer," I am trying to prejudice you in favor of the one I prefer. Nevertheless, there is some basis for the distinction. The so-called "newer" approach relates both to newer developments in psychoanalytic theory and to newer views of Shakespeare. Freud discovered first the unconscious and its freight of rather sordid wishes. In the twenties, however, psychoanalysis became increasingly concerned, not so much with the unconscious, as with the various strategies the mind uses to direct unconscious wishes into acceptable channels. This approach to the mind leads quite naturally to considering a work of literature, not as a single unconscious wish, but as a totality or *Gestalt* of competing unconscious wishes, the showplace of an interior drama in the minds of the playwright or his audience. Similarly, this so-called "newer" psychoanalytic criticism follows on the antirealistic, antibiographical trends in Shakespearean criticism. Looking through a Shakespearean tragedy to the author's biography is a nineteenth century pastime. Looking at the characters as real people or staging Shakespeare with real rabbits hopping about on real grass, these are nineteenth century approaches to realism. In our own sublimely enlightened century, we tend to play down Shakespeare's realism and consider instead the formal interrelations between the various parts of the play, the wholeness of it, and this is what the "newer" kind of psychoanalytic criticism has also begun to do.

It is no surprise, then, that this newer or motivational researcher's approach first turns up in relation to those aspects of Shakespearean tragedy that are least realistic, the ghosts, for example, in *Julius Caesar, Macbeth,* and *Hamlet.* These ghosts, Otto Rank early decided,[1] are all associated with father figures (Banquo being a surrogate for Duncan). The ghosts represent a dual wish. Most obviously, they are the quite literal fulfillment of a wish to see the father dead, but they also represent the "immortality," the persistence of one's childhood feelings toward the father. Thus, they represent a second wish, that these infantile attitudes were as questionable as a ghost and could be laid to rest like a ghost.

Another point of nonrealism which lent itself to this newer psychoanalytic approach was the old chestnut planted by Rymer and Coleridge: Is Iago realistic or not? The answer the newer approach gives[2] is that Iago is neither real nor unreal, but the projection of doubting impulses. That is, Othello represents to the unconscious of the audience an impulse toward idealizing, toward absolute purity, uncontaminated by any cynicism; Iago represents an impulse of absolute disillusionment, uncontaminated by any idealism.

In other tragedies besides Othello, the characters are regarded as projections of different unconscious feelings. For example, in *Julius Caesar,* there is a single father, Caesar himself, but there are three "sons." Brutus is a son who embodies both love and hatred toward the father. Cassius embodies only hatred, and he also projects in his repeated talk about suicide the self-punishing impulse of a "bad"

son. Antony embodies only love for the father and the desire
to vindicate and identify with the father. Similarly, *Hamlet*
can be taken as a configuration of different attitudes toward
the father. There are five father figures: the ghost is the
idealized father; Polonius the doting father; Claudius the
criminal father; old Fortinbras the murdered father; Fortinbras's uncle, the sick, impotent father. Similarly, Laertes and
Hamlet represent different aspects of the son. Laertes is the
dutiful son, eager to revenge his father's murder, but he is
subordinate to Hamlet who represents the son as a rival of the
father.

In *Macbeth*, Freud himself pointed out, Macbeth and
Lady Macbeth are like two halves of a dissociated personality:
after the murder of Duncan he becomes defiant, she remorse-
ful; together they exhaust the possibilities of response. Ludwig
Jekels analyzed the role of Macduff as a counterpart of
Macbeth.[3] That is, Macbeth is a bad son murdering the king-
father. Macduff also defies, rebels against, and ultimately
kills the king-father, but in his case it's all right.

Even these "new" psychoanalytic critics, however, as these
examples suggest, tend to talk mostly about plot and character and rather less about the language. Very recently,
however, one psychoanalyst, Dr. Robert Fliess,[4] has tried
to deal with the texture of Shakespeare's verse. He suggests
that Shakespeare's images keep the mind of the audience
in a constant state of change, fluctuating, as it were, up
and down the levels of the unconscious from the earliest
stages of childhood to the latest. For example, Fliess contributes a novel approach to the textual crux as to whether
that flesh of Hamlet's that might melt is "solid," "sullied," or
"sallied." In any case, Fliess argues, the image of melting
flesh suggests the relaxation and flow upon the satisfaction
of the rigid tension of a man's sexuality. The "self-slaughter"
'gainst which the Everlasting has fixed his canon disguises a
sexual "self-abuse" outlawed by the Everlasting, be he God
or father. The image contributes its mite to the totality of a
play which deals with the complex relation of father and
son.

Nevertheless, as even this brief summary must suggest,
what I am calling the newer psychoanalytic approach is not
yet fully developed. It does indeed deal with a Shakespearean
tragedy as a totality, a configuration or *Gestalt* of plot and
characters, but it tends to neglect the poetry. Further, the

psychoanalytic critic, even one studying the play as a totality, does not always make it clear that he is considering it in relation to the mind of the audience. Like our student with the phallus on his mind, he too often contents himself simply with saying that something going on in the tragedy is like something psychoanalysts experience in practice. He often fails to go on to draw a conclusion about some particular mind; he sometimes reverts to an earlier approach and refers the total configuration of the play to the author's mind or a character's.

Even though this newer approach is not yet applied fully to Shakespeare, it does emerge very sharply and clearly in one area of psychoanalytic criticism—the popular arts, myth, folktale, movies, television, and the like, where no single author clearly appears. We can expect this third approach in Shakespearean criticism if for no other reason than that Shakespeare was once—in some quarters still is—a popular artist. The line between *Romeo and Juliet* and *I married a Teen-Age Necrophiliac* is not as sharp as some middlebrows would have it.

As for the three methods of psychoanalytic criticism, there is no particularly sharp line between the first, or peeping-Tom, approach (referring the work to the author's mind) and the third (referring it to the audience's mind); in psycho-analytic theory, the audience's response to a work of art recapitulates *mutatis mutandis* the author's act of creation. The sharp line runs between, on the one hand, those two methods which consider the work as a totality and, on the other, the psychoanalytic approach which considers only a part of the work, the mind of a single character. In treating a literary character as a human being the critic assumes that an author finds or invents a reality and then copies it in his work of art (perhaps the most famous critics of this school were the burghers of Rembrandt's *Night Watch*). In treating the work as an indivisible whole the critic assumes that the work of art is to be itself savored as a final reality, not as a filtered version of something else. In psychological terms, the critic who looks at a single character in isolation assumes that a literary work portrays the stimuli and responses of some fictitious people; the critic who looks at the work as a total configuration considers it as itself the stimulus to the very real responses of very real people—the audience. In other words, we have come to an old crux in Shakespearean

criticism, the case of A. C. Bradley vs. G. Wilson Knight, two
different conceptions of what the bard is doing. Is Shakespeare writing Galsworthian naturalism or verse drama? Is he
writing realistic plays about realistic people or is he dealing
in the demonic wisdom of folktale?

This difference about the author carries over into the
question of what the audience is doing, what kind of cove-
nant, what gesture of "as if," we make when we are watching
a play. Dr. Johnson held that we credit a drama "with all the
credit due to a drama," that is, we recognize that it is a fiction
but credit it as "a just picture of a real original." Coleridge
held that "we pass no judgment either way," but rather make
"that willing suspension of disbelief for the moment, which
constitutes poetic faith." The real division in the psychoanalytic approaches, then, is: When we see a Shakespearean
tragedy, do we agree to believe or do we simply agree not
to disbelieve?

The notion that we pretend that plays (or any work of
art) are real will fit the naturalistic theater and fiction of the
late nineteenth century and after well enough; but it will not
accommodate a whole host of other genres that the suspension-of-disbelief approach will: myth, folktale, lyric poetry,
morality plays, allegory, surrealist and abstract painting,
music, and so on. Also, the suspension-of-disbelief approach
corresponds to the general psychoanalytic description of the
way art seduces its audience: because the ego function of
reality-testing is, as it were, bought off by artistic convention,
our unconscious responses are free to come through. The more
we consciously tell ourselves, "This is not reality, but a play,"
the more the ego suspends its function of belief or disbelief,
and the more we are free to respond unconsciously. The only
basis for applying the psychoanalytic description of the mind,
not to the real mind of the audience, but to the fictional minds
of the characters, is the old Aristotelian one of probability.
In effect, when Freud or Jones says that Hamlet cannot kill
Claudius because of his Oedipal feelings, they are saying
that Hamlet's delay is probable, lifelike, or human under the
circumstances. Yet, probability in Aristotle's sense simply
begs the question. It is not at all clear whether by "probability" Aristotle—or we—mean what is human or lifelike under
the circumstances or what is probable or necessary in terms
of the internal logic, the *mythos,* of the tragedy as a whole.

Perhaps most important, the psychoanalytic study of a

literary character must end with simply that. The newer psychoanalytic approach, considering the play as a whole with respect to the audience's mind, is, in that grimmest of social scientists' terms, heuristic. It puts us in a position to go on and answer some of the fundamental questions about tragedy in general and Shakespearean tragedy in particular. The basic assumption of psychoanalysis in general is: There are certain patterns in infantile fantasies and drives which we modify in growing up, yet these infantile patterns persist unmodified in the unconscious mind of the adult, and from them he derives his emotional or "gut" reaction to things. We find underneath the shaped and ordered surface of works of art these same infantile patterns. Therefore, says this newer psychoanalytic approach to art, we must understand the emotional response of an adult audience to a Shakespearean tragedy—or any work of literature—in terms of these more or less concealed infantile patterns.

Given this set of hypotheses, we can answer such basic questions about tragedy as the one Aristotle asked: How is it that the dramatist makes the unpleasant catastrophes of tragedy into a source of pleasure for the audience? The answer, in psychoanalytic terms, is that the dramatist dredges up the terrors and chaos of childhood to impose on them the order of art and the resoultion of the tragic ending. In other words, catharsis, in a psychoanalytic sense, means mastering both the fears from childhood and the adult's pity for the individual (himself) suffering those fears. This pity and fear is reordered and reunderstood into the coherence of art. More specifically, a tragedy acts out two wishes: the first is the child's wish to rebel against the authority of his parents (which the tragedy projects as fate, God, or the social order). The second wish is the ayenbite of inwit, the wish to be punished for this rebellion. Thus, the audience at a tragedy feels fear for its own audacity in rebelling and pity for its own suffering for that rebellion. In the last act of a Shakespearean tragedy—as opposed to a modern tragedy—these inconsistent demands, to rebel and to be punished for it, are reintegrated into a moral order, albeit somewhat bruised, which the tragic ending re-establishes.

Thus, this newer psychoanalytic approach suggests what is unique in Shakespearean tragedy, what makes it different from, say, Greek tragedy, or French, or modern. One special attribute of Shakespearean tragedy is the use of plot parallels.

As Ludwig Jekels suggested, the extra plots give us other versions of the wish which the tragic hero projects. For example, in *Macbeth*, the hero wishes to replace the king-father; in fact, he does, and that causes all the trouble. Macduff also defies, rebels against, and ultimately kills the king-father, but in his case we feel that it is all right because he is getting rid of a tyrant. In other words, Jekels says, the actions of the secondary hero give us another form of the major tragic wish of *Macbeth*, a form in which it is toned down, made socially acceptable. The parallel gives us, in effect, a more grown-up form of the wish projected by the main plot. Similarly, as Robert Fliess suggests, Shakespeare's verse with its vast deluges of images and metaphors keeps the unconscious of the audience in a constant state of ferment. In every word and every line, the poetry ranges through all kinds of unconscious patterns, dredging them up so the tragedy can order them into coherence. In short, psycho-analysis finds the special elements in Shakespearean tragedy its range and depth, the complexity with which it develops and handles different levels of unconscious fantasies and wishes in a single play. The "new psychoanalytic criticism" thus leads into the bases of aesthetic value, though people often say (quite erroneously) questions of value are beyond the scope of psychoanalysis.

This newer psychological approach can also tell us something about the characters, specifically, the tragic hero. Aristotle said the tragic hero should be a man neither wholly good nor wholly bad. In a psycho-analytic sense, the tragic hero is a projection or repre-sentation of a wish which (presumably) all the members of the audience feel to a greater or lesser extent. In the case of Lear, the hero acts out a childish longing to be everything. Coriolanus tries the hopeless task of winning the love of a cold, demanding mother by doing high deeds. Hamlet longs to rise above a world which he finds diseased and distasteful. Instead of a man who is neither wholly good nor wholly bad, the psychoanalytic view presents us with a *wish* which can be either good or bad. For example, Macbeth projects a wish to replace the king-father, a bad wish. Othello, however, projects a wish for complete possession of complete and wonderful purity, surely a good wish. But in all these cases the wish is a *partial* wish—and this is the psychoanalytic form of the ambiguity Aristotle noted—the wish is only half the story; is is a wish uncorrected by conscience or any sense of reality. Contrast the case of comedy. The comic hero often projects the same kind of wish as a tragic hero, one which may be either good or bad, but is uncorrected by a sense of reality. In comedy the social or cosmic order, the rest of the play in other words, bends to grant this wish; in tragedy, the rest of the play rather cruelly teaches the hero his folly.

From such answers to basic issues of tragedy, the pleasure in pain, the nature of the tragic hero, the special quality of Shakespearean tragedy, it should be clear that psychoanalytic criticism need not be the narrow, jargon-ridden technic it so often is. Psychoanalysis offers a rich, dynamic approach to all aspects of literature from the minutiae of particular words to the grand hermetic mysteries of literary value—but only if the critic recognizes two things. He must refer his findings to some mind, and of the three minds available, the one to use is not necessarily the best or most nimble but the most real, the one most certainly there: the audience's, in the last analysis, his own.

## NOTES

[1] *Das Inzest-Motiv in Dichtung und Sage,* 2d. ed., Leipzig, 1926, K. VI. One of the finest of psychoanalytic literary studies, this work has not yet been translated into English.

[2] Maud Bodkin, *Archetypal Patterns in Poetry,* 1934; Vintage ed., 1958, Chap. V. J. I. M. Stewart [Michael Innes], *Character and Motive in Shakespeare,* London, 1949, Chap. V.

[3] Ludwig Jekels, "The Riddle of Shakespeare's *Macbeth*" (1916), "The Problem of the Duplicated Expression of Psychic Themes" (1932), in *Selected Papers,* New York, 1952.

[4] In a book with (for literary critics) the unlikely title *Erogeneity and Libido,* New York, 1957, *passim* and p. 198.

*John Skinner**

# LEWIS CARROLL'S ADVENTURES IN WONDERLAND

The life of Lewis Carroll is the story of a Wonderland which he created for Alice and shared with her, the Dormouse, the Mad Hatter and the March Hare. Yet Wonderland was also a real world; a land of wonder may be a world in which the imagined is real and the real sometimes imagined, while people assume a dual role. The imaginative story is not only a product of creative genius, for creation, but also serves a purpose for the author who is his own first audience, and the fantasy of Lewis Carroll is intelligible only after study of his life plus a consideration of what he was trying to achieve when he wrote the nonsense stories intended for children but now so jealously cherished by adults.

*Alice's Adventures in Wonderland* have become world property, and the story has been published in France, Germany, Italy, Russia, Sweden, Spain, and Holland. It was printed in Arabic and Chinese, although the book was banned in Hunan Province because the Chinese felt that the human personality was degraded when animals were given the power of speech. The story was immediately popular in America and Great Britain, and an American collector paid $150,000 for the original manuscript, while over 400,000 people visited a display of Carroll manuscripts when they were exhibited in Philadelphia.

The world appeal of the fantasy of Lewis Carroll suggests that the story has values beyond entertainment for children or mere storytelling, for the themes of Alice's adventures have been used in the adult world of motion picture, ballet, and the ice show. The characters have appeared in advertising,

* JOHN SKINNER is a psychoanalyst and the author of many professional articles.

and our speech reflects adopted phrases. Stuart Chase used quotations from the book as chapter headings in a book about the never-never land of economics.

Apparently the fabric of the story contains the thread of old themes which are universally appealing and which can be understood clearly only after we have applied modern psychological understanding to the life of the author and attempted to understand the fantasies which produced the story. We are indebted to Sigmund Freud for our knowledge of the psychological value of wit or humor, of fantasy or fairy tale, and these devices are all familiar in the stories of Lewis Carroll.

In the analysis of wit and humor, Freud found that certain psychological processes which were common to dreams or other unconscious mental activity, were also common to humor and wit. Symbols were condensed into one word or object, as in the portmanteau words of Lewis Carroll or even in his characters, for Alice was able to telescope her appearance from large to small and back again through the use of magic food, and there is a combination of adult and childish attitudes in her behavior. Many forbidden impulses are permitted in nonsense which are prohibited the adult, and there is a varied indulgence of childhood wishes in the stories of Lewis Carroll. Freud felt that the playful use of nonsense words, puns, or jokes of speech permitted an enjoyment of euphoric glee not unlike the unsuppressed autointoxication of a child who is drunk with laughter because of his own humorous thoughts. Freud was of the opinion that wit represented an accomplishment of wishes on a more realistic level than dreams, which he found to be of a different sphere of mental life, so that humor and wit are considered to be the result of a higher plane of consciousness with a greater realization of impulses than are found in the passive enjoyment of dreams. If these formulations are accurate, we should be able to find evidences of the use which Lewis Carroll made of his nonsense writing and to assess some of the wishes he hoped to realize by writing.

Paul Schilder has called attention to the sadism and anxiety which he felt the stories of *Alice's Adventures in Wonderland* and *Through the Looking-Glass* contained, but he felt that the facts of Lewis Caroll's life were incomplete and not of great value in attempting to understand the author and his stories. However, this is not an entirely satisfactory answer or analysis. Even incomplete facts should gain new weight when compared with the stories and may give some additional understanding of the creator of these modern fairy tales. Little is known about the authors of primitive myths or fairy tales, but we have an opportunity here to compare the life of the author with the fantasy which he produced in his stories. There is a certain historical parallel between the production of the primitive myth and the stories of Lewis Carroll, for he told them verbally first and wrote them later, just as the earliest stories were probably first spoken and written later. Often the written version is censored and changed when it is time for the author to perpetuate himself on paper, and Lewis Carroll consciously deleted one chapter of the story of Alice and suppressed references to the dreamlike quality of the world in which Alice moved.

Lewis Carroll was born Charles Lutwidge Dodgson, on January 27, 1832, the first child of a cleric in the Church of England. His father has been described by a relative as a scholarly but stern man with a grave disposition. He married his cousin when he was thirty years of age, and the family lived in a small parish in Yorkshire, two miles from a village of one hundred people. The father was pious, reserved, a storyteller, and a man of humor.

Lewis Carroll's mother was a quiet, reserved woman whom everyone is said to have loved, if we can believe her son. There were eleven children, eight of whom were girls, although none of the biographers has given a great deal of information about the relationships of the brothers and sisters. The three other sons were all ordained as clergymen in the Anglican Church; and Lewis Carroll might as well have been, for he studied for the church, although he never accepted final ordination.

We expect that ten younger children must have constituted a constant threat to the priority of the oldest son; and while he must have enjoyed a special position in an English family, because he was the firstborn and a son, he must also have felt an early displacement because of the orderly production of other children who demanded the time and attention of the mother.

Lewis Carroll was a serious, quiet, withdrawn child who invented games, plays, stories, and magic to amuse himself and his brothers and sisters. He used the same devices as an adult in his private life and in his writing. He usually provided the other children with precise rules for the games, and this early sense of exactness is reflected in his later behavior. He developed a hobby of puppets, built a toy theatre, became interested in photography, and loved to play with snails, caterpillars, or other small animals which he endowed with the ability to speak and think. This animistic attitude toward animals, dolls, or other objects is seen in the play of all children but is particularly significant in the life of Lewis Carroll, since it is a form of imagination which persisted through all of his adult life and which was not abandoned with the close of childhood. It is also important that this withdrawn, imaginative play is embraced when the child feels himself apart from the living world of parents and brothers and sisters. It is usually the lonely child who populates the world with imaginary creatures to defeat his loneliness and isolation.

After attending school in his home neighborhood until twelve, Lewis Carroll was sent to Rugby when he was fourteen, but he did not enjoy either school and hated to live with other boys. The following letter was written to his sisters when he was in residence at Richmond School near his home:

I hope you are all getting on well, as also the sweet twins. The boys I think that I like best, are Harry Austin and all the Tates of which there are seven besides a little girl who came down to dinner the first day, but not since. . . . The boys have played two tricks upon me which were these—they first proposed to play at "King of the Cobblers" and asked if I would be king, to which I agreed. They then made me sit down and sat (on the ground) in a circle round me, and told me to say "Go to work" which I said, and they immediately began kicking and knocking me on all sides. The next game they proposed was "Peter, the red lion," and they made a mark on a tombstone (for we were playing in the churchyard) and one of the boys walked with his eyes shut, holding out his finger, trying to touch the mark; then a little boy came forward to lead the rest and led a good many near the mark; at last it was my turn; they told me to shut my eyes well, and the next moment I had my finger in the mouth of one of the boys, who had stood (I believe) near the tombstone with his mouth open. For two nights I slept alone, and for the rest of the time with Ned Squire. The boys play me no tricks now. The only fault (tell Mama) that there has been was coming in one day to dinner just after grace. . . .

Hazing the new boy was accepted practice when Lewis Carroll entered Rugby; the food was poor, and the educational pattern was that of Tom Brown. In later life Lewis Carroll felt indignant about the tyranny among schoolboys, and the persistence of this feeling seems to be the adult echo of his earlier unhappiness and fears.

While at school, Lewis Carroll wrote a number of small newspapers, one of which was called *The Rectory Umbrella* and another *Mishmash*. These papers were written and illustrated by hand, and many of the symbols of the later stories were first expressed here. One issue contained a whimsical article on the potentiality of photography for changing a personality from negative to positive, which gives some clue to Lewis Carroll's lifelong interest in photography.

Lewis Carroll stammered, a trait common to all the children in the family, and yet in his stories there is a preoccupation with long, complicated words, many of which the author invented, with rules for pronunciation. He did not always stammer when he became an adult and never while he was playing with children, although the speech defect became activated if another adult interrupted the play with children. While he often laughed about his stammer, he felt concerned enough to try to correct his speech by reading long passages from Shakespeare aloud. A recent biographer states that he was originally left-handed, and the correlation between the change from left-handedness is commonly related to speech disorders. This is also one of the early evidences of reversal of behavior which is consistently seen in the life of Lewis Carroll.

He entered Christ College, Oxford, when eighteen and the following year became a resident, where he remained for forty-seven years with only brief absense during holiday. He was outstanding in his studies, and his instructors in mathematics and theology wrote to his father to tell him that his son was a genius. He studied thirteen hours a day and worked all night before his oral examinations, coming up third on the list. He won a scholarship during the first year and graduated in 1854 when twenty-two.

Lewis Carroll seemed to enjoy Oxford more than his experiences at boarding school. He was freer in his friendships, wrote a great deal of humorous verse, attended the theatre, and was less serious. He had planned to become ordained in the church but did not complete his orders because he felt a conflict between his secular and spiritual interests. His speech may have been a factor in his rejection of the church, since he could not preach easily, but there was also an inability to indulge himself in the theatre or social life and at the same time feel comfortable in the church. He was notably interested in the children's theatre, and most of his friends were young girl actors. He cared less for the adult theatre and has recorded enjoyment of only one production, *Henry VIII,* which he felt was "dreamlike."

He wrote "The Jabberwocky" at the age of twenty-three, while at Oxford, and it was first published in his magazine, *Mishmash.* It was included in the story of Alice's adventures later, when he was thirty-nine. He continued writing at Oxford, and his later pamphleteering on mathematics, antivivisection, and architecture may represent an extension of the interest which he expressed in his personal magazines.

He was not fond of the usual adolescent activities and preferred intellectual games, writing, or long solitary walks. He changed his name to Lewis Carroll when he was twenty-five, ostensibly for the purpose of publication, but it seems also to have been an attempt to satisfy the demands of a nagging conscience.

He had been reporting for the college newspapers, and after he became an editor he began to use the name of Lewis Caroll. He had considered Dares for his pen name, the first syllable of his birthplace, Daresbury, but later he invented Lewis Carroll from Ludowicus, the nearest Latin name to Lutwidge combined with the Latin for Charles, or Carolus. Although he was named Charles Lutwidge Dodgson, he reversed the order in creating Lewis Carroll but omitted the use of a paternal name, Dodgson. This rejection of a symbol of the father seems to have been necessary at a time when his secular interests were not compatible with the church, and during all of his life he felt guilty about the fact that he could not decide to enter the church and become fully ordained, which may point to some essential, unconscious conflict with his father.

As an adult, Lewis Carroll developed many peculiar, seemingly unrelated eccentric habits and attitudes. Mr. Charles Collingwood, a relative, says that he suffered from unconscious periods which were like an attack or seizure. It was the sight of an epileptic man which caused Lewis Carroll to become interested in anatomy, and as a result of his feeling

against medical experimentation on the human body he
became an ardent antivivisectionist. He wrote pamphlets on
the subject and sent angry letters of complaint to the newspapers.

His rooms at Christ Church, in "The House," were comfortable and meticulously neat and clean. He decorated the walls
with the pictures of the girl children whom he photographed,
but there were no pictures of boys or babies. He kept a file
of all his letters, and he is said to have received over one
hundred thousand. He registered each letter in a ledger,
recorded the date of his answer, and his correspondence was
apparently voluminous. He seems to have felt compelled to
answer the letters he received, although the replies were
sometimes written several years after the original letter was
received.

He bought notepaper in nine graduated sizes so that he
could always write a letter which would be no longer than
both sides of a sheet of paper but which would exactly fill
both sides of the paper. One biographer states that he wrote
mathematical treatises in black ink and stories in violet ink.
He kept a large collection of pencils, pencil sharpeners, and
mechanical pencils of which he was very proud.

His closest friends were young girl children with whom
he maintained warm friendships until they were thirteen or
fourteen years old. Most of his collected letters are to these
friends and give additional understanding of Lewis Carroll's
personality which was in distinct opposition to the characteristics of Charles L. Dodgson. If he maintained an interest in
his child friends beyond puberty, he often wrote them letters
urging them to maintain spiritual well-being; but these letters
contained little of the sparkling humor that he had written to
them as children and he often says that he can hardly imagine
that they are no longer children. There is no record of love
for an adult woman, other than for Ellen Terry, whom he
had seen act when he was a child, and for whose nieces he
held a particular affection.

Lewis Carroll often invited his friends to his rooms for dinners or parties, where he photographed them in costumes
which he kept in the rooms for this purpose. He kept small
toys and games for their amusement and invented music
boxes which would run backward. He always kept a floor
plan for each party, showing where each guest sat, and a
menu book of the food served. He enjoyed planning dinners

for others but ate very little himself. His lunch usually consisted of sherry, a biscuit, and a slice of melon. When he was entertained in a friend's home, he took his own sherry bottle with him and asked to be served only from his own supply.

He was conservative in his choice of clothing and wore black suits with black or gray gloves. He said that gloves were of especial significance because they have "love" inside them, and when a child once carried off one of his gloves he sent her a humorous bill for the expense and trouble she had caused him. He refused to wear an overcoat and if invited to dinner never wore a dinner jacket, for he would not change his clothes once he had dressed for the day.

We are not given a great deal of information about his choice of vocation, and yet there is evidence of some conflict because he remained a don and did not become a minister. As the oldest son, there was probably a strong family desire for him to carry on the clerical tradition of the family, for the other sons were ordained in the church, which probably only increased Lewis Carroll's guilt at his defection. If this is true, he accepted a part of the tradition when he could not embrace the whole, for he was ordained a deacon and preached in the university church although never fully ordained. He preached logical and serious sermons, without humor, and it was said they were simple enough for a child to understand. He was unorthodox in religion, and disliked the Anglican tenets which disapproved of ministers who attended the theatre or were interested in secular activities. He always expressed a guilty love for the theatre and yet he did not feel that he could give up this interest and enter the church. His speech impediment may also have played a part in his decision against an active church life, so he avoided a clean-cut solution by side-stepping the basic issue and preaching occasionally.

Lewis Carroll seemed modest and disliked success, protesting any recognition of his ability. He once wrote his mother that he was tired of being recognized for his achievements at Rugby, saying he felt he could not have gained more notoriety if he had shot the dean. Following the success of the Alice stories, he avoided celebrity collectors by saying that Charles L. Dodgson and Lewis Carroll were two different persons and that Lewis Carroll was unknown at Oxford, becoming angry if he were unmasked as Lewis Carroll in a group which knew him as Professor Dodgson. He became increasingly shy, aloof, and introspective, with a tendency to be easily offended and to show little interest in other adults.

The character of Lewis Carroll reverses at every point the behavior which was so well known in Professor Dodgson, bachelor don at Oxford College. Professor Dodgson was precise and careful, while Lewis Carroll was inclined to be absent-minded and to forget easily. He once failed to recognize his host of the previous day with a convenient amnesia which is apparent to all of us. Professor Dodgson was austere and cold, but Lewis Carroll was known as the man who loved children and who approached strange adults on the streets, in railroad coaches, or at the beaches to ask if he might play with the children. He carried toys and puzzles in his traveling bag for their entertainment and gained his greatest fame as the author of stories for children.

Although Professor Dodgson was cold, pedantic, and logical, Lewis Carroll wished for an artistic career, and Tennyson and Ruskin were among his friends, as were most of the famous artists and authors of England. His photography of children and famous friends is delicate, sensitive, and intuitive, with a clear perception of color, light, and the personality of the person whom he photographed.

Lewis Carroll was slight physically, wore his hair longer than was usual for the period, and was somewhat boyish-looking even after his hair had grayed. He spoke in a high voice and walked with a slight limp caused by housemaid's knee. He has been described as prim and old-maidish in habit and attitude. A friend who was an artist commented on the fact that he seemed to have two profiles. He is also said to have had a tremor in his upper lip, a slow, precise manner of speech, probably related to his speech disorder, and deafness in one ear.

He was jealous of the attention of parents to their children and often became angry if his play with children was interrupted. It distressed him to hear children make errors in speech, and he corrected them if they pronounced words poorly. He preferred children with straight hair, and there is an indication of a fetish about hair, for he seemed to have an exaggerated interest in this physical characteristic. He said he could imagine no pleasure greater than to brush the hair of Ellen Terry, and he carried small scissors with him to snip souvenir locks of hair from children he met.

Lewis Carroll seems to have shown no interest in little

boys, never photographed them, and was not interested in them as child actors. He did not like exaggerated speech or coarse jokes and was offended if a man dressed in woman's clothing in the theatre. He once left a play in which a man appeared as a woman, but he did not seem to have any feeling about girls who dressed in boy's clothing, common practice in the children's theatre.

We are familiar with the baby who was nursed by the Ugly Duchess in the noisy kitchen while she sang a paradoxical lullaby to the child who was supposed to sleep in the pepper-filled room:

> Speak gently to your little boy
> And beat him if he sneezes.
> He only does it to annoy
> Because he knows it teases.
> I speak severely to my boy,
> I beat him when he sneezes,
> For he can thoroughly enjoy
> The pepper when he pleases!

We are not surprised when the baby turns into a pig if we also know how Lewis Carroll felt toward children who were unfortunate enough to be born as boys, also his unhappy fate. When Alice reflects on the curious metamorphosis of the baby, the symbol of the pig as child is clear:

> If it had grown up . . . it would have been a dreadfully ugly child: but it makes a rather handsome pig, I think.

It is impossible to gain conscious understanding of the life of Lewis Carroll or of the meaning of his written fantasy unless a psychoanalytic approach is used in the study. One of the outstanding characteristics of the stories of Alice is the dreamlike quality of the writing and of the situations Alice and others encounter. Lewis Carroll admitted this when he first wrote the manuscript, but discarded all references to dreams when he rewrote the book for publication. However, the verse which opens the book makes the intention clear:

> The dream child moving through a land
> Of wonders wild and new,
> In friendly chat with bird or beast—
> And half believe it true.

Lewis Carroll seems to have escaped from harsh world realities into his stories as others escape from painful situations in dreams. The story of *Alice's Adventures in Wonderland* was consciously designed for the entertainment of the children of Dean Liddell, the friend of the author at Oxford, and Lewis Carroll characterized his stories as love gifts. However, he was not conscious of the motivation of the stories or of the source of their inspiration. The explanation of the fantasy came much later than the original creation, and Professor Dodgson was often hard put to explain what he had meant when he wrote as Mr. Carroll. "The Hunting of the Snark" was always a mystery, for audience and author, and in one of the letters he wrote some years after the verse was published, Lewis Carroll says:

In answer to your question, "What did you mean the Snark was?" will you tell your friend that I meant that the Snark was a Boojum. I trust that she and you will now feel quite satisfied and happy. To the best of my recollection, I had no other meaning in my mind, when I wrote it; but people have since tried to find the meaning in it. The one I like best (which I think is partly my own) is that it may be taken as an Allegory for the Pursuit of Happiness.

Although he made this explanation as "partly my own," it had been suggested in a letter written to him by three American children and represented the value which they had seen in the allegory rather than the meaning Mr. Carroll had given it. He seems glad of an explanation, though made by another, and there is other evidence that he was never able to explain the meaning of the poem sufficiently, either to himself or others, for he also says:

"Of course you know what a Snark is? If you do, please tell me: for I haven't an idea of what it is like."

Lewis Carroll was as ignorant of the source of his material as we are often ignorant of the wellspring of the bizzarre dreams of sleep:

. . . I added my fresh ideas, which seemed to grow of themselves upon the original stock; and many more added themselves when, years afterward, I wrote it all over again for publication . . . but whenever or however . . . *it comes of itself*. I cannot

set invention going like a clock, by any voluntary winding up.
. . . Alice and the Looking Glass are made up almost wholly of
bits and scraps, single ideas which come of themselves.

Lewis Carroll liked to invent portmanteau words which
carried a double meaning and which telescoped several ideas
into one word, just as a number of incidents may be symbolized in one event in a dream, but his explanation of these
words were also made sometime after the word had been
unconsciously written and given meaning. He writes the
following explanation of the words in the Jabberwock, but
it does not indicate a controlled, rational invention of words
so much as a later analysis of meaning, which Mr. Carroll
may mistrust even as he explains:

I'm afraid I can't explain "vorpal blade" for you—nor yet
"tulgey wood"; but I did make an explanation once for "uffish
thought": . . . It seems to suggest a state of mind when the
voice is gruffish, the manner roughish, and the temper huffish.
Then again, as to "burble": if you take the three verbs "*b*lest,"
"mu*r*mur" and "var*ble*," and select the bits I have underlined, it
certainly makes "burble"; though I am afraid I can't distinctly
remember having made it in that way.

He has said that the Snark was a mythological creature
which was half-snake and half-shark, and this verse was
written in reverse, in a sense, for the first line which occurred
to him was the last line of the written poem:

For the Snark was a Boojum, you see.

There is a relationship between the two poems "The Hunting
of the Snark" and "The Jabberwocky," for some of the
nonsense words are common to both poems. The following
explanation of the words in "The Jabberwocky" was made in
*Mishmash* in 1855, one of the newspapers Lewis Carroll
wrote while at Oxford:

*Bryllyg.* (derived from the verb to *Bryl* or Broil) the time of
broiling dinner, i.e., the close of the afternoon.
*Slythy.* (compounded of *Slimy* and *Lithe*) smooth and active.
*Tove.* A species of badger. They had smooth white hair, long
hind legs, and short horns like a stag; lived chiefly on cheese.
*Gyre.* verb. (derived from *Gyaour* or *Giaour,* "a dog") to scratch
like a dog.

*Gymble.* (whence *Gimblet*) to screw out holes in anything.
*Wabe.* (derived from the verb to *Swab* or *Soak*) the side of a hill. (from its being *soaked* by the rain).
*Mimsy.* (whence *Mimserable* and *Miserable*) unhappy.
*Borogrove.* An extinct kind of parrott. They had no wings, beaks turned up, and made their nests under sun-dials; lived on veal.
*Mome.* (hence *Solomome, Solemone,* and *Solemn*) grave.
*Rath.* A species of land turtle. Head erect; mouth like a shark; the fore-legs curved out so that the animal walked on its knees; smooth green body; lived on swallows and oysters.
*Outgrabe.* Past tense of the verb to *Outgribe.* (it is connected with the old verb to *Brike* or *Shrike* from which are derived "shriek" and "creak") squeaked.

Hence the literal English of the passage is: "It was evening, and the smooth active badgers were scratching and boring holes in the hill-side; all unhappy were the parrots; and the grave turtles squeaked out."

There were probably sun-dials on the tops of the hill, and the "borogroves" were afraid that their nests would be undermined. The hill was probably full of the nests of "raths" which ran out squeaking with fear, on hearing the "toves" scratching outside. This is an obscure, but yet deeply affecting relic of Ancient Poetry."

Lewis Carroll described this as Anglo-Saxon poetry, and in *Carroll's Alice,* Professor Harry Morgan Ayres, Columbia University, traces characters and illustrations to an Anglo-Saxon source. He feels that "Haigha" and "Hatta" in *Through the Looking-Glass* are prototypes for the Hatter and the March Hare in *Alice's Adventures in Wonderland.* He believes that Haigha is a name coined from the name of an English authority on Angle-Saxon, Daniel Henry Haigh. He also found the word "hatte" used in the Anglo-Saxon manuscripts, which may have been mistaken by Lewis Carroll as a family name, although it is a translation of a verb, "is called."

Professor Ayres shows further that some of the costume detail in the Tenniel drawings is similar to the drawings in the early Anglo-Saxon manuscripts, particularly in the cross-gartering and the design of the shoes of Haigha and Hatta. His thesis is further supported by Lewis Carroll's references to "Anglo-Saxon attitudes" of "skipping and wriggling with great hands spread out on each side," which is an exact description of the flat, awkwardly articulated drawings in the early Anglo-Saxon manuscripts. (Lewis Carroll called it an "attitude," with perhaps an intentional pun on the word of "hatte," thus making it "(h) attitudes".) There are other evidences that his imaginative characters were based on friends and acquaintances or other people who are familiar to all of us—teachers, nurses, butlers, gardeners, and other adults.

The practice of reversal permeates the life of Lewis Carroll, his stories and his hobbies. Alice found herself in a world which reversed the accepted patterns of the world, and the story of the Looking-Glass is a story of complete reversal of the real world. In his own life, Lewis Carroll was obliged to write with the right hand rather than the left, and to reverse the character of Charles Dodgson in order to become Lewis Carroll. Everything worked backward for Alice, too, when she fell down the rabbit hole into another world or when she stepped into the land behind the looking-glass. Lewis Carroll liked to write in reverse, and sent letters which could be read only when they were held up to a mirror. He wrote the verse about the Jabberwocky in reverse and the last line first.

One of the letters to a child friend was written with the signature of Charles Dodgson as salutation, and opens:

"C. L. D. Uncle loving your"

The letter is somewhat acid in tone, for Lewis Carroll was writing about a birthday gift which had not pleased him:

It was so nice of you to give me that pretty Antimacassar you had made for my grandfather. And how well it has lasted.

His life seems to indicate that he did not like his adult, masculine character and that he wished to change himself into a small, adventurous girl because he could not reverse the inexorable force which propelled him toward adult life. If he could have reversed his order in the family constellation, he could have displaced the progression of ten brothers and sisters who forced him to become the oldest child. He is clear in stating his feeling toward boy babies, and an important boy character, Bruno, appears in only one story, *Sylvie and Bruno,* although he is more like a little girl than like a little boy and Lewis Carroll did not complete the story until after twenty years of work. There are clear expressions of hostility toward boys, and the letters of Lewis Carroll in-

clude only one letter to a boy. It is full of rejection, with
little friendliness in the tone:

> I would have been very glad to write to you as you wish, only
> there are several objections. I think when you have heard them,
> you will see that I am right in saying "no." The first objection is.
> "I've got no ink. . . ." The next objection is, "I've no time." You
> don't believe that, you say? Well, who cares? . . . The third and
> greatest objection is, my great dislike for children. I don't know
> why, I'm sure: but I hate them—just as one hates armchairs and
> plum pudding. . . . So you see, it would never do to write to
> you. Have you any sisters? I forget. If you have, give them my
> love. . . . I hope you won't be much disappointed at not getting
> a letter from
>                                         Your affectionate friend,

Much of the humor of Lewis Carroll is based on reversal
of the intention of an original thought, and he parries the
aggression of others by thrusting it back upon his opponent.
The logical, childlike arguments of Alice are a perversion of
adult logic, and Lewis Carroll used this same device in some
of his correspondence:

> In some ways, you know, people that don't exist are much
> nicer than people that do. For instance, people that don't exist
> are never cross; and they never contradict you; and they never
> tread on your toes! Oh, they're ever so much nicer than people
> that do exist. However, never mind; you can't help existing; and I
> daresay you're just as nice as if you didn't.

Such logic is the peculiar delight of children who trap and
overcome the restrictive adult by extending the original
promise to an infinite, illogical, never-to-be-expected conclusion. It is also a sadistic, verbal revenge, and we are all
familiar with the person that cannot be convinced because
of the illogical logic that protects him.

This tendency seems closely related to the teasing which
we find in many of Lewis Carroll's letters and which is often
openly hostile. He wrote the little boy a letter because he felt
a compulsion to answer all letters and he pretended to meet
the request, yet he denies he has written the letter, asks that
the boy not feel too disappointed, while at the same time
he inquires about the boy's sisters to whom he sends his love.
It is significant that he signed some letters "Sylvie"; but he
never used the name of Bruno, which further suggests his

identification with his small girl characters rather than with the boys. He could never overcome this aversion to boys, and writes in another letter:

My best love to yourself—to your Mother kindest regards—to your small, fat, impertinent, ignorant brother my hatred.

He does not seem to have enjoyed being a boy, although he remembers:

Once I was a real boy

just as the Mock Turtle laments:

Once I was a real turtle.

He was once asked to teach in a boy's school, and wrote the following reply:

To me they [boys] are not an attractive race of beings (as a little boy I was simply detestable) and if you wanted to induce me, by money, to come and teach them, I can only say you would have to offer more than 1,000 pounds per year.

A recent biographer, Florence Becker Lennon, feels that the verse of Lewis Carroll sometimes indicates an unresolved Oedipus conflict with a strong attachment to the mother. "Solitude," written when Lewis Carroll was twenty-one, seems to support Mrs. Lennon's analysis:

I'd give all wealth that years have piled,
The slow result of life's decay,
To be once more a little child
For one bright summer day.

Although Mrs. Lennon does not frankly admit a Freudian analysis of this verse, there is sufficient symbolism in this poem and in another, "Stolen Waters," to support the thesis that Lewis Carroll remained at a childish level in his emotional life:

I kissed her on the false, false lips—
That burning kiss I feel it now!

"True love gives true love of the best;
Then take," I cried, "my heart to thee!"

The very heart from out my breast
I plucked, I gave it willingly:
Her very heart she gave to me—
Then died the glory from the west.
In the gray light I saw her face,
And it was withered, old and gray;
The flowers were fading in their place,
Were fading with the fading day.

Lewis Carroll offers a solution to the insoluble dilemma of
adulthood by substituting a state of childish existence, aimed
not at the realization of a mature adult life, but fixed at a
level of innocence in life until the adult-child passes into the
larger innocence of death:

Be as a child—
So shalt thou sing for very joy of breath—
So shalt thou wait thy dying,
In holy transport lying—
So pass rejoicing through the gate of death,
In garment undefiled.

There is a further indication of an unsolved emotional
problem in Lewis Carroll's choice of young girls as love
objects; young girls who were sisters; sisters who were young
girls and thus one step removed from the mother who may
not be loved because of the taboo of the father and of society.
He stated his ideal as that of a young girl but stipulated that
they must be young girls from outside the family. We have
also seen that when Lewis Carroll reversed the family name
he omitted adoption of the paternal name but maintained
the perversions of the mother's family name, just as his
identifications remained with girl children instead of with
boys. He seems to have solved his adolescent conflict by
putting adult sexuality aside, and remaining a passive, com-
pliant son who did not protest the loss of his masculine
adulthood openly but who apparently never loved an adult
woman.

If this is true, his repression of feeling must have been
deep and unrealized, which may explain in part the elaborate
defenses which he created to protect himself from anxiety.
We have seen that he created two personalities for himself
and that he lived as Charles L. Dodgson or Lewis Carroll
with equal facility and enjoyment. In the final analysis, we
can expect that it was through such a defense that life

became tolerable for him and that he escaped eventual illness by splitting his personality into two forms. Paul Schilder felt that the anal-sadistic content of the stories of Lewis Carroll were significant and that most of the compulsions which he displayed are related to the retentive, hoarding, inflexible character of the anal personality which seems to be supported in his dress, the cataloguing of letters and papers, the neatness of his room, his choice of notepaper in graduated sizes, his scanty diet, his clean gloves, and the general neatness and precise exactness of his life. The exaggerated control of his environment seems to mirror a fear of the volatile and explosive unconscious wishes which he felt. Neither could he be certain what to expect from uncontrolled, free, and less restricted people in the world, so he shunned them and sought security in the presence of children who are also immature adults. In later years his fears bordered on the pathological, for he refused to dring from a sherry bottle other than his own and he cut the pages of his manuscripts into strips when he mailed them to the illustrator, who was instructed to use a guide, mailed by separate post, in reassembling the manuscript.

There is a persistence of sexual feeling which cannot be denied, however, and Lewis Carroll was aware of some guilt in his relationships with his young friends, for he always felt that Mrs. Grundy was looking over his shoulder:

(being now an old man who can venture on things that "Mrs. Grundy" would never permit to a younger man) have some little friend to stay with me as a guest. My last friend was the little girl who lately played Alice.

Mrs. Grundy is a further censor of his activities in the following letter, which was written with so much nervousness that the original is hardly legible. It is a letter full of apology and fear but also full of persistence and anxious expectation when he invites a child to visit him:

You were so gracious the other day that I have nearly got over my fear of you. The slight tremulousness which you may observe in my writing, produced by the thought that it is you I am writing to, will soon pass off. Next time I borrow you, I shall venture on having you alone: I like my child friends best one by one: and I'll have Maggie alone another day, if she'll come (that is the great difficulty!). But first I want to borrow (I can scarcely

muster courage to say it) your eldest sister. Oh, how the very
thought of it frightens me! Do you think she would come? I don't
mean alone: I think Maggie might come, too, to make it all
proper. . . .

This letter is almost hysterical, pleading, and suppliant,
with mixed fear that he may be misunderstood and a
further fear that he may lose the love of one child when he
asks her to act as his intermediary with her sister. There is
some biographical material which indicates that some parents
were unwilling to permit their children to visit Lewis Carroll,
and he objected if the parents did not wish children to visit
him unchaperoned. There was an open, unspecified disagreement between Mrs. Liddell and Mr. Dodgson which must
remain mysterious until his diaries are published or until there
is further biographical information concerning him. In addition to preferring his visitors alone, and resenting the interruption of parents, it was difficult for Lewis Carroll to share
his friends with others. He sent the following gentle repri-
mand to one of the children whom he knew:

Oh, child, child! I kept my promise yesterday afternoon, and
came down to the sea, to go with you along the rocks: but I saw
you going with another gentleman, so I thought I wasn't wanted
just yet; so I walked about a bit, and when I got back I
couldn't see you anywhere, though I went a good way on the
rocks to look.

His interest in figure drawing seems a further sublimation
of his sexual interest in children. This never became a
conscious sexual interest and yet his preoccupation with girl
children can scarcely be understood in other terms. A woman
friend who was also an artist worked with him to secure
suitable models, and states that he considered twelve the
ideal age for his drawing, for he considered children too thin
who were younger. In later years, Lewis Carroll developed
a close friendship with Harry Furniss, the artist who illustrated several editions of his stories, and in one of his
letters, Lewis Carroll confesses his wish and the accompanying fear of social taboos:

I wish I dared dispose with all costume: naked children are
so perfectly pure and lovely, but Mrs. Grundy would be furious—
it would never do. Then the question is, how little dress would
content her.

Although he wrote about "children" in the letter, he did not mean all children, but only little girls, for he states in another letter:

I confess I do not admire naked boys, in pictures. They always seem to need clothes—whereas one hardly sees why the lovely forms of girls should ever be covered up.

His interest in the figures of little girls and his love of little girls was the eventual expression of his denial of adult sexual life. There is a cohesion in the pattern if we recall his interest in photography, the costumes in which he dressed his young friends, his summer vacations at the beach, and the actual celibacy which he chose for himself, further enforced by his association with the church.

Love may assume many aspects when denied, and Schilder has identified the sadism, unconsciously expressed in the fairy tales of Lewis Carroll. This can be further illustrated in many of his letters, which contain moralistic advice, corrections of speech and grammar, or playful complaints when his young friends do not give him the love and attention which he demands.

In one letter, he writes to apologize for having failed to congratulate a child on her birthday and although he called when no one was at home he imagined the following scene as preparation for the child's party:

I had just time to look into the kitchen, and saw your birthday feast getting ready, a nice dish of crusts, bones, pills, cotton-bobbins, and rhubarb and magnesia. "Now," I thought, "she will be happy!" And with a smiling face I went away.

He was very conscious of birthdays, and some of his letters are complaints about the gifts he received. They are usually complaints couched in coy terms, but the harshness is there, though disguised and softened:

Thank you very much for the napkin ring, but do you know I never use anything of the sort, so I hope you won't mind giving it to somebody else instead, and if you really want to make something for me, make me a little bag (say a square bag about the size of this note sheet); *that* would be really useful, and I should be really glad to have it.

At another time he had been promised a gift which had not
been sent him, so he wrote the following letter to complain,
although he reversed his feeling and wrote the letter as though
he were writing to thank his young friend for the birthday
present:

> I have waited since January 27 to thank you for your letter
> and present, that I might be able to say the "scales" had come—
> but as they still don't come, I will wait no longer. Thank you for
> all your birthday wishes and for the "scales," whatever they are.

Although he was timid in his behavior, he dreaded the
rejection that the timid person always fears, and the following letters show his anger when he is neglected, although he
also pretends that the loss of a friend more or less could mean
little to him. There is also interesting incidental information
about his voluminous letter writing:

> *Please* don't suggest to her to write, poor child. If she had
> got, as I have, more than 800 entries in her letter-register for
> this year, she wouldn't be particularly keen about adding one
> to the list.

Despite his friendships there is a complaint of ultimate
poverty of love in the wistful confession which Lewis Carroll
made in another letter:

> Of course there isn't much companionship possible, after all,
> between an old man's mind and a little child's—what there is, is
> sweet—and wholesome, I think.

He once wrote a child that he forgot what the story of Alice
was about but he said: "I think it was about malice."

Some may feel that too great an emphasis has been placed
on slight, incidental information about Lewis Carroll, as
given in letters and articles, and yet it is precisely the slight
and incidental that gives the deepest understanding of the
forces which prompted him to fashion his life as he did. It
is the chink in the armor which is dangerous, the vulnerable
break in the defense, but it may also be the avenue to the
heart and a true understanding of the individual.

There is a good deal of evidence which traces the characters in the stories of Alice to people known to Lewis Carroll.
The following description of the White Rabbit might almost

be a description of the personality of Lewis Carroll, and seems to indicate the manner in which he introjected himself into his stories:

And the White Rabbit, what of him? Was he framed on the Alice lines or meant as a contrast? As a contrast, distinctly. For her "youth," "audacity," "vigour," and "swift directness," of "purpose," read "elderly," "timid," "feeble," and "nervously shilly-shallying" and you will get *something* of what I meant *him* to be. I think the White Rabbit should wear spectacles. I am sure his voice should quaver, and his whole air to suggest a total inability to say "Bo" to a goose!

There is a persistence in Lewis Carroll's feeling that his writing should have meaning, even though he could not always give it, and it is the Red Queen who reminds Alice that: "Even a joke should have meaning." It is important for our understanding, then, to relate the other clues concerning characters to the origins which Lewis Carroll has defined. Canon Duckworth accompanied Lewis Carroll on the boat trip the day he first told the story to the Liddell children, and later Carroll sent a copy of the book to the Canon, with the inscription: "The Duck from the Dodo." The Duck and the Dodo in Wonderland seem to have been created from the first syllables of the two names, Duckworth and Dodgson. It is also interesting to recall the symbol of the Dodo bird which is stupid, ineffective, and aimless, which may be related to the stammering, ineffectual life Lewis Carroll lived and which in turn may also be related to his speech, for a stammered pronunciation of Dodgson produces "Dodo" as the first syllable.

When the Dormouse tells the story of the three little girls who lived in the treacle well—Elsie, Lacey, and Tilly— he uses variations of the names of the children Lavinia, Alice, and Edith. Elsie is a pronunciation of the initials of Lavinia Charlotte; Lacie is an anagram for Alice; and Tillie was the pet name used for Edith. Later, "Lory," the parrot, may be traced to Lorina, and "Eaglet" is a childish pronunciation of the name Edith.

It is possible to recognize the prototype of many familiar people in the stories of Lewis Carroll and to populate them with acquaintances whom we also wish to caricature. The reader may do this unconsciously, and yet Lewis Carroll seems to have written many of his stories as an overt expression of malice, clothed in the socially acceptable form of whimsy. The inconsistency of the adult world is always apparent, but also apparent in the inconsistencies of the life of Lewis Carroll and of his acquaintances. The stories are filled with an endless procession of people in masquerade and somewhat ridiculous as a result; queens, kings, footmen, servants, teachers, gardners, and other everyday people of everyday life.

Lewis Carroll suffered from insomnia, although he sometimes denied it, and one of his young friends said that his most absurd ideas came to him when he was almost asleep. He walked long distances during the day and invented a system of cryptograph writing which enabled him to write his thoughts in the dark. Although he worked hard during the day and exhausted himself physically, he was often unable to fall asleep and he wrote "Pillow Problems" to provide ways of occupying his mind when he was sleepless.

It was perhaps on the threshold of sleep that Lewis Carroll felt most keenly his discovery that if "live" is spelled backward it becomes "evil," for it is in this period of mental dusk that the darker thoughts of the mind threatened to penetrate into consciousness. Lewis Carroll expressed this same sentiment in speaking of the Snark:

I engage with the Snark—every night after dark—in a dreamy delirious fight.

He could never explain this creature of his imagination, searched for but never found, although he realized that it was not quite all nonsense:

Still, you know, words mean more than we mean to express when we use them: so a whole book ought to mean more than the writer meant.

He never found a role for himself in the world, either, and remained with a portmanteau personality, now open as Lewis Carroll, now closed behind the armor of Charles L. Dodgson. He could not gasp the essential role of an adult, masculine person and he fumbled for his identity only to find it was usually expressed in a soft, feminine, plastic identification with young girl children. He was a pedantic, forbidding adult as Charles L. Dodgson, and in this role openly presented himself to the world, but as Lewis Carroll he became an adult, unmarried, secluded male spinster. In later years, he became more openly the character of Lewis Carroll, and the querulous and complaining characteristics of his behavior were said to be more pronounced.

Lewis Carroll was not a quiet, shy, passive person in all respects, but his revolt was expressed in a bland, limited, and inhibited way. Stories are made from words, and words are intended to be spoken, so Lewis Carroll lived and protested through his stories while Professor Dodgson lived and protested in pamphlets or letters to the newspapers. Overt displacement of the shadowy authority of the father was never realized; but Lewis Carroll was created from the spiritual rib of Charles Lutwidge Dodgson, and authority became divided and diluted so seemed less threatening.

There was a similar dilution in his own personality, and his basic sexual conflict remained unexpressed, his sexual wishes disguised by his interest in young girls, while he guarded against overt sexuality by discarding his friends when they became adolescents. If women were necessary, they were necessary as mothers or sisters, not as wives or friends, which may bring us close to the basic source of the creative impulse of Lewis Carroll.

He could never slay the dragon and become the hero, the traditional role of the young hero in classic myths, for there is no hero in "The Hunting of the Snark." At the crucial moment the hero disappears, vanishes, and admits that he cannot even identify his enemy or find him:

> But if ever I meet with a Boojum, that day
> In a moment (of this I am sure),
> I shall softly and suddenly vanish away—
> And the notion I cannot endure!

This is perhaps the only solution of the dilemma of Charles Lutwidge Dodgson who did not dare to become adult. Martin Grotjahn, in a psychological analysis of "Ferdinand the Bull" had shown a similar inclination in this modern, mythical character who refused to become an adult bull, fighting in the bullring, and so remained the eternal child sitting quitely under the paternal corktree, smelling the beautiful flowers. Grotjahn explains the appeal of the book to the adult when he says:

Adults like to read this book to children, telling them in this way that Ferdinand enjoys everlasting love, peace and happiness so long as he behaves like a nice little calf who does not grow up. In this case the book is used as a clear-cut castration threat like most famous books for children (*Struwwelpeter, Alice in Wonderland*).

Lewis Carroll also remained a child, and in this role solved the problem which we all have faced when growing up. It is perhaps this unconscious identification with him which makes us understand him when he speaks to us through his stories and which will also make Alice live forever as a child of the collective world-unconscious.

## BIBLIOGRAPHY

1. *Carroll's Alice,* Harry Morgan Ayres, New York, Columbia University Press, 1936.
2. *Life of Lewis Carroll,* Langford Reed, London, Foyle, 1932.
3. *The Life and Letters of Lewis Carroll,* Stuart Dodgson Collingwood, London, Unwin, 1898.
4. The Lewis Carroll Book, Richard Herrick, Dial Press, 1931.
5. *The Russian Journal and Other Selections from the Work of Lewis Carroll,* John Francis McDermott, Dutton, 1935.
6. "Lewis Carroll," in *The Eighteen Eighties,* Walter De la Mare, Cambridge University Press, 1930.
7. *The Story of Lewis Carroll,* Isa Bowman, London, 1899.
8. *The Basic Writings of Sigmund Freud,* Random House, 1937.
9. *Complete Works of Lewis Carroll,* Modern Library, Random House, 1937.
10. "Ferdinand the Bull," Martin Grotjahn, *American Imago,* 1, No. 1 (1940), "Psychoanalytic Remarks About a Modern Totem Animal."
11. "About the Symbolization of Alice's Adventures in Wonderland," Martin Grotjahn, *American Imago,* 4, No. 4 (1947).
12. "Psychoanalytic Remarks on Alice in Wonderland and Lewis Carroll," Paul Schilder, *Journal of Nervous and Mental Disease,* 87, No. 2 (1938).

Mark Kanzer*

# THE "PASSING OF THE OEDIPUS COMPLEX" IN GREEK DRAMA

## I

The attention focused by Freud on Sophocles' *Oedipus Tyrannus* has not been transferred, strangely enough, to the sequel, *Oedipus at Colonus*, which is integrally related to the problems of the earlier play. Whereas *Oedipus Tyrannus* confronts men with the disastrous results of their fundamental unconscious drives, *Oedipus at Colonus* depicts the process of restitution and social application of the same forces in a manner which anticipates and closely resembles Freud's own formulations as to the passing of the Oedipus complex through superego development.

The career of Oedipus did not end when he blinded himself after discovering that he had inadvertently carried out the prophesy that he would murder his father and marry his mother. He later went into exile from Thebes, the city he had ruled, and for twenty years (a generation!) wandered miserable and homeless through many lands, accompanied only by his daughter Antigone. *Oedipus at Colonus* deals with the refuge and peace which he finally found, and with his death.

At the beginning of the play, Oedipus and Antigone rest momentarily in a grove at Colonus outside Athens. The natives warn them that they have committed sacrilege in entering the holy place of the Eumenides and are completely horrified when they discover that the stranger is the notorious Oedipus. The exiled king feels, however, that his accidental intrusion into the haunts of the Fates, or Eumenides, is a signal he has awaited from the gods that his trials are over, and implores the alarmed populace to summon the Athenian

---

* MARK KANZER is the author of many professional articles in the field of psychoanalysis and literature.

king, Theseus. While awaiting Theseus, a second daughter of Oedipus, Ismene, arrives with the message that oracles have recently proclaimed that the grave of Oedipus will have great powers and that consequently rival disputants for the throne of Thebes will seek to gain possession of him. Oedipus rejoices that "the gods who overthrew him now sustain him" but entertains only bitterness to the Thebans who drove him into exile. When Theseus arrives and shows himself well disposed, Oedipus offers him the promised power of his grave if the Athenian king will provide him with refuge and protection for the remainder of his days. Theseus agrees, and the stage is set for two dramatic interviews with the contending rulers of Thebes.

The first encounter is with Creon, maternal uncle and ancient enemy of Oedipus. When his blandishments fail to win over his blind nephew, he seizes the daughters and lays hands upon Oedipus himself. Theseus intervenes in time and drives off Creon ignominiously. Then Polyneices, a son of Oedipus, arrives to beg his father's aid. In the dramatic highpoint of the play, Oedipus rebukes his son for his previous indifference and, in a violent diatribe, curses Polyneices and his brother Eteochles as undutiful sons and predicts their death in battle at each other's hands.

Lastly, a thunderstorm arises, and Oedipus senses a message from the gods that his time has come. He summons Theseus for the third and last time and grants him alone the privilege of witnessing his last moments and final resting place on earth. Then the old hero disappears in a mysterious manner, and Theseus, guarding the secret, assumes the obligation of a father to the bereaved daughters.

## II

The grove of the Eumenides as the scene of the action is of key importance. As Oedipus himself points out, his wandering to this spot is an omen that the gods are ready to grant him forgiveness and peace. The Eumenides are the Furies or Fates who, in Greek mythology, are older and stronger than the gods. They are female spirits, representative of the prehistorical matriarchy and the savage customs of an earlier period. The rise of the father state was paralleled by the evolution of a hierarchy of gods who symbolized the need for reason and discipline so characteristic of the later Greek culture. Throughout the patriarchal period, however, secret cults dedicated to the more primitive gods continued to flourish. The sins of Oedipus in killing his father and committing incest with his mother were crimes against the two fundamental taboos of the tribe, and his punishment and sufferings were regarded as sentences executed upon him by the Furies, who torment the violators of family morals. Polyneices, subtly hinting at his spiritual as well as biological relationship to his father, declares, "I believe that the Furies that pursue you were indeed the cause (that I too was driven from my native city and I have become a wanderer, inasmuch as I have forfeited the right to dwell within the family)."

The question then arises as to why Oedipus felt that his entrance into the holy place of the Furies was a sign of the end of his torments. Here we must recall the special history of the Furies in the mythology of Athens and their role in the Greek drama of the period. Aeschylus had recorded the sufferings of Orestes who had killed his mother for instigating the murder of his father. Although the deed of Orestes was approved by the gods of the father state, the Furies pursued him with merciless ferocity which could not be averted by the gods themselves. Finally, a trial was held at Athens in which the Furies were persuaded to reconcile themselves with the rule of the gods, in token of which their names were flatteringly changed to "The Eumenides," or "The Gentle Ones." This superb repressive mechanism did not change the dread in which these powerful and passionate spirits were held, and in *Oedipus at Colonus* they are referred to as "most feared daughters of darkness and mysterious earth," and the grove into which Oedipus has wandered as "the inviolate thicket of those whom it's futile to fight, those whom we tremble to name. When we pass we avert our eyes, close our eyes, in silence, without conversation, shaping our prayers with our lips." The Furies evidently represent the dread forces of the unconscious which must be appeased by the reasonable mind and, in the imagery of Sophocles, have their abode in the womb of the mother. That Oedipus dares to enter the forbidden region is indeed the characteristic of Oedipus; but why should this action now be in accord with the divine will and not an affront to the gods as on the previous occasion? His blindness cannot be the extenuating circumstance, since his earlier incestuous deed had been carried out unwittingly and even in accord with the prophesies of the oracles.

The difference between the two occasions must be inferred

as the drama proceeds. First we find Oedipus, the proud and arrogant, paying obeisance at this spot to the rightful king, Theseus, and obtaining his permission to dwell here with his daughter Antigone until his death. In this act, we may see a familiar rite of homage of vassal to sovereign, duplicating the dutiful relationship of the son to the father. In this traditional ceremony, the subject places his life and all his property at the disposal of the king and at once receives them again at the hands of the benevolent ruler. What Oedipus receives from Theseus is analogous to the real meaning of the ritual of homage, namely, forgiveness for rebellion and the right to a partial satisfaction of his desires as long as he accepts the laws of the community. Through his acknowledgement of Theseus as his ruler, Oedipus undoes the crime of parricide and restores to life the figure of the father. He has been freed of the first of his two sins. As a reward for giving up his independence, which has long since lost its attractions, he is granted protection, a home and security for his daughter Antigone.

The figure of Antigone requires our study. We recall that after the blinding and exile of Oedipus, he wandered over the earth, shunned by all men and accompanied only by this faithful daughter. There is here a complete allegorical account of a neurosis following a traumatic experience. In giving up his kingdom and his eyesight, Oedipus renounces the gratification of his drives in the outer world and, dominated by feelings of shame and guilt, regresses to a more infantile relationship to the mother. The self-inflicted blindness by the man who solved the riddle of the sphinx, namely, the mysteries of intercourse and birth, points to a primal scene which gave him knowledge and instigated his desires. In yielding his power of sight, Oedipus subjects the memory of the primal scene to infantile amnesia and to a dwelling place in the unconscious, as do countless children who have repreated his experiences in more attenuated form in real life. Antigone here plays the role of the mother—a familiar distortion of the unconscious. In the period of expiation which corresponds to his neurosis, Oedipus has clung to incestual satisfactions with all the more vigor for the disguise, just as symptoms regularly embody the return of the repressed in the measure of defense.

In Oedipus at Colonus, we see the basic drives of Oedipus repeating themselves as they do in every neurosis, with an

effort to master the original trauma. Again he horrifies the
populace by wandering with his mother-daughter into a
sacred region which symbolizes her genitals. His blindness
reverses the original deed, which was visual, just as the
father-daughter relationship reverses the original family ties.
The act is a signal that the good will of the gods is in store
for him instead of their displeasure, and is to be followed
by a treaty of friendship with the father instead of deadly
combat. The psychopathology of this process is closely allied
to the normal passing of the Oedipus complex into the
latency phase.

Secure in the pact with the father, Oedipus can confront
a repetition of the old traumatic experiences. Creon himself
appears, his mother's brother and the very man who had
played such a vital role in exposing and punishing Oedipus
on the occasion of his earlier transgression. Again Creon seeks
to separate him from a mutual female relative, now Antigone
instead of Jocasta, and to drive him forth from a home which
he has found. In Creon's determination to seek "the power of
his grave" may be found a death threat with implications of
castration. The situation now terminates differently; it is
Creon who is convicted of behavior offensive to society and
who is driven off. That Oedipus summons Theseus for this
task shows that he no longer depends upon the infantile
omnipotence of earlier days but has delegated his powers to
the father as the child ordinarily learns to do in his latency
period. Social implications of this action relate not only to
the course of the individual with respect to the authority of
the community but, in the specific sense of the Athenian
drama, with the triumph of the father state, represented by
Theseus, over the supreme authority of the matriarchy, the
mother's brother Creon.

The appearance of Polyneices at this point provides the
cue to the supreme emotional climax of the play, the curse
of Oedipus upon an undutiful son. The undoing of the
crimes of Oedipus reach a culmination when he can only
defend himself against his former accuser, Creon, but sits
in judgement himself upon the man who is guilty of his own
sins. In Polyneices, Oedipus confronts the projected image
of his former self, and the merciless hatred which he pours
forth is a reaction formation which shows how far he has
gone in the identification with his father. Oedipus as guardian
of the family morality has proceeded still further along the

road of undoing his evil deeds. He has accepted completely
the customs and interests of the father and, in Freudian
terminology, has formed a superego.

Creon and Polyneices provide two great tests of the pact
between Theseus and Oedipus. He has refrained from the
use of his infantile omnipotence in his dealings with Creon,
and has renounced his former goals in his rejection of Polyneices. The third and last manifestation of his loyalty to
Theseus is in his complete surrender of individuality by death
and transmission of his powers to the king. The ensuing
drama of the passing of Oedipus is obviously a puberty rite
in which father and son each renounce their death wishes
against each other, and only one man emerges from the
ceremony. The mysterious burial place and powers of Oedipus are in Theseus, who "alone has witnessed the secret
passing of Oedipus" and who now addresses Antigone as
"my daughter." Symbolically, Theseus, who represents the
reason and culture of Athens, has mastered but still bears
within himself the passion of a more primitive phase of
development. Oedipus will still provide him with powers in
critical times; where reason finds its limits, the driving force
and prophetic insight derived from the forgotten Oedipal
experiences will still be of service.

On the stage at the end are Theseus and Antigone, and
now the last meaning of the drama reveals itself. The puberty
rites and the identification of father and son have terminated
in a wedding ceremony. The setting at the entrance to the
womb has been robbed of its terror by the purifying action
of the drama. On the stage, throughout the play, at the
opening of the grove has been the equestrian status of
Colonus, ancestor of the natives. The totemic significance
of the figure has been borne out throughout the drama by
repeated reference to the horses and olive trees for which
Colonus is famous. These emblems of male and female
fertility, animal and vegetable, flourish in this region which
had long been a sacred spot marked by many temples and
altars. Colonus, "the white columns," derives its name from
its setting on two white hills which guard the road into
Athens. Poseidon, the god of horses, and Athena, goddess of
olives, were supposed in Greek mythology to have contended
for possession of the place. Theseus and Polyneices both
appear upon the stage after having made sacrifices to Poseidon. The wedding ceremony requires that the man shall be

freed of his Oedipal guilt. It is the sanctified Theseus, not the youth of unbridled passions, who may be the bridegroom. And for Antigone, the site is a reminder of how the untamed female spirits here became the "gentle ones" and thrived and were honored in the form of the goddess of spinning and domestic arts. Antigone, "daughter" of Theseus, and Athena, daughter of Zeus, reincarnate the conditions of marriage in the patriarchy, where the women shall take the dependent role and yield to men the precedence which they enjoyed when they were mothers.

## III

*Oedipus at Colonus* is regarded as the last of Sophocles' plays, written when he was eighty-nine years old. There is a legend that the aged man was once hailed before a tribunal by his son, Iophon, on the ground of mental incompetence and the need for a guardian for himself and his estates. Iophon, a tragedian like his father, is said to have been jealous of the preference which the old man showed for an illegitimate son. At a hearing before the court, Sophocles defended himself solely by reading portions of the *Oedipus at Colonus*, which he was then writing, and was acquitted without further dispute. This tale, which is reported in Cicero's *De Senectute*, has been regarded as of doubtful validity, but shows a remarkable resemblance to the action of the play.

Certainly the picture of Oedipus finding peace and death at the end of his journey would serve as an appropriate valedictory from Sophocles, and the imagery of resurrection and reunion with the ancestors would be in a fitting vein. The locale of the drama, Colonus, was actually the birthplace of Sophocles, and as such provides a natural "unity in place" for a play whose "unity in time and action" is a sweeping survey of life and death expressed in symbols which condense and integrate all the stages of existence. How aptly the Oedipal theme may represent the problems of each phase of development: the infantile omnipotence, the latency period, puberty and marriage rites; the characteristic perpetuation in the mature man through preference for the daughter and hostility to the son; and finally, even at the brink of the grave, in reincarnation and perpetuation in the successor.

Not that Oedipus would ordinarily come to mind as the prototype of Sophocles, who was known rather as "The Serene." His entire life seems to have been marked by success

and serenity, and he was famed for his pleasant disposition.
The character in the play who really resembles the dramatist
is Theseus, the temperate and cultured Athenian. Perhaps in
the metaphor that Theseus "knew the final resting place of
Oedipus" is to be found the hidden source of the drives and
insight which found their sublimation in the tragic plays in
which Sophocles gave play to his imagination. We are given
pause by the casual comment placed in the mouth of Jocasta,
that "many men dream that they have slept with their
mothers." Plato quotes Sophocles as welcoming old age
because it gave him freedom from the passions—a statement
that does not accord with traditional picture of serenity.
Perhaps it is not without significance that it was the aging
dramatist, presumably rejoicing at his liberation from physical
drives, who created the *Oedipus Tyrannus* with the violent
and tragic conflicts of the hero who is forced by fate to
renounce his sexual life.

Finally, the political situation in Athens was certainly not
without its influence on the Oedipus plays. *Oedipus Tyrannus* was written soon after Athens had begun her long and
disastrous war with Sparta, and the theme of the play is
primarily political: How has this evil befallen our state and
what sins have our rulers committed that the gods should
punish us in this way? *Oedipus at Colonus*, conceived during
the final decline of Athens, invokes the spirit of her ancestral
hero, the victorious Theseus, and annihilates with imprecations the foes of the city. His last play contains the parting
message of the oracle, "Those who come to terms with
Oedipus will triumph; the others will be doomed by their
guilt."

# FREUD AND LITERATURE

## I

The Freudian psychology is the only systematic account of
the human mind which, in point of subtlety and complexity,
of interest and tragic power, deserves to stand beside the
chaotic mass of psychological insights which literature has
accumulated through the centuries. To pass from the reading
of a great literary work to a treatise of academic psychology
is to pass from one order of perception to another, but the
human nature of the Freudian psychology is exactly the stuff
upon which the poet has always exercised his art. It is therefore not surprising that the psychoanalytical theory has had a
great effect upon literature. Yet the relationship is reciprocal,
an the effect of Freud upon literature has been no greater
than the effect of literature upon Freud. When, on the
occasion of the celebration of his seventieth birthday, Freud
was greeted as the "discoverer of the unconscious," he corrected the speaker and disclaimed the title. "The poets and
philosophers before me discovered the unconscious," he said.
"What I discovered was the scientific method by which the
unconscious can be studied."

A lack of specific evidence prevents us from considering
the particular literary "influences" upon the founder of psychoanalysis; and, besides, when we think of the men who
so clearly anticipated many of Freud's own ideas—
Schopenhauer and Nietzsche, for example—and then learn
that he did not read their works until after he had formulated
his own theories, we must see that particular influences
cannot be in question here but that what we must deal with
is nothing less than a whole *Zeitgeist,* a direction of thought.
For psychoanalysis is one of the culminations of the Romanticist literature of the nineteenth century. If there is perhaps

* LIONEL TRILLING is one of America's best-known literary
critics and the author of *The Liberal Imagination* among many
other books and articles.

251

a contradiction in the idea of a science standing upon the shoulders of a literature which avows itself inimical to science in so many ways, the contradiction will be resolved if we remember that this literature, despite its avowels, was itself scientific in at least the sense of being passionately devoted to a research into the self.

In showing the connection between Freud and this Romanticist tradition, it is difficult to know where to begin, but there might be a certain aptness in starting even back of the tradition, as far back as 1762 with Diderot's *Rameau's Nephew*. At any rate, certain men at the heart of nineteenth century thought were agreed in finding a peculiar importance in this brilliant little work: Goethe translated it; Marx admired it; Hegel—as Marx reminded Engels in the letter which announced that he was sending the book as a gift— praised and expounded it at length; Shaw was impressed by it; and Freud himself, as we know from a quotation in his *Introductory Lectures,* read it with the pleasure of agreement.

The dialogue takes place between Diderot himself and a nephew of the famous composer. The protagonist, the younger Romaneau, is a despised, outcast, shameless fellow; Hegel calls him the "disintegrated consciousness" and credits him with great wit, for it is he who breaks down all the normal social values and makes new combinations with the pieces. As for Diderot, the deuteragonist, he is what Hegel calls the "honest consciousness," and Hegel considers him reasonable, decent, and dull. It is quite clear that the author does not despise his Rameau and does not mean us to. Rameau is lustful and greedy, arrogant yet self-abasing, perceptive yet "wrong," like a child. Still, Diderot seems actually to be giving the fellow a kind of superiority over himself, as though Rameau represents the elements which, dangerous but wholly necessary, lie beneath the reasonable decorum of social life. It would perhaps be pressing too far to find in Rameau Freud's id and in Diderot Freud's ego; yet the connection does suggest itself; and at least we have here the perception which is to be the common characteristic of both Freud and Romanticism, the perception of the hidden element of human nature and of the opposition between the hidden and the visible. We have too the bold perception of just what lies hidden: "If the little savage [that is, the child] were left to himself, if he preserved all his foolishness and combined the violent passions of a man of thirty with the lack of reason of a child in the cradle, he'd wring his father's neck and go to bed with his mother."

From the self-exposure of Rameau to Rousseau's account of his own childhood is no great step; society might ignore or reject the idea of the "immorality" which lies concealed in the beginning of the career of the "good" man, just as it might turn away from Blake struggling to expound a psychology which would include the forces beneath the propriety of social man in general, but the idea of the hidden thing went forward to become one of the dominant notions of the age. The hidden element takes many forms, and it is not necessarily "dark" and "bad"; for Blake the "bad" was the good, while for Wordsworth and Burke what was hidden and unconscious was wisdom and power, which work in despite of the conscious intellect.

The mind has become far less simple; the devotion to the various forms of autobiography—itself an important fact in the tradition—provides abundant examples of the change that has taken place. Poets, making poetry by what seems to them almost a freshly discovered faculty, find that this new power may be conspired against by other agencies of the mind and even deprived of its freedom; the names of Wordsworth, Coleridge, and Arnold at once occur to us again, and Freud quotes Schiller on the danger to the poet that lies in the merely analytical reason. And it is not only the poets who are threatened; educated and sensitive people throughout Europe become aware of the depredations that reason might make upon the affective life, as in the classic instance of John Stuart Mill.

We must also take into account the preoccupation—it began in the eighteenth century, or even in the seventeenth —with children, women, peasants, and savages, whose mental life, it is felt, is less overlaid than that of the educated adult male by the proprieties of social habit. With this preoccupation goes a concern with education and personal development, so consonant with the historical and evolutionary bias of the time. And we must certainly note the revolution in morals which took place at the instance (we might almost say) of the *Bildungsroman,* for in the novels fathered by *Wilhelm Meister* we get the almost complete identification of author and hero and of the reader with both, and this identification almost inevitably suggests a leniency of moral judgment. The autobiographical novel has

a further influence upon the moral sensibility by its exploitation of all the modulations of motive and by its hinting that
we may not judge a man by any single moment in his life
without taking into account the determining past and the
expiating and fulfilling future.

It is difficult to know how to go on, for the further we look
the more literary affinities to Freud we find, and even if we
limit ourselves to bibliography we can at best be incomplete.
Yet we must mention the sexual revolution that was being
demanded—by Shelley, for example, by the Schlegel of
*Lucinde*, by George Sand, and later and more critically by
Ibsen; the belief in the sexual origin of art, baldly stated by
Tieck, more subtly by Schopenhauer; the investigation of
sexual maladjustment by Stendhal, whose observations on
erotic feeling seem to us distinctly Freudian. Again and
again we see the effective, utilitarian ego being relegated to
an inferior position and a plea being made on behalf of the
anarchic and self-indulgent id. We find the energetic exploitation of the idea of the mind as a divisible thing, one part of
which can contemplate and mock the other. It is not a far
remove from this to Dostoevski's brilliant instances of ambivalent feeling. Novalis brings in the preoccupation with the
death wish, and this is linked on the one hand with sleep and
on the other hand with the perception of the perverse, self-
destroying impulses, which in turn leads us to that fascination
by the horrible which we find in Shelley, Poe, and Baudelaire.
And always there is the profound interest in the dream—
"Our dreams," said Gérard de Nerval, "are a second life"—
and in the nature of metaphor, which reaches its climax in
Rimbaud and the later Symbolists, metaphor becoming less
and less communicative as it approaches the relative autonomy of the dream life.

But perhaps we must stop to ask, since these are the components of the *Zeitgeist* from which Freud himself developed,
whether it can be said that Freud did indeed produce a
wide literary effect. What is it that Freud added that the
tendency of literature itself would not have developed
without him? If we were looking for a writer who showed the
Freudian influence, Proust would perhaps come to mind as
readily as anyone else; the very title of his novel, in French
more than in English, suggests an enterprise of psychoanalysis, and scarcely less so does his method—the investigation of sleep, of sexual deviation, of the way of association,

the almost obsessive interest in metaphor; at these and at many other points the "influence" might be shown. Yet I believe it is true that Proust did not read Freud. Or again, exegesis of *The Waste Land* often reads remarkably like the psychoanalytic interpretation of a dream, yet we know that Eliot's methods were prepared for him not by Freud but by other poets.

Nevertheless, it is of course true that Freud's influence on literature has been very great. Much of it is so pervasive that its extent is scarcely to be determined; in one form or another, frequently in perversions or absurd simplifications, it has been infused into our life and become a component of our culture of which it is now hard to be specifically aware. In biography its first effect was sensational but not fortunate. The early Freudian biographers were for the most part Guildensterns who seemed to know the pipes but could not pluck out the heart of the mystery, and the same condemnation applies to the early Freudian critics. But in recent years, with the acclimatization of psychoanalysis and the increased sense of its refinements and complexity, criticism has derived from the Freudian system much that is of great value, most notably the license and the injunction to read the work of literature with a lively sense of its latent and ambiguous meanings, as if it were, as indeed it is, a being no less alive and contradictory than the man who created it. And this new response to the literary work has had a corrective effect upon our conception of literary biography. The literary critic or biographer who makes use of the Freudian theory is no less threatened by the dangers of theoretical systematization that he was in the early days, but he is likely to be more aware of these dangers; and I think it is true to say that now the motive of his interpretation is not that of exposing the secret shame of the writer and limiting the meaning of his work, but, on the contrary, that of finding grounds for sympathy with the writer and for increasing the possible significances of the work.

The names of the creative writers who have been more or less Freudian in tone or assumption would of course be legion. Only a relatively small number, however, have made serious use of the Freudian ideas. Freud himself seems to have thought this was as it should be: he is said to have expected very little of the works that were sent to him by writers with inscriptions of gratitude for all they had learned from him. The Surrealists have, with a certain inconsistency, depended upon Freud for the "scientific" sanction of their program. Kafka, with an apparent awareness of what he was doing, has explored the Freudian conceptions of guilt and punishment, of the dream, and of the fear of the father. Thomas Mann, whose tendency, as he himself says, was always in the direction of Freud's interests, has been most susceptible to the Freudian anthropology, finding a special charm in the theories of myths and magical practices. James Joyce, with his interest in the numerous states of receding consciousness, with his use of words as things and of words which point to more than one thing, with his pervading sense of the interrelation and interpenetration of all things, and, not least important, his treatment of familial themes, has perhaps most thoroughly and consciously exploited Freud's ideas.

## II

It will be clear enough how much of Freud's thought has significant affinity with the antirationalist element of the Romanticist tradition. But we must see with no less distinctness how much of his system is militantly rationalistic. Thomas Mann is at fault when, in his first essay on Freud, he makes it seem that the "Apollonian," the rationalistic, side of psychoanalysis is, while certainly important and wholly admirable, somehow secondary and even accidental. He gives us a Freud who is committed to the "night side" of life. Not at all: the rationalistic element of Freud is foremost; before everything else he is positivistic. If the interpreter of dreams came to medical science through Goethe, as he tells us he did, he entered not by way of the *Walpurgisnacht* but by the essay which played so important a part in the lives of so many scientists of the nineteenth century, the famous disquisition on Nature.

This correction is needed not only for accuracy but also for any understanding of Freud's attitude to art. And for that understanding we must see how intense is the passion with which Freud believes that positivistic rationalism, in its golden-age pre-Revolutionary purity, is the very form and pattern of intellectual virtue. The aim of psychoanalysis, he says, is the control of the night side of life. It is "to strengthen the ego, to make it more independent of the superego, to widen its field of vision, and so to extend the organization of the id." "Where id was"—that is, where all the irrational, nonlogical, pleasure-seeking dark forces were —"there shall ego be"—that is, intelligence and control. "It is," he concludes, with a reminiscence of Faust, "reclamation work, like the draining of the Zuyder Zee." This passage is quoted by Mann when, in taking up the subject of Freud a second time, he does indeed speak of Freud's positivistic program; but even here the bias induced by Mann's artistic interest in the "night side" prevents him from giving the other aspect of Freud its due emphasis. Freud would never have accepted the role which Mann seems to give him as the legitimizer of the myth and the dark, irrational ways of the mind. If Freud discovered the darkness for science he never endorsed it. On the contrary, his rationalism supports all the ideas of the Enlightenment that deny validity to myth or religion; he holds to a simple materialism, to a simple determinism, to a rather limited sort of epistemology. No great scientist of our day has thundered so articulately and so fiercely against all those who would sophisticate with metaphysics the scientific principles that were good enough for the nineteenth century. Conceptualism or pragmatism is anathema to him through the greater part of his intellectual career, and this, when we consider the nature of his own brilliant scientific methods, has surely an element of paradox in it.

From his rationalistic positivism comes much of Freud's strength and what weakness he has. The strength is the fine, clear tenacity of his positive aims, the goal of therapy, the desire to bring to men a decent measure of earthly happiness. But upon the rationalism must also be placed the blame for the often naïve scientific principles which characterize his early thought—they are later much modified —and which consist largely of claiming for his theories a perfect correspondence with an external reality, a position which, for those who admire Freud and especially for those who take seriously his views on art, is troublesome in the extreme.

Now Freud has, I believe, much to tell us about art, but whatever is suggestive in him is not likely to be found in those of his works in which he deals expressly with art itself. Freud is not insensitive to art—on the contrary—nor does he ever intend to speak of it with contempt. Indeed, he speaks of it with a real tenderness and counts it one of the true charms of the good life. Of artists, especially of writers, he speaks with admiration and even a kind of awe, though perhaps what he most appreciates in literature are specific emotional insights and observations; as we have noted, he speaks of literary men, because they have understood the part played in life by the hidden motives, as the precursors and coadjutors of his own science.

And yet eventually Freud speaks of art with what we must indeed call contempt. Art, he tells us, is a "substitute gratification," and as such is "an illusion in contrast to reality." Unlike most illusions, however, art is "almost always harmless and beneficent" for the reason that "it does not seek to be anything but an illusion. Save in the case of a few people who are, one might say, obsessed by art, it never dares make any attack on the realm of reality." One of its chief functions is to serve as a "narcotic." It shares the characteristics of the dream, whose element of distortion Freud calls a "sort of inner dishonesty." As for the artist, he is virtually in the same category with the neurotic. "By such separation of imagination and intellectual capacity," Freud says of the hero of a novel, "he is destined to be a poet or a neurotic, and he belongs to that race of beings whose realm is not of this world."

Now, there is nothing in the logic of psychoanalytical thought which requires Freud to have these opinions. But there is a great deal in the practice of the psychoanalytical therapy which makes it understandable that Freud, unprotected by an adequate philosophy, should be tempted to take the line he does. The analytical therapy deals with illusion. The patient comes to the physician to be cured, let us say, of a fear of walking in the street. The fear is real enough—there is no illusion on that score—and it produces all the physical symptoms of a more rational fear, the sweating palms, pounding heart, and shortened breath. But the patient knows that there is no cause for the fear, or rather that there is, as he says, no "real cause": there are no machine guns, man traps, or tigers in the street. The physician knows, however, that there is indeed a "real" cause for the fear, though it has nothing at all to do with what is or is not in the street; the cause is within the patient, and the process of the therapy will be to discover, by gradual steps, what this real cause is and so free the patient from its effects.

Now, the patient in coming to the physician, and the physician in accepting the patient, make a tacit compact about reality; for their purpose they agree to the limited reality by which we get our living, win our loves, catch our trains and our colds. The therapy will undertake to train the patient in proper ways of coping with this reality. The patient, of course, has been dealing with this reality all along, but in the wrong way. For Freud there are two ways of dealing with external reality. One is practical, effective, positive; this is the way of the conscious self, of the ego which must be made independent of the superego and extend its organization over the id, and it is the right way. The antithetical way may be called, for our purpose now, the "fictional" way. Instead of doing something about, or to, external reality, the individual who uses this way does something to, or about, his affective states. The most common and "normal" example of this is daydreaming, in which we give ourselves a certain pleasure by imagining our difficulties solved or our desires gratified. Then, too, as Freud discovered, sleeping dreams are, in much more complicated ways, and even though quite unpleasant, at the service of this same "fictional" activity. And in ways yet more complicated and yet more unpleasant, the actual neurosis from which our patient suffers deals with an external reality which the mind considers still more unpleasant than the painful neurosis itself.

For Freud as psychoanalytic practitioner there are, we may say, the polar extremes of reality and illusion. Reality is a honorific word, and it means what is *there;* illusion is a pejorative word, and it means a response to what is *not there*. The didactic nature of a course of psychoanalysis no doubt requires a certain firm crudeness in making the distinction; it is after all aimed not at theoretical refinement but at practical effectiveness. The polar extremes are practical reality and neurotic illusion, the latter judged by the former. This, no doubt, is as it should be; the patient is not being trained in metaphysics and epistemology.

This practical assumption is not Freud's only view of the mind in its relation to reality. Indeed, what may be called the essentially Freudian view assumes that the mind, for good as well as bad, helps create its reality by selection and evaluation. In this view, reality is malleable and subject to creation; it is not static but is rather a series of situations which are dealt with in their own terms. But beside this conception of the mind stands the conception which arises from Freud's therapeutic-practical assumptions; in this view, the mind deals with a reality which is quite fixed and static, a reality that is wholly "given" and not (to use a phrase of Dewey's) "taken." In his epistemological utterances, Freud insists on this second view, although it is not easy to see why he should do so. For the reality to which he wishes to reconcile the neurotic patient is, after all, a "taken" and not a "given" reality. It is the reality of social life and of value, conceived and maintained by the human mind and will. Love, morality, honor, esteem—these are the components of a created reality. If we are to call art an illusion, then we must call most of the activities and satisfactions of the ego illusions; Freud, of course, has no desire to call them that.

What, then, is the difference between, on the one hand, the dream and the neurosis, and, on the other hand, art? That they have certain common elements is of course clear; that unconscious processes are at work in both would be denied by no poet or critic; they share too, though in different degrees, the element of fantasy. But there is a vital difference between them which Charles Lamb saw so clearly in his defense of the sanity of true genius: "The . . . poet dreams being awake. He is not possessed by his subject but he has dominion over it."

That is the whole difference: the poet is in command of his fantasy, while it is exactly the mark of the neurotic that he is possessed by his fantasy. And there is a further difference which Lamb states; speaking of the poet's relation to reality (he calls it Nature), he says, "He is beautifully loyal to that sovereign directress, even when he appears most to betray her"; the illusions of art are made to serve the purpose of a closer and truer relation with reality. Jacques Barzun, in an acute and sympathetic discussion of Freud, puts the matter well: "A good analogy between art and *dreaming* has led him to a false one between art and *sleeping*. But the difference between a work of art and a dream is precisely this, that the work of art *leads us back to the outer reality by taking account of it.*" Freud's assumption of the almost exclusively hedonistic nature and purpose of art bar him from the perception of this.

Of the distinction that must be made between the artist

and the neurotic Freud is of course aware; he tells us that the artist is not like the neurotic in that he knows how to find a way back from the world of imagination and "once more get a firm foothold in reality." This however seems to mean no more than that reality is to be dealt with when the artist suspends the practice of his art; and at least once when Freud speaks of art dealing with reality he actually means the rewards that a successful artist can win. He does not deny to art its function and its usefulness; it has a therapeutic effect in releasing mental tension; it serves the cultural purpose of acting as a "substitute gratification" to reconcile men to the sacrifices they have made for culture's sake; it promotes the social sharing of highly valued emotional experiences; and it recalls men to their cultural ideals. This is not everything that some of us would find that art does, yet even this is a good deal for a "narcotic" to do.

## III

I started by saying that Freud's ideas could tell us something about art, but so far I have done little more than try to show that Freud's very conception of art is inadequate. Perhaps, then, the suggestiveness lies in the application of the analytic method to specific works of art or to the artist himself? I do not think so, and it is only fair to say that Freud himself was aware both of the limits and the limitations of psychoanalysis in art, even though he does not always in practice submit to the former or admit the latter.

Freud has, for example, no desire to encroach upon the artist's autonomy; he does not wish us to read his monograph on Leonardo and then say of the "Madonna of the Rocks" that it is a fine example of homosexual, autoerotic painting. If he asserts that in investigation the "psychiatrist cannot yield to the author," he immediately insists that the "author cannot yield to the psychiatrist," and he warns the latter not to "coarsen everything" by using for all human manifestations the "substantially useless and awkward terms" of clinical procedure. He admits, even while asserting that the sense of beauty probably derives from sexual feeling, that psychoanalysis "has less to say about beauty than about most other things." He confesses to a theoretical indifference to the form of art and restricts himself to its content. Tone, feeling,

style, and the modification that part makes upon part he
does not consider. "The layman," he says, "may expect
perhaps too much from analysis . . . for it must be admitted
that it throws no light upon the two problems which
probably interest him the most. It can do nothing toward
elucidating the nature of the artistic gift, nor can it explain
the means by which the artist works—artistic technique."

What, then, does Freud believe that the analytical method
can do? Two things: explain the "inner meanings" of the
work of art and explain the temperament of the artist as man.

A famous example of the method is the attempt to solve
the "problem" of *Hamlet* as suggested by Freud and as carried out by Dr. Ernest Jones, his early and distinguished
follower. Dr. Jones's monograph is a work of painstaking
scholarship and of really masterly ingenuity. The research
undertakes not only the clearing up of the mystery of
Hamlet's character but also the discovery of "the clue to
much of the deeper workings of Shakespeare's mind." Part
of the mystery in question is of course why Hamlet, after
he had so definitely resolved to do so, did not avenge upon
his hated uncle his father's death. But there is another
mystery to the play—what Freud calls "the mystery of its
effect," its magical appeal that draws so much interest toward
it. Recalling the many failures to solve the riddle of the
play's charm, he wonders if we are to be driven to the
conclusion "that its magical appeal rests solely upon the
impressive thoughts in it and the splendor of its language."
Freud believes that we can find a source of power beyond
this.

We remember that Freud has told us that the meaning
of a dream is its intention, and we may assume that the
meaning of a drama is its intention, too. The Jones research
undertakes to discover what it was that Shakespeare intended to say about Hamlet. It finds that the intention was
wrapped by the author in a dreamlike obscurity because it
touched so deeply both his personal life and the moral life
of the world; what Shakespeare intended to say is that
Hamlet cannot act because he is incapacitated by the guilt
he feels at his unconscious attachment to his mother. There
is, I think, nothing to be quarreled with in the statement
that there is an Oedipus situation in *Hamlet;* and if psychoanalysis has indeed added a new point of interest to the

play, that is to its credit.* And, just so, there is no reason
to quarrel with Freud's conclusion when he undertakes to
give us the meaning of *King Lear* by a tortuous tracing of
the mythological implications of the theme of the three
caskets, of the relation of the caskets to the Norns, the
Fates, and the Graces, of the connection of these triadic
females with Lear's daughters, of the transmogrification of
the death goddess into the love goddess and the identification of Cordelia with both, all to the conclusion that the
meaning of *King Lear* is to be found in the tragic refusal
of an old man to "renounce love, choose death, and make
friends with the necessity of dying." There is something
both beautiful and suggestive in this, but it is not *the*
meaning of *King Lear* any more than the Oedipus motive
is *the* meaning of *Hamlet*.

It is not here a question of the validity of the evidence,
though that is of course important. We must rather object
to the conclusions of Freud and Dr. Jones on the ground
that their proponents do not have an adequate conception of what an artistic meaning is. There is no single
meaning to any work of art; this is true not merely because
it is better that it should be true, that is, because it makes
art a richer thing, but because historical and personal experience show it to be true. Changes in historical context
and in personal mood change the meaning of a work and
indicate to us that artistic understanding is not a question
of fact but of value. Even if the author's intention were,
as it cannot be, precisely determinable, the meaning of a
work cannot lie in the author's intention alone. It must
also lie in its effect. We can say of a volcanic eruption on
an inhabited island that it "means terrible suffering," but if
the island is uninhabited or easily evacuated it means some-

---

* However, A. C. Bradley, in his discussion of Hamlet (*Shakespearean Tragedy*), states clearly the intense sexual disgust which
Hamlet feels and which, for Bradley, helps account for his uncertain purpose; and Bradley was anticipated in this view by
Löning. It is well known, and Dover Wilson has lately emphasized
the point, that to an Elizabethan audience Hamlet's mother was
not merely tasteless, as to a modern audience she seems, in
hurrying to marry Claudius, but actually adulterous in marrying
him at all because he was, as her brother-in-law, within the forbidden degrees.

thing else. In short, the audience partly determines the
meaning of the work. But although Freud sees something
of this when he says that in addition to the author's intention we must take into account the mystery of *Hamlet*'s
effect, he nevertheless goes on to speak as if, historically,
*Hamlet*'s effect had been single and brought about solely
by the "magical" power of the Oedipus motive to which,
unconsciously, we so violently respond. Yet there was, we
know, a period when *Hamlet* was relatively in eclipse, and
it has always been scandalously true of the French, a people not without filial feeling, that they have been somewhat
indifferent to the "magical appeal" of *Hamlet*.

I do not think that anything I have said about the inade-
quacies of the Freudian method of interpretation limits the
number of ways we can deal with a work of art. Bacon remarked that experiment may twist nature on the rack to
wring out its secrets, and criticism may use any instruments
upon a work of art to find its meanings. The elements of
art are not limited to the world of art. They reach into life,
and whatever extraneous knowledge of them we gain—for
example, by research into the historical context of the
work—may quicken our feelings for the work itself and even
enter legitimately into those feelings. Then, too, anything
we may learn about the artist himself may be enriching and
legitimate. But one research into the mind of the artist is
simply not practicable, however legitimate it may theoretically be. That is, the investigation of his unconscious
intention as it exists apart from the work itself. Criticism
understands that the artist's statement of his conscious intention, though it is sometimes useful, cannot finally determine meaning. How much less can we know from his
unconscious intention considered as something apart from
the whole work? Surely very little that can be called conclusive or scientific. For, as Freud himself points out, we
are not in a position to question the artist; we must apply
the technique of dream analysis to his symbols, but, as
Freud says with some heat, those people do not understand his theory who think that a dream may be interpreted without the dreamer's free association with the
multitudinous details of his dream.

We have so far ignored the aspect of the method which
finds the solution to the "mystery" of such a play as *Hamlet*
in the temperament of Shakespeare himself and then illu-

minates the mystery of Shakespeare's temperament by means of the solved mystery of the play. Here it will be amusing to remember that by 1935 Freud had become converted to the theory that it was not Shakespeare of Stratford but the Earl of Oxford who wrote the plays, thus invalidating the important bit of evidence that Shakespeare's father died shortly before the composition of *Hamlet*. This is destructive enough to Dr. Jones's argument, but the evidence from which Dr. Jones draws conclusions about literature fails on grounds more relevant to literature itself. For when Dr. Jones, by means of his analysis of *Hamlet*, takes us into "the deeper workings of Shakespeare's mind," he does so with a perfect confidence that he knows what *Hamlet* is and what its relation to Shakespeare is. It is, he tells us, Shakespeare's "chief masterpiece," so far superior to all his other works that it may be placed on "an entirely separate level." And then, having established his ground on an entirely subjective literary judgment, Dr. Jones goes on to tell us that *Hamlet* "probably expresses the core of Shakespeare's philosophy and outlook as no other work of his does." That is, all the contradictory or complicating or modifying testimony of the other plays is dismissed on the basis of Dr. Jones's acceptance of the peculiar position which, he believes, *Hamlet* occupies in the Shakespeare canon. And it is upon this quite inadmissible judgment that Dr. Jones bases his argument: "It may be expected *therefore* that anything which will give us the key to the inner meaning of the play will *necessarily* give us the clue to much of the deeper workings of Shakepeare's mind." (The italics are mine.)

I should be sorry if it appeared that I am trying to say that psychoanalysis can have nothing to do with literature. I am sure that the opposite is so. For example, the whole notion of rich ambiguity in literature, of the interplay between the apparent meaning and the latent—not "hidden" —meaning, has been reinforced by the Freudian concepts, perhaps even received its first impetus from them. Of late years, the more perceptive psychoanalysts have surrendered the early pretensions of their teachers to deal "scientifically" with literature. That is all to the good, and when a study as modest and precise as Dr. Franz Alexander's essay on *Henry IV* comes along, an essay which pretends not to "solve" but only to illuminate the subject, we have something worth having. Dr. Alexander undertakes nothing more

than to say that in the development of Prince Hal we see the
classic struggle of the ego to come to normal adjustment,
beginning with the rebellion against the father, going on to the
conquest of the superego (Hotspur, with his rigid notions of
honor and glory), then to the conquests of the id (Falstaff,
with his anarchic self-indulgence), then to the identification
with the father (the crown scene) and the assumption of
mature responsibility. An analysis of this sort is not momentous and not exclusive of other meanings; perhaps it does
no more than point up and formulate what we all have
already seen. It has the tact to *accept* the play, and does not,
like Dr. Jones's study of *Hamlet*, search for a "hidden motive"
and a "deeper working," which implies that there is a reality
to which the play stands in the relation that a dream stands
to the wish that generates it and from which it is separable;
it is this reality, this "deeper working," which, according to
Dr. Jones, produced the play. But *Hamlet* is not merely the
product of Shakespeare's thought; it is the very instrument
of his thought, and if meaning is intention, Shakespeare did
not intend the Oedipus motive or anything less than *Hamlet;*
if meaning is effect then it is *Hamlet* which affects us, not
the Oedipus motive. *Coriolanus* also deals, and very terribly,
with the Oedipus motive, but the effect of the one drama is
very different from the effect of the other.

## IV

If, then, we can accept neither Freud's conception of the
place of art in life nor his application of the analytical
method, what is it that he contributes to our understanding
of art or to its practice? In my opinion, what he contributes
outweighs his errors; it is of the greatest importance, and it
lies in no specific statement that he makes about art but is,
rather, implicit in his whole conception of the mind.

For, of all mental systems, the Freudian psychology is
the one which makes poetry indigenous to the very con-
stitution of the mind. Indeed, the mind, as Freud sees it, is
in the greater part of its tendency exactly a poetry-making
organ. This puts the case too strongly, no doubt, for it seems
to make the working of the unconscious mind equivalent to
poetry itself, forgetting that between the unconscious mind
and the finished poem there supervene the social intention
and the formal control of the conscious mind. Yet the
statement has at least the virtue of counterbalancing the

belief, so commonly expressed or implied, that the very opposite is true and that poetry is a kind of beneficent aberration of the mind's right course.

Freud has not merely naturalized poetry; he has discovered its status as a pioneer settler, and he sees it as a method of thought. Often enough he tries to show how, as a method of thought, it is unreliable and ineffective for conquering reality; yet he himself is forced to use it in the very shaping of his own science, as when he speaks of the topography of the mind and tells us with a kind of defiant apology that the metaphors of space relationship which he is using are really most inexact since the mind is not a thing of space at all but that there is no other way of conceiving the difficult idea except by metaphor. In the eighteenth century Vico spoke of the metaphorical, imagistic language of the early stages of culture; it was left to Freud to discover how, in a scientfic age, we still feel and think in figurative formations, and to create, what psychoanalysis is, a science of tropes, of metaphor and its variants, synecdoche and metonymy.

Freud showed, too, how the mind, in one of its parts, could work without logic, yet not without that directing purpose, that control of intent from which, perhaps it might be said, logic springs. For the unconscious mind works without the syntactical conjunctions which are logic's essence. It recognizes no *because,* no *therefore,* no *but;* such ideas as similarity, agreement, and community are expressed in dreams imagistically by compressing the elements into a unity. The unconscious mind in its struggle with the conscious always turns from the general to the concrete, and finds the tangible trifle more congenial than the large abstraction. Freud discovered in the very organization of the mind those mechanisms by which art makes its effects, such devices as the condensations of meanings and the displacement of accent.

All this is perhaps obvious enough and, though I should like to develop it in proportion both to its importance and to the space I have given to disagreement with Freud, I will not press it further. For there are two other elements in Freud's thought which, in conclusion, I should like to introduce as of great weight in their bearing on art.

Of these, one is a specific idea which, in the middle of his career (1920), Freud put forward in his essay *Beyond*

*the Pleasure Principle.* The essay itself is a speculative attempt to solve a perplexing problem in clinical analysis, but
its relevance to literature is inescapable, as Freud sees well
enough, even though his perception of its critical importance is not sufficiently strong to make him revise his earlier
views of the nature and function of art. The idea is one
which stands besides Aristotle's notion of the catharsis, in
part to supplement, in part to modify it.

Freud has come upon certain facts which are not to be
reconciled with his earlier theory of the dream. According
to this theory, all dreams, even the unpleasant ones, could
be understood upon analysis to have the intention of fulfilling the dreamer's wishes. They are in the service of what
Freud calls the pleasure principle, which is opposed to the
reality principle. It is, of course, this explanation of the
dream which had so largely conditioned Freud's theory of
art. But now there is thrust upon him the necessity for re-
considering the theory of the dream, for it was found that
in cases of war neurosis—what we once called shellshock—
the patient, with the utmost anguish, recurred in his dreams
to the very situation, distressing as it was, which had precipitated his neurosis. It seemed impossible to interpret
these dreams by any assumption of a hedonistic intent. Nor
did there seem to be the usual amount of distortion in
them: the patient recurred to the terrible initiatory situation with great literalness. And the same pattern of psychic
behavior could be observed in the play of children; there
were some games which, far from fulfilling wishes, seemed
to concentrate upon the representation of those aspects of
the child's life which were most unpleasant and threatening
to his happiness.

To explain such mental activities Freud evolved a theory
for which he at first refused to claim much but to which,
with the years, he attached an increasing importance. He
first makes the assumption that there is indeed in the psychic
life a repetition-compulsion which goes beyond the pleasure
principle. Such a compulsion cannot be meaningless; it must
have an intent. And that intent, Freud comes to believe,
is exactly and literally the developing of fear. "These dreams,"
he says, "are attempts at restoring control of the stimuli by
developing apprehension, the pretermission of which caused
the traumatic neurosis." The dream, that is, is the effort to
reconstruct the bad situation in order that the failure to meet

it may be recouped; in these dreams there is no obscured intent to evade but only an attempt to meet the situation, to make a new effort of control. And in the play of children it seems to be that "the child repeats even the unpleasant experiences because through his own activity he gains a far more thorough mastery of the strong impression than was possible by mere passive experience."

Freud, at this point, can scarcely help being put in mind of tragic drama; nevertheless, he does not wish to believe that this effort to come to mental grips with a situation is involved in the attraction of tragedy. He is, we might say, under the influence of the Aristotelian tragic theory which emphasizes a qualified hedonism through suffering. But the pleasure involved in tragedy is perhaps an ambiguous one; and sometimes we must feel that the famous sense of cathartic resolution is perhaps the result of glossing over terror with beautiful language rather than an evacuation of it. And sometimes the terror even bursts through the language to stand stark and isolated from the play, as does Oedipus's sightless and bleeding face. At any rate, the Aristotelian theory does not deny another function for tragedy (and for comedy, too) which is suggested by Freud's theory of the traumatic neurosis—what might be called the mithridatic function, by which tragedy is used as the homeopathic administration of pain to inure ourselves to the greater pain which life will force upon us. There is in the cathartic theory of tragedy, as it is usually understood, a conception of tragedy's function which is too negative and which inadequately suggests the sense of active mastery which tragedy can give.

In the same essay in which he sets forth the conception of the mind embracing its own pain for some vital purpose, Freud also expresses a provisional assent to the idea (earlier stated, as he reminds us, by Schopenhauer) that there is perhaps a human drive which makes of death the final and desired goal. The death instinct is a conception that is rejected by many of even the most thoroughgoing Freudian theorists (as, in his last book, Freud mildly noted); the late Otto Fenichel in his authoritative work on the neurosis argues cogently against it. Yet even if we reject the theory as not fitting the facts in any operatively useful way, we still cannot miss its grandeur, its ultimate tragic courage in acquiescence to fate. The idea of the reality principle and the idea of the

death instinct form the crown of Freud's broader speculation
on the life of man. Their quality of grim poetry is characteristic of Freud's system and the ideas it generates for him.

And as much as anything else that Freud gives to literature, this quality of his thought is important. Although the
artist is never finally determined in his work by the intellectual systems about him, he cannot avoid their influence;
and it can be said of various competing systems that some
hold more promise for the artist than others. When, for
example, we think of the simple humanitarian optimism
which, for two decades, has been so pervasive, we must see
that not only has it been politically and philosophically
inadequate but also that it implies, by the smallness of its
view of the varieties of human possibility, a kind of check
on the creative faculties. In Freud's view of life no such
limitation is implied. To be sure, certain elements of his
system seem hostile to the usual notions of man's dignity.
Like every great critic of human nature—and Freud is that
—he finds in human pride the ultimate cause of human
wretchedness, and he takes pleasure in knowing that his
ideas stand with those of Copernicus and Darwin in making
pride more difficult to maintain. Yet the Freudian man is,
I venture to think, a creature of far more dignity and far
more interest than the man which any other modern system
has been able to conceive. Despite popular belief to the
contrary, man, as Freud conceives him, is not to be understood by any simple formula (such as sex) but is rather an
inextricable tangle of culture and biology. And not being
simple, he is not simply good; he has, as Freud says some-
where, a kind of hell within him from which rise everlastingly
the impulses which threaten his civilization. He has the
faculty of imagining for himself more in the way of pleasure
and satisfaction that he can possibly achieve. Everything that
he gains he pays for in more than equal coin; compromise
and the compounding with defeat constitute his best way of
getting through the world. His best qualities are the result
of a struggle whose outcome is tragic. Yet he is a creature
of love; it is Freud's sharpest criticism of the Adlerian
psychology that to aggression it gives everything and to love
nothing at all.

One is always aware in reading Freud how little cynicism
there is in his thought. His desire for man is only that he
should be human, and to this end his science is devoted.

No view of life to which the artist responds can ensure the quality of his work, but the poetic qualities of Freud's own principles, which are so clearly in the line of the classic tragic realism, suggest that this is a view which does not narrow and simplify the human world for the artist but on the contrary opens and complicates it.

# A. Bronson Feldman[*]

# ZOLA AND THE
# RIDDLE OF SADISM

A new translation of Zola's *The Human Beast* by Louis
Coleman—a rough paraphrase of the novel by George Mil-
burn, done for our contemporary rough readers, the subway
passengers addicted to the pocket books known to the trade
as "breast-sellers"—and Hollywood's production of the *Beast*
in technicolor, perhaps a tridimensional superepic version,
with Zola's locomotives driving right over our heads—these
testimonials of the novel's timeliness bring one back to it
with the curiosity to discover what insights it may hold for
the world today.

*La Bête humaine* was produced in 1890, when Zola was
fifty, and his France was turning from a surfeit of naturalism in literature to the orgy promised by symbolism. In this
book he gave the country and the Continent, indeed the
entire West, the dominant symbol of passion for the next
fifty years. Tolstoi had unconsciously suggested the artistic
utility of the locomotive in the death of Anna Karenina. Joris
Karl Huysmans anticipated Zola in *Against the Grain* but
he did no more than toy with the erotic facet of the symbol.
His master displayed its economic and ethical sides as well.
It required the systematic exploitation method of Zola to
make Europe and America see the significance of the railroad
engine as an emblem of fundamental emotions, the prevailing
drives of humanity in present-day industrial circumstances.

With characteristic romantic American chastity Frank
Norris in *The Octopus* worked on the economic facet exclusively. Glimpses of the thing's ethical meaning flashed
across William Ellery Leonard's autobiography, *The Locomotive God*. Leonard's individual emphasis on the theme
of paternal tyranny and its relation to the machine left barely

---

[*] A. Bronson Feldman is Director of the Mental Hygiene
Division of the Psychological Services Center in Philadelphia. He
is the author of *The Unconscious in History*.

more than a hint of its other aesthetic values. We have to
return to Zola before we can realize its power as a prism of
our time.

The protagonist of *The Human Beast*, Jacques Lantier,
is a locomotive engineer. He does not appear in the original
genealogy that Zola drew up for the Rougon-Macquart
chronicle to which the novel belongs. Yet the idea of a story
of railroad life had been in the writer's mind from the first
design of the series, when he was twenty-eight. He said at
that time, "I want to do 'big machines.' " It did not occur
to him that he wished to emulate by art his father Francesco,
the artillery officer who became an engineer-builder of canals
and roads. In 1877, when *The Dive* (*L'Assommoir*) came
out with the story of Gervaise Macquart and her seduction
by Lantier's father, only two illegitimate children were mentioned, Claude and Etienne. Their creator could not bring
himself to conceive the tragedy of Jacques until he himself
became a father, not just the Father of Naturalism, but the
procreant of an illegitimate daughter. She was born in the
spring of 1889, a year in which Zola surprised his admirers
and critics by publishing nothing. He spent the following
spring collecting material for *The Human Beast*.

The spur to creation of this book came, I think, from the
newspaper reports of the butchery of women in the White-
chapel slums of London, which were all blamed on the half-
legendary "Jack the Ripper."

Whenever Jacques Lantier or his author attempts to explore the sources of the lust for murder that drives the
hero to his doom, it is traced to an "ancient wrong" committed far back in the infancy of the human race. Zola explicitly defines the wrong as a betrayal and infidelity, an
act done by woman—"in the caves"—in defiance of her mate,
and frightfully avenged by him. This primitive unfaithfulness
and its chronic punishment, Zola imagines, kept a spark of
hate for the perfidious sex burning in the memories of
Lantier's masculine ancestors, and they more or less unconsciously bequeathed it to their sons. When it emerged
in the young railroad engineer's brain it burst into the fire
that we see smoldering and raging through the swift history
of *The Human Beast*. To kill the beloved—that, he thinks,
is the sole way to hold her utterly his own. Even before he
can possess her, at the moment when he feels the woman

yielding to his warmth, the desire to destroy her seizes him
and flight alone can rescue his hand from crime. The novelist
neglects to trace the conscience of Lantier to the "caves."
Zola is satisfied with explaining it as a product of moral
training and a sturdy proletarian education. Clearly he
never dreamed that the hero's conscience had roots in common with the motives that impelled his frenzy to kill, and
would perish if separated from the sadism.

Today we have no difficulty in recognizing under the
scientific veneer of Zola's concept of heredity the old religious
conviction of "original sin." The artist has given it a
peculiar twist. Instead of conceiving the origin of the
deathward drift of man as a simple temptation to union with
woman, he pictures it as an action in which feminine desire
predominates, and forever fickle, provokes murderous jealousy.

It would be a mistake to brush aside as fantastic the
explanation offered by the novel for Lantier's blood lust.
The fantasy itself calls for explanation. And the novel
supplies us with plenty of the clues necessary to solve it.

In the first place we find the mysterious fact that in
Lantier's thought his ardor for Severine Roubaud is fast
connected with the memory of the murder of President
Grandmorin, in which he suspects she was an accomplice.
He knew the dead railroad magnate by reputation only, and
the feat of the old man's destruction made Severine tower
in his mind like a giantess. He coveted her above all other
women. The knowledge that she was married to a man who
could cut a rival's throat for jealousy, far from lessening
his love for her, intensified it with the challenge of danger.
In the downfall of Grandmorin he sensed the accomplishment of an ancient wish, one that stirred not only his infancy
to the depths but the infancy of the whole race. The tragedy
leaves us without doubt of the significance of the President
as an imago, indeed a model, of paternal authority.

To bring this lone father of the story in blood to dust is
an act so gratifying to the rest of the characters—all under-
lings and children—that not a single utterance of regret is
heard anywhere. Their sterile bodies exult over the great
man's death. Lantier loves Madame Roubaud because she
assisted in the performance of a murder the like of which
he must have yearned to do in his childhood. To his brain her
crime was father-murder. Its patricidal nature is stressed by

the novelist, who, early in the *Beast,* throws out the hint that Severine may have been Grandmorin's daughter. Readers of *The Dive,* remembering the parentage of Jacques Lantier, will comprehend how he could have developed so deep a hate for his father, and fearfully repressed it.

The death wish against the father springs in childhood out of the soil of thwarted acquisitiveness, from the little boy's impotent fury against the man who deprives him of absolute possession of the mother. In the beginning it is the incest wish: the child blindly craves reunion with the woman who gave it birth and sustained its life with her milk. I say "it" since the incest drive shows no distinction of sex in the earliest years. In *The Human Beast* the drive manifests itself most plainly in the girl Severine, whose outrage on hearing Roubaud say that she might be the daughter of Grandmorin indicates the energy of her obsession with the thought. It is easier for her to endure the guilt of her adultery with the old man.

Her husband's jealousy, which leads to the assassination of Grandmorin, bears no clear sign of incestuous origin. But Roubaud stands shamefacedly like a son in relation to the President, his patron. The idea that the President has known Severine as a "mistress" maddens the mechanic to the point where he can devise his patron's death. Such an anger could rise only from the unconscious where the infantile, the primeval, and the insane exist as one. The killing of Grandmorin, then, represents the triumphant arrival of his foster boy Roubaud at the imaginary monopoly of his boyhood dreams, the domination of the woman whom he frantically refused to share—with his "father."

No sooner does the assassin behold himself in undisputed possession of Severine than he falls a prey to guilty brooding over his crime. Consumed by shame he gives up his wife without a struggle to his young countryman Lantier. Roubaud lacks the strength to take a father's place.

The mechanic's sexual impotence is paralleled by his political weakness. He makes gestures of revolutionary republicanism against the government of Napoelon III but collapses into servility as soon as his bluff is called. To strike down a boss in hot blood is one thing: to take and maintain the dictatorship of society—that is a feat for the Roubauds fulfillable only in dreams and the illusions of Bastille Day parades.

The contrast that Zola produces between the husband's moral breakdown after the murder and his wife's increase of courage and vivacity remind us of the similar (though sexually reversed) situation in *Macbeth.* In that tragedy of regicide, as Dr. Ludwig Jekels brilliantly pointed out, Shakespeare seems to have split a single personality into Lord and Lady Macbeth. In the same manner Zola appears to have divided one creature of his fantasy to form the incestuous Severine and her "father"-killing partner. The latter alone is endowed with the standard human equipment of a conscience.

Jacques Lantier is less of a man, more of a child than poor Roubaud. Look how the engineer pets his locomotive Lison, which gives the illusion of coming felinely alive under his strokes. The fascination that feminine breasts exert on Jacques provides us a glimpse of the baby-survivals in his mind, an insight that expands in scope when we observe him weeping, near the end of the novel, while he tells of his affair with Severine to a courtroom crowded with motherly souls. His tears drop from self-pity, for the loss of love he had to suffer in cutting Severine's throat. The deed filled him for a moment with a vision of himself as one of virility and grandeur, as if he had dared a godlike heroism. The illusion vanishes. The urge to kill women again revives in him. This proves that in killing Madame Roubaud he was endeavoring to kill someone else, whom his knife could never reach, a ghost-woman of the mental "caves" of his infancy. In a word, the central urge in Lantier is matricide.

Just as his countryman Roubaud looks like a father in comparison with him, the fiery Severine strikes his unconscious as a magnet of maternal comfort and terror. The incestuous character of his love for her is revealed by the location of her death. He murders her in the bed where she had slept with the paternal despot Grandmorin. The crime thus stands for a revenge on the part of a son who hates his mother for having surrendered herself to his father.

The method of the imaginary matricide testifies to the force of a baby impulse in Lantier: he tears his victim's neck with a substitute for a tooth. (At the beginning of his story we see him eager to sink a pair of scissors into another woman's bosom.) Zola discerned a caveman in his hero; he overlooked the cannibal.

The brute in the engineer lives forever in dread of the loss of his manhood. It is the threat of unmanning him that drives him to madness, to murder. Where a Roubaud would expect this menace from a father figure, Lantier expects it from women, from his mother surrogates. Why this is so the novel never discloses. We are left to guess, on the basis of meager facts such as the allusion to Lantier's mother Gervaise as a major influence in his life: he cost her "so many tears." His father is scarcely mentioned, and yet his longing for maleness must be at the root a wish to equal his father. Lantier's industrial conscience—he is a good workman, happy in his employment, elated by the responsibilities of his job—this points to the working-class training of his father. But his rebellion against his conscience is a revolt against the female element in it. One link between the maternal prototype in his conscience and his castration-terror may be detected in the young man's yearning to dig a pit in the women who allure him. The hole in Grandmorin's neck haunts him. Possibly it meant to his imagination a vagina, the void he was afraid that women might create in himself. His passion for killing them, therefore, can be said to get its energy from a triple motive—the wish to retaliate against the maternal menace of castration; revenge for maternal "infidelity" (the one factor Zola himself is dimly aware of); and finally the rage of the mouth-thwarted child, a craving to rip, perhaps to devour, the mother.

This combination of horrors is revealed as fixed in Lantier's unconscious by the coupling in his conscious thought of sexual intercourse with bloody violence. It is well known that children preserve their earliest memories of parental copulation as scenes of aggression and rape. To make love like father, consequently, is identical in the infant head with sadism, especially when it beholds the mother treated elsewhere as a drudge or cheap toy. Zola illuminates the sadistic ideals of his hero by setting the stage of his last encounter with Madame Roubaud by her foster-father's bed, in a room whose prevailing color is red.

Attention should also be called to the fact that the weapon Lantier wields against his love is the property of her elderly husband. It symbolizes the son's imaginary capture of his father's privilege. But the knife is a gift from Severine. This suggests the ancient belief of boys that their mothers possess the male organ, or once possessed it and were deprived by some occult savagery. The growing firmness of Severine's character, contrasted with the enfeeblement of her husband, sharpens our perception of the male side of her self.

The heroine's love for Latiner may be accounted for by an aborted maternal tendency. She plays at motherhood with him to the extent of behaving like one of those Greek matriarchs of old who encouraged their sons to slay their detested husbands. Severine's deepest pleasure in her relation with Lantier rises from the belief that he is actually inside her. This womb fancy in a girl who never wants a child covers the prime desire of her life—to own a penis. She too suffers from "castration" anguish. It is alleviated by Lantier only by his subjection to her will, by his becoming an instrument of her sex. She senses in his presence a danger, yet cannot believe that the peril is embodied in her darling obedient boy. She dies because she fails to understand that her game of maternity has to end when she tries to make a "man"—that is, a husband—of him.

The boy is scared to delirium by her insistence on the murder of old Roubaud. It reminds him that she belongs to a stranger; she was "unfaithful" to him, like the mother whom he cost so many tears. His love for her lasted so long as he retained the unconscious conviction that she was a sister-soul, who had killed a father for the sake of incest as he had always wished to do. From the hour when Severine alters in his view from an equal to a superior, from a sister to a mother, she wakes the triple terror and fury of his infancy. He strikes her dead, and his "eternal desire" is fulfilled: "She did not, and never would belong to anyone." Standing over her body he remembers the corpse of President Grandmorin: "the two murders had joined together, for was not one the logical mate of the other?"

When Zola pictured his protagonist's amazement at the sight of the stabbed Severine he must have experienced an echo of *Macbeth*. Lantier, he wrote, "would never have believed she [his maternal idol—F.] had so much blood." In the same way Macbeth's queen, wondering about her royal victim, who resembled her father in sleep, cries out, "Yet who would have thought the old man to have had so much blood in him?" The two tragedies, Shakespeare's and Zola's, join their currents in the whirlpool of incest- and parricide-lust that Freud discovered and named the Oedipus complex.

Jacques Lantier's locomotive Lison is fancied as feminine. He rides the giantess like a little boy gleefully propelling his mother from her shoulders. Zola, however, is not content with this idyllic fantasy. The iron mare represents more than the might of maternal sex. It turns in the novelist's hand to an image of paternal economy. The transition is achieved by means of the old illusion of the mother having the organ of the male. The ridden emerges as projectile, embodying the aggressive energy of labor, transforming the good mother earth. Against the modern landscape the locomotive glows as a symbol of labor mastered, a symbol of capital. It belongs to the Grandmorins. Since the Grandmorins run the country the machine comes to represent the state, once depicted as a ship. It is La Belle France herself that we find at the finish of *The Human Beast* racing, bereaved of her engineer and fireman, straight to disaster. The train is carrying the sons of the fatherland to the battlefield of the Franco-Prussian War. And the fatherland is without a father. The Emperor Napoleon III was merely a usurper, a rebellious prodigal son, the nephew mimicking his uncle.

The train wreck that Zola anticipates at the end of the novel is foreshadowed by the wreck in the middle. He dwells with pitiless detail on the havoc, the mangling and burning of humans and the earth, the broken locomotive. These visions of devastation recall the fondness of Zola for images of fecal glee and ferocity. For the oral sadism expressed in his visions of biting and consuming gives way in his railroad catastrophes to the sadism of the opposite orifice. Now he blasts and smirches and piles up carnage. It is impossible to miss his exultation over the ruin and the filth, like the glee of a god reducing a universe to waste matter.

In both forms of sadism the object of the author's wrath is primarily maternal, a robust woman or the round and fertile earth. The locomotive is his phallic weapon, always punished, shattered, for its audacity, and always resurrected. Manipulating it in imagination gives him a sense of social power infinitely richer than the magic of the pen, which writers would like to believe is mightier than the sword.

The likeness between Emile Zola and Jacques Lantier can be traced without much difficulty. Both are marked, in the terms of the Rougon-Macquart genealogy, by "Election de la mère; resemblance physique du père." The engineer

is a native of the town of Plassans, which Zola modeled
after Aix, the Provencal town where he was taken at the
age of two and lived until he was eighteen. When Lantier
was six his parents moved to Paris, leaving him with a god-
mother. When Zola was six his father passed away. Emile
found himself suddenly transported from prosperity to
poverty, for which he doubtless blamed his mother. Toward
her he behaved with childish cruelty up to the time of his
literary success. He cost the widow many tears, like Jacques
Lantier with his deserted mother. The hero of *The Human
Beast* was about sixteen when the idea invaded his brain
that he was destined "to avenge some very ancient offense."
Zola was the same age when his grandmother died; she took
charge of the household after the death of his father and
cared for him with mixed austerity and tenderness. He
could not bear being alone with his mother. Whenever he
had the chance he left home to wander in woods with his
friend Paul Cézanne. Emile's favorite haunt was a cemetery. Here he forgot his troubles in the nostalgic poetry of
Musset and the other Romanticists. We learn extremely
little about Jacques Lantier's adolescence. He was trained
to become a locomotive driver, and he did. Zola's real concern is with his hero's love-life rather than with his work.
Jacques falls in love with Severine Roubaud, born Aubry, the
ward of President Grandmorin. Her maiden name instantly
recalls the name of the novelist's mother, Emilie Aubert.
Severine suggests *severing* (the castration anxiety again).
The suffix *-ine* makes one think of the woman Zola married,
Alexandrine Mesley, who had been the mistress of another
man, a medical student, before she allowed Zola to love
her illicitly. Like young Lantier he appeared incapable of
loving any but another man's woman, and then only when
the woman was abandoned by the more masterful rival.
The romance of Zola with Jeanne Rozerot, his wife's servant,
who bore him his first child, began as a secret adultery. He
became a father by stealth.

"Our century suckled at the breast of Romanticism," said
Zola, summoning the intellectual youth of France to revolt
against the old sweet ideals. He tempted them with the raw
victuals of Naturalism, and they swarmed to his banquet.
Literature became "slices of life." The insurrection of Symbolism was too metaphysical and frail to last; it amounted to no
more than a swerve; its ultimate masterpieces (Proust,

Mann, Joyce) moved in circuits back to what Tennyson called "the troughs of Zolaism." The fiction of our own period, following two "Franco-Prussian" wars of global scale, lingers both gladly and grimly in the shadow of the master of *The Human Beast*.

*Heinz Kohut**

# "DEATH IN VENICE"
# BY THOMAS MANN

## A STORY ABOUT THE DISINTEGRATION
## OF ARTISTIC SUBLIMATION

Thomas Mann was born in Lübeck in northern Germany in 1875. His father, a senator and vice-mayor of this old Hanseatic city, died, comparatively young, of septicemia, when Thomas Mann was fifteen. The mother was born in Rio de Janeiro. Her father was a German planter, her mother a Brazilian of Portuguese and Indian stock. After the early death of her mother she was, at the age of seven, taken to Lübeck where she remained. In her youth she was considered to be very beautiful, though for northern Germany a foreign, exotic southern type. Thomas Mann was the second of the five children of these parents, of whom the eldest, Heinrich, became well known as a novelist.

Thomas Mann's early childhood seems to have been influenced mainly by women. As the family was well-to-do, summers were spent on the shores of the Baltic. He remembers that he dreaded to go back to the city when the summer was over. He hated school and the discipline which it imposed on him during the winter. During his schooldays he had a homosexually tinged "crush" for a classmate, apparently the boy Hippe later described in *The Magic Mountain.*

His first major work, *Buddenbrooks,* was written in Italy in 1901. He records that he burned his hand severely when sealing the parcel containing this manuscript to send it to the publisher. As there was compulsory military training in Germany, he was to have been inducted into the army. After

* HEINZ KOHUT is a psychoanalyst and the President of the American Psychoanalytic Association. A brief version of this paper was first presented in 1948 in a seminar on Psychoanalysis and Literature conducted by Dr. Helen V. McLean at the Chicago Institute for Psychoanalysis. Numbers in parentheses in this article indicate references at the end of the essay.

being twice rejected because of cardiac neurosis, he was finally accepted. Three months later he was given a medical discharge because of an inflamed tendon.

In 1905, at the age of thirty, he married Katja Pringsheim, the only daughter of an old, respected German-Jewish family. His marriage was apparently a very happy one. Of his six children, the youngest girl, Elisabeth, became her father's favorite. In 1910, one year before *Death in Venice* was written, his sister Carla committed suicide. The effect on him of this tragic event was great, and many years later he described its detailed circumstances with much emotional vividness in the novel *Doctor Faustus* (1947). When in 1927 —five years after the death of his mother—the other sister, Julia, also ended her life by suicide, Mann, as if to reassure himself, commented: "It seems that the nourishing love has given more resistance to life to us, the sons, than to the girls."

Despite this assertion, the doubts remained. Earlier, in comparing himself with his sister Carla, he stated that they were made of similar stuff. Both he and his biographers note a certain "mental laziness" and a tendency to withdraw into sleep in times of stress. He states that he always reassured himself when he began a new work by telling himself that the task would be short and easy. When he had finished it he superstitiously pretended to himself that it had little value. He closed his autobiography (9) by saying: "I assume that I shall die in 1945, when I shall have reached the age of my mother." Even from such slender evidence it is apparent that his rational ego was, in times of stress, forced to surrender to archaic magical beliefs.

*Death in Venice* was written in such a period of stress, and it is the aim of this essay to try to trace in part how the emerging profound conflicts of the author were sublimated in the creation of an artistic masterpiece. With this purpose in mind we shall first examine the content of *Death in Venice*. In the English translation the short novel is divided into five chapters, following the earlier German editions. While the author abandoned this division in later German editions, the following abstract adheres to it for the purpose of greater clarity.

In the first chapter, all is not well with the hero, Gustav Aschenbach, an artist and writer, as he struggles to maintain his ability to work. In order to carry on, he has to take refuge

in frequent interruptions that restore his strength; therefore,
he takes naps in the middle of the day and goes on walks[1]
to recuperate. The walk on which we find him in the beginning of the story leads him by chance to a cemetery. The
reader, however, is given the impression that Aschenbach
has reached a destination—that something meaningful and
preordained is happening. This impression is accentuated by
Aschenbach's sudden encounter with a man, the first of a
series of men of hidden significance he is to meet in the
story.

The seemingly intuitive conclusion reached by the reader
that something of mysterious import is involved, here and
later, is prepared by the author through one or more of the
following devices. First, the man at the cemetery, for example,
arrives on the scene with a silent suddenness that creates the
impression of an apparition rather than an approach. Second,
the intense emotional response that this and the other encounters evoke in Aschenbach is out of proportion to the
factual significance that any of them should have for him as
a person or to the events portrayed in the story. This is a
clever maneuver which allows the reader to discard mystical
connotations from the framework of the story itself and
attaches the mysticism to Aschenbach. In other words, the
writer of the story detaches himself from his hero and describes a man who is emotionally impelled by forces which
are beyond his reason or control. This is a technique which
is rather characteristic of Thomas Mann's fiction. In his later
novels the detachment is enhanced by the more deliberate
intrusion of the writer in the form of expressed irony. The
third device used in *Death in Venice* to underline the significance of the various figures Aschenbach encounters is their
detailed delineation, which, again, is out of proportion to
their ostensible import to the hero or the plot.

Returning to the story, the man in the cemetery is
described as having his chin up, so that his Adam's apple
looks very bald in the lean neck. He is red-haired, with a
milky, freckled skin. Standing at the top of the stairs leading
to the mortuary, he is sharply peering up into space out of
colorless, red-lashed eyes. The man has a bold and domineering, even ruthless, air, and his lips are curled back,
laying bare the long, white, glistening teeth to the gums.
Aschenbach has, at first, a vague unpleasant feeling which
suddenly changes to an awareness of such hostility in the

stranger's gaze that he hastily walks away. He is then seized by a passionate longing to travel which overcomes him so swiftly that it resembles "a seizure, almost a hallucination." He sees a tropical landscape with a crouching tiger ready to jump on him, and he experiences terror. The hallucination subsides, and his self-discipline transforms his yearning into a reasonable desire for new and distant scenes, a "craving for freedom, release, forgetfulness." The emotional events following the encounter with the stranger fall into a sequence: first, panic, and the irrational impulse toward flight; then the repression of this ego-alien, dissociated impulse and its replacement by a reasoned, egosyntonic decision to travel.

The second chapter begins with a description of Gustav Aschenbach's personality and an account of his life. One is soon led to assume that the author is drawing quite consciously from his own biography. Even such a detail as the foreign background of his mother, for example, is only thinly disguised. Aschenbach owes certain foreign traits in his appearance to his mother, the daughter of a Bohemian musician. But there are other traits as well that ring a familiar note to any reader of Thomas Mann's autobiographical essay, especially the description of Aschenbach's struggle against forces within himself that interfere with his artistic creativeness. It sounds like a complaint, near to the author's own heart, when he says of his hero: "From childhood up he was pushed to achievement . . . and so his young days never knew the sweet idleness and blithe *laisser aller* that belong to youth." But Gustav Aschenbach forces himself to work, despite great inner resistances, and he resorts to certain ceremonials that permit him to keep on producing: "He began his day with a gush of cold water over chest and back; then setting a pair of tall wax candles in silver holders at the head of his manuscript, he sacrificed to art, in two or three hours of almost religious fervor, the powers he had assembled in sleep." Aschenbach's attitude expresses a masochistic pride in suffering. His "new type of hero" is St. Sebastian who, pierced by arrows, ". . . stands in modest defiance. . . ." His style of writing is one of "aristocratic self-command"; he is ". . . the poet-spokesman of all those who labor at the edge of exhaustion; of the overburdened, of those who are already worn out but still hold themselves upright; . . . who yet contrive by skilful husbanding . . . to produce . . . the effect of greatness." We learn that selections from his works

are adopted for official use in the public schools and that a
patent of nobility was conferred upon him on his fiftieth
birthday.

Other aspects of Aschenbach's character are not autobiographical. After a brief period of wedded happiness his
wife had died.[2] Aschenbach's married daughter remained
to him, but he never had a son. One gets the impression that
all these details of Aschenbach's life, including his advanced
age, tend to prepare the way for the progressive dissolution
of the restraining, reasonable forces in his personality—almost
as if the poet tried to excuse his hero by showing that there
are no responsibilities or strong emotional bonds that would
tie him to his old existence.[3]

Others have noted that the description of Aschenbach
resembles in physical, facial attributes the Bohemian composer Gustav Mahler, who had died just at the time when the
story was written. A further reference to Mahler is the use of
the first name Gustav and perhaps also the introduction of
a Bohemian conductor as maternal grandfather (2).

In the third chapter the "reasonable flight" from the man
in the cemetery is effected. The reader is still given the
feeling of the preordained, the vague impression that reason
is helplessly succumbing to infinitely stronger irrational
forces; that the man in the cemetery is a power within
Aschenbach from which there is no escape through external
flight.

Outwardly, however, Aschenbach acts quite rationally. He
plans his trip to last only a few weeks, tells himself that he
needs relaxation and intends to return refreshed to his work.
He plans originally to stay on a small island in the Adriatic;
yet, even without considering the title of the story, one
gathers that the final destination is elsewhere. And so it
happens; the weather is bad, the crowd at the hotel is
boring, and suddenly it becomes clear to Aschenbach that
Venice is his destination.

The man from the cemetery, however, cannot be evaded
by flight. On his way to Venice another apparition appears as
if to remind the fugitive of the foolishness of his subterfuges.
The man on the trip to Venice is a dandy, loudly dressed,
with rouge on his cheeks, a wig of brown hair on his head,
and rings on his fingers. When he laughs he shows an "un-
broken row of yellow teeth," obviously false; yet, underneath
makeup and costume, and behind the loud laughter designed

to feign youthfulness, he is an old man. Aschenbach is "moved
to a shudder" as he watches the disgustingly playful way
in which the old man behaves toward his young male
companions. He tries to avoid him by moving to the other
side of the ship, finally escaping by going to sleep. Aschenbach sees him once more, as the old man is leaving the boat.
He is pitifully drunk, swaying, giggling, fatuous; licking the
corners of his mouth, he teases Aschenbach with remarks
about Venice that sound clearly as if they were concerned
with the love for a woman and not for a city. "Give her our
love, will you," he says, "the p-pretty little dear"—(here his
upper plate fell down on the lower one), the ". . . little
sweety-sweety sweetheart. . . ."

Aschenbach's third encounter takes place after his arrival
in Venice; it is with a gondolier who takes him, against his
will, directly to the Lido. In contrast to the description of the
dandy on the boat, but resembling the man in the cemetery,
the gondolier is more fearsome than disgusting. The gondola
is "black as nothing on earth except a coffin"; the man, who
is "very muscular" and has "a brutish face," mutters to himself during the crossing, and the effort of rowing "bared his
white teeth to the gums." It occurs to Aschenbach that he
might have fallen into the clutches of a criminal; but, as
before, he withdraws into passivity when his fear is mounting.
He becomes indolent and dreamy, and lets matters take their
course. Nothing happens; yet, after Aschenbach's arrival,
it becomes evident that his misgivings had not been entirely
unjustified: the gondolier is "a bad man, a man without a
license," who is sought by the police.

After the preceding encounters the stage is set and the
contrast prepared for what constitutes, in the other sense,
the goal of the voyage. Aschenbach is scarcely settled in his
hotel when the decisive meeting takes place. The antithesis
could not be more extreme. The object of his journey is
Tadzio, a fourteen-year-old Polish boy of perfect beauty. He
is "pale," shows "a sweet reserve," is "godlike," of "chaste
perfection" and "unique personal charm." In contradistinction,
the boy's three older sisters are described in a disdainful,
superior, and almost pitying way. Tadzio is overwhelmingly
the favorite of his mother and his governess as revealed by
his beautiful attire and by his "pure and godlike serenity."
The sisters, on the other hand, are dressed with "almost
disfiguring austerity"; "every grace of outline was wilfully

suppressed," and their behavior was "stiff and subservient."
Aschenbach concludes that the boy is ". . . simply a pampered
darling . . . the object of a silf-willed and partial love . . ."
from the side of the mother. It is significant, in terms of
narcissistic fulfillment, that the major emphasis is on the
child. No father is present or implied. The mother's manner
is described as "cool and measured." She has the ". . .
simplicity prescribed in certain circles whose piety and
aristocracy are equally marked." Something "fabulous" about
her appearance is attributed to pearls, the size of cherries.

Gustav Aschenbach is at first not aware of the impression
which Tadzio has made on him. Preconscious signals of
anxiety, however, follow directly. He feels tired, has "lively
dreams" during the following night, and is, in general, "out
of sorts." He blames the weather for his "feverish distaste,
the pressure on the temples, the heavy eyelids"; and considering the possibility of not remaining in Venice, he does
not unpack his luggage completely. But all the self-deception
is in vain; the fascination is growing. He observes Tadzio
innumerable times, at first through chance encounters, later,
as his defenses give way, by passionately following him whenever he can; yet he never speaks to him; he remains always
alone.

In the engulfing passion for Tadzio there is also expressed
a love for the sea which is paraphrased as a "yearning to seek
refuge . . . in the bosom of the simple and vast, . . . for the
unorganized, the immeasurable, the eternal—in short, for
nothingness." Both appear to Aschenbach as one—the perfection of Tadzio's beauty and "nothingness . . . [which is] . . .
a form of perfection." He observes that Tadzio's teeth are
imperfect, and with a pleasure which he does not try to
explain to himself he concludes that the boy is "delicate"
and that he will "most likely not live to grow old."

Aschenbach does not give up the fight without a last effort.
Pretending to himself that he must get away from climatic
conditions that seem to portend disease, he makes a valiant
attempt to escape from Venice and from his growing infatuation but cannot tear himself away. There is the smell
of germicides, a hint about the danger of infection, but "the
city's evil secret mingled with the one in the depths of his
heart." Certain rumors, mentioned in the German papers,
were officially denied. But, "Passion is like crime; it does not
thrive on the established order. . . ." Everything within him

had been waiting for a chance to turn back, and all the author can do for his hero is to provide him with an excuse which allows him to postpone the moment of recognition for a little.

The moment comes when all pretext is cast aside and, seemingly with sudden change of mind, he decides to stay, triumphantly and "with a reckless joy." "With a deep incredible mirthfulness" Aschenbach gives in to the regressive disease of his emotions. With the crumbling of his moral and rational defenses there is now no more need and no longer the possibility of his deluding himself about his true motivations. He acknowledges that it was because of Tadzio that the leave-taking had been impossible.

In the fourth chapter, Aschenbach is no longer trying to deceive himself. He has yielded to his passion for Tadzio, and he accepts and enjoys it. He is able to see the boy many times every day. Some of these meetings occur by chance, but mostly they are deliberately and cunningly arranged. The only defenses which Aschenbach keeps to the very end, even in his dreams, are those for which his past as an artist has equipped him best: sublimation and idealization. The sight of the beautiful boy spurs him to philosophical reflections on the nature of beauty. He summons up the memory of an ancient prototype of his love, of Socrates for Phaedrus. He writes an essay on a "question of art and taste," trying, in this work, to translate Tadzio's beauty into his style. But his defensive struggles are only partially successful and the instinctual forces cannot be entirely desexualized; after finishing his brief work Aschenbach feels strangely exhausted, as if after a debauch.

Tadzio soon notices the extent to which he has caught Aschenbach's attention, and a tacit understanding is established between them. The child's behavior is dignified, yet seductive. When he recognizes the small signs of response, hints of a secret understanding with the boy, Aschenbach's enthusiasm is, at first, well concealed and controlled. A sudden encounter with Tadzio, however, and an unexpected lovely smile almost tear down his last reserve. All Aschenbach can do is to escape into the darkness where he breathlessly ". . . whispered the hackneyed phrase of love and longing . . . impossible in these circumstances, absurd, . . . ridiculous enough, yet . . . not unworthy of honor even here: 'I love you!' "

The final chapter, while continuing the description of Aschenbach's love and the disintegrating effects it has on his personality, deals, in appearance at least, mainly with the influences of an external event, an epidemic of Asiatic cholera which has broken out in Venice. Population and city officials alike try to conceal the news of the spreading disease, knowing well that the foreign travelers will leave if they find out about it. More and more of the visitors, however, discover the alarming truth, and depart from Venice. Tadzio and his family, apparently unaware of what is happening, stay on; hence, Aschenbach remains, sensing the sickness of the city to be a fitting frame for the sickness within himself, the passion to which his reasonable self is succumbing. This defeat of reason and control is now nearly complete. One night he presses his head against the door leading to Tadzio's bedroom, "powerless to tear himself away, blind to the danger of being caught in so mad an attitude." While he is not detected on this occasion, he has become conspicuous at other times, and he notices more than once that mother and governess find reasons to call the child away from his proximity. His pride rebels feebly at such an affront, but it is no longer a match for his desire.

To Aschenbach's encounters with the man in the cemetery, the dandy on the boat, and the gondolier, there is now added a fourth encounter with a symbolic male figure, a street musician. Many features in the sketch that the author gives us of him strike us as familiar. He is red-haired; "the veins on his forehead swelled with the violence of his effort"; his gesticulations, "the loose play of the tongue in the corner of his mouth," and the strikingly large and naked-looking Adam's apple are described as brutal, impudent, and offensive. After cemetery, senile perversion, and the gondola "black as a coffin," Aschenbach now faces the final symbolic representation of regression and disintegration in the form of a strong smell of carbolic acid, the odor of death.

Although Aschenbach soon knows the whole truth about the epidemic in Venice, he does not warn Tadzio's mother. He reflects that Tadzio will die soon, and this assumption, uncontradicted by his love, even fills him with a strange pleasure.

Toward the end of the story, and just before Aschenbach's death, he has a nightmare. Its ". . . theater seemed to be

his own soul, and the events burst in from outside, violently
overcoming the profound resistance of his spirit; . . . [leaving]
the whole cultural structure of a lifetime trampled on,
ravaged, and destroyed." The emotions which the dreamer
experiences are, at first, "fear and desire, with a shuddering
curiosity." He heard "loud confused noises from far away"
and a howl resembling Tadzio's name.

. . . He heard a voice naming though darkly that which was to
come: "The stranger god!" . . . he recognized a mountain scene
like that about his country home. . . . The females stumbled over
the long, hairy pelts that dangled from their girdles. . . . They
shrieked, holding their breasts in both hands; coiling snakes with
quivering tongues they clutched about their waists. . . . Horned
and hairy males . . . beat on brazen vessels . . . troops of beardless
youths . . . ran after goats and thrust their staves against the
creatures' flanks, then clung to the plunging horns and let themselves be borne off with triumphant shouts . . . his will was
strong and steadfast to preserve and uphold his own god against
this stranger . . . his brain reeled, a blind rage seized him, a
whirling lust, he craved with all his soul to join the ring that
formed about the obscene symbol of the godhead, which they
were unveiling, monstrous and wooden . . . they thrust their
pointed staves into each other's flesh and licked the blood as it ran
down . . . yet it was he who was flinging himself upon the
animals, who bit and tore and swallowed smoking gobbets of
flesh— . . . and in his very soul he tasted the bestial degradation
of his fall.

This dream portrays the depth of Aschenbach's spiritual
degradation. The downfall of the standards of his waking
life, while less drastic, is not less humiliating. What just
recently aroused his contempt when he saw it in another, he
now has yielded to, himself.

Soon thereafter the inevitable happens. On one of his
walks, trying to follow Tadzio, Aschenbach loses his way.
Exhausted from the heat and wishing to refresh himself, he
buys and eats some strawberries, "overripe and soft," obviously the carriers of the deadly germ. Two days later,
fatally ill, he learns that Tadzio is about to leave Venice. He
sees him once more, on the beach, just before his death. The
last impression of the dying writer, symbolizing and idealizing
his death, is of Tadzio, who, moving out into the open sea,
waves with his hand as if to invite him outward "into an
immensity of richest expectation."

In the analysis of Mann's novel, which forms the last part of the present essay, the artist's literary work will, in the main, be viewed as an attempt by the author to communicate threatening personal conflicts. The emphasis of the preceding outline of *Death in Venice* was, therefore, placed on those aspects of the story that appear to contain the most significant unconscious or preconscious patterns. A number of biographical data concerning Thomas Mann which could serve as a basis for establishing a link between the artist and his work have also been stated. Some additional material referring to the specific circumstances under which *Death in Venice* was written will now be presented.

*Death in Venice* appeared first in 1912 in the German literary periodical *Die neue Rundschau*. It had been written a year earlier, in 1911. Thomas Mann was then thirty-six years old. He had been married for about six years. His father had been dead twenty-one years. His mother was living, and his sister Carla had recently committed suicide. Venice, the stage on which the action of the story takes place, had shortly before been visited by the author. The epidemic of cholera and the attitude of the city officials with regard to it were actualities of the then recent past. A more personal connection with infectious disease was the fact that the author's wife had developed tuberculosis in 1911. She was forced to stay at a sanatorium, and Thomas Mann finished *Death in Venice* while living alone with his children in Tölz.

As has already been mentioned, the figure of the composer Gustav Mahler has been woven into the story (2). It is tempting to speculate on the reasons that induced Thomas Mann to introduce some of Mahler's features in the creation of his hero. The only manifest connection is the fact that Gustav Mahler's death occurred in 1911, the year in which *Death in Venice* was composed. One is, however, led to assume either that there was a personal relation between Thomas Mann and Gustav Mahler or that an intimate, perhaps intuitive knowledge of Mahler's personality led the author to avail himself of external characteristics where a more profound similarity between Mahler and Aschenbach was to be implied. To establish the reasons for the special significance of Mahler's death would be an intriguing endeavor.[4]

We have, however, at our disposal important information about another theme which occupied Thomas Mann's atten-

tion during the period before the artistic ideas expressed in
*Death in Venice* were fully developed. We know (2) that
his original plan was to write about a singular episode in
Goethe's life, namely, how the seventy-four-year-old renowned poet had fallen in love with a young girl—almost
a child by comparison—Ulrike von Levetzow, who was then
only seventeen. It is well known that Goethe finally was
able to submit to the necessity of tearing himself away from
his passion. The celebrated trilogy of poems, *Die Marienbader
Elegie,* is an enduring monument to this event in Goethe's life.

As has been pointed out (6), death is a theme which
occurs repeatedly in Mann's works. One of the first stories
he wrote (at the age of sixteen or seventeen, about a year
after his father died) bears the title "Death." It is no exag-
geration to maintain that in almost all his subsequent writings
death remains one of the principal themes either as an
important part of the action or, in a more disguised form,
as recurring metaphysical speculation.

It is not only the frequency with which Thomas Mann
returns to the theme of death in his work that reveals its
importance to the writer. A more specific connecting link
with the author are his protagonists who are often manifestly
autobiographically conceived, in particular when Mann tells
about the life and the problems of artists. It is the attitudes of
these fictitious personalities toward life and death which
constitute an important source of information about the
author who created them. In the story "Tonio Kröger," as
well as in other early works of Thomas Mann, death, or the
sympathy for death, seems to gain its significance not so much
from any expressed value of its own but rather from an
aristocratic negation of life (6).

Tonio Kröger feels it necessary to divorce himself from
life; he can remain artistically active and creative only inasmuch as he ceases to be a human being (6). If an adolescent assumes such an attitude as a defense in his struggle
against overwhelming instinctual demands, we are inclined
to regard it as temporary. As Anna Freud has pointed out
(3), the asceticism of youth has to be considered as a normal
phenomenon. The author of *Death in Venice,* however, was
a mature man of thirty-six with a wife and children. The
artists in Thomas Mann's stories are influenced by the
progress-negating philosophy of Schopenhauer and Nietzsche
and subscribe to the creed of the German romanticists that

there is a close affinity between beauty and death (8). The
romantic artist must be dead, symbolically, in order to be
able to create a work of beauty. This tendency is particularly
evident in the hero of *Death in Venice*. The very name
Aschenbach (brook of ashes) clearly evokes, at least in the
original German, the association with the river of the dead in
classical mythology (5). To enable himself to work, Aschenbach is described as resorting to the ceremonial of placing
lighted candles at the head of his manuscript which creates
a distinctly funereal impression; in addition he feels compelled to mortify the flesh by self-abnegation and by a strong
need to isolate himself (6).

At the time this novel was written, only two important
members of the author's family were dead: the father, who
had died many years ago, and the beautiful sister Carla, who
had recently committed suicide. One is immediately inclined
to assume that identification is with the dead father and not
with Carla for the simple reason that the heroes of Thomas
Mann's earlier stories are struggling with problems similar
to Aschenbach's and that these stories were written before
Carla's suicide. Apart from such negative reasoning, which
tends to exclude the sister from consideration rather than to
establish the father for the role, there is, it seems, more
positive proof to be obtained within the story itself.

The literary commentators (1, 2, 5) are in accord about
the fact that the four men whom Aschenbach encounters are
messengers of his impending death; and it is plausible to
assume that this symbolism was consciously intended by
Thomas Mann as he wrote the story. By contrast, the interpretation offered in the present essay is that the four appari-
tions are manifestations of endopsychic forces, projected by
Aschenbach as the repression barrier is beginning to crumble.
The four men are thus the ego's projected recognition of the
breakthrough of ancient guilt and fear, magically perceived as
the threatening father figure returning from the grave. Three
of these four figures, the man in the cemetery, the aged freak
on the boat, and the gondolier, are described as baring their
teeth in a strange way which has been pointed out (5) as
calling to mind the idea of the skull of a skeleton: death or
a dead man. The gondolier in a gondola, black like a coffin,
seems to be an allusion to the figure of ancient mythology,
Charon, who ferries the dead across the River Styx to Hades
(2). The first man arises from the cemetery with the sudden-

ness of apparition—the most unambiguous portrayal of someone deceased who threateningly returns. The last one, a street
singer, carries about him the odor of death. All except the
dandy on the boat are described as powerful and dangerous,
and a more or less clear inference of free, unhampered aggression and sexuality can easily be drawn. When we read in the
description of the street singer that the veins on his forehead
were swollen, we may interpret this detail as an allusion to
either or both of the aforementioned standard attributes of a
feared father: sexual excitement or rage. The old man dressed
up to give the deceptive impression of youth suggests a
parallel with a dead man who comes back to life. The vary-
ing combinations of fear and contempt which are experienced
by Aschenbach in these encounters express the original hostile
and loathing attitude toward a father figure with the secondary fear of retaliation from the stronger man; also included is
probably the ego's reaction against the emerging superstitious
fear of the returning dead, an attempt at self-reassurance by
ridicule.

In this context it is illuminating to remember Thomas
Mann's confession that he could not free himself entirely
from very superstitious attitudes and beliefs. For example,
he attached special significance to the date and hour of his
birth; certain numbers had a particular magical meaning for
him; and the fact that his children were born, as he said,
"in pairs" (girl and boy; boy and girl; girl and boy), constituted for him a lucky omen (9). The coexistence of such
superstitious beliefs with extreme rationality is characteristic
of compulsive personalities. That the archaic ego of the
compulsive is particularly prone to believe in the magical
powers of the dead is also a well-established fact.

Another peculiarity of the compulsive personality is the
predominance of strongly ambivalent attitudes, particularly
toward the father and father surrogates. In this connection,
light is shed on Mann's preoccupation with the aged Goethe,
who certainly represents the father figure of father figures for
any German writer. The ascertained fact that the topic of
Goethe's infatuation with a young girl was in the writer's
mind just before the Aschenbach story was taking shape
adds, though indirectly, to the evidence for the assumption
that the central theme underlying *Death in Venice* is the
father conflict. Reverence for Goethe usually prevents
biographers from dwelling on the ridiculous aspects of his

last love affair; at most, the tragic impossibility of the
liaison is stressed. Both of these opinions are stated in *Death
in Venice:* the latter, in the author's attitude toward Aschenbach's passion for Tadzio (". . . impossible in these circumstances, absurd,—ridiculous enough, yet . . . not unworthy
of honor even here . . ."); the former, expressing straight-
forward ridicule and disgust, in the portrayal of the old
dandy on the boat.

In general, one can say, that the father theme is dealt with
in *Death in Venice* by splitting the ambivalently revered and
despised figure and by isolating the opposing feelings that
were originally directed to the same object—a typical compulsive mechanism. The bad, threatening, sexually active
father is embodied in the four men Aschenbach encounters.
With the good one, who foregoes threats and punishment
and heterosexual love—with the father, that is, who loves
only the son—Aschenbach identifies himself, portraying in
his love for Tadzio what he wished he had received from his
father. This device, however, is not entirely successful:
Aschenbach's ambivalence is intensified by the narcissistic,
envious recognition that another is getting what he really
wished for himself, and hostile, destructive elements enter
into his feelings toward Tadzio. He not only experiences a
strange pleasure at the thought that Tadzio will die early,
but indirectly he also exposes the beloved boy to great
danger by not warning his family about the epidemic. On
the whole, however, it remains true that the destructive
impulses toward Tadzio are secondary, arising only in so
far as the narcissistic identification with the boy and the
enjoyment of love by proxy are not entirely successful. The
basic hostility is not directed against the boy (as jealousy
against a brother) but against the hated father image. The
ferociousness of this hatred is revealed in Aschenbach's last
dream in which his unsuccessful struggle with the bad
father, the foreign god of the barbarians, the obscene symbol
of sexuality, the totem animal, is killed and devoured. By
the law of talion, which is the immutable authority for the
archaic ego of the compulsive, death must be punished by
death and Aschenbach has to die.

The decisive threat to Aschenbach's defensive system is,
however, neither caused by the traces of envious hostility
against Tadzio nor by the hatred against the father but by the
breakdown of sublimated homosexual tenderness and the

nearly unchecked onrush of unsublimated homosexual desire in the aging writer. Aschenbach's last dream is an expression of the breakdown of sublimation; it describes the destruction of "the whole cultural structure of a lifetime."

The material that builds up the dream comes from three sources. First, we can discern remnants of sublimatory ego activity; they account for the formal aspects of the dream which retains something artistic and impersonal, as if it were a beautiful fable from classical mythology. Second, we recognize the portrayal of the disintegration of Aschenbach's personality; it finds expression specifically in relation to his now unconcealed sexual desire for Tadzio. The former sweetness of Tadzio's name has been transformed into "a kind of howl with a long-drawn u-sound at the end." Third, the undisguised emergence of a primal scene experience allows us to draw conclusions about the traumatic impact of the observation of the sexual activities of adults upon the child.

The sequence of curiosity, mounting sexual tension, wish to participate in the sexual activity, and the fear of being annihilated by participation in the sadistically misinterpreted sexual activity of the adults are clearly described. There is little doubt, too, that the homosexual desires and fears must have originated during such experiences—that the child must have been partially identified with the mother and must have wished for the sexual love of the father. The dread of castration (death), aroused by the wish to participate in the violent activity of the adults and, especially, by the passive attitude toward the father, must have led to an attempt to abandon the libidinal striving for participation and may have initiated the building up of "the whole cultural structure of a lifetime."

We may well find the origins of Aschenbach's artistic attitude in the dangers of the primal scene experience. At the beginning of the primal scene the child is an observer, not yet threatened by traumatic overstimulation, passivity, and fear of mutilation. Could it not be that the child, as the dread becomes overwhelming, returns by an internal tour de force to the original role of the emotionally uninvolved observer, and that further elaborations of such defenses against traumatic overstimulation make important contributions to the development of creative sublimation?

To prevent misunderstanding, these considerations are not

intended to furnish a complete explanation of artistic creativity, not even to those limits that apply in general to genetic constructions. The hypothesis that artistic creativity may be related to the feminine principle and that artistic creativity may in certain instances derive its energy from the sublimation of infantile wishes does not need support from the material which has been presented. Suffice it to say that Aschenbach's homosexual organization and feminine identification are fully compatible with this old and well-substantiated psychoanalytic thesis and that the waxing and waning of artistic productivity in Aschenbach seems to run parallel with the predominance either of the sublimated or of the unsublimated homosexual strivings.

The specific hypothesis that is advanced here refers to certain features of the artistic attitude in an individual instance. Primal scene experiences, creating overstimulation, dangerous defensive passive wishes, and castration anxiety, may lead to the attempt to return to the emotional equilibrium at the beginning of the experience and prepare the emotional soil for the development of the artistic attitudes as an observer and describer. This hypothesis seems particularly compatible with certain qualities of Mann's art, his detachment and irony. It is possible that similar considerations apply, beyond Aschenbach, to other artistic personalities and, more generally, that it is perhaps a genetic factor in the development of an ironical attitude toward life.

Beyond the portrayal of problems posed by the mother identification and by the ambivalently passive attitude toward the father, the trend toward union with the mother can also be discerned in Mann's writings. This wish, however, is more strongly repressed and seems to evoke even deeper guilt than the ambivalent attitude toward the father. Rarely does it, therefore, reveal itself in a sublimated, egosyntonic form of object love and, if instances of this type occur, they are by no means unambiguous. One might speculate that perhaps the Slavic features of Tadzio (or of Hippe and Claudia Chauchat in *The Magic Mountain*) contain a hint of effectively sublimated love for the mother who, in real life, was an "exotic type." Yet almost always when we encounter the wish for the mother we find it presented either in vague, deeply symbolic terms or in the regressive form of "identification" rather than as object love. In addition some kind of punishment, mostly in the form of death or disease, is expressed or implied. This holds true not only for Thomas Mann's literary productions but also for his actual beliefs, as can be inferred from his superstitious prediction that his life would come to an end in 1945, when he should have reached the age at which his mother had died.

The wish for the mother expresses itself, more frequently than in the forms discussed above, in even more regressive, diffuse, highly symbolic yearnings. It seems that this is the only way in which this deeply guilt-provoking wish is permitted to occur repeatedly in the consciousness of the writer and of his literary figures and is allowed to be accepted by the ego with a certain degree of pleasure. The pleasure, however, is a rather melancholy one for in many of Thomas Mann's works the wish for the mother emerges disguised as a longing for death. In *The Magic Mountain* it is the immensity of an alluring snow landscape which attracts Hans Castorp and almost leads to his death by freezing. In *Death in Venice* the mother symbol seems to be represented first of all by the sick city itself from which Aschenbach cannot extricate himself; it is not only a city, but also the sea, and death—the whole atmosphere of Venice, death, and the sea together—toward which Aschenbach's deepest wishes are directed. As death is overtaking him, Aschenbach sees Tadzio, beckoning him outward into the open sea, "into an immensity of richest expectation." This picture, then, establishes clearly not only the symbolic identity of death and the sea but also the connection between the boy, Tadzio, and the sea-death-mother motif.

We are faced with the final task of examining the specific circumstances in the author's life that might have activated his conflicts and thus provided the impulse for writing *Death in Venice*. The recent suicide of the sister Carla, an old competitor for parental love, might have precipitated feelings of guilt. Perhaps, too, Carla constituted an object of strivings which were displaced from the mother to the sister, a speculation that finds support from the fact that Mann treated the incest motif between brother and sister in the short story "*Wälsungenblut*," written in 1905 (7).

Of greater importance was probably the concurrent illness of Mann's wife which may have forced the author into closer affectionate ties with his young children. The possibility may also be entertained that his wife's illness may have necessitated a period of sexual abstinence which, in turn, led to increased conflicts concerning homosexual regression.

As we follow the sequence of Mann's publications we can, it seems, discern that, with his increasing success as a writer and with the reassuring stability of his position as husband and father, his original "sympathy with the aristocracy of death" began to be counterbalanced more and more by an actively participating acceptance of life. This more affirmative attitude toward life finds expression in most of Mann's writings after the First World War (6). Settembrini, in *The Magic Mountain,* is certainly an advocate of active participation in life and an outspoken enemy of any sympathy with death or disease; and there can hardly be any doubt that the author's conscious affection was for Settembrini and not for Naphtha, his adversary; yet, the old conflict between progressive and regressive forces was never fully resolved. Mann's preoccupation with death and disease continued to be expressed in his last writings, despite his admirably courageous attitude in the political events preceding and during World War II.

In his preface (10) to a volume of stories by Dostoevski, Mann recognized that he, like the great Russian, received much of the impetus for his productivity from a deep sense of guilt and that, in a way, his literary productions served as expiations. Glover mentions (4) that some obsessional neurotics fear that analysis will destroy their sublimatory capacities and that, in fact, the sublimated activities of the ego are equated with sexual potency by them. One of Mann's lifelong preoccupations was the struggle to maintain his artistic creativity which seemed forever threatened and precarious and which he tried to protect with superstitious magic. Paradoxically, the successful sublimation of passive feminine attitudes into artistic creativity must have called forth the guilt of masculine achievement.[5] And like the artist-hero in one of his last novels, *Doctor Faustus* (1947), who sells his soul to the devil and accepts disease and early death in return for a measure of active living in artistic productivity, Thomas Mann, too, seems to have to assure the threatening father that he has not really succeeded, and that his sublimations are breaking down. Aschenbach in *Death in Venice* and Leverkühn in *Doctor Faustus* allowed Mann to spare himself, to live and to work, because they suffer in his stead.

## SUMMARY

In the preceding essay the attempt is made to establish a correlation between some known biographical data, certain trends in the writings of Thomas Mann, and the plot of his short novel, *Death in Venice*. The influence of unconscious guilt and, possibly, the role of early sexual overstimulation for the development of an (ironical) artistic personality are discussed. The disintegration of the creative processes in the principal character of the story is seen as a return of unsublimated libido under the influence of aging, loneliness, and guilt over success. It is assumed that the author displaced his personal conflict on the protagonist of the story and thus was able to safeguard his own artistic creativity.

## NOTES

1 The translation "walk" for the German *Spazierengehen* is inadequate; there is however, no exact English equivalent. *Spazierengehen* is an expression of pointed leisure corresponding to the ride in a carriage of the aristocracy. It is perhaps an imitation of this aristocratic habit by the middle class, on foot.

2 Mann's wife had to go to a sanatorium because of tuberculosis approximately at the time of the composition of *Death in Venice*.

3 The mechanism here may be compared to dreams of failing an examination which, in reality, one has successfully passed long ago (12). Aschenbach's progressive disintegration appears to be based on the fact that he has no object-libidinal ties to reality. This may have served as a reassurance to Mann who, despite temporary loneliness, felt that he had sufficient emotional closeness to his family to preserve him from Aschenbach's destiny.

4 A letter written by Freud to Theodor Reik (II) establishes the fact that Mahler had consulted Freud and was "analyzed for one afternoon . . . in Leyden" less than a year before Mahler's death. Freud alludes to Mahler's withdrawing of libido from his wife and to Mahler's "obsessional neurosis." The latter is especially interesting in view of the obsessional features of Thomas Mann, discussed in the present essay. Dr. Bruno Walter, the distinguished conductor, who knew both Thomas Mann and Gustav Mahler intimately, expresses his firm conviction that Mann and Mahler did not know each other personally at any time (Bruno Walter in a letter to the author of December 13, 1956).

5 We remember in this context that he burned his hand severely when sealing the package containing the manuscript of the novel (*Buddenbrooks*) that was to bring him fame, and we recall the ceremonials of magical expiation that characterize Aschenbach's working habits.

REFERENCES

1. Lydia Baer, *The Concept and Function of Death in the Works of Thomas Mann*, Philadelphia, privately printed, 1932.

2. Arthur Eloesser, *Thomas Mann, sein Leben und sein Werk*, Berlin, S. Fischer, 1925.

3. Anna Freud, *The Ego and the Mechanisms of Defense*, London, Hogarth Press, 1937.

4. Edward Glover, *The Technique of Psychoanalysis*, New York, International Universities Press, Inc., 1955.

5. Martin Havenstein, *Thomas Mann, der Dichter und Schriftsteller*, Berlin, Wiegand & Grieben, 1927.

6. Hans Kasdorff, *Der Todesgedanke im Werke Thomas Manns*, Leipzig, H. Eichblatt, 1932.

7. Thomas Mann, *Wälsungenblut*, Munich, Phantasus-Verlag, 1921, privately printed.

8. ——, *Betrachtungen eines Unpolitischen*, Berlin, S. Fischer, 1918.

9. ——, *"Lebensabriss,"* in *Die neue Rundschau*, Berlin, S. Fischer, June 1, 1930, pp. 732, ff.

10. ——, "Dostoevski—in Moderation," in *The Short Novels of Dostoevski*, New York, Dial Press, Inc., 1945, pp. vii-xx.

11. Theodor Reik, *The Haunting Melody*, New York, Farrar, Straus and Young, 1953.

12. Wilhelm Stekel, *"Beiträge zur Traumdeutung,"* *Jahrb. psychoanalytische & psychopathologische Forschungen*, I (1909), p. 458.

*Harry Slochower**

# INCEST IN
# "THE BROTHERS KARAMAZOV"

In *The Brothers Karamazov,* Mitya publicly competes
with his father for Grushenka. And Dostoevski criticism
has accepted Grushenka as the incest figure in the novel.
However, the main plot of the story and Mitya's major inner
dilemma center, not in Grushenka, but in another woman:
Katerina or Katya. And this essay will attempt to show that
Katya is the deeper of Mitya's incest burdens. The paper
would also suggest that although Freud's study of Dostoevski
never mentions Katya, she appears there in a veiled form.

Freud names *The Brothers Karamazov, Hamlet,* and
*Oedipus Rex* three literary masterpieces, dealing with patricide, motivated by sexual rivalry. He regards three of Fyodor
Karamazov's sons guilty of patricide, and sees Grushenka as
the object of the sexual contest between Fyodor and Mitya.[1]

Now, *The Brothers Karamazov* is a later, more complex
form of the Oedipal situation than are *Oedipus Rex* and
*Hamlet.* In Sophocles, Oedipus actually commits incest and
patricide. Shakespeare's modern, sophisticated scene presents
more tangled relations. There is a scene in Hamlet's mind
between his father and Claudius, between his mother and
Ophelia, and between himself, as the son, and Gonzago "the
nephew" (in the play between the play).[2] In Dostoevski,
the pattern becomes still more intricate. We have three father
figures: Fyodor Karamazov, Grigory (who brings up Mitya
and Smerdyakov), and Father Zossima; three or four sons:
Mitya, Ivan, Alyosha, and Smerdyakov, who divide the
patricidal guilt. But most complex of all is the problem of
incest. Grushenka is the manifest object of Mitya's desire. The
hidden and more troublesome incest figure is Katya.

* HARRY SLOCHOWER has written widely in the field of psychoanalysis and literature.

Katya is pivotal not only for the plot. She is also the
source of Mitya's obsessive feeling of his "debt" to her. His
inability to return the money he took from Katya is the chief
ground of his emotional disturbance. This is the reason,
Mitya says, "why I fought in the tavern, that is why I
attacked my father." Here, Mitya associates his patricidal
impulse with his "debt" to Katya. What tortures him when he
is arrested is not the false charge that he murdered his father,
nor so much the thought that he killed Grigory, but "the
damned consciousness" that he had not repaid Katya and
had become "a downright thief." (In passing, we might note
that Mitya recalls that as a boy he stole twenty kopecks from
his mother which he returned three days later) (430). Why
does Mitya feel that this is "the most shameful act of my
whole life," that his very *"life"* depends on his returning the
3,000 rubles to Katya? (523, 720).[3]

## KATYA AS MOTHER IMAGE

Dostoevski gives Katya features which he also assigns
to Mitya's mother, Adelaida. Both belong to a fairly rich
and distinguished family and become heiresses. Both possess
an imperious beauty and are described as strong, vigorous,
and intelligent. Mitya's mother was "a hot-tempered, bold,
dark-browed, impatient woman," and according to rumor
used to beat her husband. She left Fyodor, running away
with a divinity student. Katya strikes Mitya as proud, reckless, defiant, self-willed. She too defies convention: She
comes to Mitya alone, impulsively offers to become his wife.

From the outset, Katya appears to Mitya as "a person
of character." Indeed, he speaks of her as a kind of goddess.
At the meeting in Father Zossima's cell, he is particularly
outraged by his father's aspersions of Katya's good and
honorable name for whom Mitya feels "such reverence that
I dare not take her name in vain." (72) (We are told that
there were everlasting scenes between Fyodor and Mitya's
mother and that after Adelaida left her husband, "Fyodor
Pavlovitch introduced a regular harem into the house.")
And just as the question is raised how Adelaida could have
married "such a worthless puny weakling" as Fyodor,
so Mitya cannot understand that Katya should choose "a
bug" like himself (5).

Mitya comes to Katya's attention by his wild exploits

which set the whole town talking. He felt that this made
him "a hero." But, he complains, Katya "didn't seem to feel
it." When she first saw him, she "scarcely looked at me, and
compressed her lips scornfully." (Mitya's mother abandoned
him when he was three years old and apparently never
"looked" at him afterward.) Thereupon, Mitya plans revenge
on Katya by humiliating her. The opportunity comes when
disgrace threatens Katya's father (a lieutenant-colonel), who
is suspected of irregularities in connection with an apparent
deficit of 4,500 rubles of government money which is held
in his account. Katya, desperately trying to save her father
from dishonor, gets word from Mitya that he will give
her the money if she comes to him alone, Mitya promising
"to keep the secret religiously."

When Katya came to him, Mitya's first thought "was
a—Karamazov one," to treat this "beauty" as a prostitute.
But she also appeared to him beautiful "in another way . . .
because she was noble . . . in all the grandeur of her generosity and sacrifice for her father." In contrast, Mitya
thought of himself as a little animal, "a bug . . . a venomous
spider." His feelings toward her comprised a mixture of
hatred and love. His hatred for Katya, he tells Alyosha, was
such as he never felt for any other woman. But it is the
kind "which is only a hair's-breadth from love, the maddest
love."

Katya's visit aroused a powerful sexual desire in Mitya.
He was so excited by the "venomous thought" of possessing
her that he nearly swooned "with suspense." Although Mitya
gained mastery over his demon, his deep guilt begins at
this point. It is as though by offering herself to him, Katya
divined his hidden wish to enter into an impermissible relation with her. But Mitya curbed his desire, gave Katya the
money (we should bear in mind that it is the money left him
by his mother). After she leaves, Mitya drew his sword,
nearly stabbing himself—"why, I don't know," he adds
(115, 117-118). Mitya's ability to control his Karamazov
sensualism in this scene is a major test of his manhood, and
*foreshadows that he will resist the other temptation, that of
killing his father.* He was held back from taking Katya by—
perhaps also despite—the thought that she was ready to
surrender herself for the sake of her father.

However, soon afterward, Mitya yielded to another en-
ticement. He took the 3,000 rubles which Katya asked

him to post and spent half of the sum on his mistress figure, Grushenka (repeating his father's act in which Fyodor attempted to keep the dowry of Mitya's mother). At about the same time, he agreed to Katya's proposal or demand that they become engaged. (How this comes about, Dostoevski-Mitya does not make clear).

The engagement takes place shortly after the incident in Mitya's room and immediately following the death of Katya's father. She offers to become Mitya's wife to save him from himself:

"I love you madly," she writes him, "even if you don't love me, never mind. Be my husband. Don't be afraid. I won't hamper you in any way. I will be your chattel. I will be the carpet under your feet. I want to love you for ever. I want to save you from yourself" [120–121][4]

Mitya makes a form of resistance, writing Katya that she is now rich (having become an heiress on her father's death), whereas he was "only a stuck-up beggar." For some unexplained reason, Mitya sends his brother Ivan to her who thereupon falls in love with Katya. This "one stupid thing," he says later to Alyosha, "may be the saving of us all now."[5]

## KATYA AS THE POSSESSIVE MOTHER

The identification of Katya with Mitya's mother lies above all in their attempt to dominate their men. Katya's authoritative character is suggested first by her outward appearance. Alyosha is struck "by the imperiousness, proud ease, and self-confidence of the haughty girl." Her love for Mitya is that of a commanding or pitying mother for a wayward son. She would be Mitya's "God," as she says. When Alyosha tells her that Mitya sends her his "compliments" (his manner of letting Katya know that her betrothal is off), she retorts:

"No, he won't recognize that I am his truest friend; he won't know me, and looks on me merely as a woman. . . . Let him feel ashamed of himself, let him be ashamed of other people's knowing (that he had not returned the money he owed her), but not of my knowing. He can tell God everything without shame . . . I want to save him for ever. Let him forget me as his betrothed."

The Pan-Slavic Mother Goddess is worshiped for her fruit-bearing and yielding qualities, not for her beauty. She is generally identified with the good Russian earth and its earthy peasant folk. Katya, with her aristocratic pride, stern virtue, and possessiveness is a distortion of this Eastern Mother Goddess. She can not produce because she cannot yield.

At one point, Katya seems almost ready to accept the role of Mitya's "friend" and "sister." When told that Mitya has gone to Grushenka, she exclaims:

"I've already decided, even if he marries that—creature . . . *even then I will not abandon him.* . . . I will watch over him all my life unceasingly. When he becomes unhappy with that woman, and that is bound to happen quite soon, let him come to me and he will find a friend, a sister. . . . Only a sister, of course, and so for ever; but he will learn at least that that sister is really his sister, who loves him and has sacrificed all her life to him."

Yet, in the same breath, she reverts to the tyrannical nature of her love:

"I will gain my point. I will insist on his knowing me and confiding entirely in me, without reserve," she cried, in a sort of frenzy, "I will be a god to whom he can pray!"

At the trial, she relates the humiliating errand on which she came to Mitya. And the author comments that such self-immolation seemed incredible even "from such a self-willed and contemptuously proud girl, as she was." She herself confesses at the trial: "I tried to conquer him by my love . . ." (151, 153, 194-196, 722, 731).[6]

Katya offers to sacrifice herself for Mitya. But she would *impose* her sacrifice on him, *would be his Mother-Savior by command.*[7] Mitya senses this. He calls Katya "a woman of great wrath . . . Hard-headed creature," realizes that "she loves her own *virtue,* not me," that she wants "to sacrifice her life and destiny out of gratitude," that her love for him is "more like revenge." The revenge consists in Katya's attempt to reform him, that is, to deprive him of the "bug" in himself which he enjoys. It is the threat of the mother engulfing the son by her all-possessive love.

Mitya keeps speaking of his "debt" to Katya and of his "disgrace." On the manifest level, he is referring to the fact that he had squandered 1,500 of Katya's 3,000 rubles on a spree with Grushenka. At first, he heatedly resists revealing this fact:

"I won't speak of that gentleman," he says at the trial, "because
it would be a stain on my honour. The answer to the question
where I got the money would expose me to far greater disgrace
than the murder and robbing of my father, if I had murdered
him."

When pressed, he reveals his "shame," stating that he stole
the money, not from his father, "but from her . . . a noble
creature, noblest of the noble." But "she has hated me ever
so long, oh, ever so long . . . and hated me with good
reason, good reason!" The "good reason" is that he asked
her to come alone knowing that she was aware of and despised his debaucheries. Even after his engagement to her,
Mitya was unable to curb his dissipations, indeed, carried
them on "before the very eyes of his betrothed!" The
"tragedy" of it, he adds, is that "these lofty sentiments of hers
are as sincere as a heavenly angel's." But Mitya did not
want to reform. He would rather vanish into "his filthy
back-alley, where he is at home and where he will sink in
filth and stench at his own free will and with enjoyment"
(121, 122).

Mitya makes desperate efforts to free himself from the
"debt" to his surrogate "God"-mother. This, although Katya
herself does not press him for the money, indeed, acts as
if she did not care what he did with it. Furthermore, Mitya
*could* get the money: Alyosha offers him 2,000 rubles and
says that Ivan would give him another 1,000. Moreover, he
could borrow from Grusha. But no! Mitya is obsessed with
the feeling that *he can rid of his "debt" to Katya only by
giving her the money which he has inherited from his mother
and which his father is withholding from him.* (Mitya's
attempts to get the money from Samsonov, Lyagavy,
Madame Hohlakov are a wild-goose chase which invite failure.) And he wants no more than 3,000 rubles, although
by his reckoning, his mother left him 28,000 rubles. If his
father would give him 3,000 rubles, Mitya tells Alyosha, he
would draw his soul "out of hell":

"Let him give me back only three out of the twenty-eight thousand . . . For that three thousand—I give you my solemn word—
I'll make an end of everything, and he shall hear nothing more of
me. For the last time, I give him the chance to be a father.[8]
[509, 720, 124-5]

## GRUSHENKA: THE HETAIRA-MAGDALENE

From this perspective, Grushenka is the lighter of Mitya's burdens. The conflict with his father over her is open and somewhat literal.[9] Mitya is ready to accept all his rivals, except Fyodor. He is not jealous of the old merchant Samsonov, or of the Pole who, Mitya declares, has priority because he was her "first lover." It is of some significance that Mitya's attitude toward Grushenka is a transference of Katya's to him. As Katya was willing to accept any conditions if Mitya would agree to be her husband, so he declares:

"I'll be her [Grusha's] husband if she deigns to have me, and when lovers come, I'll go into the next room. I'll clean her friends' goloshes, blow up their samovar, run their errands." (124)

However, Mitya does not want to force his love on Grusha. And, it is his hope that she may be the means by which he can free himself from Katya. Her soft, voluptuous, noiseless movements contrast with Katya's bold and vigorous step, her simple "child-like good nature" with Katya's complex ironic consciousness.

Mitya speaks of Grusha's "infernal curves." Yet, the story does not have a single erotic scene between them. Even at his "wedding" with Grusha at Mokroe, Mitya does not go beyond kissing his beloved (154-155, 630). Dostoevski himself remarks that Grusha is Russian in that her beauty is only of the moment. Russian literature, as Berdyaev notes, does not know the erotic motifs of the West. It has no stories comparable to Tristan and Isolde or Romeo and Juliet. The attraction of Russian women (as of the Russian Mother Goddess) lies not in their seductiveness but in their earthy productivity.

Mitya's meeting with Grushenka at Mokroe is the poem of *The Brothers Karamazov*, the lovers' Dionysian song to life. For the first and only time, the two are united, at one with "the people," the Russian peasants, over whom they reign as King and Queen. It is their Eden where all is love, kindness, forgiveness, and generosity. To the rhythm of children's songs, Mitya, and his bride themselves act like children. Everything—down to the language and mood—is simple, elemental, and earthy. Here, all are equal (except for the

"foreigners," the Poles, who leave before the high point of
the revel is reached).

But it is a Karamazov-Eden, and the celebration takes
on the character of a delirious orgy. Mokroe is the scene
of Mitya's and Grushenka's "wedding." It takes place at
about the same time when the father is murdered and after
Mitya thought he may have killed his surrogate father Grigory. At this point, "society" steps in and arrests Mitya.

Like many of Dostoevski's women, Grushenka turns from
the hetaira to the Madonna. Her transformation begins
during Aloysha's visit when his kindness frees her for a
generous, overflowing love of the "soul," becoming "more
loving than we," as Alyosha puts it. The change takes on a
stable form after Mitya's arrest. Now, there were

> signs of a spiritual transformation in her, and a steadfast, fine and
> humble determination that nothing could shake. . . . There was
> scarcely a trace of her former frivolity.

Through Grusha's love, Mitya declares, he has "become a
man himself" (372-373, 597, 630).

## MITYA'S NEED OF THE TWO WOMEN

Although Mitya states that Grusha has made "a man"
of him, it appears that she does not completely fulfill his
needs. She is the permissive figure who *accepts Mitya as he
is.* But Mitya also needs the authoritative, censorious conscience, especially since his father lacks this quality altogether. Fyodor is a satyr figure, embodies an amorphous,
chaotic sensualism intent solely on the pursuit of pleasure.
And Mitya has only a distant relation to Father Zossima, Alyosha, and Ivan, the religious and rational superegos in the
novel.

This may explain why Mitya cannot and does not want
to free himself from Katya, why he kneels and prays "to Katya's image" in Grusha's presence (162). When she produces
the letter which virtually condemns him, Mitya cries out:

> "We've hated each other for many things, Katya, but I swear, I
> swear I loved you even while I hated you, and you didn't love
> me!"[10]

When, at the trial, Katya tells of her visit to Mitya and her
bow to him, Mitya sobs: "Katya, why have you ruined

me? . . . Now, I am condemned" (723). Does her re-
cital reactivate his incestuous desire for her? Does her attempt to save him again put him in her "debt"?[11]

Even as Mitya turns towards Grushenka, he remains bound
to Katya. Following the trial, he seems concerned only about
seeing Katya. Alyosha tells her:

"He needs you particularly just now . . . he keeps asking for you.
. . . He realizes that he has injured you beyond reckoning. . . .
He said, if she refuses to come, I shall be unhappy all my life."

When Katya appears in the doorway of his prison cell,

a scared look came into his face. He turned pale, but a timid,
pleading smile appeared on his lips at once, and with an irresistible
impulse he held out both hands to Katya.

And now, the two confess their mutual tie. Katya tells him:

"Love is over, Mitya! but the past is painfully dear to me. . . . I
shall love you for ever, and you will love me; do you know that?
Do you hear? Love me, love me all your life!" she cried, with a
quiver almost of menace in her voice.

Mitya replies:

"I shall love you . . . All my life! So it will be, so it will always
be . . ."

He pleads with her that she forgive him for having wanted
to humiliate her, for his desire to have "the proud aristocratic girl" appear as "the hetaira." His plea is met in Katya's
final resignation, in her words to the rival Grushenka: "Forgive me . . . Don't be anxious, I'll save him for you"
(804-805, 810-12).

In his book *Hamlet and Oedipus*, Ernest Jones gives
examples of the mythic process of decomposition in which
the tyrannical figure is broken up into several characters,
some of whom may be veiled as beneficent. Applying this
strategy, one may say that Dostoevski-Mitya divide the
mother figure into Katya and Grushenka. The decomposition may be due to Mitya's repressed feelings about his own
mother who was apparently unconcerned about abandoning
him when she left Fyodor. Mitya moves from the commanding

goddess-mother to the yielding mistress-mother. In the end,
he needs both: "the proud aristocratic girl and the hetaira."
Grusha can only follow, but not guide. He needs both,
moreover, for the mixture of elements in each. Grusha is
submissive. Yet, in the scene with Katya, Mitya recognizes
in her "the queen of all she-devils." Katya is defiant, haughty,
and domineering. Yet, Alyosha notes that her face can beam
"with spontaneous good-natured kindliness, and direct warm-
hearted sincerity" (698, 161, 153). She would be Mitya's
"God," but is also ready to sacrifice herself to help him. In
the end, the two women figures tend to merge.

Mitya almost marries Katya and nearly kills Fyodor.
Like Hamlet, he wrestles with the demon driving him to
violate the primary taboos. Mitya too shows no hesitation
to "act," except where it concerns Katya and Fyodor. His
promise lies in his gradual awareness of the nature of his
"debt" and guilt, awareness that his involvement with Katya
was injurious to her and himself.

## FREUD'S ANALYSIS OF A KATYA FIGURE IN ZWEIG'S STORY

In his essay "Dostoevski and Parricide" (*Collected Papers*, Vol. V), Freud does not refer to Katya at all. And,
while he does not mention Grushenka by name, he is clearly
referring to her when he writes that, in Mitya's case, "the
motive of sexual rivalry [with his father] is openly admitted."

That the master of the Oedipal analysis should have missed
the major incest figure in the novel seemed incredible to
me. Careful scrutiny discloses, however, that Freud after
all does "analyze" Katya. But he does so "unconsciously":
This analysis appears in Freud's discussion of Stefan Zweig's
story "Four-and-Twenty Hours in a Woman's Life," which
he inserts in his essay on Dostoevski. His manifest purpose
here is to illuminate Dostoevski's gambling mania and its
connection with the novelist's onanistic burden. But what
Freud says about the woman in Zweig's story applies—with
some allowance for digressive "free association"—to Dostoevski's Katya.

Theodor Reik, in his essay on Freud's "Study on Dostoevski," pays tribute to his "original insight into the life
and creation of the great novelist," making only some minor
criticisms. One of these is that Freud's summary of Zweig's
story is too long. "We cannot help feeling," Reik observes,

that Freud's long digression is "an error in proportion" (*From Thirty Years with Freud*, New York, 1940). In a letter (cited in Reik's essay), Freud grants "that the parenthetical Zweig analysis disturbs the balance." Yet—as though Freud sensed that this digression *was* somehow relevant—he continues: "If we look deeper, we can probably find what was the purpose for its addition." Freud's discussion is "an error in proportion," if we limit ourselves to his avowed intention. But, if as Freud suggests, "we look deeper," that is, if we examine it for clues to Freud's unconscious "purpose," it is not at all too long, but not long enough, is not "parenthetical," but central.

Freud summarizes the Zweig story in the following way:

An elderly lady of distinction tells of an experience she had more than twenty years earlier. "She had been left a widow when still young and is the mother of two sons, who no longer need her." In the gambling rooms of Monte Carlo, into which she wanders aimlessly, she is attracted by the hands of an unlucky gambler, who evidently leaves the gambling rooms in the depths of despair, with the evident intention of ending his hopeless life:

"An inexplicable feeling of sympathy compels her to follow him and make every effort to save him . . . she . . . finds herself obliged, in the most natural way possible, to join him in his apartment at the hotel, and finally to share his bed." She "exacts a most solemn vow from the young man . . . that he will never play again, provides him with money for his journey home . . . is ready to sacrifice all she has in order to keep him." But instead, "the faithless youth had gone back to his play. She reminds him of his promise, but, obsessed by his passion, he calls her a spoil-sport, tells her to go and flings back the money with which she had tried to rescue him. She hurries away in deep mortification and learns later that she has not succeeded in saving him from suicide."

Transposed into the relationship between Katya and Dmitry:

Katya's father dies while she is still young. She tries to be a mother to two of Fyodor's sons, Mitya and Ivan, neither of whom "need her." Katya learns that Mitya has been leading a "gambling" life and that he is in despair. After the death of her father (who is analogous to the woman's husband in the Zweig account), she comes to Mitya's room.

She does not share his bed, except in Mitya's fantasy and
perhaps also in her own. Katya attaches herself to him, gets
his promise to reform and gives him money, expressing her
readiness to sacrifice everything to save him. But, here too,
the hero surmises the woman's actual motivation and goes
back to his "play." He is now seized with the obsession
to return the money to her, who would interfere with his
gambling life. At the end, Katya learns that she did not
succeed in saving Mitya.

In the course of his analysis of Zweig's story, Freud
writes:

The equation of the mother with the prostitute, which is made
by the young man in the story . . . brings the unattainable within
easy reach. The bad conscience which accompanies the fantasy
brings about the unhappy ending.

The woman wants to save the young man's soul. But this
is a disguised façade. To be sure:

faithful to the memory of her husband, she has armed herself
against all similar attractions; but—and here the son's fantasy is
right—she did not, as a mother, escape her quite unconscious
transference of love on to her son, and fate was able to catch
her at this undefended spot.

Earlier, Freud speaks of

Dostoevski's burden of guilt [which] had taken a tangible shape
as a burden of debt, and he was able to take refuge behind the
pretext that he was trying by his winnings at the tables to make
it possible for him to return to Russia without being arrested by
his creditors.

Most of this applies to Mitya's relation to Katya.[12]

## FREUD'S MARTHA AND THE MATRIARCHY

The question occurs: How explain Freud's omission of a
central figure of the Oedipal situation?[13] The answer would
probably entail a thorough analysis of Freud's life work.
But perhaps some light may be thrown by considering briefly
one personal factor in his life and its bearing on his an-
thropological outlook.

As is well known, Freud's Oedipal scheme centers in the patriarchal cycle of human history. It has little to say about the matriarchy beyond noting that "the maternal inheritance is older than the paternal one" (footnote to "The Savage's Dread of Incest" in *Totem and Taboo*). In his essay "The Heart of Freud" (Haldeman-Julius Publications, 1951), A. Bronson Feldman suggests that this may be connected with the fact that in his own life, Freud "had never experienced a mother's dictatorship." In his biography of Freud, Ernest Jones speaks of Freud's mother as "indulgent." Where "the father stood for the reality principle," Jones states, the mother stood for "the pleasure principle" (page 7). Freud's conception of what women and mothers are or should be corresponds roughly to the nineteenth century German conception: the soft, giving, noncompetitive figure.[14] He writes to his wife:

Nature has determined woman's destiny through beauty, charm and sweetness. Law and custom have much to give women that has been withheld from them, but the position of women will surely be what it is: in youth an adoring darling and in mature years a loved wife [Jones, page 176].

Now, ironically enough, we learn from Jones's account that Freud did experience some measure of a "mother's" dictatorship. The most prominent women in Freud's life were, aside from his mother (about whom Jones gives very little), Martha Bernays, who became his wife, and her mother. Martha's mother was the head of the family and, according to Jones, Freud found in her "too masculine an attitude." Freud himself says of her that she is "fascinating, but alien, and will always remain so to me . . . she exacts admiration" (Jones, page 116). Freud had some bitter quarrels with this strong-willed woman and even threatened to break with Martha unless she defied her mother. Later, however, Freud got on quite good terms with the mother.

Now, Freud wanted to think that Martha was not like her mother. "If, for instance," he writes to his wife

I imagined my gentle sweet girl as a competitor it would only end in my telling her, as I did seventeen months ago, that I am fond of her and that I implore her to withdraw from the strife into the calm uncompetitive activity of my home [Jones, page 176].

And again: "I seek similarities with you [and her mother],
but hardly find any" (Jones, page 116).

"Hardly any," yet some. For, referring to a photograph
Martha sent him, Freud sees in her face "an almost masculine
expression, so unmaidenly in its decisiveness." Jones adds
that Freud was painfully to discover that "she was not at
heart docile and she had a firmness of character that did not
readily lend itself to being molded" (page 102).

Actually, Freud's courtship was no simple idyl. There
were years of separation; passion alternated with resentment
and with torturing doubts about Martha's love for him of
which Freud needed repeated reassurance. It too was at
first a "secret" relationship, jeopardized by the displeasure
of Martha's family. In his first letter to her, shortly before
their betrothal, Freud would assure her "of a relationship
which perhaps will have for long to be veiled in secrecy.—
How much I venture in writing that!" (Jones, page 106).
Only once did Freud allow himself to express some public
resentment against his fiancée. This happened in connection
with the Cocaine Episode in which Freud held her indirectly
responsible for the delay in publishing his manuscript on
cocaine. In his Autobiography, Freud would explain

how it was the fault of my fiancée that I was not already famous
at that early age . . . but I bore my fiancée no grudge for her
interruption of my work.

Jones comments that Freud's excuse is "somewhat disin-
geneous," that "it does not tally very closely with the facts,"
and that it "must cover a deeper explanation" (page 79).

According to Jones, Freud thought of Martha as a truly
noble character in whose presence one could not have a
mean or common thought. He refers to Freud's feeling of
being in "debt" to Martha:

when he said he would be in her debt when he died he had more
than one reason for his gratitude. She protected him from any
kind of meanness, and he would do nothing improper or unworthy
even in order to gain her in marriage. [page 125]

This feeling of "debt" should be considered alongside what
Jones calls Freud's "great dislike of helplessness and his love
of independence." Yet, Jones observes that "in all major
personal issues," Martha "proved stronger than Freud and

held her ground." He speaks of "a remarkable concealment in Freud's love life," and that in his relation to Martha, Freud "often needed to express some hardness or adverse criticism before he could trust himself to release his feelings of affection" (pages 129, 122, 124).[15]

However, Martha was not only "masculine." Jones notes that "Martha's tact and sweetness," again and again, "succeeded in smoothing things over." Thus, it was possible for Freud to see in Martha that which he wanted: "the gentle sweet girl." But the competitive "masculine" strain was there, in Martha and more so, in her mother. It constituted a threat to Freud's ideal conception of woman, and he tried to keep it out of his sight. Here may be one of the roots for his failure to appreciate the historic function of the matriarchy. And here may be the explanation why Freud did not consciously recognize Katya's dominating personality as a mother figure.[16]

## NOTES

[1] Mitya, in particular, can be likened to Oedipus and Hamlet in that his character spells his fate. He too is more intent on uncovering the truth than is anyone else. In doing so, he likewise arouses suspicion against himself and contributes most to his condemnation. Father Zossima's act of kneeling before Mitya (seen by a member of his order as the elder's sensing that Mitya is contemplating the murder of his father) is a kind of warning, such as the oracle gives Sophocles' Oedipus. Mitya's celebration with Grushenka at Mokroe (it is their "wedding") takes place after his near attempt to kill Fyodor and after he thought he had killed Grigory.

[2] For a psychoanalytic interpretation of Oedipus and Hamlet along these lines, see my essays "Oedipus: Fromm or Freud" (*Complex*, Spring, 1952) and "Shakespeare's Hamlet. The Myth of Renaissance Sensibility," *American Imago*, Vol. 7, No. 3.

[3] The numbers refer to pages in the Modern Library Giant edition of *The Brothers Karamazov*.

[4] Dostoevski offers but scanty material for the motivation of Katya's humiliating herself before Mitya whom she regarded as a profligate and gambler. He does suggest some identification between Katya's father and Mitya. Both were lieutenants, are in disgrace and "gamble" away their honor and that of the family. Katya conceives her role to be that of saving both, first her father and later Mitya.

[5] A related "strategy" occurs in Thomas Mann's *Doctor Faustus* where Leverkühn sends a friend to woo Marie, whereupon the friend and Marie fall in love with each other.

6 Katya would also impose her will on Grushenka. She invites the rival to her house and would have her be "an angel" who will give up Mitya because that is best for him. Alyosha feels that Katya has fastened on Mitya because "a character like Katerina Ivanovna's must dominate, and she could dominate someone like Dmitry, and never a man like Ivan" (153–155, 161–162, 193).

7 In this sense, there is something to the point made in Komarowitsch's *Die Urgestalt der Brüder Karamasoff* (München, 1928) that Katya's love demands the same unlimited subservience as the Grand Inquisitor's. Komarowitsch refers to Dostoevski's comment in his Notebooks: "Katya: Rome, unique objet de mon ressentiment." The line is taken from Corneille's *Horace* and is spoken by a heroine who curses her native land. Incidentally, Grusha calls Katya "mother" (in a derogatory sense). Garnett regrettably translates the Russian word *matj* as "my girl" (812).

8 The number 3 is a leading motif in *The Brothers Karamazov* as it is in the Oedipus dramas, the *Divine Comedy, Don Quixote, Faust,* and other mythopoesis. In Dostoevski's novel, it has a diabolic sign (the violence of the 3 brothers, the abandonment of Mitya when he was 3 years old, the 3,000 rubles, the 3 blows with which Smerdyakov kills Fyodor, Ivan's 3 interviews with Smerdyakov, and the devil's 3 visits with Ivan); and its resurrectory sign, his 3 ordeals, his arrest on the 3rd day of his struggle to save himself.)

9 As Fyodor would buy Grusha with 3,000 rubles, so Mitya offers the Pole 3,000 rubles if he would release her. Grusha herself is at first attracted to or binds herself to father figures: Samsonov, the Pole, and Fyodor, whom she does not discourage at first.

10 Mitya himself is not aware of his complex involvement with Katya. She is, indeed, the great "secret" of his life and of the novel. She comes to Mitya secretly, asks him to send off the 3,000 rubles secretly; Mitya would keep the fact secret that he spent half of her money on Grushenka. Above all, the nature of his "debt" to Katya is Mitya's "great secret" and "disgrace."

11 Earlier Mitya declared that what he wants is "to have done with her and with father." It seems to Mitya that he could be freed from Fyodor if his father returned the heritage his mother left him. Would Mitya be getting his "mother" back from Father in this way and thus be liberated from the temptation to kill him? And would he be released from the "debt" to the surrogate mother by giving her his own mother's money?

12 Freud's letter to Reik contains a sentence which is a kind of quick summation of the Katya-Mitya relation. Dostoevski, Freud notes, "really only understands either crude, instinctive desire or masochistic submission and love from pity."

13 There is another surprising omission in Freud's essay. As

mentioned, Freud sees the patricidal guilt distributed among Mitya, Ivan, and Smerdyakov, but exempts "the contrasted figure of Alyosha." To be sure, Dostoevski himself consciously intended to portray Alyosha as his saintly "hero" who believes in "active love." However, Alyosha is at most an unheroic hero. To begin with, Dostoevski, the artist, draws him with less power, pours less of his artistic blood into him than he does into his criminal brothers. And this has aesthetic "justice." For Alyosha does almost nothing that affects the central problem. And he can do nothing since he loves and forgives everybody for everything. That is, *he is unable to choose* and is therefore unable to act. Furthermore, the psychology of the savior figure suggests hidden guilt feeling which extends beyond the theological ground. Alyosha constantly *invites punishment*, and like Father Zossima begs "forgiveness." Now, unlike Father Zossima, Alyosha has not yet sinned in his personal life, has done nothing for which he needs to atone. Does he feel guilty only because of his impotence in relation to the problem of the Karamazovs? The passage in which Alyosha begs to be forgiven offers another clue. It comes immediately following the death of his surrogate Father Zossima. In this scene, he embraces, kisses, and wets the earth (the Russian "Mother Earth" in Dostoevski's terminology), "vowed passionately to live it, to love it for ever and ever." Gazing at the coffin of the elder, "he longed to forgive every one and for everything, and to beg forgiveness. . . . He had fallen on the earth a weak boy, but he rose a resolute champion. . . ." (380–381). The last point was suggested to me by Larry Goldsmith.

14 Interestingly enough, in Teutonic mythology, women are distinguished, not by their beauty or softness, but by their bravery and warrior role, e.g., the Walküre.

15 Did Martha's firmness and nobility represent a concealed threat to Freud's love of independence (similar to that which Mitya felt in Katya)?—A possible clue may be contained in Freud's dream of the Botanical Monograph (*The Basic Writings of Sigmund Freud*, New York, 1938, pp. 241–246). In his analysis of the dream, Freud writes that he reproaches himself for remembering so seldom to bring his wife flowers, "as she would like me to do," and is reminded "that we often forget in obedience to a purpose of the unconscious." His next association is the monograph on the coca plant. (We know that he indirectly blamed Martha for interruption of his work on this subject.) He further notes that the genus *Cyclamen* which Freud remembers having seen next morning is "my wife's favorite flower." And he associates his dreaming of the "dried specimen of the plant, as though from a herbarium" to his having become "a *book-worm* (cf. *herbarium*)." Erich Fromm would seem to be on the right track in commenting that "the monograph about the cyclamen stirs up his feeling that he fails in that aspect of life which is symbolized by love and

tenderness" (*The Forgotten Language*, New York, 1951, p. 92).
Might one further suggest that Freud's desire for "independence"
appears in the dreamer seeing a "dried specimen of the plant"
instead of a "blooming" cyclamen? In his analysis of the dream,
Freud twice mentions the fact that the cyclamen is "my wife's
favorite flower."

16 Some of the following data in Jones's biography may offer
material for other analogies between Freud and the problem in
*The Brothers Karamazov*:

Martha was a "pure noble beauty" to Freud, who "could both
love and hate passionately." Before his marriage, he expressed
doubts on being worthy of Martha, saying to himself: "You have
won the dearest girl quite without merit of your own." He fan-
tasied that his admired friend Fleischl (who was a close student
of physics and mathematics) could make Martha happy. Freud
became engaged to Martha about two years after the death of
her father, and we learn that Freud found pleasure in the fact
that Martha saw a resemblance between him and her father (pp.
162, 102, 110, 89–90).

*Frederic Wertham**

# AN UNCONSCIOUS DETERMINANT IN "NATIVE SON" †

Psychoanalytic studies of works of literature have often been undertaken. But the author of the work of literature was usually dead or unavailable. This has reduced such studies to the dangerous field of psychoanalysis without psychoanalysis. There is a great temptation to speculate about the self-revelation of an author in the hero of his play or novel. Freud himself succumbed to such speculation in the case of Shakespeare.

If we want to arrive at valid conclusions about the psychology of literary creation, we must have access to the living author. As far as I know, no psychoanalytic study of a literary creation based on analytic study of its author has ever been undertaken.

What I shall present to you today is based upon one of the great novels of our time. We can recognize greatness in a work of art by the way its fame spreads over national boundaries. *Native Son* is popular in many countries. A leading Soviet critic, Yermilov, has compared Richard Wright to Dostoevski.

Wright is interested in psychopathological problems in relation to writing. He had to be deeply conscious of each step of progress he made as a writer and he wanted to know the uses of technical devices involved. Out of discussions we had on the relationship of psychiatry to literature, we decided to undertake an experiment to determine where certain elements in *Native Son* were derived from. Wright accounted for a certain element in this novel in a manner which was

* FREDERIC WERTHAM is a well-known psychiatrist and the author of many books and professional articles, among them *Seduction of the Innocent, The Circle of Guilt,* and *The Show of Violence.*

† Read before the American Psychopathological Association's 34th Annual Meeting in New York City on June 9, 1944.

rational and fitted a political and social framework rather
than a true emotional personal one.

There is an obvious advantage in working with an author
for free associations to the symbols in his work. It is, in fact,
the only scientific method for such a study. But there is also a
grave disadvantage. One naturally does not feel free to reveal
too much personal data about someone who is in the public
eye. For this reason I am limiting what I present to you to a
fragment which of necessity has to be severed from the
context. While I was handicapped in my study of *Hamlet*[1]
by the fact that Shakespeare was dead, I am handicapped in
writing openly about *Native Son* by the fact that Richard
Wright is alive. This fragment, however, is enough to state
and demonstrate certain definite conclusions about the
psychology of the process of literary creation.

In 1938 Wright published an autobiographical sketch "The
Ethics of Living Jim Crow."[2] Recently he has written a much
fuller account of his life, "Black Boy,"[3] which is coming out
this fall. This autobiography is of considerable interest here.
It has taught me one thing about autobiographies: they may
be a literary disguise almost as hard to penetrate as a novel.

Wright himself attempted to interpret *Native Son* in a
booklet he called "How Bigger Was Born."[4] Is this interpretation by the author himself correct? That is how one may
formulate one aspect of my study.

That there is an identification between Bigger Thomas and
his creator is evident. It becomes even more clear to anyone
who reads *Native Son* and the autobiography "Black Boy."
How far this identification goes is a special problem in itself.
It has always to be kept in mind that "a literary creation is
not a translation but a transmutation of human experience"
(*Dark Legend*).

Just as I believe that in *Hamlet* the key scene is the appearance of the father's ghost in the mother's bedroom, so the
key scene in *Native Son* is when Bigger Thomas unintention-
ally kills Mary Dalton in the presence of her blind mother.
(Bigger, as you will remember, is employed as a handyman
in the house of the Dalton family.)

Had the author any knowledge or remembrance of a
situation where a boy like Bigger worked in a white household, where there was a tense emotional atmosphere between
the dramatis personae? Was he conscious of any fantasies or
daydreams from which threads would lead to the key scene

and its setting in the novel. The answer to both these questions is "No."

In the process of analysis a stage was reached where associative material, vague and fragmentary, was forthcoming, which was related to such scenes. But Wright did not know whether these scenes and figures were memories or fantasies. "Did I invent these people?"

The overcoming of resistance led to the emergence of more and more concrete and coherent situations. Fantasies became linked to living memories. It became evident to me that they had actually occurred in Wright's life. But even at this stage his sense of memory, if I may so call it, was still incomplete and lacked reality character. Fortunately, through two relatives living near the places involved, the real existence of persons, names, and places could be checked. Speaking of one letter of verification he said: "I knew it and I didn't know it. It is strange when you see it black on white in front of you." Only some time after this were these experiences fully remembered and acknowledged by him. Then he said: "I am sure that this . . . was the soil out of which *Native Son* came. The moment it came I recognized it." These facts Wright had completely forgotten for eighteen years. In other words, the root experiences intimately related to the key scene of the novel were unavailable to his consciousness at the time of the novel and at the beginning of our experiment when he reflected on the sources of his inspiration for the creation of the Dalton household.

As an adolescent of fifteen, Wright went to public school and worked mornings and evenings for a white family. The lady of the house was young and pretty. She lived with her husband and her mother. Her real name was highly significant in the analysis, and as a common English word had definite symbolic meaning. In his memory the figure of the mother is very unclear. She used to get the breakfast every morning. The daughter, the lady of the house, was friendly to young Richard, and he felt this was a second home to him. She lent him money to make a down payment on a new suit for a special school function.

His chief duty was to tend the fireplace. He chopped wood and brought in the coal. I need not point out the definite relationship of these circumstances to those in *Native Son*. The fireplace corresponds of course to the furnace in the novel, in which the Dalton girl's body was burned.

Further associative material led to the recollection of a special scene. In the early morning young Richard would carry scuttles of coal and wood into the house. On one such morning when he was carrying out his usual routine, he opened the door and came suddenly upon the lady of the house before she had dressed. She reprimanded him severely and told him he should always knock before entering. These recollections had great emotional power. They were related to much earlier emotional experiences.

I may cite here a fragment of a dream produced during the analysis: "I was passing through a factory yard on my way home. A white man volunteered to conduct me through the factory grounds. As I walked with him I remarked that it was good to have short-cuts, for they saved a lot of time in getting home." Associations to this dream led to an early experience. On his way home from school, the shortest route was through a park, a "white park," where colored boys were reluctant to go for fear of being molested by older white boys. Once he saw a drove of white Mexican children on a road. One little Mexican girl was nude. His mother commented on Mexicans. Other episodes went back to his fourth year.

Mary's mother, Mrs. Dalton, is a very interesting figure. In actual memory she corresponds to the mother of the young woman in whose house he had a job. He said that his memory of her remained "nebulous" even after the whole scene was clearly recalled.

You will remember that in the novel Mrs. Dalton is blind and cannot see. But at the crucial moment she is present and becomes aware that something extraordinary is going on.

Who is the woman who is blind but not blind enough, who does not see but who watches the secret acts of the hero? In Wright's life it may be sufficient to say that the ego ideal was largely derived from the mother, and not from the father. And the very symbol of the seeing eye that is blind fits the mother image.

An analysis of this scene in *Native Son* would be incomplete without an account of how he came to use the name Dalton for the white family. At the beginning of our experiment he could not account for it. But sometime later he said he recalled from the days when he worked in a medical research institute that "Daltonism" is a form of blindness. Had the name Dalton perhaps something to do with the blindness of Mrs. Dalton? There is also a deeper and more dynamic association. Daltonism—and that is what he did not remember—is of course a technical term for a form of color blindness. I need not point out to you how emotionally charged the expression "color blind" is in relation to a novel that plays in the South.

While hitherto it has only been assumed, on the basis of more or less valid reasoning, that the unconscious plays an important role in literary creation, the present study gives proof in a specific instance. The data presented here are sufficient to show that unconscious material enters definitely into a work of art and can be recovered by analytic study. Only unconscious factors with a high emotional value are significant in literary creation. The dream process runs through the creative process.

Comparison of the long-forgotten memories presented in this study with the self-explanation of *Native Son* in "How Bigger Was Born" shows that the latter is a conscious rationalization. Psychoanalytic studies of works of literature in which the author was not available may also in many instances have been such rationalizations based mainly on theory.

## NOTES

1 "The Matricidal Impulse. Critique of Freud's Interpretation of Hamlet," *Journal of Criminal Psychopathology*, II (4), 1941, 455. *Dark Legend*. Duell, Sloan & Pearce, New York, 1941.

2 In *Uncle Tom's Children*, Harper, New York. 1938.

3 Harper, 1944.

4 Harper, 1940.